'A SEDITIOUS AND SI

'A SEDITIOUS
AND
SINISTER TRIBE'
THE CRIMEAN TATARS AND
THEIR KHANATE

DONALD RAYFIELD

REAKTION BOOKS

Published by
Reaktion Books Ltd
Unit 32, Waterside
44–48 Wharf Road
London N1 7UX, UK

www.reaktionbooks.co.uk

First published 2024
Copyright © Donald Rayfield 2024

All rights reserved

No part of this publication may be reproduced, stored in a retrieval system
or transmitted, in any form or by any means, electronic, mechanical,
photocopying, recording or otherwise, without the prior permission
of the publishers

Printed and bound in Great Britain by Bell & Bain, Glasgow

A catalogue record for this book is available from the British Library

ISBN 978 1 78914 909 8

CONTENTS

GLOSSARY

ağa	Ottoman honorary title for senior, influential, rich individuals
akçe	(= little white) common Ottoman coin, by seventeenth century, *c.* 3 grams of silver
Alans	Iranian ethnos, later the Osetians
Arğın	a major clan in many Turkic nations
Barın	Mongol and Tatar clan
bey	governor of district
beylerbey	chief governor
bulqaq	period of anarchy
Chersonesus	ancient city outside today's Sevastopol
daruğa	chief of police
Deşt-i-Qıpçaq	(= Qıpçaq wilderness/steppe), the Mongol–Tatar empire of Eastern Europe, western Siberia and Central Asia
emir	Arabic term for monarch, prince, general
Hiwi	(from German *Hilfswillige*, 'volunteer') euphemism for forced indentured labourer
Horde	(from Turkic *orda*, 'camp') major Turco-Mongol state, the 'Golden Horde', soon splitting into 'Blue', 'White', 'Great Hordes' and so on
jizya **or** *ciziye*	tax paid by non-Muslims in lieu of military service
Khakan	khan of khans
Khazars	rulers of eighth-century Turkic empire based on Volga and north Caucasus
kıta	short poem in couplets, often of praise
koşma	felt prayer rug; genre of lyrical poem, often Sufic
kurgan	Iranian burial mound in southern Russia
kuruş	silver Ottoman coin from 1648, replacing the *akçe*
Mangıt	Noğay and Crimean Tatar clan
Mansur	Mongol and Tatar clan
meclis	Turkic parliament or other political assembly
medrese	school
mirza	Persian title of distinction; prince(ling); *bey*'s equerry
mufti	senior Islamic jurist, able to issue a fatwa
mühtesib	market inspector
naib	court clerk

Noğay	Tatar ethnos, largely nomadic, from Caspian Sea to mouth of Dnepr
nuker	(Mongol term) hired warrior, personal bodyguard
nureddin	'light of the faith': second deputy to, and usually close male relative of, Crimean khan
Or Qapı	'gate to the moat/dyke': fortress, built 1509, protecting isthmus between Crimea and Ukraine
öşr	tax on agricultural produce
paşa	governor of Ottoman province, also magnate in general
Pechenegs	Turkic and possibly Hungarian ethnos
Perekop	'ditch': Russian name for Or Qapı
qadı	judge
qadıasker	'military judge'; in fact, chief justice
qalğa	first deputy to, and usually close male relative of, Crimean khan
qaraçı	electoral status of Crimean Tatar clan; originally Mongol non-royal nobility
Qıpçaq	Turkic ethnos, dominant in the Mongol–Turkic empire
qurultay	Mongol and Turkic parliament or constituent assembly
Sarmatians	largely Iranian ethnos in southwest Ukraine
Schuma	(from German *Schutzmannschaft*) Nazi-organized defence units in occupied territory
sejm(as)	Polish-Lithuanian parliament
sekban	(from Farsi *sagban*) 'dog-handler', in Ottoman empire elite squad of riflemen
Selcüq	major Turkic dynasty and ethnos, originally dominating Anatolia
seyyid	descendant of the Prophet
shariat	Islamic common law and custom
Siciut	Mongol–Turkic clan
Şirin	Turkic clan, dominant in Crimea
şişlik	'skewer', or sheep tax
sultan	Ottoman: absolute hereditary monarch; Crimea: son of a khan
tamğa	Tatar–Mongol national symbol (trident); sales tax
töre	unwritten pre-Islamic code of Turkic law, regulating personal, social, political relations and customs
tudun	Khazar governor
tuğra	sultan's calligraphic seal
ulus	province, country, homeland
yarlıq	monarch's written decree
Yaşlav	Crimean Tatar clan, only later receiving *qaraçı* status

zabit	Crimean police official
-zade	(from Farsi) son of
zakat	tax on wealthy to benefit the poor

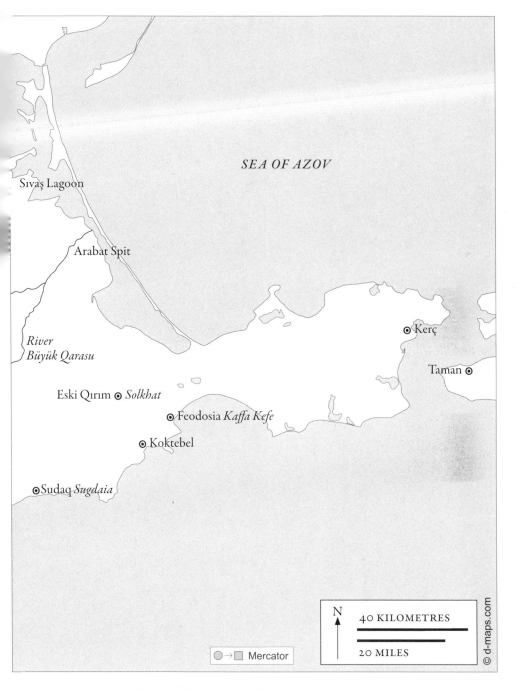

SEA OF AZOV

Sıvaş Lagoon

Arabat Spit

*River
Büyük Qarasu*

⊙ Kerç

Taman ⊙

Eski Qırım ⊙ *Solkhat*

⊙ Feodosia *Kaffa Kefe*

⊙ Koktebel

⊙ Sudaq *Sugdaia*

N

40 KILOMETRES

20 MILES

⊙→▣ Mercator

© d-maps.com

MAP 1 Crimea, ancient and modern. River names and ancient names in *italics*.

INTRODUCTION

This is a history of a nation, the Crimean Tatars. It was formed primarily from the Turkic Qıpçaq people, many of whom came west from Central Asia early in the modern era, and later with the forces of Genghis Khan and his Golden Horde. As the Golden Horde broke up in the fourteenth century into various khanates and adopted Islam, the Crimean Khanate arose. The Crimean peninsula, with its complex ethnic mix of Turkic, Greek, Italian and Gothic peoples, its connections with Byzantium and with the Ottomans who were superseding them, had maritime connections that favoured intercontinental trade, and a geography that made invasion difficult. It was ideally suited to become an independent state. The khanate that took shape in the 1440s, and which came under Ottoman tutelage in the 1470s, survived for some 350 years, whereas the other inheritor states of the Golden Horde were all swallowed up by Russia before the sixteenth century ended. Why the Crimean Khanate not only survived, but flourished for so long, is one of the themes of this history. The reasons include a formidable military might (based on cavalry and archers of unparalleled skill), a durable constitution, in which a khan's absolute power was moderated by influential clans of nobles (the *beys*), and a complex yet fair taxation and judicial system. To these factors we must add a steady income from tribute paid by (and often extorted from) neighbouring states, subsidies from the Ottoman government for military services rendered, and a productive economy that exported everything from salt to slaves all round the Black Sea. The stance adopted by the Crimean khans was that, as the direct descendants of Genghis Khan, they were the freeholders of all the lands north of the Danube and east of the River Bug that Genghis had conquered in the thirteenth century. Therefore, the rulers of Poland, Lithuania, Ukraine and Russia all seemed to the Crimean khans mere leaseholders who had to pay annual ground rent to the Genghisid freeholder, or suffer the penalty of invasion, destruction and enslavement.

The positive aspect of this arrangement was that the Crimean Tatars cleverly maintained a balance between their 'leaseholders', supporting the weaker against the stronger: thus this tiny nation, never more than two million strong (and at times, after epidemics or wars, far smaller), shaped the borders and the policies of nations ten times bigger.

The decline and fall of the Crimean Khanate was determined by the same factors as its rise: by the end of the seventeenth century the 'lease-holders' had become strong enough to defy the 'freeholder' and cut off the payments that sustained the khanate. The Tatars' virtuosity with bow and arrow was eventually outdone by the artillery, the navy and sheer numbers that the Russian army developed and which the Tatars could not rival. Unlike their imperial neighbours, the Crimean Tatars made war without attempting to acquire their neighbours' territory: they used attack as a means of defending their own, but never expanded. What antagonized the Crimean Tatars' opponents most was their systematic capture of civil- ians to sell as slaves, or to ransom as hostages. Other nations did the same, but not on the same scale, especially where white Christians were involved. The Tatars also acquired ill repute for savagery: the fact that they were no more cruel than any of the warring powers of the seventeenth century was overlooked. The final factor in their decline was the failure of their patron: the khanate's chief paymaster and supporter, the Ottoman empire, stopped expanding and fell into decline at the end of the seventeenth century. The symbiosis of Tatar and Turk collapsed.

Much of Crimea's success depended on the talents of the reigning khans. The Crimean Tatars were unique in having just one dynasty, the Giray family, from whom a khan had to be chosen, even though an Ottoman sultan, rather than the Crimean people, might dictate the choice. The Girays rarely married outside their own aristocracy, and Crimean Tatars generally were endogamic, that is they tended to marry among themselves (with an occasional admixture of their Caucasian associates, the Circassians). The Crimean Tatars thus were free from the strengths and weaknesses of most medieval monarchies, who by international marriages created for them- selves not just alliances, but disputed inheritances and wars of succession.

The Crimean Tatars' best historian, the early eighteenth-century Seyyid Muhammed Riza, author of *Seven Planets*, identified the seven khans (we can now add an eighth) whose intelligence, personality and charisma strength- ened or even saved the khanate. The last years of the khanate's existence, from 1770 to 1783, however, saw a succession of khans who had neither the political and military support nor the strength of character needed to prevent the Russian empire from swallowing up and destroying one of Europe's most extraordinary, if controversial civilizations.

The final chapters are a concise chronicle of that destruction, which has rightly been classified as a slow genocide. It may, with Russia's invasion of Ukraine, now be reaching its conclusion.

This book is by no means the first history of the Crimean Khanate. In English we have the work of Alan Fisher and Brian Glyn Williams, who focus primarily on the fate of the Crimean Tatars under Russian and Soviet rule. Not since 1855, however, the time of the Crimean War, when Reverend Thomas Milner, a talented geographer, summarized histories by the Austrian orientalist Joseph von Hammer-Purgstall, has the English reader had access to a history of the khanate. In the 1880s the formidable Russian historian and orientalist Vasili Smirnov combed through every available manuscript source in Turkish, Crimean Tatar, Arabic and Farsi to produce his *Crimean Khanate under the Supremacy of the Ottoman Porte* (two volumes revised and reprinted in 2005). Despite its pro-Russian and 'orientalist' stance, Smirnov's masterpiece is a classic that no historian can afford to overlook. The Ukrainian historian Oleksa Haivoronsky, with a lighter touch, published *The Rulers of Two Worlds* (2007–9), taking the khanate's story from its beginnings to about 1640 CE. The major recent Western work in English is Dariusz Kołodziejczyk's 1,000 pages on the relations between the khanate and Poland-Lithuania, even broader than its title suggests. Generally articles and other publications by Polish, Russian, German, Hungarian, Turkish and French scholars over the last fifty years, as the Bibliography shows, provide an enormous amount of detailed information and thought-provoking ideas not accessible to every English-speaking reader: one object of this history is to give an insight into this research.

Russian physical destruction of Crimean Tatar writing, from histories to poetry, began with the burning of the khan's libraries and archives in the 1730s and was taken further by the Russian civil service in 1833, when every piece of Crimean Tatar writing was ordered to be burnt or confiscated. (Further losses occurred in the Soviet purges of the 1930s and the Nazi occupation of Crimea in 1941–4.) Consequently we know just the titles of some major works by Crimean Tatars, whose khans themselves were in several cases major writers. Every now and again, however, in manuscript collections from Leiden to Tehran, from St Petersburg to Cairo, lost works are found again, such as the full records of the Crimean courts in the seventeenth century or works by long-buried poets. Future researchers will be able to fill some of the gaps.

In the 1990s, when Crimean Tatars were able to return from exile in Central Asia, a frantic era of publication began in centres of Crimean Tatar learning, notably in Simferopol. Many of these publications are now hard to acquire, some have been pulped (together with their authors and publishers) by Putin's acolytes. Much, however, has been made available on the Internet by Tatar scholars and should be downloaded while the opportunity exists. Among them are the four volumes of *The History of the Crimean Tatars* by the late Professor Evgeni Vozgrin, a Russian from Simferopol and an advocate for, as well as lifelong student of, Crimean Tatar culture.

One problem when writing a history of Crimean Tatars is finding the right transliteration for names of places and persons. Crimean towns were first known by Greek names, which were replaced by Turkic ones as the khanate established itself, and then by Russian names by Catherine the Great (not to mention Soviet mania for ideological renaming). I have tried to use the name appropriate to the period written about and to make cross-references to modern names to minimize confusion. Names of persons are complicated by the fact that, like many Muslims, Crimean Tatars did not usually have surnames, so that the flurry of Mehmeds and Ahmets are sometimes hard to distinguish from one another and require extra definition. The ultimate problem is that of alphabet: until 1928 Crimean Tatar, like Turkish, was written in Arabic script. Transliterating this into the Latin alphabet is sometimes problematic: Turkic languages often have eight different short vowels, while Arabic provides for only three (*a, e/i, o/u*), which are normally indicated only by 'points' in the Qur'an or primary school books. Crimean Tatar in Arabic script (unlike Farsi) often does not distinguish *p* from *b*, *k* from *g* or *ng*, and gives only hints of a vowel's nature by a choice between an 'emphatic' or a 'normal' version of an Arabic consonant that precedes it. Even transliterations by skilled orientalists, like the recent publication of Seyyid Muhammed Riza's *Seven Planets* in Kazan, have ambiguities. I have done my best with the help of the Ottoman Turkish dictionaries available, but in the end we are faced with the fact that Mehmed and Muhammad are in Arabic script identical, and I have had to choose the pronunciation most likely in Bağçasaray or Istanbul.

Finally, the Crimean Tatar language has three dialect 'zones'. On the coast, where the Ottomans controlled many of the ports, Crimean Tatar is very close to Ottoman Turkish; in the northern steppe zone it is a distinctly

Qıpçaq Turkic language, not always intelligible to an Ottoman speaker, while in the mountain range that separates the steppes from the coast an intermediary form has persisted. (Crimean Tatars living in Romania and Bulgaria have themselves developed dialect differences.)

Grammars of Crimean Tatar exist, but the projected three-volume Crimean Tatar–Russian–Ukrainian dictionary has stopped publication after volume one. A Crimean Tatar–English dictionary is badly needed, however good online Crimean Tatar–Russian dictionaries may be.

In this history, Russian words are given in the usual Library of Congress transliteration, Ukrainian names of persons and places, likewise. (There are complications with cities like Lviv, which have belonged to various jurisdictions in the past, and in this case has been also known as Lvov, Lwów or Lemberg.) Crimean Tatars still use the Cyrillic alphabet in tandem with the new 1997 Latin alphabet, which closely follows Turkish and is more and more commonly used (as in most Turkic languages of the former USSR). The peculiarities of Crimean Tatar are that, in addition to the letters of the modern Turkish alphabet, it uses *q* to indicate a *k* pronounced far back in the throat, *ñ* to indicate English *ng*, and, particularly in words of Arabic origin, *â* to indicate that the preceding consonant is softened (like the first *n* in *onion*). Tatar and Turkish use *j* (pronounced as in French) mainly for foreign words. Both languages use *c* to indicate an English *j* sound, *ç* to indicate an English *ch*, and *ş* an English *sh*. *Ğ* in Turkish has no sound of its own (it merely lengthens and darkens a preceding vowel), but in Tatar it has the sound of a Parisian *r*. The undotted *ı* in both Turkish and Tatar indicates an *i* pronounced back in the throat like the Russian *ы*, or reduced to a neutral vowel.

Not all quotations in this narrative are referenced, for example those that are to be found in well-indexed and standard sources, such as D. Kołodziejczyk, *The Crimean Khanate and Poland-Lithuania: International Diplomacy on the European Periphery (15th–18th Century)* (Leiden, 2011), and V. Smirnov, *Krymskoe khanstvo pod verkhovenstvom Otomanskoi porty* (Moscow, 2005).

1

CRIMEA BEFORE THE CRIMEAN KHANATE

Crimea has long been a uniquely attractive habitat for Europeans and Asians. A peninsula (in fact, almost an island, since a narrow isthmus is its only solid land connection to the steppes of southern Ukraine), not much bigger than the island of Sicily, its short winters and long summers are milder than the ferociously cold or hot steppes. It has a northern savannah zone, good for grazing cattle and, given skilled tilling, growing grain; a southern mountain chain runs from southwest to northeast, providing protection against natural and human forces, as well as numerous streams and Eastern Europe's largest ancient broadwood forest; and a rocky Black Sea coast with several good harbours. Even more than Sicily, in antiquity Crimea attracted a bewilderingly mixed succession of immigrants before a dominant ruling culture (Turkic in Crimea, Italian in Sicily) moulded them into a governable community. With its fertile soil and its protection from attackers thanks to a dyke, or rampart and moat, cut across the Or Qapı (Perekop) isthmus, its only land approach, Crimea was, like Sicily, well placed on international trading routes. For millennia goods were most easily moved overseas or overland between Europe and Central Asia, even China and Iran, through Crimean ports and entrepôts.

The name Crimea might be supposed to be derived from one of its early inhabitants, the Iranian Cimmerians; the etymology deriving Crimea from a Turkish root meaning 'defence' or defensive ditch is more plausible. In any case, the Turkic form *qırım* is not recorded before the thirteenth century CE. At first the east Crimean town of Solkhat was renamed Eski Qırım ('old Crimea') by the Mongol–Tatar invaders. Its meaning, 'old ditch', may well be simply a translation from the original name of the town, Solkhat, deriving from Italian *solcata*, 'furrowed'. It is notable, however, that Slavs in medieval times referred to the Crimean Tatars as the *Perekop* Tatars (Tatars of the ramparts or dyke).

Archaeology, by studying ornamented stone tombs and barrows, shows that Crimea has been inhabited since prehistory. Not until around 500 BCE, however, do Greek historians and geographers help us identify who the Crimeans were. The earliest were the Cimmerians, whom Homer believed to live in thick fog. They may, like the Scythians, be one of the Iranian semi-nomadic peoples who roamed the steppes before Turkic and Slavic tribes displaced them. Place names stemming from the Cimmerians are even today widespread from the Balkans to the Don River, and their influence was strong, for their metallurgy brought the Crimea out of the Bronze Age into the Iron Age. Horses provided them with transport, meat and milk; they had no personal property except for a sword and a chalice, their commerce was by barter, not money, and they were reputed to be the 'most honest' of 'barbarian' nations.

Between 1000 and 500 BCE the Cimmerians were ousted by, or merged with, or developed into the Taurideans. The word 'Tauridean' (and Tauris for the Crimea itself) appears to come from the Greek *tavros* ('bull'), because of the use of bull's blood in the Tauridean sacrifices to the virgin goddess Artemis. Possibly the name is connected with Anatolian words for 'mountains', and certainly the Taurideans were located in the mountainous south of the Crimea, where they practised shepherding on land and piracy at sea. Unlike the Cimmerians, the Taurideans had a fearsome reputation, killing and sacrificing any foreigner they captured. By 500 BCE they were confined to the Crimean mountains by a more powerful Iranian group, the Scythians, who together with the Greeks had formed a kingdom and a trading port on the mainland to the east of the Crimea, near today's Taman.

The syllables of the very few surviving names of Cimmerian and Tauridean leaders and tribes, such as the Cimmerian *Teupsha* or the Tauridean fief *Sinkhi*, suggest that, whatever Iranian genesis they had, there was a substratum from northwest Caucasian peoples, such as Circassians. Their disappearance is as obscure as their origin. It is most likely that they gradually lost their identity to a Turkic majority in the Crimea.

The next wave was Scythian, so powerful that the Black Sea became known as the Scythian Sea. It was enough to forge a dual empire, thanks to migrants from Greek cities who set up trading posts all around the Black Sea. The Pontic Bospor empire in the northeast, under the control of a succession of emperors called Mithridates, is a unique example of Greek and Scythian joint rule. The Scythians, unlike the peaceful Cimmerians and violent Taurideans, were all-rounders, producing wool, meat, wheat and manufactured goods, including remarkable jewellery. They developed in

Crimea a complex society in which warriors, farmers, industrialists, shipbuilders, architects, traders and government officials all played a role (Greek being the lingua franca). Nomads now coexisted with settled and urban communities. By the beginning of the Christian Era, Roman writers had to concede, 'These Scythians are far better educated than other barbarians; you can find very clever and enlightened persons among them, in a nation which always has a weapon in its hands.' Like their predecessors (a wave of Iranian tribes, the Sarmatians) Scythians in Crimea were eventually assimilated by later Turkic immigrants. But local people's pride in a supposed Scythian ancestry remained even when the Crimea formed a Turkic khanate.

The Scythian influence was so strong that when the Roman empire in 45 CE finally included Crimea and Roman citizens settled there, the settlers preferred to spend the summers in Scythian-style yurts, rather than build villas. The Crimean markets, however, were full of goods that met the massive demands of the Roman army and which were weighed out with Roman measures and scales. The Roman military executed pirates and made Black Sea trade safe. Crimea prospered: it produced not just salt and newly introduced olives, but the fermented fish sauce *garum* that the Romans loved. Crimeans learnt how to make glass and to organize a fishing fleet. The Crimean economy was now short of labour, yet slavery was abolished in favour of better-motivated paid workers. The Romans in the Crimea, however, faced constant attacks from Taurideans and were never assimilated despite their forts and a whole network of roads. In the fourth century CE, when the Roman empire was contracting, they abandoned their furthest outposts. The empire split into a western Roman and an eastern Byzantine empire. It was the Greeks of the Byzantine empire who stayed on in the Crimea, first as traders and eventually as would-be rulers.

The remains of a Jewish cemetery indicate that Jews began emigrating to Crimea as early as the first century BCE. There were further waves much later, when Jews were subjected to persecution in the Byzantine empire. If, as is generally supposed, the Turkic Khazar aristocracy converted to Judaism towards the end of the first millennium, then the Jewish Karaim ('readers') soon outnumbered orthodox rabbinical Jews in Crimea, whose earliest known synagogue was built as recently as 1309.

Under Byzantine sovereignty, Crimea still had regular tides of immigrants, but from the sixth century onwards these were more refugees than invaders. The first influx was of Ostrogoths: like the Visigoths they were émigrés from the overcrowded Baltic island of Gotland, but unlike the Visigoths, who headed for Rome and sacked it before establishing an empire in the Iberian peninsula, the Ostrogoths first threatened the Byzantines on the Danube, then, as later, the effective northern border of the Byzantine empire, and after negotiations were incorporated as mercenaries and as borderland settlers. (Large numbers of Ostrogoths, however, roamed further east to the Don in the third century CE and in alliance with, or opposition to, various Iranian groups followed the Black Sea coastline, fought Roman and Greek garrisons and ravaged large areas of Anatolia, before disappearing from history.)

The Goths were driven south by a population explosion, crop failures and famines that reduced them to a diet of beech nuts and grass roots. Their long journey south to the promised land took them two centuries, crossing Russia (where they gave the Slavonic natives Gothic words for sword and bread), before reaching the sea. They settled first in modern Moldavia, before negotiating submission to Byzantine authority, accepting Christianity and settling in the well-fortified southwest of Crimea, in a province called Gothia by St John Chrysostom, who ordained a later Crimean bishop. This Gothic–Greek principality had a capital called Doros or Dori, built on an impressive and impregnable limestone plateau. As farmers and villagers, rather than nomads, the Goths found it easier than earlier immigrants to build and inhabit permanent settlements, even though they cautiously chose steep mountain slopes rather than easily tilled flat lands vulnerable to subsequent invaders. By the sixth century, it is estimated that some 60,000 Goths were established in southwest Crimea and could provide 3,000 trained soldiers for the Byzantine army.

The Goths effortlessly overcame the resistance of the established population. Taller and leaner than the Iranian nomads, they were also more sophisticated and flexible: even though the version of Christianity they adopted in the fourth century was, at first, a heretical Aryan one that denied Christ the immutable and eternal status of God the Father, conversion integrated the Goths with the ideology of the Byzantine empire. Adherence to the Aryan heresy effectively rejected the Trinity and might eventually have made it simpler for Goths in the Crimea to convert to Islam. By the eighth century, however, the Goths had Greek bishops and became fully Orthodox Christians. Literacy and the adoption of the imperial religion gave the Goths an advantage over all the other former 'barbarians' under Byzantine tutelage. Sixth-century Byzantine scholars praised the Goths as 'fine warriors, energetic and skilful farmers, distinguished for being the most hospitable of all people'. The Goths established the Crimea's modern reputation for growing fine fruit in abundance. Under their missionary-bishop Ulfilas (whom Emperor Constantine II called 'the Moses of our time'), the Goths quickly adapted the Greek alphabet for their own language and produced a version of the New Testament that remained in use in the Crimea for at least five centuries. (Gothic inscriptions in stone are still being discovered in Crimea; in 1582 Ogier Ghislain de Busbecq, Flemish ambassador to the Ottomans, with the aid of his German-speaking servant, transcribed some eighty words and a song from two speakers of Crimean Gothic, and, to judge by a report from a visiting Catholic archbishop, the Gothic language may have persisted until the late eighteenth century in remote mountain villages.) They also wore traditional Scandinavian dress and jewellery, and built houses in stone and wood exactly as they had in Gotland.

Over the next centuries the Crimean Goths had to defend themselves, sometimes without Byzantine help, against new invaders. They fought off the Khazars in the eighth century and in 833, in alliance with Khazars, were threatened by the Russian prince Bravlin, who looted churches and palaces in the southwest ports and captured and enslaved thousands of Goths and other Crimeans. In the tenth century the Gothic viceroy (*toparch*) went to Kiev to negotiate peace with Russia and, recognizing Byzantium's weakened powers, accept a degree of Russian suzerainty. We know little of Gothic fortunes in Crimea until the thirteenth century, when Guillaume de Rubrucq reports 'teutonic'-speaking Crimean cities, now paying tribute to Turkic Cumans. After the Mongol invasion the Goths, as 'owners of Theodor and the Coast', were assigned power, together with Genoese merchants, over the southern Crimea. Both nations lost power only when the Ottomans invaded in the 1470s, with artillery and a policy of ruthless slaughter.

The Gothic heritage in Crimea is not just visual. Even today there are Crimean Tatars, blue-eyed, fair-haired, who look as if they have stepped out of an Ingmar Bergman film, and the Crimean Tatar language itself has Gothic relics: fair-haired men are called *Gottfrieds*, wooden buttresses *paivander*, roof rafters *razn*, warm rooms *stube* and pantries *keler*.

At the end of the fourth century CE Europe was flooded by the first wave of ferocious nomads from East Asia, the Huns, almost certainly a people known to the Chinese as Xiong-nu. We know very little of their composition – their armies were almost certainly federations of Turkic as well as other Asian nations – or of their language: to judge by the names of known Huns, they adopted Indo-European, even Germanic and Slavonic, as well as Turkic and perhaps Tungusian names. The novelties they brought to Europe were the stirrup and the runic alphabet (although we have no extant Hunnic writing). After conquering half of Europe, on the death of their leader Attila they seemed to vanish. A relict group attacked the Crimean Goths and subsequently merged into the Crimean population, perhaps as its first Turkic-speaking element. Like many other invaders, however, they left few traces of their language or culture. The first effect of their incursions into Crimea came in the 520s, when they cut off the transport of locally grown grain to the Constantinople populace, caused famine in Byzantium and strangled trade in Chersonesus. As the Byzantines reached a precarious truce with Hunnic tribes, they appointed their leaders as provincial viceroys. Across the Kerç straits, a Hun leader, Grod, was installed in the Graeco-Iranian city-state of Bospor. He may have been about to accept Christianity, for he began destroying the gold and silver idols of his Hunnic subjects, who then rose up and murdered him, together with his entourage and the Byzantine military mission protecting him.

At the last stages of Hunnic dominance, a kind of Turkic khanate was formed, incorporating various groups including the Oğuz, who would a thousand years later dominate Anatolia and the Balkans. This loose union of nomadic warriors centred on the lower reaches of the Volga and Don, and stretched from China to the Black Sea. When they made a brief incursion into Byzantine territory in the fifth century Emperor Zeno tried to use these tribes as a force against the Ostrogoths. This Turkic union became known as Greater Bulgaria (Turkic migrants to the Danube and Balkans also gave the name Bulgaria to a Slavonic kingdom). The Bulgars, like other Turkic tribes, were nomads and cattle-herders, and had an undemanding religion that alternated worship of Heaven with shamanism and ancestor-worship. Some arrived in Crimea and adopted a settled life, at first living in primitive dugouts and using unfired pottery. Only later did they learn to make wooden houses on stone foundations and to vary their diet of meat with small amounts of home-grown grain. As they became farmers, they revived the economy of the countryside and raised the level of pottery, producing the typically Crimean roof tiles decorated with symbolic animals or Greek letters.

On the Black Sea, the sixth century was largely peaceful and trade with Anatolia and European Byzantium brought Crimea prosperity. The Crimean coast was protected by fortresses, such as those at Aluşta (then Aluston) and Gurzuf (Gorzibitoi), which were built by Sarmatian or Alan settlers. (Deformed skulls found in burials testify to their Iranian origin.) On the southwest coast, the port of Chersonesus (near today's Sevastopol) became the major city and port for the whole of Crimea. Built on a grid plan with numerous public spaces and buildings, some built from imported marble, it had sewers, piped drinking water and paved streets. A Russian archaeologist reconstructs a typical Chersonesus house:

> Separated from the lane by a stone wall, a low gate, with a stone cross set into the wood as a talisman, leads to a small courtyard, where a Chersonesus citizen spends most of his life. Women grind corn by hand, cook over an open fire or, in richer households, in stoves made of broken tiles and built on brick. The household cattle – cows, sheep and donkeys – live under a wooden roof. A stone food trough is fixed to the courtyard wall. One rich household has a small bathhouse with underfloor heating, as in Armenia and Georgia ... In one corner there is usually a low stone shed for equipment, typically fishing gear ... The house, usually single-storey, sometimes two-storeyed, is at the back of the courtyard and has several rooms and a single or double tiled roof. The lower storey is always stone, the upper, reached by a stone or wooden staircase, is usually wooden, or a wooden framework with mud bricks ... Walls were plastered with clay and then whitewashed, rich houses having tapestries. One ground-floor room always has steps leading down to a pantry, sometimes with cisterns for salting fish. Here you find grain in enormous pythoi, half-buried in the ground, or large amphorae, also used for salted fish and wine. Drinking water is kept here.[1]

Even though the Crimean population remained obstinately pagan, Christianity was spreading westwards from Kerç, where a Christian necropolis was established in the fourth century. Christian mausolea were built in an Iranian style; all over the coastal zone there were churches, even basilicas, with frescos and mosaic floors.

The western population of this first Turkic khanate, intermingling with Iranian Sarmatians of the Balkans, were one element in the composition of the Khazars. The Khazars by the ninth century would expand into a mighty khanate, dominating the North Caucasus and bordering the Crimea. It had absorbed the Bulgars and many other Turkic groups. At first the attacks of the Khazars coincided with chaos and decline in Byzantium, where iconoclasm split church and state into opposing sides, and where the rise of Arab Islam brought devastating attacks to the gates of Constantinople. The Khazars took advantage of Byzantine disarray and Crimea suffered badly, but Chersonesus was spared from Khazar attack. The Khazars were soon stopped in their tracks by the arrival of the Arabs and the militant expansion of Islam, which in less than two centuries had reached the Caucasus (but not the eastern or northern coasts of the Black Sea) and demolished or subjugated every political entity in their path. The Khazars took a fatal step in 737, when their Khan Obadia and the Khazar elite decided they needed the protection of an established Abramaic religion but, to avoid taking sides with Muslims or Christians, chose Judaism, a religion with no state or army to defend its followers. (The Khazar army and many of the common people, however, preferred Islam.) The Khazar ruling class adopted the simple Karaite version of Judaism, based on the first five books of the Old Testament.

The result was a rebellion that sent the Karaim Khazar Khan and his elite into exile: many of them settled in Crimea, where they became a distinct ethnos. (A few hundred survive to this day, with a version of Judaism so discrete that even the Nazis decided not to classify them as Jews. They speak and write a Turkic dialect distinct from the Crimean Tatar language that had begun to act as a unifying force for the peninsula.)

In the ninth century eastern Crimea was recovering from turbulence, but Byzantine influence was severely weakened when the Goths of Theodoro province rebelled against feudal landlords, in particular the prosperous monasteries (the iconoclastic movement had in part been a farmers' rebellion against exploitation by monasteries). This may be why many Crimean monks sought shelter in monasteries made by carving caves into the limestone mountains. Byzantium was too preoccupied with hostilities in Anatolia and on the Danube frontier to intervene. By 900 CE the arrival of former Khazars, like that of Goths and Greeks, also drove the majority of the Crimean population into villages and towns or farms. Nomadic cattle-herders became a minority, however important as a warrior and ruling class.

In the early tenth century another Turkic (and possibly Ugric (Hungarian)) tribal group, known as the Pechenegs, consolidated its incursions into the steppes between the Dnestr and Dnepr. Their banditry and violent cavalry attacks exterminated those Khazars still remaining there. The Pechenegs had advanced tactics and used stirrups and bridles that allowed them to fire off volleys of arrows at both fleeing and pursuing foes. Their enemies usually tried to appease them, which gave the Pechenegs enormous power both in Russia and in Byzantine territories, where they assisted or opposed Russians or Greeks with blatant opportunism. In a century of proxy wars, Slavs, Vikings and Pechenegs, constantly changing sides, helped to inflame the antagonism between the weakened Byzantium and a resurgent Kievan Russian empire: in 972 the Pecheneg Khan Kuria, whose seat was in Crimea, drank from a ritual chalice fashioned from the skull of the Kievan prince Sviatoslav.

It took a century for the Pecheneg menace to be crushed: in 1091 Emperor Alexius I Comnenus surrounded the Pecheneg army and slaughtered 30,000 men, women and children. The survivors scattered, some of them ending up in the Russian army. Although they were hated for the destruction they wrought on many towns, a minority of the Pechenegs stayed in Crimea and integrated with the existing Turkic population, taking up trade and farming, and even becoming literate. Byzantium learned to live with Pechenegs as a counterbalance to the new Russian menace. The Byzantine emperor Constantine VII Porphyrogennetos wrote in his *On Administering the Empire*, 'When Rome [Byzantium] is at peace with the Pechenegs, neither Russians nor Turks can attack.' The emperor was well aware of the importance of Pecheneg ties with Crimea: 'In order to survive, Chersonites have to come to Byzantium to sell skins and wax bought from Pechenegs.'

Chersonesus was by now the effective capital of Crimea: its prosperity faltered only when its Byzantine viceroy Strategos Simeon was murdered at the end of the ninth century. As Byzantium's power waned, thanks to Selcüq Turks in Anatolia, the Qıpçaqs became the dominant economic movers. Arab sources testify that Crimean trade in the eleventh century focused on Sudaq on the southeastern coast: 'furs from the North, cotton and silk from Trabzon'. Russian traders came down the Dnepr river to join Greek and Qıpçaq merchants.

Most influential were these new tenth- and eleventh-century Turkic invaders, the Qıpçaqs (also known as Cumans and Polovtsians), who had migrated from the Altai mountains, following the tracks of the Oğuz and Selcüq Turks in Anatolia. The Qıpçaqs would, as they spread from the Urals to Europe, give their name to the entire Turkic-speaking steppes of Central Asia, Russia, Ukraine and Poland, the *Deşt-i-Qıpçaq* (literally, 'Wilderness of the Qıpçaqs'). Though nomadic herders like their predecessors, the Qıpçaqs had a more elaborate system of pastorage, as well as conducting looting raids on weaker tribes and settlements. Under Prince Vladimir Monomakh the Russian principalities managed to break off their internecine fighting for long enough to reduce the Qıpçaqs to isolated groups or to exile. In the twelfth century a large Qıpçaq army crossed the Caucasus and with their families was integrated into the Georgian army of King David the Builder. In the Crimea the Qıpçaqs were safe from Russian incursions; they settled as traders and were reinforced by an even larger wave of Qıpçaq migration in the wake of the Mongol invasion of the thirteenth century. That chaotic wave of refugees was described by a Flemish observer as 'such an enormous quantity that they were devouring one another, the living the dead ... we saw no settlements, only enormous numbers of Qıpçaq graves.' The Qıpçaqs determined much of the vocabulary and grammar of the Crimean Tatar language, as they shaped other written and spoken Turkic languages of Central Asia and Russia (such as Kazakh and Kyrgyz). The first manual of the Qıpçaq language, the Codex Cumanicus, prepared in Kaffa by Catholic missionaries in the thirteenth century in order to communicate with the Crimean Tatars, is also one of the earliest documents to call the Turkic-speaking inhabitants of the peninsula Tatars (the term dates back to the seventh century, and was used to denote both Turkic and Mongol tribes: its etymology is disputed). Turkic peoples of Crimea and the Volga regions would soon be called Tatars by themselves and their Slavic neighbours.

Byzantium ceded its power in Anatolia to Turkic states, predominantly Selcüq, which accepted Islam in the eleventh century and formed a group of allied or warring states collectively known as Rum. When Byzantium was at its weakest, sacked by the Latins who had invaded as the Fourth Crusade, the Greek emperors came to terms with Selcüq sultans who had lost a war with more powerful rivals: Izz-ed-Din Kaikavus II, expelled from Konya, was given refuge in the western Black Sea province of Dobruja, where his Selcüqs established three Muslim cities and then turned on their Byzantine protectors. By the mid-thirteenth century the whole *Deşt-i-Qıpçaq* had succumbed to the Mongol invasion. Genghis Khan's grandson and Juchi's son, Khan Berke of the Golden Horde, whose empire was based at Sarai on the lower Volga, offered the European Selcüqs a safe haven in eastern Crimea: their force of 12,000 sabres was a valuable acquisition for the Golden Horde. Sultan Kaikavus II was given the towns of Sudaq and Solkhat as a hereditary fief, thus making his son Ğiyas (from Arabic *Ghiyath*) ed-Din, 'helper of the faith', a future khan of Crimea.

The Selcüq Turks, despite conflicts with Qıpçaq and other Crimean Tatars, integrated well and opened up Black Sea trade by regular communication with their relations and fellow-traders in Sinop on the Anatolian coast. Selcüqs, influenced by their Greek and Gothic neighbours, adopted Christianity; some even became priests, albeit keeping Turkic names such as Toktemir, Sultan or Alaçı. Most new arrivals, however, remained Muslim and ensured that Crimea would be a mainly Muslim state, inclusive of most sects, while Islam would be interpreted in the Hanafi fashion with minimal prohibitions. Religious diversity and tolerance was to be typical of the

Crimean Khanate. Further waves of Selcüq immigration to Crimea came over the centuries, whenever rebellions or oppression in the Ottoman empire generated refugees. The result in shaping the Crimean Tatar language was to create zones, in which the northern steppe zone was fully Qıpçaq in its phonology and morphology, and the southern coastal zone spoke a dialect very close to Ottoman Turkish, while the mountainous interior was a compromise between the two.

A major change in the orientation of Crimea, bringing it into close contact with Western Europe, came at the end of the twelfth century, when Emperors Manuel I and Isaac Angelos sold a monopoly of Crimean maritime trade to the Genoese, who were then, with their rivals the Venetians, the Mediterranean's main seafarers. The Genoese made Chersonesus their capital in the 1220s, but paid taxes to Trebizond, a breakaway from the Byzantine empire, partially under Georgian control. The Genoese allied themselves with fellow Christians, the Gothic and Greek province of Theodoro, which became for the next 250 years a virtually independent principality. Crimea began to split up into a number of small feudal fiefs and principalities. The northern Qırq-Yer (later the Jewish settlement of Çufut Qale) was first ruled by Christian Hellenized Sarmatians and Alans, before passing into the hands of a *bey* appointed by a Noğay Tatar khan. In 1154 the Arab geographer Idrisi counted some forty castles on the coast from Chersonesus to Sudaq, and reported that the ports of Gurzuf, Aluşta and Kerç were prospering. Russians, some of them refugees from Pecheneg attacks on Kiev, also stimulated trade.

In 1223 the first surviving Crimean literary work, a poem on the traditional Turco-Persian Qur'anic subject of Yusuf and Zuleika, was written by Mahmud Qırımlı. The Crimean Tatar original has been lost, but a translation into early Ottoman Turkish was made around 1230 (two copies were discovered in the twentieth century). No doubt Mahmud Qırımlı was one of a number of Crimean Tatar poets, virtually all of whose work was destroyed by Russian soldiers in the 1730s or civil servants in 1833. Its existence implies the development of a literate society at an early stage in the *Deşt-i-Qıpçaq*.

Other nationalities completed the ethnic potpourri of Crimea: Jewish tombstones survive from the first century BCE, and Talmudic and rabbinical Jews formed a compact ethnos, mostly in the fortress city of Çufut Qale, where they specialized in crafts and occupations avoided by Muslims, but never suffered discrimination until Russians and then Nazi Germans conquered the peninsula. The Talmudic Jews became known as *qrımçaq* and spoke a distinct dialect, but used Hebrew as their written language. Some former Khazars and in later centuries Ashkenazi and Sephardic Jews who had been expelled from Europe fled to Crimea and became *qrımçaq*. Their relations with the 'Judaizing' *karaim*, believed to be former Khazars, were uncontentious. Tatars knew the *karaim* as *züfütsiz*, and rabbinical Jews as *züfütlü çufut* (Jews without and with sidelocks).

Political prejudices have distorted assessments of Russian and Slavic involvement in the evolution of the Crimean Khanate. After the Novgorod pagan prince Bravlin's incursion, 'quasi-apostolic' St Vladimir, Grand Duke of Kiev, was the next Russian to invade Crimea in the course of his war on Byzantium: in 988 CE he was stopped in the city of Chersonesus (also known as Korsun, now Sevastopol), where, after a truce, he agreed to convert his court and his entire country to Christianity, receiving as a reward marriage to Anna, the sister of the Byzantine emperors Basileos II and Konstantinos VIII. Vladimir then looted Korsun, removing its ecclesiastic treasures for his new cathedral in Kiev, and slaughtered many of its Christian inhabitants. Although he promised to help defend Byzantium against rebellion, he was not, *pace* nationalist Russian historians, given any rights to remain in Crimea. Later, in 1793, officials working for Catherine the Great 'found' a stone plinth in Tmutorakan, across the Sea of Azov, with an inscription apparently by a medieval Russian who had measured the distance across the straits to the Crimea. Tmutorakan, without doubt, was a Byzantine Greek-speaking city in which Russian merchants appeared from time to time. The plinth is an eighteenth-century forgery. Russian trade with Crimea before the sixteenth century was one-sided: Crimean goods appeared in Moscow, but there is little evidence of Russian trade with, or presence in, Crimean ports.

By the time the Mongol invasion transformed the steppes, Crimea's demography had stabilized. The only other new element was that of Armenian traders and craftsmen, refugees from their homeland, perpetually torn between Iranian, Turkic and Western powers: in the 1060s some 20,000 Armenians had fled from Turkic Selcüq conquerors across the Black Sea to Slavic and Byzantine territory (largely to Crimea). Before the Mongol invasion and the conversion to Islam of Berke, khan of the Golden Horde, probably in 1257, many Tatars remained shamanists, while Iranian immigrants persisted with fire-worship. Islam was still a minority religion in Crimea: Christianity, whether Orthodox, Catholic or Armenian Monophysite, was dominant. The oldest extant Crimean church is that of St John the Baptist in Kerç, built in 717 CE when the Khazars ruled the city. A Greek list of the 730s shows that Crimea had four autocephalous eparchies, while that of Doros, known to the Greeks as Gotthias, had seven bishoprics, including one for Huns and one for the Cuman-like Onoğur Turks. (The first Crimean synagogue may have been built in Chersonesus in the first century BCE; later synagogues were *kenasas*, serving Karaim, rather than rabbinical Jews.) Despite the influx of Selcüq Turks from Anatolia, the oldest mosque was constructed well after the Mongol invasion, under the patronage of the Golden Horde Özbek Khan in 1314.

The prosperous port of Sudaq produced a thirteenth-century *synaxarion* (collection of lives of the Saints) with marginal notes listing many Greek Orthodox parishioners who were Cumans or bore Turkic and even Mongol names.[2] After the establishment of Genoese ports, when Crimea became more a federation than a colony, the Christian bishoprics established new boundaries to match the political ones.

The Mongol invasion

The life of almost all of Asia and much of Europe was catastrophically changed by an invasion whose traumatic violence was unforeseen. In 1223 a reconnoitring Mongol–Tatar force appeared at Sudaq and caused severe damage. Although Genghis's conquests had begun a decade earlier, his victims still did not realize that the first invasion, however devastating, was merely a rehearsal. Genghis Khan's army returned, this time to stay, in 1238 and again in 1248. Sudaq had a Mongol governor, and the town of Solkhat (renamed Qırım) followed suit. Not until 1299, when the Mongols ruined the densely populated Chersonesus and totally destroyed Qırq-Yer, did they take over the whole of Crimea. Byzantium had collapsed, thanks to the Latins of the Fourth Crusade; Chersonesus was in economic decline. Now there could be a total transformation of Crimea. It became a key province (*ulus*) of the new Mongol–Tatar empire and eventually part of the Golden Horde of Genghis's grandsons. The Crimeans would be seen by the outside world as Tatars, Qıpçaqs loyal to the Horde, invaders and aggressors. Peace was at an end. It took, however, decades before the indigenous Qıpçaqs of North Crimea and Qıpçaqs from Central Asia, the bulk of the Mongol army, saw one another as one people.

The Great Horde first established itself at its capital Sarai on the lower Volga under Genghis's grandson Khan Batu, whose long reign (1227–55) gave the Horde enough stability to maintain an empire that stretched from the Urals to the Carpathians, from Russia's forest zone to the Black Sea:

Batu was for a short time (1235–41) khan of the entire Mongol empire. After Batu's death, his cousin Hülagü conquered the Caucasus, Iran, Iraq and Syria, and became khan of the Southern Horde, beginning a disintegration that would within a century irretrievably weaken the Mongol–Tatar empire. In 1257 Batu's younger brother Berke was the last khan of an intact Great Horde: thereafter it became the Golden Horde. Berke immediately appreciated Crimea's resources and trade: he exacted fair taxes and exerted imperial control bloodlessly. Berke's skills, enhanced after his accession by a declaration of Islamic faith, which did not compel the Mongol–Tatar elite to convert to Islam, extended his reign to 1255. Mengu-Timur, Batu's grandson and Berke's successor as khan of the Golden Horde, reverted however to traditional Mongol–Turkic shamanism: this led him to make blunders obnoxious to Muslims: for instance, having rescued the Anatolian sultan Izz-ed-Din Kaikavus II from Byzantine captivity and installed him in Kaffa, he tried after the sultan's death to make his son Masud marry his stepmother, Izz-ed-Din's widow, a normal action in Mongol mores. Horrified, Masud fled to Anatolia and became a Selcüq ruler, and Anatolia shunned all contact with Mengu-Timur. Mengu-Timur maintained, however, Berke's moderation, even pacifism, and renewed Genghis Khan's pledge to exempt Orthodox Christian clergy from tax and persecution. He even asked in one royal decree (*yarlıq*, an edict, a formal regulation) for his Christian subjects to pray for and bless the Mongol race and forbade, on pain of death, any abuse of Christianity. In 1266 Mengu-Timur appointed a nephew, Oran-Timur, as his viceroy in Kaffa and at the same time licensed the Genoese to conduct Kaffa's commercial affairs. In 1278 Crimea welcomed its first foreign diplomat, a Venetian consul. Posterity called Mengu-Timur *kelek khan*, the just khan. Mengu-Timur died young in 1280 from clumsy surgery: he left at least three widows and ten sons, who fought over the succession, but thanks to whom Mengu-Timur's brother Tuka-Temur (both were grandchildren of Genghis Khan and sons of Juchi) would be the forefathers of the Crimean khans.

Mengu-Timur's triumphant heir was not his son, but a cherished close relative, whose career was marred only by his grandfather's illegitimacy, even though this grandfather was the first-born of Genghis's son Juchi. This was Noğay, an army general (*temnik*) and famous warrior who never actually won a pitched battle, but preferred persuasive negotiation. He did, however, attack unruly Crimean cities, the first being Chersonesus in 1248, and he insulted Byzantine ambassadors bearing gifts (although he had once been a Byzantine ally).

On Mengu-Timur's death, Noğay, as a purely military leader, had to play a double game in the competition between the late khan's brother and nephew for power, a game that ended with Noğay's complicity in the murder of Tuda-Mengu, the late khan's brother. In the 1290s a series of fratricidal murders ended with a seventeen-year-old Toqta becoming khan and Noğay, his *éminence grise*, the effective ruler of most of Eastern Europe. By 1296 Noğay was minting coins in his own and his son's names, even though he was not a khan. Toqta showed his resentment by summoning the overbearing Noğay to his camp: Noğay attacked him with an enormous army, but dared not seize the khan. As a result the Golden Horde territory was divided, Noğay inheriting the Black Sea coast and Crimea, which he now had to subdue. He sent his grandson Aq-Taiji as viceroy to Eski Qırım to make the population swear fealty. The Genoese suspected that Noğay, unable to pursue Toqta, was bluffing: they made Aq-Taiji drunk and murdered him. Noğay's army besieged and burnt Kaffa, and then did the same to several other coastal forts, some of which, such as Sarı-Kermen and Eski Kermen, were never rebuilt. His fury assuaged, Noğay pardoned one city and insisted on freeing prisoners, a step too far for his generals, who thus lost potential ransom payments. Three of Noğay's grandsons deserted Noğay and went over to Khan Toqta, but Noğay's sons pursued and killed them. The turncoats then murdered one of Noğay's sons. Noğay had lost all authority, and his underlings and appointees in the Balkans also defied him. Noğay then committed treason by seeking help from the ruler of Persia. To escape Toqta's wrath, Noğay claimed to be mortally ill, but his pretence was exposed, and in 1300 this heroic figure – tall, but now fat, with eyebrows that covered his eyes – was killed.

Khan Toqta took over Noğay's Crimean interests. Here he undertook his first war against a foreign power by attacking Kaffa, because the Genoese had rounded up starving Tatar nomads, indebted to the Italians, and were now selling them as slaves. The Genoese dared not fight; instead they set fire to the port and embarked for Italy. Toqta took revenge by confiscating all Genoese property in Sarai and other centres of the Golden Horde. The Genoese were not allowed to return until Khan Üzbek came to power in 1313–14; they meekly accepted his forgiveness (the *Deşt-i-Qıpçaq* trade was too lucrative for them to suspend any longer) and did not ask for reparations.

Toqta then standardized coinage in the Horde's realm and forbade Crimea to mint its own coins. The empire that followed the break-up of the Great Horde was now known as the Golden Horde. The Golden Horde was characterized by constant in-fighting. After 21 years in power, Toqta

Khan died in 1312, aged 42, either drowned in an accident on the Volga, or poisoned by his successor Üzbek Khan, who reigned until 1341. Üzbek and after him Canı Beg Khan (*reg.* 1342–57) restored order by installing viceroys in the *ulus* of the southwest and southeast corners of the empire. Thus Crimea and Hacı Tarhan (near today's Astrakhan) became dominions of the Golden Horde, which was based on the central Volga. Maintaining the Horde's integrity required constant manipulation and occasional armed intervention to stop the new *ulus* declaring themselves as khanates in their own right.

The Crimea under Mongol dominance was still far from unified: nomadic Qıpçaqs effectively controlled the northern steppe zone – the *bey*s of their clan, the Yashlav, would only later become a core constituent of the Crimean Khanate's aristocratic structure. As the Golden Horde's grip weakened, major clans – the Şirin (whose *bey*s claimed descent from Genghis Khan), the Barın and the Arğın – claimed power and landholdings in the central parts of Crimea, as they did in other *ulus* of the Golden Horde.

These clans, or ruling tribes, were known as *qaraçı*, a Mongol term that originally implied nobility not related by blood to the Genghisids. (Over the centuries the largest clan, the Şirin, won the privilege of marrying Genghisid princes, and thus could claim descent from Genghis Khan.) Apart from the Şirin, who were more numerous, powerful and wealthy than the others, the dominant *qaraçı* clans were at first the Barın, Arğın and Siciut. A Qıpçaq clan in later years gave way to a Mansur or Mangıt clan, in which Noğay Tatars played an important part. As their names imply, these *qaraçı* clans were of much earlier origin than the Golden Horde or, in some cases, even than Genghis Khan. The Şirin derived their name from the Persian for 'sweet', which was usually a woman's name, but among Tatars could also be a man's: they were known to have originated as an Iranian, probably Osetic or Alan, tribe, like other Iranian peoples caught up in the transformation of Central Asia into a Turkic-speaking region. The *qaraçı* clans limited, even dictated, the accession, deposition and power of their khans: their leaders – *bey*s or emirs – could not be deposed by a khan, or killed without serious cause. Khans were traditionally inaugurated by a Şirin leader lifting them on a white felt rug to the throne. True, in the anarchic period (the *bulqaq*) of the second half of the fourteenth century, when khans fought each other often for illusory power, clan leaders had less influence. In peaceful times, however, their ability to summon up private fighting forces, their landowning wealth and, above all, the prestige of their antiquity made them all-powerful. The Qıpçaq clan dated back to the eleventh century; the Arğın were of Mongol ancestry, and just as long established; the Barın were a Mongol clan dating from at least the thirteenth century. The Şirin, oddly enough, were of much more recent origin, although a clan called Az, presumably also of Iranian origin, is recorded in the eighth century: the Şirin achieved dominance thanks to a fourteenth-century leader, Rüktemir (or Örök Tämär), an ally of Khan Tokhtamir. Tokhtamir allowed Rüktemir to marry Aysulu, the widow of Mamai, and thus made the Şirin leader a Genghisid by marriage. Rüktemir was killed fighting Timur Leng in 1396, but Tekene, the son of Rüktemir and Aysulu, was the Şirin *bey* instrumental in bringing Hacı Giray from Lithuania and establishing him as the first fully autonomous khan of Crimea. Once Crimea was an independent khanate, the power of the clans, above all of the Şirin, was unshakable. The Şirin could imitate the khan in the way they governed their fiefs, and could send their own embassies to foreign countries. They owned land from the isthmus of Or Qapı right to Kerç at the southeast corner of the peninsula: the clan *bey*s were never properly feudal lords: their farmers paid a moderate tithe, but were free from obligations, apart from military service in times of war. Although later khans created armed forces directly under their control, or the command of the Ottomans, the Crimean monarchy remained a limited monarchy, constitutional if we recognize as such an unwritten agreement between the clans and the monarch.

Meanwhile, the Graeco-Gothic Theodoro behaved like a self-governing principality, and the Genoese ports of Kaffa and Sudaq, together with representatives of other Italian trading republics, Venice and Pisa, concluded mutually favourable tax and trade agreements with the Mongols and controlled much of the hinterland.

When Khan Berke accepted Islam, there was stiff resistance from many Mongol and Qıpçaq leaders; not until Khan Üzbek's reign was Islam made compulsory and a hundred or so recalcitrant pagans were executed. In Crimea other religions flourished. Urged on by Pope Clement VI, whose name was carved into the gates of Kaffa in 1348, an Italian and French priesthood urged Armenians and Greeks to convert to Roman Catholicism. They were successful in appealing to the converts' self-interest, largely because the popes in Rome and the missionaries and traders from Western Europe had established good relations with the Mongol empire. The Mongols in theory tolerated all religions, but Orthodox Christianity was suspect, being associated with countries like Muscovy and Byzantium that resisted the Mongols, whereas Roman Catholics had warmly acclaimed the Mongols as liberators of Jerusalem and slaughterers of heretics and Muslims, so that a Mongol delegation was invited to Rome to attend the Papal Jubilee celebrations in 1300.

The Golden Horde khans largely stayed away from Crimea, but their *beylerbeys*, best seen as governor-generals, took active steps to repress rebellion and collect unpaid taxes. There were also frequent inter-ethnic conflicts. A Greek *synaxarion* (an ecclesiastic register of deaths and other events) records a massacre in 1278 by Tatars of Greeks in Sudaq, the Tatars tormenting the city for two further years. In 1299 Noğay (who would give his name to the Noğay Tatars, close but untamed relatives of Crimea's Qıpçaqs) came and razed most of Sudaq. More than thirty years later the Arab traveller Ibn Battuta visited Sudaq and noted, 'Its harbour is one of the biggest and best. The city used to be large, but most of it was destroyed because of internecine fighting.' In 1260 Niccolò and Matteo Polo (father and uncle of Marco Polo) passed through Sudaq and approved of it as a commercial centre. A few decades after Noğay's punitive raid the city revived. Qıpçaq *beys* and *mirzas* (princelings) ruled over a flourishing Sudaq that had been granted tax exemptions by the Horde. The Qıpçaqs were now generally known by the term Tatars (originally a Mongol term for Turkic peoples) and were the dominant nationality after Khan Üzbek's Islamization extended to Crimea. Non-Turks and non-Muslims were heavily taxed. The Greek farmers who tilled the soil had to pay *jizya*, a tax which at least exempted them from military service. On the proceeds, local rulers built palaces that would house future Crimean khans.

The Crimeans tried to maintain a foreign policy of their own. Sultan Baybars 'Great Panther', the Mameluk ruler of Egupt, a Qıpçaq whose parents had both been slaughtered by the Mongols, defeated a Mongol army in 1260. Nevertheless he made peace with the khan of the Golden Horde and paid for the mosque that Üzbek Khan built in Solkhat (Eski Qırım) in 1314. Eski Qırım flourished as the Crimea's most cosmopolitan city in the fourteenth century. Armenians, who called it Holy Cross (*Surb-khach*), made it a centre for ceramics and reinforced their colony with Armenian refugees from Anatolia; in the forested hills overlooking the city they built a monastery, which became a famous scriptorium.

Not only in Kaffa (Feodosia) did the Genoese flourish. They now had the port of Cembalo (today's Balaklava), from which they expelled their Greek rivals. They began to export soap and almonds to Muscovy and grain to Constantinople. Despite earlier prohibitions, they traded in slaves (largely Caucasian, Polish or Russian prisoners of war, but also Tatars). The Genoese built ships, wooden galleys with metal plating. In 1390 they were permitted to mint coins, notably 3-gramme silver *aspra*, with the arms of Genoa on the obverse and the Mongol trident *tamğa* symbol on the reverse. Genoese rule was well organized: a consul was appointed annually from Genoa, and a state council of eight men and sixteen judges, helped by military and policing committees, kept a tight rein on the port of Kaffa.

In the first half of the fourteenth century the Golden Horde, and consequently Crimea, experienced unprecedented peace under Khan Üzbek (Öz Beg, a grandson of Mengu-Timur), a man who in his long reign was acclaimed as a Mongol Justinian or Constantine I. Öz Beg faced some of his predecessor's problems, for instance the sale in Kaffa of Tatar citizens into slavery, but this time not by Italians, but by Circassians. Not until the 1350s were the Italian traders taught a lesson, this time by Öz Beg's successor, Canı Beg Khan. The Genoese behaved like feudal lords, as did the Venetians in their new colony of Azov (then Tana). When a certain Andreolo Civrano murdered a Tatar merchant, Hoca Omar, there was a riot in which many Europeans were robbed and forced to flee. Porto Pisano at the mouth of the Don was, like Tana, then closed to Italians for five years. The Venetians themselves arrested Civrano and surrendered him to the mercy of Mongol–Tatar law, but they rashly demanded compensation for their losses. Canı Beg Khan's siege engines failed to breach Kaffa's walls, so moved to the west Crimean port of Cembalo (later renamed Balaklava), protected only by an earth rampart, and burnt the city down. The Tatars returned to Kaffa and catapulted a corpse, riddled with plague, over the walls, to which everyone then attributed the 1348–9 outbreak of plague in Crimea and then in Europe. Nothing, however, would induce the Italians to bow down: Genoese and Venetians were now at war with one another, and goods belonging to Tatar merchants were damaged during a naval clash The subsequent prolonged legal wrangling was supervised by Canı Beg Khan's *daruğa* (police chief). Generous exchanges of compensation and bribes settled the matter, and the Venetians were handed another harbour near Kaffa, which they called Provato. Canı Beg Khan needed Venetian bribes to pay for the Horde's foreign wars: he could not afford scruples.

By the 1350s Tatars were becoming not only settled, but urbanized. On a plateau in the mountainous interior, near today's Bağçasaray, which in the sixteenth century would become the capital of the Crimean Khanate, the town and necropolis of Eski Yurt ('old homeland') and fortress of Qırq-Yer were built on the site of an eighth-century Alan Christian settlement, and also of the Jewish settlement of Çufut Qale. Here Nenekey-Hanım, the Christian daughter of the Golden Horde Khan Tuqtamış (Tokhtamysh), had her mausoleum. This well-protected and well-watered plateau and valley nurtured the embryonic Crimean Khanate.

Perhaps greater than any political or military disaster, the epidemic of plague, the 'Black Death' in 1346–9, had a traumatic effect on the Crimea: probably a third of the population of a quarter of a million died, often within days, even hours, of infection from bacteria carried by a louse, originally infesting rodents, but also bales of wool. Plague struck all the ports, but especially Kaffa, where people and wool from the Golden Horde's steppes were then shipped across the Black Sea and Mediterranean. Thanks to the Crimea's crucial role as a hub for trade, Constantinople would be depopulated (5,000 deaths a day) and Italy then ravaged. This epidemic was the worst in history. A treatise by the Arab historian Ibn al-Wardi, who himself died of plague in 1349, identifies Canı Beg Khan's Horde as the source of the infection and estimated that in Crimea 1,000 died every day in 1346. The plague was a major factor in the destabilization and disintegration of the Horde after 1350: the disappearance of the Volgo-Bulgarian literary language, and the suspension of written Chağatai, suggests severe depopulation. The reduction in the Mongol–Turkic taxable population, let alone of tax collectors, was disaster enough.[3] An Italian lawyer from Piacenza records in 1348 that Tatars began attacking Christians, who fled with their possessions onto a battleship and sought refuge behind the walls of Kaffa. The Tatars besieged Kaffa, allegedly infecting the Genoese of the city, some of whom transported the plague to Italy via Constantinople. Plague recurred more frequently in Crimea than anywhere else on earth: in 1386; in 1389 when *beylerbey* Noğay's forces invaded; in 1435–8, later killing even khans; and at the end of the eighteenth century, infecting Russians. Only the prolific child-bearing of a polygamous society enabled Crimea to recover its losses within a generation.

The ultimate effect of the epidemic, in Crimea as in Europe, was to make the labour of surviving farmers and soldiers more valuable and to remove some of the causes for warfare. On the other hand, plague depleted the number of judges, *mirza*s and administrators who could maintain order. Only earthquakes could match the destructive power of plague: in 1292 an earthquake badly damaged Sudaq.

The Crimeans owed their relative freedom from central control not only to plague, but to chaos and rebellion in the Horde. In birth and death, the new dominant figure, Mamai, a khan's brother, was a Crimean Tatar, born in Eski Qırım. Despite his obscure birth (he was not a descendant of Genghis Khan) and small physique (his skeleton suggests he was just under 1.5 metres

(4.9 ft) tall), in the 1350s he fought his way to become the viceroy of Crimea and the Black Sea coast. After the battle of Kulikovo, where he was routed by Dmitri Donskoi, whom Mamai had installed and later removed as Grand Duke of Muscovy, Mamai retreated, badly wounded, to Crimea. There he lost a battle (apparently at Kalka on the Dnepr, just where the Mongols had defeated the Russians in 1223).

Canı Beg Khan died in 1357, reputedly poisoned and replaced by his ruthless son Berdibek. Mamai was a childhood friend and later son-in-law of this short-lived tyrant, who was probably the last khan of the Golden Horde accepted as a legitimate heir. Berdibek tried to placate or dispose of any official appointed by his father. Mamai was made all-powerful *beylerbey* of Crimea in 1359. No sooner had Mamai begun sending Crimean ambassadors to Moscow than Berdibek died of debauchery or assassination, and Mamai was dismissed from his post, somehow surviving the rapid succession of vindictive conspirators and murderers who now took over the Golden Horde. In 1363 Mamai was menaced by a new clan who had taken power in the east and intended to overthrow all the descendants of Batu Khan: Mamai took refuge in Eski Qırım, and a year later regained power under a puppet khan Abdallah. Mamai then attacked Azov, killing its Italian consul Iacobo Cornaro (who was also the Venetian ambassador to the Golden Horde).

The Golden Horde's disarray encouraged Lithuanian princes to attack in 1362. Grand Duke Algirdas's army defeated three Crimean princes, Kutluğ Buga, who governed Eski Qırım, Hacı-bek the viceroy of Qırq-Yer and Demetrius, prince of Theodoro. The defeated Mamai and Khan Abdallah were dismissed from the Horde's capital Sarai: they then negotiated with Moscow for recognition as the true rulers of the Horde, for a reduction of Moscow's annual tribute payments and for an alliance with Russian grand-duchies friendly to Moscow. This new alliance enabled Mamai to regain control of Crimea and even of Venetian Azov, but during his absence Crimea was attacked by a certain Hacı Çerkes, who backed a usurper in Crimea and proclaimed him khan. Mamai responded and by 1369, when Khan Abdallah died, so many claimants had been eliminated that there was nobody still willing to declare themselves khan of the Golden Horde. Mamai appointed his own wife, Berdibek's daughter, as regent to an eight-year-old boy, Muhammad. Encouraged by the boy's survival, Mamai proclaimed him khan and himself as first minister to the world: the Egyptian sultan welcomed this first step by the Horde towards legitimacy.

Mamai's defeats in the stormy 1370s, when Russian principalities and Mongol–Tatar clans were at daggers drawn, were in fact a blessing for Crimeans, whose attackers were all engaged elsewhere. In 1375 Mamai was horrified to find that the Genoese had expanded their landholdings right to the border of his capital in Eski Qırım: he repossessed eighteen villages and, for the first time in the history of the Horde, built fortifications all round his Crimean base. But disaster struck. In 1380 Mamai, utterly defeated by the Russians, fled to Kaffa and then to Eski Qırım, both of which denied him refuge. In theory Mamai still had Crimea and the coast of the Sea of Azov to rule (he is still commemorated by the names of two villages in western Crimea), but he was soon captured and murdered by Tuqtamış, the new khan, the first for thirty years to have a firm grip on power. Tuqtamış took over Mamai's harem, gave Mamai a respectful burial in a traditional *kurgan* (a barrow only recently excavated) and offered Mamai's son a government post. Good relations were re-established with the Genoese, and eighteen settlements that Mamai had confiscated were returned to them. Once again foreign income flooded the Crimean coast.

Tuqtamış and his expansionary zeal had angered his future nemesis, the Central Asia 'Iron Cripple', Timur Leng. The first half of the 1390s was taken up by war with Timur Leng, which raged from the Black Sea to Iraq. Tuqtamış sometimes prevailed, but his allies were often defeated. During lulls between Timur Leng's attacks Tuqtamış laid claim to Crimea, but the effective ruler of Crimea, Taş-Timur, being a direct descendant of the Genghisid Tuga-Timur dynasty, had such strong support among Crimean Tatars that Tuqtamış had to yield power to him. The descendants of Mengu-Timur exploited the power vacuum and claimed Crimea: Crimean Tatars accepted their legitimacy. Tuqtamış won over the powerful Emir Idiki (Edigü) and by 1393 felt secure enough to demand both territory and tribute from his nominal subjects, the Polish-Lithuanian commonwealth: his letter to the Lithuanian Grand Duke Jogaila, demanding payment for the Horde territories that the preceding Grand Duke Algirdas had seized forty years previously, was fruitful and Lithuania would go on paying tribute until the 1650s. Timur Leng fought on, each campaign more devastating than the previous, until in 1395 he had conquered the whole territory of the Horde – including Crimea – and installed a puppet khan. Tuqtamış managed to recover Crimea in 1396, deposing and either expelling or killing Taş-Timur. He besieged Kaffa the following year, but in 1397 was chased out of the Crimea, which would accept descendants of Mengu-Timur, but not the invader. Tuqtamış then approached Lithuania's Grand Duke Vytautas the

Great, so deferentially as to call him 'father' and pay him tribute. Lithuania began an involvement with the Horde in general and Crimea in particular that persisted for centuries. But the new alliance was badly routed in battle by Edigü. A great number of leading Lithuanians, Russians and Poles were killed along with Tuqtamış's men. Tuqtamış fled to Siberia, made his peace with Timur Leng and had the satisfaction of outliving him, before being himself killed in battle with Edigü. Nevertheless, Tuqtamış had focused his attention on the Crimea: he was a Golden Horde aspirant and, arguably, the first khan of Crimea.

In his old age, in 1419, Edigü fled to Crimea and, desperate to protect himself from Tuqtamış's offspring, tried to appease Grand Duke Vytautas of Lithuania: 'Let us devote the rest of our days to peace . . . the flames of war have cleansed our hearts of spite.' There was no reply. Lithuania supported a rival claimant to power in Crimea, Kadır-Berdi. In hand-to-hand fighting Kadır-Berdi and Edigü mortally wounded one another. Edigü became the subject of Tatar heroic oral poetry and his men survived to form the core of a new khanate, that of the Noğay, who would eventually be allies or subjects of Crimean khans.

The vacuum in the Horde was filled in 1419 by a Crimean descendant of Tuga-Timur, a Muhammad who would be known as Ulu (great) Muhammad Khan. This new khan was forced to flee to Lithuania, where he held out for some years, hoping for a second chance to seize power, which came when Vytautas judged the Horde so weakened by quarrels that Ulu Muhammad could be reinstated and take over all Crimea as its khan. But a stronger claim to Crimea was asserted by Muhammad's cousin Taş-Timur, whose son Devlet Berdi would be the uncle of the first Giray Khan of Crimea (Ğiyas ad-Din, Devlet Berdi's brother and the first Giray Khan's father, is presumed to have perished in war with Tuqtamış or Edigü). Taş-Timur disappeared after 1396. Devlet Berdi lasted until 1427, when he tried to seize the Golden Horde capital of Sarai. He is reputed to have petitioned the sultan of Egypt for help, in verse letters written in such ornate Qıpçaq Turkish that their recipients in Cairo could not decipher them. Similarly, a few years later, Ulu Muhammad, temporarily occupying the Golden Horde throne, sent triumphant letters to the Turkish Sultan Murad II and to the sultan of Egypt, but his use of the old Uighur script baffled both sultans. Disappointed, Ulu Muhammad pondered an alliance with the Holy Roman Emperor Sigismund and the Magister of Livonia; he also renewed his alliance with Vytautas. His ambitious international efforts came to naught: a new rival, another Muhammad, this time *küçük* (lesser) Muhammad, was supported by the Mangıt clan of Tatars. Ulu Muhammad's stance meanwhile offended Tekene, the chief *bey* of the powerful Şirin clan, at a time when the Mongol–Tatar Horde was distracted by the question whether to support Yuri or Vasili II as Grand Duke of Muscovy.

Tekene, the Şirin *bey*, lost the argument and retreated to his Crimean landholdings, still plotting to oust Ulu Muhammad and install a grandson of Tuqtamış, Seyyid Ahmad, as khan of the Horde. In Lithuania Vytautas was briefly succeeded by his cousin Švitrigaila, once supported, but now opposed, by Ulu Muhammad. In the mid-1430s there was an uneasy stand-off between the two Muhammads and Seyyid Ahmad. So bewildered was the Grand Duke of Moscow that he paid tribute to all three claimants to the khanate. The ruler of Kazan, another Ğiyas ad-Din, took advantage of the confusion and tried to capture Sarai, but was killed by *küçük* Muhammad, while Ulu Muhammad fled to Lithuania. Seyyid Ahmad retained supreme power in Crimea until 1431.

2
THE CRIMEAN KHANATE
IS BORN

By the start of the fifteenth century the instability of Eastern Europe and the Golden Horde, after the Black Death and the ravages of Timur Leng, led to a new alignment of political powers and the emergence of successor states. Before and after Timur Leng's invasions, Crimean viceroys of the Golden Horde, all with claims or pretensions to be legitimate heirs of Genghis Khan, had each declared themselves khans of their fief, but had been swept away by their rivals or by their own ambitions to control the vestigial centre of the Golden Horde on the Volga. A major new factor was the emergence of the Grand Duchy of Lithuania, which from 1413 was ruled by the same monarch as Poland and had a parliament, a *sejmas*, which sat jointly with the Polish *sejm*. Lithuania rapidly expanded over Baltic, Slav and Qıpçaq lands to take over an enormous territory from the Baltic to the Black Sea. Lithuania was not only erecting a barrier to halt the Horde's expansion westwards: it was becoming a refuge and a base for Tatars who had been exiled by or who sought refuge from other aggressors on the Horde's territory. Lithuania traded asylum, even landholdings and military posts, in exchange for recognition, military help and guarantees from its Tatar guests.

Lithuania initiated its relations with the Crimea at a remarkable battle in 1362 at Yabgu, then a fortress near the lower Dnepr river, controlled by Crimean rulers. For the first time, Western swords and spears defeated Tatar bows on horseback. In the 1380s Vytautas, the nephew of Grand Duke Algirdas, settled some four hundred Karaim Tatar families near his fortress-palace at Trakai, near Vilnius; Muslim Tatars followed. They enjoyed tolerance, for Lithuania was still slowly converting from its own paganism to Christianity (and periodically back again). The Tatar community, known to this day as *Lipka* Tatars, found common ground with Lithuanians in resisting the Horde and its successor states, notably Muscovy.

Grand Duke Vytautas's first dealings with Khan Tuqtamış were not pleasant. Tuqtamış in 1393 demanded annual compensation for old Horde territories that the Lithuanian Grand Duke Algirdas had conquered many decades earlier. In 1397 Tuqtamış was suddenly deprived by Edigü's forces of any hope of becoming khan of the Golden Horde. Tuqtamış held on to Crimea only long enough to kill its would-be khan Taş Timur, and was then given refuge and substantial landholdings by Vytautas. Together they concocted an agreement to make them rulers of all Eastern Europe. 'Let us go', the proposal (as a Ruthenian chronicler records) began,

> to capture all Tatar land. Let us conquer Khan Temir-Kutlu and share his treasure and estates and install Khan Tuqtamış to rule over the Horde, in Kaffa, in Azov, in Crimea, in Astrakhan, in the Horde beyond the Urals, and all along the coast, and in Kazan, and it will all be ours and so will the Khan, and we shall rule not only Lithuanian and Polish land, but the North and Veliki Novgorod and Pskov and the Germans, as well as all the Russian grand duchies and we shall have tribute and tithes from all the Russian grand dukes.[1]

At first Vytautas and Tuqtamış were successful. At the battle of Vorskla on 12 August 1399, however, although the Lithuanians had the advantage of gunpowder and artillery, the allies failed to coordinate their attack. Routed by Edigü, they blamed one another. Tuqtamış fled to Siberia, but when Timur Leng quarrelled with Edigü, Tuqtamış wrote to the Iron Cripple, apologized for his hostility and promised to serve him. It was too late, however: Timur died in 1405, and Edigü caught up with Tuqtamış the following year.

Lithuania still held the cards, as far as Crimea's fate was concerned. Among the refugees was an infant boy, the future Hacı Giray. His father Ğiyas-ad-Din was killed in the Crimea in 1397 by Edigü's forces, and although Ğiyas's brother Devlet Berdi (who can be called the first legitimate Crimean khan, if only for a few months in 1427–8) survived the conflict, a servant rescued Ğiyas's only child and took him to Lithuania, safe from Edigü's revenge. We know little about Hacı Giray's early days: his rescuer seems to have found him a foster-father, an *atalık*, who in Tatar tradition would raise him to be a warrior until he reached puberty. He may have been called Hacı not because he found a way, in those turbulent years, to perform the *hajj* by travelling across the Black Sea and Anatolia to Mecca, but because his *atalık* had done so. (Other accounts state that the influential *hajji* in Hacı's life was the *atalık* of Ǧiyas ad-Din. It was this man who later persuaded Hacı to endow his family with the dynastic name of Giray.) If Hacı had been a real pilgrim to Mecca, an *el-hajji*, we would expect him to bear a Muslim name: Hacı must have been his given name. As for Giray, no convincing derivation has been suggested. The word is not Turkic, and only one Ottoman lexicologist, Ahmed-Vefik-Paşa, ventured to define it as 'authentic', making it an honorific title parallel to Ottoman Turkish *efendi* (from the Greek *authentes*, 'lord'). The written form of Giray can also be read as Kerey (the god of hell in a Siberian Turkic language); transliteration into Russian and Polish, however, confirms it was pronounced Giray (and later, Girey). The least implausible explanation is a popular etymology, one contemptuously dismissed by serious scholars: it is said that Hacı Giray lived so long in Lithuania that later, when asked to approve any proposition, he would reply in Lithuanian '*Gerai!*' ('all right, good, OK'). The nickname, as happened in other medieval dynasties, was adopted as a dynastic title by subsequent khans of Crimea.

Despite his descent through thirteen generations from Genghis Khan, attested by Turkish and Arab scholars, Hacı Giray spent the first forty years of his life making futile attempts to claim his patrimony. His rivals also benefited from Lithuanian protection. The young Ulu Muhammad left Lithuanian exile in 1424 with Vytautas's approval and conquered Crimea briefly. Seyyid Ahmad who, supported by some *beys*, tried to rule Crimea in the 1430s, was almost certainly a son of Tuqtamış and thus a refugee for some years in Lithuania.

Supported by Grand Duke Vytautas, Hacı Giray appears to have made a first return to his homeland around 1426, presumably encouraged by the prospect of his uncle Devlet Berdi's restoration. A letter from a Franciscan monk in the Genoese community, sent to Vytautas, promised that Devlet Berdi intended to maintain good relations with the Genoese; the letter was intended to be delivered to Lithuania by Hacı Giray. (This is the earliest written record of Hacı's presence in Crimea.)

At this period Hacı Giray, together with his cousin Canai (Devlet Berdi's son), had to flee from the wrath of a khan, more likely to be Seyyid Ahmad than Ulu Muhammad, who, supported by Grand Duke Vytautas, had conquered most of Crimea. Both persecutors, Seyyid and Muhammad, tried to exterminate rival heirs to the khanate. Pursued by a hail of arrows shot by the Horde, a legendary account goes, Hacı, Canai and a servant crossed the Dnepr at high water, clinging to their horses' manes. Canai crossed unharmed; Hacı's horse was struck by an arrow and he had to swim;

his servant surrendered his own horse to Hacı and drowned, begging Hacı to take care of a now fatherless family. When the cousins reached the deserted steppes on the right bank, then the Lithuanian side of the Dnepr, they rode at random for three days. They encountered a nomad and claimed to be Crimean gentry who had escaped slavery. Asked for directions, the nomad gave them crusts of bread and told them to rest while he watched over their horses. The two fell asleep with exhaustion. When they woke in the morning they found their horses and all their possessions had been stolen. Canai was too exhausted to walk further. Hacı wandered on foot for two days, met more nomads and claimed to be a destitute merchant's son, robbed and orphaned by bandits. This time the nomads escorted Hacı to the care of a Sufi. The Sufi's wife exploited Hacı, making him work all day and sleep on straw with a stone for a pillow. The Sufi, however, suspected that their new slave was of noble origin; over the next few years news spread that Hacı was alive. Tekene of the Şirin clan, rebelling against Seyyid Ahmad, was looking for an acceptable candidate for the khanate of Crimea and sought out Hacı. Canai then reappeared (one account states that Canai had joined a merchant caravan travelling to Kazan, another that he was killed by a Crimean *bey*).

According to other accounts, the Lithuanian court gave Hacı at various times estates and refuge either at Trakai (the centre for exiled Tatars, said by some chroniclers to be Hacı's birthplace) or at the Belorussian town of Lida. Hacı's mother Asya, a rich *mirza*'s daughter, remained in Crimea, yet escaped the vengeance of her husband's killers. History records her visiting Kaffa in old age, when Hacı was already established as khan in Crimea. She was displeased on a second visit that the Genoese did not give her gifts as valuable as on her first visit. When calling on the Genoese consul, Hacı's sons came dressed as paupers to extort as presents a horse and a purse full of money. The consul forbade Kaffa's Italian citizens to have anything to do with the khan's emissaries.[2]

Meanwhile, in 1427, the Egyptian chronicler Bedr-ed-Din El Ayni records the receipt by the sultan of Egypt of a letter from Devlet Berdi in 1427, claiming to control Crimea and its surroundings. The Golden Horde reacted violently: Khan Ulu Muhammad immediately invaded. The Şirin clan changed sides, allying itself to the more powerful invader. Devlet Berdi, as the paucity of coins minted in his name suggests, was driven out within months. In September 1429 Ulu Muhammad reported to Vytautas that he had conquered the entire empire of the Horde. Ulu Muhammad's assurances of security were undermined the next year when Dario Grillo, a Genoese ambassador sent from Kaffa to Lithuania to discuss trade, reported that he was robbed of his money, horses and goods on the road by Muhammad's Tatars. It took the Genoese sixteen years to settle the complaints about the robbery. Other Italians fared worse: a Venetian expedition to Azov was ship-wrecked, and in 1432 a second expedition was taken prisoner by the Genoese in Kaffa, as the two city states were now at war. The Venetians were secretly helped and encouraged by Alexei I, prince of the Graeco-Gothic state of Theodoro, who planned an Orthodox uprising against Catholic Genoese Cembalo (today's Balaklava). Only in spring 1434, under Carlo Lomellini, did a Genoese fleet of twenty ships and 8,000 men bring the novelty of several cannons, which breached Cembalo's walls. The Venetian rebels were, after a bloody encounter, defeated. The city was looted and then burnt. Most prisoners were executed, but Prince Alexei's son was spared.

Away from the coast, around the fortress-city of Qırq-Yer, Canike-hanım, Khan Tuqtamış's daughter and, from 1395, Edigü's wife, ruled a fief that was entirely hers after Edigü sided with Timur Leng. (The betrayal so infuriated Tuqtamış that he killed Canike's mother and spared Canike only because she was out of reach.) She was an exceptional woman for her times – in 1416, independently of Edigü, she performed the *hajj*, more to demonstrate her political power than her piety. She had already sent her young brother to Qırq-Yer to save him from Edigü's murderous intentions, and after Canike's brother killed Edigü, the widowed Canike ruled the north of Crimea. As a Genghisid, she intended that Hacı Giray should inherit Crimea, regardless of claims by Tuqtamış's other descendants, Küçük Muhammad and Seyyid Ahmad.

By 1434 Hacı Giray had reappeared. After Vytautas's death and the brief rule of his nephew Švitrigaila (an ally of Seyyid Ahmad), Hacı, regarded as the most trustworthy ally among the contenders for power in Crimea, now had the support of not only the four Tatar *qaraçı* clans, but also of Canike-hanım in Qırq-Yer, of Sigismund, king of Poland, and of the Grand Duke of Lithuania. Hacı came with an army, reputedly of 16,000 men, and the support of the major *mirza*s as well as of Tekene, chief *bey* of the Şirin clan and thus the Crimea's kingmaker. Hacı managed to conquer Solkhat (Eski Qırım) across the bay from Kaffa and, inland, was welcomed to the well-defended Qırq-Yer: he is said by a Byzantine historian, Laonikos Chalcocandylae, in connection with Lomellini's punitive expedition that year, to have imposed heavy taxes on the inhabitants of both Gothic Theodoro and Genoese Kaffa. The Italians complained, but sent gifts; Hacı Giray reacted by attacking the city, and part of Lomellini's forces are said to have gone inland to confront the Tatars. What is certain is that they ravaged Chersonesus, and then in June, to take vengeance on Hacı's Tatars, attacked Eski Qırım with a convoy of 612 wagons and siege engines, backed by an equally large force from Kaffa. The Genoese army stopped to rest for the night and was attacked from the hills by small groups of Tatar horsemen. The Tatar bowmen killed most of the Genoese cavalrymen and routed the rest, before the main Tatar army came and slaughtered or enslaved the entire Genoese army, moving later to Solkhat with the Italians' guns and equipment for a celebratory feast. 'The survivors hid among the corpses, pretending to be dead, and then ran to the city, but there were very few who had fewer than three wounds, from arrows, swords or spears,' the Italians reported.[3] This triumph at Solkhat (Eski Qırım) proved to the world Hacı Giray's cunning and the efficiency of his horsemen's Genghisid tactics.

For all his success, Hacı Giray still held only the eastern part of Crimea and had to maintain an uneasy peace with the Christian inhabitants of the Graeco-Gothic principality of Theodoro and the Genoese at Kaffa. In Kaffa there was a Tatar *tudun* (governor-general) with authority to tax non-Italians and limited powers to control the Genoese's expansionary instincts. The prince of Theodoro, as the weaker of the two Christian centres, needed Hacı's support against their Catholic neighbours, and Hacı, using Tatar tactics of maintaining a balance between prospective enemies, supported the weaker of the two potential adversaries. In turn, the Italians called Hacı *timor*, 'terror', and the Theodoro prince *dubius*. Italians and Tatars needed each other, however, as sources of income and for access to overseas trading partners and resources.

Despite his triumph over the Kaffans and the enormous reparations he extorted from them, Hacı Giray came under pressure from Khan Seyyid Ahmad and had to retreat once more to Lithuania. In 1437 Canike-hanım died: Qırq-Yer, in the hands of the quarrelling khans of the Horde, was still out of Hacı Giray's reach.

Seven or more years passed before Seyyid Ahmad, whose endless devastating wars with rivals such as Ulu Muhammad enraged the Şirin clan, moved north into the steppes. Tekene *bey* proclaimed Hacı as the sole legitimate khan: in 1441 this new ruler of the Crimea was brought back from Lithuania, lifted onto a white felt rug and elevated to the throne in a typical Genghisid election of a khan by the *beys*. The date of 1441 is confirmed by the first coins that Hacı minted and by the first mention of an 'Agicarei' in Genoese correspondence.

From the start Hacı was popular, and not only with his Tatar subjects. Reputedly handsome, he was a sophisticated cosmopolitan by the Horde's standards: he was fluent not only in Lithuanian, but in Polish and Ruthenian Russian, the administrative languages of the dual kingdom. He included the Virgin Mary in his prayers to Allah, he was as tolerant of Jews as of Christians and held ecumenical views of Muslim sects, building mosques and medreses, and patronizing Sufis. Next to his palace at Qırq-Yer stood a Greek monastery: Hacı sold two of his horses to pay for the monastery's wax candles. The Qur'anic motto on Hacı's seal read, 'O Allah, ruler of kingdoms, thou givest power to whom thou wishest.' He was nicknamed *melek*, 'angel', by his subjects.

Grand Duke Kazimieras of Lithuania (after 1447 also Kazimierz, king of Poland) became an even closer ally of Hacı, as Seyyid Ahmad kept raiding southern Lithuania, eventually reaching Lvov in 1452. Crossing the Dnepr on his retreat to Horde territory, Seyyid was intercepted by Hacı's forces. Seyyid escaped, but those of his men who survived were drafted into the Crimean Tatar army, in the first of a series of recruitments by Hacı that repopulated Crimea and strengthened its forces. Once in Lithuanian territory Seyyid Ahmad shocked Lithuania by attacking the citizens of Kiev. He was arrested by Lithuanian nobles who now went back on their initial plan to use the Horde to seize power in Lithuania. In 1456 Seyyid, would-be khan of the Horde, was removed to Kaunas as an 'honoured' prisoner; some of his sons joined the Tatar community at Trakai, others fled to Moldavia, whose ruler promised to keep them imprisoned until Poland-Lithuania asked for them. At last Tuqtamış's descendants were no longer a threat to Crimea. Hacı Giray could claim to be the legitimate ruler of the entire Horde, a claim that he and future Girays asserted from time to time, taking or inheriting for a while the new khanates of Kazan and Hacı Tarhan (Astrakhan). Hacı continued to support Poland and Lithuania, in 1453 helping Kazimierz to put down a rebellion by his nobles.

In 1453 Constantinople fell to Sultan Mehmed II Fetih (the Conqueror). The Byzantine empire was now totally extinct. The Ottomans had inherited its territories including, in theory, Crimea, over which Byzantium exercised only a nominal hold. The territory controlled by Hacı Giray already had a sizeable Ottoman community, refugees from Anatolia and enterprising traders. He understood the implications of the new superpower. The Ottomans were known to revere the memory, descendants and lands of Genghis Khan, but this deference did not necessarily imply recognition of Genghisid independence. Even before Constantinople fell, on 8 March 1453,

Hacı sent a decree adorned with gold insignium and a red khanate seal: it was a certificate exemption, a *tarhan yarlıq*, to be borne by Hakım Yahya, a visiting senior Ottoman official.[4] The decree was, strikingly, written not in Ottoman, but in Qıpçaq Turkish and may not have been intelligible to all its recipients. (In a decree of 1456 Hacı Giray used the pre-Islamic formula for his oath, a Turkicized version of the Mongolian *möngke t(e)ngri-yin küçündür*, 'by the power of eternal God'.[5]) The *tarhan yarlıq* is of historical interest because of its extensive list of taxes and officials for which the recipient was given exemption and immunity. It warns everyone from the khan's *beylerbey* to scribes and customs officers and military police that all administrative sanctions and charges are to be suspended. The taxes include those on mowing, pasturage, draught horses, sales of goods or of animals and slaves, inns, postage, cheetah-handlers and falconers; Hakım Yahya was to be allowed to go where he wanted and to express himself freely: as for anyone contravening the terms of this *tarkhan yarlıq*, 'let misfortune be with him'. The impression gained from this document is of a highly organized and well-policed state with an elaborate tax system. It also reveals that Eminek, grandson of Tekene, and now chief of the Şirin clan and commander of the khanate's army, was on his way to becoming chief vizier to Hacı and his successor.

Hacı Giray expanded his effective rule over two of the three Noğay Tatar clans who roamed the steppes from the Dnestr to the Caspian, and over the coastal Circassian clans who lived west of the Kuban river, just as he increased his population and army at the expense of defeated minor Tatar rulers all over the steppes.

Ottoman hegemony demanded a compromise to save Crimea from either conflict with or absorption into Sultan Mehmed's empire. In summer 1454 an enormous Turkish fleet of sixty ships (crewed by ethnic Greek sailors, commanded by the admiral Temir-Kaya) entered the Black Sea, primarily to reconnoitre and intimidate the Italian colonists. Repulsed by the Moldavian port of Cetatea Alba, which was protected by strong walls and a contingent of Genoese mercenaries, the fleet went to Chersonesus, where they burnt a ship, looted the port and took Genoese hostages. Then they sailed on to Kerç, the furthest point of Crimea, and crossed the Sea of Azov to the Greek city of Vosporo, where they intercepted a moored Turkish boat that had taken Hacı Giray's emissary to Constantinople for discussions about the dispatch of the armed Ottoman fleet. The boat's crew disembarked, took up piracy and looted Vosporo. They were confronted and boarded by a Genoese sea captain. Thirty-seven of the pirates who had not drowned were sent to Kaffa: seventeen were Caucasian tribesmen (Getians) and were promptly hanged; seven Tatars were sentenced to row galleys; and thirteen Turks were handed over to Temir Kaya when his fleet came back to Kaffa. When Temir Kaya moored within cannon range of the city, Kaffa's inhabitants were at first worried about the vulnerability of their ruined city walls. The Turks disembarked to consult with Hacı Giray. Shortly after, groups of sailors disembarked, allegedly to take on provisions: the Genoese consul Demetrio Vivaldi allowed them to enter the city, but magistrates intervened when Armenians and Greeks hurled themselves at the Turks who were looting the market. Armed Turks landed, lost a dozen men in an attempt to scale the city walls, and the fleet moved closer from its moorings to the port. At this point Hacı Giray and 6,000 Tatars appeared, outnumbering Temir Kaya's forces. The Genoese began negotiating with Temir Kaya. Hacı Giray, with bodyguards and interpreters, went down to the ramparts and demanded to talk to Temir Kaya. In the end the Turks received provisions, and Hacı Giray extorted 3 per cent of Kaffa's customs dues, while the Genoese paid both Hacı and Temir Kaya a fine of nearly 5,000 gold liras. Sultan Mehmed's envoy, it turned out, had been living in Kaffa since April, trying to deter Demetrio Vivaldi from violent action, and negotiating the stringency of Ottoman control proposed for Kaffa. Laden with presents and with messages to the sultan, assuring the Ottomans of Genoese submission, the ambassador was sent home with Temir Kaya. When the fleet returned to base, Temir Kaya apparently complained to Sultan Mehmed that he had been badly treated by Kaffa's people, but that the city should still be designated the main port of the northern Black Sea.

This had been a reconnaissance expedition, ostensibly with merely diplomatic and trading aims. When the Ottomans returned, they had established their reputation for ruthlessness that would ensure compliance from the Genoese. Nevertheless, the Genoese completely restored the city walls, at a cost equal to the tribute they had paid to Hacı Giray. Fortunately, the canny Genoese had transferred all their convertible wealth to the Bank of St George, whose directors helped them finance the fortifications. Genoese acquiescence in Hacı Giray's extortions, however, hastened their doom, for the Bank of St George calculated that Kaffa was unlikely to repay its debts, now that traders' ships could reach the Black Sea from the Mediterranean only by running the gauntlet of Turkish cannon in the Bosphorus. The Catholic bishop of Kaffa, Iacobo Campora, wrote to Genoa, complaining of Consul Vivaldi's weakness. The vulnerability of the Genoese in Kaffa only increased the authority of the city's Tatar prefect (*tudun*, an old Khazar title), who was charged with looking after the khan's interests.

Hacı Giray had in summer 1456 to face the consequences of his extortions: his name disappears from Genoese correspondence and is replaced by that of his son Hayder, who conspired with the Genoese and seized power. In autumn the Tatar *bey*s intervened and Hayder fled to Lithuania. Khan Seyyid Ahmad of the Horde may have taken advantage of the breach between Kaffa and Hacı Giray; the latter had briefly to seek refuge either in Lithuania or in Ottoman territory. The prospect of Ottoman domination of the Crimea seemed, however, to alarm both Hacı Giray and the Genoese, for both sides asked a reluctant Grand Duke Kazimierz for armed support.

Hacı's letter of 1461 to Grand Duke Kazimierz of Poland-Lithuania demonstrates a bolder mindset: he considered that, given the collapse of Seyyid Ahmad's authority, he was now the lawful heir to the entire Golden Horde territory. He regarded himself as the freeholder of those lands that had over the past fifty to eighty years been recovered from the Mongol yoke by Polish, Lithuanian and Russian rulers. Moreover, by driving Seyyid Ahmad out of Crimea in 1456, Grand Duke of Muscovy Ivan III came to regard Hacı Giray as a potential ally against the Horde's attacks. In 1464 Hacı proved his worth to the Russians by interposing his Crimean forces when Seyyid Ahmad attempted to ford the Don into Ivan's territory.

Unlike his rivals, such as Ulu Muhammad, Hacı was too cautious to assert his wide-ranging claims to be the ruler of the Golden Horde by invading the central Horde lands. If he felt so disposed, he could allow Lithuania, as he allowed Moscow, the use of territories he nominally owned, but they had, if not paying annual tribute, at least to acknowledge his sovereignty as part of the seemingly generous terms of the lease:

> This is the word of Hacı Giray Khan:
>   To the ulans and lords counsellors of our right and left hand, to the princes, monks, laymen, and commoners of the Ruthenian state [*sic*]:
>   As previously our elder brother [Tuqtamış], when his horse was growing sweaty [beneath him], would come seeking hospitality to Grand Duke Vytautas, in Lithuania, and he enjoyed great sincerity, we have firstly granted Kiev along with all [dependencies] to the Lithuanian state, to our brother, Grand Duke Kazimir. And as the Lithuanian lords have requested from us, we have granted their request and – in accordance with the acts of the first khans – [we

have granted] namely: Kiev along with all incomes, lands, waters, and their profits.

There then follows a list of some twenty towns and regions stretching from northwest Russia to Moldova and the Black Sea:

> 1 And seeing great friendly acts [on your part], we have granted [all this] to our brother, Grand Duke Kazimierz, the lords, princes, counsellors, [and] to the Lithuanian state Pskov and Veliki Novgorod along with all castles and all their incomes and profits, and [their] villages along with their incomes and profits.
> 2 And [as concerns] the castles that are registered above, the lords of these castles along with the boyars, as they previously [used to serve] our brother, Duke Vytautas, they will now serve you, our brother, Duke Sigismund, and our brother, Duke Kazimierz.

The threat behind this generous grant then appeared: 'They should also pay taxes invariably, as they used to serve previously from these castles and villages. And if they do not obey, nothing good awaits them.'[6]

Grand Duke Kazimierz had in fact requested this letter from Hacı: he was prepared to pay his 'ground rent', because the document was proof to his enemy, Muscovy (also subject in theory to the Horde's territorial claims), that Poland-Lithuania was the authorized ruler of these largely Russian or Ruthenian lands.

When he needed income, Hacı could easily find a pretext to fine the Genoese enormous sums (as much as 2,400 gold liras – a total of 17 kilograms (36 lb)) for encroachment and damages, as well as taxes, and they could afford to buy him off. But in the 1450s the Ottoman Turks, as merchants and soldiers, were hostile to the Italians and able to block their access to the Black Sea at the Bosphorus or the Dardanelles. The Italians' prosperity was in jeopardy. Hacı Giray decided to open his own ports and, in collaboration with Prince Alexei of Theodoro, built Inkerman in the bay of Kalamita. Graeco-Goth merchants protested at this breach of their monopoly, but Alexei told them the new port was under the khan's protection. Sensing that the Ottomans would also disapprove of this expansion, Pope Paul II, the Patriarch of Antioch and Holy Roman Emperor Friedrich III urged Hacı Giray to resist the Ottomans. Hacı was reminded that Theodoro, as a Christian principality, must not be invaded. The proposal was not as outlandish as it might seem: some Muslim Turkic principalities in Anatolia had already united with Western Europe against the Ottoman empire. Hacı Giray, however, politely refused to join the West: Mehmed II was conducting *ghazavat*, a holy war that every Muslim was obliged to support. As a concession, Hacı did decree that, were Poland-Lithuania to join an anti-Ottoman coalition, he would support it. Approached by Western diplomats, Kazimierz was tempted to join such an alliance, but felt on reflection that it was dangerous to provoke such a powerful neighbour as Sultan Mehmed Fetih.

In the early 1460s Hacı Giray faced new enemies: Mahmud, son of the late Küçük Muhammad, khan of the steppes between the Volga and the Urals, quarrelled with his brother Ahmad and defeated him. Mahmud then moved west to the Don, heading either for Moscow or the Crimea. Mahmud proposed to Sultan Mehmed II an Ottoman–Horde alliance against Crimea. The sultan was at the time holed up in the country to escape plague in Constantinople, and did not receive the letter. Hacı, too canny to show anti-Ottoman feeling, struck and defeated Mahmud's eastern Horde, informing Pope Paul II's envoys to the Crimea on 10 September 1465. Some of Mahmud's men went over to Ahmad; others joined Hacı Giray's army and settled in Crimea. By accident, Hacı Giray had achieved a goal that had eluded his ancestors: access to the now empty throne of the Horde.

Hacı Giray died in 1466, before he could take advantage of his victory. Some suspected that, despite his nearing seventy years of age, he had been poisoned, a fate not unusual in fifteenth-century Crimea. In the 1440s Prince Alexei of Theodoro is known to have ordered poisoned sugared almonds from Venice: when asked why he needed them, he replied 'for fighting the infidels'.

Mengli Giray Khan

Like his father Hacı, Mengli repeatedly seized and lost power for over a decade before finally securing the khanate. He met with hostility from not only khans of the Great Horde, the Crimean *qaraçı beys* and the Genoese of Kaffa, but the newly arrived Ottoman Turks and his own brothers. As in the Ottoman empire, succession in the Crimean Khanate was complicated by rivalry between an inordinate number of full and half-brothers. Sultan Mehmed Fetih ordained that the eldest brother should, on succeeding, execute his male siblings; that was never a rule, and rarely a custom in Crimea, where the *qaraçı beys* (or, in later years, the Ottoman sultan) would choose a candidate from the surviving Giray family. Hacı Giray had seven or eight surviving sons: the eldest, Nur Devlet, was the first to claim the khanate, but Hacı may have had another son, Mengli, in mind. While Ottoman Turks expected the senior wife's eldest son to succeed, the Mongol tradition differed: the eldest three sons, if they were adults, might already have been allotted senior posts, so that a fourth son could occupy the vacant throne. Mengli was probably the fourth surviving son of Hacı's first wife (whose identity we do not know).

Hacı gave only one of his sons a common Islamic name – Nur Devlet; others were traditional Turkic, such as Kutluğ Zaman 'Happy Times', Yamğurça 'Fallow Deer' and Hayder 'Lion'. Mengli was, however, the only son to be given the dynastic name Giray. The name Mengli was rare, for it means '[born] with a birth mark'. In the old Turkic religion, a birth mark (*menge* in Mongolian, *beng* in modern Crimean Tatar), even if concealed by clothing, was a matter of pride: it showed that a child had been marked by the swan goddess Umai, the supreme female divinity who determined the birth, prosperity and death of those whom she protected. (Tatars never killed swans.)

Despite a dynastic name and divine birth mark, Mengli, only 21 years old, could not at first enjoy undisputed power. Within months of his father's death, Mengli had to oust his brother Hayder, who had attempted a coup ten years earlier. Two *tarkhan yarlıq* (decrees of exemption) written for Ottoman subjects in 1467 and 1468 show that Mengli soon exerted authority. Şirin clan *bey*s, the well-known Eminek and Mamak, consistently supported Mengli. Nevertheless, the eldest son, Nur-Devlet, supported by other *bey*s, claimed the throne; at first Mengli and Nur-Devlet tried an uneasy division of power, before Mengli, hoping for armed support, retreated to the fortress of Mangup, the capital of the Graeco-Gothic principality of Theodoro (where the polyglot population spoke Tatar as well as Greek and Gothic).[7] Nur-Devlet sent an embassy to Poland-Lithuania, assuring Kazimierz that the Crimean Khanate was still his ally. Simultaneously, in what seemed a renunciation of former victories, Nur-Devlet wrote to Khan Ahmad of the Great Horde, asking for confirmation of sovereignty over Crimea. Such deference lost Nur-Devlet the support of many Tatar *bey*s and of the Genoese in Kaffa. Mamak, the new Şirin *beylerbey*, supported Mengli, as did the Genoese. Kaffa's consul Gentile Camilla invited Mengli and Mamak to his inauguration.

In his youth Mengli may have spent some years in Kaffa: he certainly knew Latin and Italian, both literary and the Ligurian dialect in which he corresponded with Kaffa's officials. He was curious about European history (and would later order books from Constantinople). Grateful, he reduced

Kaffa's annual tax and, with a Genoese regiment, rode to Qırq-Yer to expel Nur-Devlet. Nur-Devlet fled to the North Caucasus, from where he lobbied a prospective ally, the Ottoman sultan, likely to be hostile to the Italians supporting Mengli. Nur-Devlet, backed by Grimaldi, a Genoese turncoat, proposed attacking Crimea by land if the sultan sent a fleet across the Black Sea. Grimaldi was denounced; the Kaffa consul condemned him to die. (Generously bribed by Grimaldi's friends, Mengli reprieved him.) Consul Camilla sent an expedition to the Circassian coast, captured Nur-Devlet and three of his brothers and imprisoned them in Kaffa (comfortably enough for them to receive guests). Only later did Mengli regret that his rivals had not been killed and induced the chief guard, Giovanni Barbo, to murder them. Nur-Devlet's servant, however, was alerted and killed Barbo. The killing of a Genoese by a Tatar caused a riot in Kaffa: the consul ordered 'Nur Devlet, five of his male relatives and two slave-servants to be put on two large armed sloops'. They were taken to an impregnable fort in Sudaq, and Genoa was asked for permission to execute them. Once again, Mengli reprieved his brothers (but asked the Genoese to imprison another brother, Melik-Emin, at Cembalo).[8]

While Sultan Mehmed was conquering the Christian Balkans, it was not only the Christians of Theodoro and Kaffa who were worried, but Mengli Giray too. For one thing, the Anatolian Turkish sultanates had already lost their autonomy to Istanbul; for another, Mengli's hostile brother Nur-Devlet was now in cahoots with the sultan. Istanbul, to judge by documents assembled at the time by Feridun-bey, did not regard either Giray brother as a legitimate khan: they spoke of Ahmad, khan of the Great Horde, as the real ruler of Crimea; Kaffa was to them just 'Little Istanbul'. (The Italian diplomat and traveller Giosafat Barbaro regarded Eminek, the all-powerful Şirin *bey*, as Crimea's real ruler.) In 1469 an Ottoman squadron landed at Kaffa, burnt some villages and took prisoners as a prelude to the expulsion of the hated Italian infidels. The Genoese appealed to Mengli Giray, 'We order our authorities in Kaffa to appeal, when necessary, to Your Radiance, as they would to a father and a senior, and to be unfailingly obedient in carrying out Your wishes.'

Mengli was then trying to secure an understanding with the Ottomans: on 25 October 1469 he wrote to the sultan with only minimal politeness after an extravagantly laudatory initial address:

We haven't managed to establish relations with you by an exchange of competent envoys who could go to see you and return to us. But we have common business which needs settling. You used to be a friend and brother to my father the Khan, and we wish you to remain one. But your man Yakub, in command of galleys, has come here; we received him with kindly words, but he arrested and took away one of my men and set two of my towns on fire . . .

he took away a large number of Kaffa's inhabitants, including one of my equerries [*nuker*]. He said, 'Kaffa people arrested my men and killed one. That's why we've taken prisoners.'

All these words are lies . . . Any damage suffered by Kaffa is suffered by us. You know best how to settle this matter.[9]

When the Şirin *beylerbey* Mamak died in autumn 1473, the succession should have been predictable: a senior male relative, approved by Mengli and by the Kaffa *tudun*, would have replaced him. The likely heir, Mengli's brother-in-law Kara-Mirza, had to compete with Eminek. Kaffa's Italians relied on Eminek and they insisted on his appointment by Mengli. Eminek bullied the khan: either Mengli would let him marry his stepmother, Hacı Giray's widow, and thus make him a member of the royal family, or the Genoese would free Nur-Devlet from Sudaq and appoint him khan instead. To reinforce his threat, Eminek promised to cut off the supply of grain to the city.

A new rival for *beylerbey*, Şeidak, the stepson of the late Mamak, announced his candidacy. In vain, Mamak's widow bribed Kaffa's senators with 1,000 gold coins. Şeidak visited the khan of the Great Horde and, in exchange for the Horde's support, offered to let the khan's young relative Canibek become khan of Crimea. This prospect made Eminek and Mengli Giray forget their differences, even though Eminek was now asking Sultan Mehmed Fetih for protection from Mengli, the Horde and, possibly, the Genoese, too. Eminek's threats to starve Kaffa aroused such popular outrage that he had to flee the country. Mengli could now lure Şeidak back to Crimea, without the protection of the Horde's army or Prince Canibek, by falsely promising to make him the Şirin *beylerbey*. This was a masterstroke, but Mengli's triumph was short-lived. A new, corrupt consul came to power in Kaffa, was bribed to appoint Şeidak *tudun* and then insisted that Mengli also appoint Şeidak *beylerbey* of the Şirins, despite the scorn the clan felt for him. Otherwise Kaffa would release and install Mengli's brother Nur-Devlet. As many prophesied, this blackmail angered both Genoese and Tatars.

Mengli's own circle, when he returned to his capital Qırq-Yer in March 1475, protested and insisted that he step down. He had to return to Kaffa, where he was received with respect, but not allowed to leave. He was helpless in the face of intrigue: Eminek, furious at the appointment of Şeidak as *beylerbey*, wrote to Sultan Mehmed Fetih inviting him to take over the Genoese ports, as long as he let the Şirins have the best of the loot. Şeidak was in hiding when the Şirin clan, led by Eminek, brought their army up to the city walls.

The sultan took note of the invitation and decided to make Crimea a vassal of the Ottoman empire, particularly as he needed the help of the Tatar cavalry for his war on Prince Stefan of Moldavia. On 31 May 1475 a fleet of five hundred Ottoman vessels under the chief vizier Gedik Ahmed Paşa approached Kaffa. It was joined by Eminek's force, but Eminek was given no reward. The Genoese were overwhelmed and surrendered. Three hundred were executed and 1,000 boys and youths were conscripted as Ottoman janissaries. This was the end of Italian power in Crimea. Not all Genoese were executed or deported. A few were retained as scribes and translators for commerce and diplomacy. Others stayed on, becoming Muslims and Tatars within a generation. In the early 1920s it became startlingly clear how well Crimean Italians had adapted when 32 peasants, speaking only Tatar and in Tatar dress, were tried by a Soviet court for hiring day-labourers: the court was astounded by their surnames, including Cambani, Parcelli, Mauro, Di-Piero and Gianuzzo.

Foreign merchants had all their wealth confiscated. After paying a large tribute, the Kaffans were ordered to go home and rebuild their walls. The same happened to the other Genoese ports. Afterwards the Turks went to Sudaq and freed Mengli's eldest brother Nur-Devlet, who set off to Qırq-Yer and declared himself khan.

Mengli fought back, but was captured.[10] He escaped execution only because the admiral felt that his sentence needed to be confirmed in Istanbul. With other high-ranking prisoners, Mengli was sent to Istanbul. Accounts vary: he was about to be beheaded when a reprieve came from the sultan who had decided either that Mengli was too handsome and noble to execute, or that he would be more reliable than Nur-Devlet as khan and cavalry commander in the Moldavian campaign. A delegation of Crimean Tatars, it is said, caught sight of Mengli offered for sale in the slave market and pleaded with Mehmed II to reinstate him as khan. What is certain is that Mengli wrote a plea to an influential Istanbul vizier. The plea is written not only in a calligraphic script, but in sophisticated Persian with Qur'anic Arabic phrases – quite unlike the Qıpçaq Turkish of Mengli's 1469 letter to Mehmed II. (Perhaps Mengli had been studying hard while in Kaffa, or he used a professional scribe, but the nobility of the Horde and its khanates, though they had forgotten the Mongol language by 1300, were usually fluent in the lingua francas of their territory: not only Qıpçaq Turkic, but Persian and Arabic, and the Horde's empires employed more translators and interpreters than any empire since.)

> While imprisoned in a dark cell, I heard about your exalted, praise-worthy qualities, and hope that salvation will come through you.
>
> Thanks to God, freed from this dark prison, I have become a subject of our Sultan. How can I pay back this debt if God does not give me the means?
>
> You must speak up to the Sultan in my defence. In Ahmed Paşa's presence I swore obedience and gratitude to the Sultan and promised to be the friend of his friends and the enemy of his enemies . . .
>
> I fear that you may believe other people's lies. Don't let yourself get angry with me before you have information from me.[11]

The subsequent transformation in Mengli's fate supports the story that the sultan adopted and housed Mengli in his palace for three years. Reluctantly or not, once confined, this Tatar warlord was turned into an educated diplomat and courtier, and a poet, too. For the time being he was unable to intervene in Crimean events and had to endure news of developments passively. Effectively a border was drawn along the range of coastal mountains from Cembalo (Balaklava) to Vosporo (Kerç), and this coastal strip became an Ottoman domain. (Nevertheless, the khan of Crimea was to receive a large portion of customs dues collected by the Ottomans.) Inland, where the khan still ruled, the *beys*, disempowering Hayder, chose Nur-Devlet as khan. The Great Horde Khan Ahmad and his nephew Cani Beg, however, threatened to overwhelm the khanate with their enormous army. Revolution struck the Şirin clan, too: Eminek was replaced by his younger brother Hacike, who was allied to Cani Beg.

Sultan Mehmed initiated the Ottoman practice of keeping 'spare' Girays close to him, in case he needed to replace a recalcitrant Crimean khan. So far he had Mengli as insurance, should Nur-Devlet prove a disappointment. Mehmed aimed to conquer Christian Moldavia and its ruler, who was disliked because of the help Moldavia had given to Prince Alexei of Theodoro. Nur-Devlet was meanwhile preoccupied with defending his territory against the Horde. On the sultan's behalf, Eminek led 10,000 men across the Dnestr, but was beaten back by the Moldavians. This defeat was exploited by Cani Beg and the Horde, who invaded the north of Crimea. Eminek had to abandon the Moldavian campaign, leaving the Ottomans in the lurch. It took a year to oust Cani Beg and it was hard to reinstate Nur-Devlet against his brother Hayder's objections. The chaos was unabated. In retrospect, Mengli's rule now seemed like a lost paradise. Eminek and Nur-Devlet both appealed to the sultan in Istanbul.

Eminek's first letter of May 1476 complained of his brother Hacike's treacherous turpitude and complicity with Cani Beg's Horde, but he promised to reinforce the Ottoman troops fighting against Moldavia. In October, after failing to come to Mehmed's aid, he had to abase himself:

> I, your wretched servant, received your honourable majesty's message about your intention to wage Holy War against Moldavia, may it be cursed by God ... We did march against the enemy with our entire army, burnt a number of infidel fortresses and took lots of loot. But on the way home we received news that the enemy [the Horde] had ravaged our country, we abandoned our loot and meant to go back to Crimea, but the infidels caught up with us and attacked. They inflicted heavy casualties, my two brothers were martyred, we lost many men, horses and arms. We took refuge in Qırım city, but have no more horses.[12]

In May 1477 Khan Nur-Devlet sent Sultan Mehmed a note asking him to ignore hostile reports, 'for my enemies are more numerous than my friends'. The following year Eminek sensed a change in the wind and advised the sultan, in Ottoman Turkish strongly flavoured with Qıpçaq, that only reinstating Mengli would restore order to Crimea:

> Now all our lords and all our people wish to have Mengli in charge; because the two other [brothers] won't come to terms, our entire country is ruined. If Mengli Giray returns, the entire population will hang on his every word, obey and respect his orders. Do us the favour of nominating Mengli Giray before the Horde's Khan approaches Crimea – then the country will be in my hands. But if you delay, we shall lose the country and its people. On my own I lack the power needed to defend it ... If the country abandons us, I shall present myself to the beauty of your august face and enter your sublime service ... Nur-Devlet is good for nothing ... the people are disgusted with him. We want you to give the following advice to

Mengli Giray: 'Busy yourself with the country's affairs and follow closely Eminek's advice.'[13]

Sultan Mehmed had lost confidence in Nur-Devlet's ability either to fight alongside the Ottoman army or to control his Tatar subjects. He duly deposed Nur-Devlet and restored Mengli. Mengli must have negotiated a superior status for himself above the sultan's viziers and other vassals, and obtained guarantees of future semi-autonomy for Crimea. No documentary evidence survives, but in the eighteenth century a fairly plausible reconstruction of a sultan–khan agreement was concocted. Among its more credible points are:

> The Sultan may never put on the Khanate's throne anyone except a prince descended from Genghis Khan. The Ottoman Porte may never on any pretext execute anyone of the Giray family. The Porte may not refuse any written request by the Khan. On any campaign the Khan must receive from the Porte 120 purses of gold for his bodyguards, and 80 for his equerries and Ottoman guardsmen.

Back in the Crimea in spring 1478, escorted with due ceremony by a senior Ottoman official as far as the Tatar-controlled port of Gözleve (today's Evpatoria), Mengli was then shipped eastwards to Kaffa. He was at first guarded by a Turkish armed escort and confined to the city, partly for his own protection, partly because Mehmed did not yet entirely trust him. A short note from Mengli complains of being housed in impoverished and ruined quarters. Shortly afterwards, Mengli managed to cross the city walls on the pretext of watching a Tatar display of horsemanship; he himself mounted a horse, gave a virtuoso demonstration of his undiminished skills, and with a crowd of applauding Tatars, in defiance of Ottoman instructions, galloped off, escorted by a hundred followers, first to Eski Qırım and then to his capital Qırq-Yer in the mountains.

Mengli was not sure that the Ottomans would respect the autonomy of his khanate; he had courageously freed himself of the tutelage of the Şirin clan *bey* Eminek, who favoured direct subordination to Istanbul. In a letter of 30 December 1481 to the exiled Genoese Bartolomeo Campofregoso and Lodizio Fieschi (sent in Greek and Latin translation to avoid scrutiny by Turks), Mengli suggested they visit him in the guise of servants of the Polish-Lithuanian king Kazimierz IV: the letter implied a conspiracy to break free of Ottoman domination and return control of Kaffa and other Christian settlements to Genoa.[14]

Mengli's brothers Nur-Devlet and Hayder fled, first to the protection of Grand Duke Kazimierz, who settled them together in Kiev, now that they were reconciled. The sultan accepted Mengli's rejection of Ottoman control, even conceding him the right to mint Crimean coinage. Generous annual subsidies to Mengli, his immediate family, his *beys* and his officials – quite apart from the mass of silver paid for military collaboration – made the independent interior of Crimea as wealthy as the Turkish coastal ports. The prospect of making war in the Balkans alongside the Ottomans did not daunt the Crimeans: unlike the Ottomans, they had no territorial ambitions, but they did relish the prospect of the trophies and slaves that victory brought.

Independently of the Ottomans, Mengli devised his own foreign policy. Poland-Lithuania was not only sheltering his treacherous brothers, but was seeking an alliance with Mengli's main enemy, the Great Horde under Khan Ahmad, in a joint move to restrain an increasingly powerful Muscovy. In Moscow Tsar Ivan III, who had in his youth defeated Khan Ahmad, was 'gathering the Russian lands'. Fortunately for Mengli, Ahmad had decided that Russia had to be defeated before he could move against Crimea. In 1480 there was an almost farcical confrontation on the frozen River Ugra: Ahmad failed to attack, partly because of the cold, partly because Kazimierz had not kept a promise to join battle. Ahmad changed directions, began to loot Lithuanian territory and was murdered in his sleep by rivals. This 'Stand on the Ugra' marked the end of the Horde's domination of Slav territory. The Horde now disintegrated into four miniature states: Kazan, Astrakhan, Siberia and Crimea. Crimea was economically, politically and militarily the best placed of the new khanates, and Mengli, like his successors, had the best claim to inherit the right to annual tribute due from Lithuanian and Russian grand duchies to Genghis Khan's original Horde.

Qırq-Yer, the capital of the Yashlav clan, lay next to the Jewish hilltop settlement of Çufut Qale and was safer than Eski Qırım, the Şirin clan's capital, which was too close to the coast. Eski Qırım began to decline: reports from Maciej z Miechowa (Mekhovsky) say that 'the houses are wretched, the town mostly abandoned.' In Qırq-Yer Mengli had a fortified palace of wooden beams and stone and baked mud walls. Here he held important prisoners: the Lithuanian ambassador in 1493, and a hostile Tatar prince, Menglişek. Like other Crimean khans, Mengli liked to travel and make temporary headquarters of other towns than his capital, or to stay with his army guarding the isthmus at Or Qapı (which was also an important centre for foreign trade and for the lucrative customs dues – 7 per cent to the khan, a lesser sum to the Şirin *beylerbey*). But he would reside principally in Qırq-Yer until in 1505 the permanent palace city of Bağçasaray was built in more spacious surroundings downstream. Meanwhile the population of this mountain zone of Crimea was increasing: Christian Greeks fled from the Ottoman-occupied coast to Mengli's religiously tolerant zone; families migrated, at first fifty at a time, from the defeated Horde. Mengli's Crimean Khanate was becoming one of Europe's most densely populated – and profitably taxed – countries. Although he had only a skeletal bureaucracy, of whom some key members were foreigners, such as the Jewish-Genoese prince Guizolfi, while others were extortioners or thugs, Mengli maintained the complex, sometimes oppressive Mongol taxation system, with extra levies on non-Muslims. He was able to tax Tatars, Armenians, Greeks and Jews even if they lived in Ottoman-administered ports such as Kaffa.

Mengli's khanate was rich in soldiers, slaves, horses, grazing, salt and arms (but not firearms). Despite tribute and subsidies from neighbouring states, Crimea was, however, short of silver: when a horse belonging to Muscovy's ambassador was accidentally let go among the Tatar herds, Mengli had to pay 3 roubles and borrow the money from the market traders. Large sums might have to be borrowed from the Ottoman merchants in Kaffa. Trade with Russia had to cross lawless steppes, where goods and sometimes traders could disappear without trace. In 1502 the Russian ambassador Alexander Golokhvastov delivered a typical 'memorandum of losses' demanding compensation from Khan Mengli Giray for confiscations, robberies and assaults.[15] That same year Crimean traders had to go to Kiev – hostile territory – to buy rye. The steppe pastures still produced little grain, and in drought years none.

Several times Mengli suggested to Moscow that their two countries should invade Lithuania at harvest time in order to loot the grain. In Crimea the land was efficiently farmed by the Greeks and Turks in the southeast of the country, close to the ports of Sudaq and Kaffa, but even so imported grain was needed. Under the Genoese, rich families, such as the Guasco, had held Tatars in feudal bondage, their ruthless exploitation symbolized by public gallows. Mengli maintained this feudalism, keeping strict control over the fishermen and salt producers of northeast Crimea. Crafts and manufacture were largely the monopoly of Greeks, Armenians and Jews, although Tatars were famed in Russia for their woven carpets and leatherwork. As the fifteenth century ended, Mengli founded new urban centres, notably Aqmescit and Qarasuvbazar, and began to build his palace at Salacıq (on the eastern edge of Bağçasaray) and border forts on the Dnepr river. He had to rely not just on money, but on masons sent by the Ottoman sultan. Furnishing his palace, he wrote to Grand Duke Ivan III, asking for silver chalices and ewers, 'because you have many and we have none'. Away from the coast, Tatars relied on slaves (often prisoners of war who might be freed after six years' work) to perform agricultural labour: richer Tatars might have twenty slaves, poorer ones five or six. Converting Tatar warrior-nomads to farmers was a slow process. It would take a century for Crimea to become more than self-sufficient in food.

Once he was installed in Qırq-Yer in summer 1478, Mengli drew up a contract with the city's leading citizens, the guildsmen, Muslims, Jews, Karaim and Armenians.[16] Mengli even imported a number of Genoese who had been deported from Kaffa to Istanbul: he settled them in the village of Süyür-Taş, where they served as his diplomatic corps: they kept their Italian and Catholic identity for two centuries, before assimilating with either the Greek or Tatar elite.

The leading citizens of Qırq-Yer were given tax relief denied to the inhabitants of the 'lower town'; slaves, at the time few in number, while exempt from tax, had limited rights. As for the prosperous 'upper town', Mengli promised to do no harm to their property or persons or to the townsfolk, and they in turn undertook to obey no authority other than his. If either side broke their oath, they would be deprived of salvation and their wives. Restored to power, Mengli Giray began sending messages and embassies to Moscow: their tone often implies that Crimea was the dominant partner. Ivan III's letters to Mengli tend to be 'petitions' (*chelobitiia*), whereas Mengli's letters to the grand duke are peremptory decrees beginning, 'My word is . . .' Although they had not taken part in the Stand on the River Ugra, Crimeans were effectively Russia's closest ally after 1480, well worth paying the tribute (called *pominki* and *vykhody* ('presents' and 'settlements')) and the cooperation. Even so, Mengli did not stop demanding annual 'presents' from Poland-Lithuania. Ivan III employed the refugee Khan Cani Beg and two of Mengli's rebel brothers, Nur-Devlet and Hayder (they were the 'others' whom Qırq-Yer's burghers now swore not to obey), at his court and in his army, thus relieving Mengli of serious threats to his power. In 1452 Ivan III's father Vasili had created, not far from Moscow, a puppet khanate of Kasimov for Qasim, the son of a khan of Kazan; Ivan III now made Nur-Devlet its khan, and Kasimov became a useful refuge for dissident and pro-Moscow Tatars, who would no longer threaten Crimea (although Ivan III could, if he wanted to undermine Mengli Giray, release Nur-Devlet and let him claim the khanate). Mengli's once troublesome brother Hayder hoped now to live as a private citizen in Moscow; Ivan III, as a precaution, exiled him to the northern city of Vologda, for centuries to come a holding pen for unwanted noblemen.

The alliance with Russia was cemented, like the alliance with Sultan Mehmed, by the diplomatic flexibility and energy of the Şirin *bey* Eminek and his brother and son, who continued, with short intervals until the end of the fifteenth century, whenever Eminek acquired other interests, to work for Mengli and for the Şirin clan as chief vizier. The new alliance had economic advantages for both sides: after the fall of Byzantium, Russia had limited trading contacts with Istanbul. Its exports – above all, falcons, narwhal horn and valuable furs – now reached the Ottoman empire via Crimea. Crimea prospered by supplying Russia with wine, salt and silk, while the Ottomans subsidized Mengli Giray personally by a generous share of the Kaffa customs dues. Mengli's army, however, needed more than cavalrymen armed with bows and sabres if it were to attack fortified towns in the north. In 1493 the Crimean Khanate used modern artillery for the first time against Lithuanian settlements: thereafter Mengli several times asked Kaffa or Moscow for muskets and cannon (and men to cast and fire them). Mengli was helped by his younger brother Yamgurça, a clever diplomat and army commander who persuaded Sultan Bayezid II to send military support when wanted, and reassured Grand Duke Ivan III of Crimean fidelity. Yamgurça was *qalğa* (designated heir to the khan), but he died after 1508. Mengli passed the post on to his sons, first Ahmat, then Muhammad. (Yamgurça's sons, however, made trouble: one, Ali Giray, assaulted his aunt Nur-Sultan and had to flee before he was killed; another, Yabunçı, sought asylum with Grand Duke Vasili III).

In September 1482 Mengli pleased Ivan III by making war on Lithuania. The Tatar army besieged Kiev, but not having artillery or siege machinery they could not storm the city walls, especially as Kazimierz had modern cannons. Instead, the khan's army set fire to the wooden suburbs and the flames spread to the city centre. Those inhabitants who did not suffocate in Kiev's caves were captured: Mengli's army went home with loot and hostages, including the city's governor-general and family. Mengli sent Ivan III a gold Eucharist chalice and tray from the cathedral of St Sophia. Kazimierz made peace, merely asking Mengli if he was now the Russian tsar's servant.

After this successful campaign, the first against Crimea's northern Christian neighbours, Mengli began to organize the Crimean state. The

Horde's power was less of a threat now that Ulu Muhammad had renounced war and modestly called himself mere khan of Kazan. The Genghisid system, like many in Western Europe, balanced a hereditary monarch against a baronial (or *beylerbey*) class, each limiting the other's power, although both sides were at times tempted to try for a monopoly of power. In Crimea the *bey* clans usually assembled together with the khan to consent to or even initiate matters of war, peace and taxation. Rarely, when in opposition, the *beys* assembled without the khan at a sacred *kaya altı*, 'lower rock'. Gradually the khans extended their powers by means of elite army groups and a class of officials. Mengli seems to have instituted the post of *qalğa*, viceroy in the khan's absence. The origin of the term is disputed: the popular explanation is that Mengli, when leaving to besiege Kiev, was asked who would look after the country in his absence. He supposedly replied, '*Büyük oğlum qalğa*,' which could be Tatar for 'Let my eldest son [Mehmed] stay behind,' but was interpreted as 'My eldest son is the *qalğa*.' The word may also be a Tatar distortion of *khalif*, 'representative, chargé d'affaires'. The post of designated heir and acting khan was permanently established, and even caught on among the *bey* clans. Mehmed Giray was given the income from tax on salt pans and part of the customs dues: he also had a small army and a base in the newly founded town of Aqmescit (today's Simferopol).

Mengli could only begin his people's transformation, so necessary given the density of population, from nomadic herders to settled tillers. Gradually towns spread in the hills around Qırq-Yer, orchards and smallholdings were established, and the steppes of northern Crimea, once pasture for horses and cattle, turned into fields of grain. Mengli himself acquired a family: already married to a Mahmut-Sultan, in 1487 he made a very advantageous marriage to a widow, Nur-Sultan, rather older than himself and with connections to the Horde. Nur-Sultan had a daughter by the Kazan Khan Halil (Ulu Muhammad's grandson), and after his death (in the Mongol tradition) married Halil's brother Ibrahim and had two sons. When Il-Khan, Ibrahim's stepson, took over Kazan, Nur-Sultan took refuge first with Tsar Ivan III, and then in the Crimea, where she had a cousin, knowing that Mengli welcomed refugee nobles from the Horde (eventually her brother, too, entered Crimean service). Nur-Sultan not only had connections: she was politically wise and proactive and, given the freedom that Crimean Tatar women then had, she was able to direct Mengli Giray's diplomacy. She advocated an alliance with Russia partly because she hoped Russia and Crimea would make her son khan of Kazan. Soon, in fact,

Il-Khan was overthrown and replaced by Muhammad-Emin, Nur-Sultan's son, so that Kazan became genealogically, as well as politically, tied to Crimea. Muhammad-Emin never met Mengli, but helped him in campaigns and called his new stepfather, as he called Ivan III, 'my brother'. In 1494–5 Nur-Sultan made the *hajj*, bringing back an Arab thoroughbred as a gift to Ivan III. She appointed Crimean officials and made grants of land; in 1510–11 she visited Moscow and then Kazan. On her initiative Crimea, Kazan and Moscow signed a peace treaty. Above all, she set an example of female collaboration for future khans and their womenfolk.

The new Ottoman Sultan Beyazid II moved closer to Mengli by appointing his own son Mehmed-Shahzade as Ottoman viceroy in Kaffa. It was to this sultan's son that the khan of the Horde, now destitute, appealed, asking to be allowed back to the Horde's old grazing grounds on the right bank of the Dnepr. Mengli and the Ottomans refused; access to the Dnepr was now blocked by Crimean and Ottoman forts and cannon. When in 1501 the Horde attacked Crimea, Sultan Beyazid tried in vain to prevent bloodshed, as did Khan Seyyid Ahmad. In vain, Mengli hoped to solve the conflict by making the Horde's men his own subjects: despite quarrels within the Horde, Mengli's army was forced to retreat to Crimea from its fort on the Don. The Horde asserted its right of access to old grazing grounds and now tried to make an alliance against Crimea with the new Polish-Lithuanian Grand Duke Alexander. The Crimeans, however, burned down the steppe grasses and the ensuing hard winter left the Horde starving: the khan's wife deserted him, as did many horsemen.

To make sure of finally defeating the Horde, Mengli, encouraged by his *divan* of Girays and *qaraçı bey*s, prepared for a new battle, this time fetching cannon and janissaries from the Ottoman viceroy Mehmed-Shahzade in Kaffa. Beyazid tried to make peace, but his emissary was murdered by the Horde. The Horde was now friendless after the Lithuanians backed out of their alliance. Mengli wanted to attack in May 1502, but hesitated because of the frozen ground: 'At this time,' he wrote to Tsar Ivan III, 'we always make hay, the larks make nests, but it's been an unusual winter.' In mid-June, reaching Samara on the Volga, ten days' ride from Crimea, he asked Ivan III for a detachment of musketeers; Ivan III never sent them, but Mengli found he did not need them against the demoralized Horde. When Mengli later moved up the Dnepr river, all he encountered were Horde horsemen surrendering to Crimeans. After the 1480 Stand on the River Ugra, the fiasco of 1502 put an end to the Great Horde's existence: its khan was left with just three hundred followers. On 15 June 1502 Mengli proclaimed, 'Glory to

God, He has given the Horde and all its territories into our hands.' He now gave himself Genghis Khan's title *Khakan* ('khan of khans'), 'Khakan of two seas and Sultan of two continents'. This was a crucial, if not universally acknowledged milestone, the beginning of the Crimean Khanate as a state to be reckoned with in European history. Nominally, the Great Horde's capital had been transferred from the Volga to Crimea. Qırq-Yer would within decades be subsumed by a new 'Garden Palace', Bağçasaray, a reconstruction of the fortified town of Salacıq, hidden by orchards, vineyards and steep rocks, watered by the Aşlama river. Mengli decided to spend the generous monetary gifts (but not the bejewelled ring) he had been given by Bayezid II on the latter's accession; Mengli suggested that Ivan III might match this with a donation of 70,000 gold pieces. The first new building was a mosque and medrese, on whose foundations and walls Mengli laboured personally. (The medrese's teachers and students were endowed with the income from 800 hectares (1,977 ac) of farmland.) The 'Hacı Giray' mosque was known as the Chain (*zincirli*) Mosque, for the heavy chain over the door that forced all who entered to bow down to knowledge and to faith. Mengli gave a speech at the opening, praising knowledge and scholarship above all. It is probably at this period that Mengli wrote Sufic poetry, of which only one short piece survives, a *kıta* equating erotic longing with the desire to see the face of God:

> How can I describe, my love, the anguish and pain of separation
>   from you?
> I have fire in my soul, tears in my eyes and daily sighs in my heart –
> In order to keep the bird of your face in my visions,
> I have turned my eyes into a cage of taut eyelashes.
> I, Khan Mengli, rule over all love's griefs and cares,
> I would not exchange love for all the kingdoms of the world.[17]

Mengli built his palace over Hacı Giray's mausoleum in Salacıq. At first this was called the Palace of Felicity, in imitation of 'The Threshold of Felicity', the sultan's palace complex in Istanbul. For the construction Mengli fetched from Venice an Italian architect, Aloisio Lamberti da Montagnana, who had been hired by Russia to rebuild the Kremlin. On their way the architect and his men were detained in Moldavia, and it took Mengli's intervention with Prince Stefan III of Moldavia as well as Ivan III's pleas to free them. After Lamberti had built Salacıq's monuments, Mengli reluctantly let the Italian travel on to Moscow. To assuage Ivan's annoyance at the delay,

Mengli sacrificed his precious rhinoceros horn ring, believed to give its wearer immunity to poison. All, however, that remains of Lamberti's Palace of Felicity is its Iron Gate, which was later removed to Bağçasaray.

The Crimean Khanate no longer resembled a mere protectorate of the Ottoman sultanate: Mengli was regarded as an equal by rulers in Istanbul and Moscow; the sultan's son Mehmed, paşa in Kaffa, called Mengli 'uncle'. The khan of the relict Great Horde still tried to gather men for revenge on Crimea: he lobbied the khans of Hacı-Tarhan (near Astrakhan) and of the Noğays, but they had no appetite for a fight. On the contrary Yamgurça and Tavakkul, the chief *beys* of the numerous and bellicose Noğay Tatars, now recognized the sovereignty of the Crimean Khanate over the Noğays. Tavakkul visited Mengli to swear an oath of loyalty. As the Noğays largely belonged to the Mangıt clan, the Crimean Mangıts now became a clan almost as powerful as the Şirins. Despite their numbers, swollen by assimilated Noğay prisoners of war (unlike most captives, neither enslaved nor ransomed), the Mangıt were considered upstarts, never fully trusted, and never attaining the lordly status of the four *qaraçı* clans. A dissident minority of Noğays tried to attack Astrakhan and, when repulsed, moved on Crimea: Yamgurça joined forces with the Crimean and Kazan armies and drove them west to the Ottoman-controlled Dnestr river. Sultan Bayezid II ordered them to return whence they came. Only fifty Noğay rebels were left. Fighting through blizzards, they headed for Lithuanian Kiev. Noğays had looted Kiev's borderlands, so the refugees were put in prison. Just like Seyyid Ahmad, confrontation with Mengli led to incarceration in Lithuania. But Sheikh Ahmad, the Noğay leader, potentially useful to Grand Duke Alexander of Poland-Lithuania, was treated as an honoured prisoner, albeit constantly guarded. Bored, the prisoner escaped and was caught in Trakai: he was for a year occasionally brought out as a curiosity for foreign diplomats and to meet his own former retainers.

In the new century Mengli played a leading role in determining the future of the Ottoman sultans. By 1507 both he and Bayezid II were over sixty. Mengli was still vigorous and had eight sons, ranging from the forty-year-old Mehmed (appointed *qalğa* after the death of his uncle Yamgurça) to the infant Sahib. All were obedient to Mengli's will. Bayezid, in failing health, had some thirteen daughters, to whom he gave the enhanced title and position of sultana; unlike Mengli, Beyazid had four surviving sons, and the elder two, Ahmed and Selim, were mature, assertive and eager for power. (The youngest prince, Mehmed, had been viceroy at Kaffa and, married to Mengli's daughter Aişa, showed no further ambitions.) Beyazid was fond of Ahmed and rightly terrified by Selim, who clearly wanted his father dead. Mengli warned Beyazid of the Tatar proverb, 'Two sheep's heads won't fit in one cooking-pot.' Beyazid made Ahmed governor of Amasya in western Anatolia, and sent Selim even further away to the Black Sea port of Trebizond, so that in the event of the sultan's death Ahmed would be nearer Istanbul and better placed to seize the throne. Selim, however, insisted on being made governor of a European province, close to the capital. For Mengli the situation became trickier when Mehmed died in 1504 and his widow Aişa married the formidable Selim, whom Mengli would now have to back in the interests of the Crimean Khanate. (Six years later, Selim told Mengli that, instead, he wanted his own son Süleyman, the future 'magnificent' sultan, to marry the widow Aişa: Selim changed his mind, however, and Mengli's daughter-in-law became Selim's wife.[18])

Mengli tried to persuade Selim to stay where he was, but the ambitious heir said, according to a letter written by Mengli in 1510 to the grand vizier Ali Paşa, that Selim wouldn't stay in Trebizond even if every stone there was a jewel. He announced that, unbidden, he was going to visit his father. He did so, first taking a ship to Crimea. His father sent out troops to stop him and Selim retreated to Kaffa, where he had warships built and demanded 15,000 men from Mengli Giray. At the same time, the rival heir Ahmed wrote to Mengli, making him a tempting offer to hand over the nine Crimean ports controlled by the Ottomans if Mengli would stop Selim's planned invasion, shackle Selim and send him to Istanbul for execution. Tatar morality, however, forbade Mengli to arrest a guest and a son-in-law: he also knew that the Ottoman army and officials preferred Selim to his more pliant brother Ahmed, and that to cooperate with Selim would ensure continued Ottoman protection for the khanate. Mengli was opposed by his own son and *qalğa* Mehmed, who was dazzled by the offer to return the Crimean ports to the khan's rule. Mengli held a banquet for Selim, and the *qalğa* boldly asked him to hand over Kaffa and the other former Genoese ports when he inherited the throne. 'Sultans take territory, they don't give it to anyone,' responded Selim, and walked out of the banqueting tent.

Mengli Giray also walked out, furious with his son, and asked Sa'adet, a less reckless son, handsome, witty and disciplined, to persuade Selim to leave Crimea. Selim immediately did so, taking Sa'adet with him to Istanbul. There Bayezid was bullied first into declaring Selim heir to the throne and then into abdicating and retiring to a distant estate, where Selim may have had him poisoned to economize on his father's pension. The new Sultan Selim, nicknamed Yavuz, 'the inexorable', took Sa'adet Giray and an army to Anatolia: Sa'adet was instructed to capture and kill Selim's brother Ahmed, an act to be rewarded by marriage to Selim's daughter. Mengli Giray was, apparently, assured of a peaceful old age under grateful Ottoman protection.

As the 1500s came to an end, the political scene in Eastern Europe changed radically. Mengli's allies, Grand Duke Ivan III, the Noğay *bey* Yamgurça, the Moldavian ruler Stefan III and Bayezid II, had all died; the cautious Polish-Lithuanian rulers Kazimierz IV and Alexander I, who had been displeased by Mengli Giray, were also dead. The Crimean Khanate remained a powerful and prosperous entity, expanding to include Noğays and, very soon, Circassians on the northeast Black Sea coast: Mengli could boast to his *bey*s of being a unifier, a new Khan Tuqtamış. But the Noğay Tatars were unruly: they lived for loot, more grazing and political anarchy. Those Noğays on the Volga who had not cooperated with the Crimeans were led by an aggressive Abd-ul Kerim. In 1509, to deal with this threat, Mengli raised an enormous army (which included unreliable Noğays), said to be a quarter of a million men: the outcome was a victory so great that it took twenty days to lead all the enslaved Noğay prisoners of war across the Or Qapı isthmus into Crimea proper.

What was ominous about this victory was that the new Grand Duke of Muscovy, Vasili III, failed to honour the Russian alliance with Crimea and did not provide the fleet he had promised to sail down the Volga and attack the Noğay base at Astrakhan. Vasili's excuse was that he was too occupied by war with Lithuania to build a fleet of river boats. In fact, Vasili was alarmed by the Crimean Khanate's growth and feared it might now be as big a threat and burden for Muscovy as the old defunct Golden Horde had been. A flurry of emissaries and spies travelled between Moscow and the Tatar south. In fact, Moscow had encouraged the Noğays to attack Mengli's khanate. Complications with Kazan angered Moscow: Mengli's stepson, Nur-Sultan's younger son Abd-ul Lâtif, was the brother of the khan of Kazan, and when he grew up, Ivan III asked for Abd-ul Lâtif to be brought to Moscow, but when in 1497 he made him khan of Kazan, he found that his new appointee, despite family links with Russia, asserted Kazan's total independence from Moscow. Abd-ul Lâtif was then deposed by Russia; Mengli and Nur-Sultan threatened to break off relations with Russia unless Abd-ul Lâtif was freed from prison into Crimean custody. Restored to the khanate of Kazan, Abd-ul Lâtif's elder brother Muhammad-Emin proved just as defiant: Grand Duke Vasili III sent an army to Kazan, and Muhammad-Emin asked the Crimean Khanate and Poland-Lithuania for help. That signalled the end of the Crimean–Russian alliance.

To the joy of King Sigismund of Poland-Lithuania, Mengli Giray decided to restore the friendly relations that the Crimean Khanate had enjoyed with Poland-Lithuania some fifty years previously. Lithuania was, however, embroiled in conflict with Vasili III's expansive Muscovy and could offer the Crimean Khanate only kind words.

In 1515 Mengli Giray died of old age at seventy, a rare achievement for a Genghisid ruler. No wonder that the historian Muhammed Riza named Mengli as the first of his 'seven planets' among the Crimean khans. His last years were overshadowed by the deaths of Yamgurça some time after 1508, and of Beti, his eldest son, who drowned in 1510 while crossing the Dnepr. Two years later, when King Sigismund of Poland-Lithuania failed to pay the annual tribute of 15,000 ducats, Mengli's sons Ahmat and Burnaş Giray, without his consent, led a raid on two Russian towns then in Lithuanian hands, and came within 160 kilometres (100 mi.) of Moscow before fleeing from an approaching Russian army. Mengli's surviving sons immediately rode to Or Qapı and ensured that the fortress on the isthmus was closed, that no-one could enter or leave Crimea by land at this vulnerable period between khans, and that news of Mengli's death would not reach the outside world until Mehmed, his successor, was enthroned.

3

TATARS AS ANTAGONISTS

Khan Mengli had given Mehmed I Giray, his son and heir, a long apprenticeship in politics and warfare. Mehmed, now fifty years old, inherited his father's energy, boldness and, to a lesser degree, intelligence. What he lacked was discretion and diplomacy. The Ottoman Sultan Selim *Yavuz*, the Inexorable (or 'Grim' as Europeans knew him), never wholly forgave Mehmed Giray's eager support for the claims of Selim's brother and rival Ahmed to the Ottoman throne, when Mehmed as an impetuous young man threw his weight behind whichever Ottoman prince he might persuade to hand over to the khanate the Turkish-controlled ports of southern Crimea. Sultan Selim had used the services of Mehmed's brother Sa'adet to ensure his own succession and to murder his brother and nephew. He knew how dangerous this was: 'I fear the Tatars worse than Persians,' he told the historian Ali-efendi, 'for if they set off, they can do a five-day journey in one day. If Sa'adet leaves his son as a hostage, fine; if not then the war arena and battlefield are ready.' Mehmed Giray, however, cautiously signed his letters to Selim from 'the modest Mehmed Giray, the weakest of all creatures', even when refusing to contribute manpower to Selim's devastating European campaigns. Mehmed, however, had unanimous support from the Crimean *qaraçi* clans, and he immediately confirmed them in the posts Mengli had granted them.

His ambitions lay not in Europe, but in restoring the Golden Horde, as the new title he awarded himself, 'Khakan of all Mongols', proved. His first concern was to stop a revived Noğay Horde, now moving from the North Caucasus to the Volga, from uniting with the Tatars of Hacı Tarhan (near today's Astrakhan) and threatening Crimea. The Noğays, as often happened, began quarrelling among themselves, however, and the losers sought asylum in the Crimean Khanate, while the winners feared that these refugees would now, supported by Mehmed Giray, attack to redress the balance.

The Noğay khan Al-Çatır offered to recognize Mehmed Giray's sovereignty by giving his sister as a wife to Mehmed and his daughter to Mehmed's son. Al-Çatır then fled in fear of a trap. Neutralizing Noğays without bloodshed was proof of Mehmed's skills.

He was less lucky with his younger brother, the lame Ahmed, whom he had appointed *qalğa*, even though the all-powerful trusted deputy to the khan was in fact Mehmed's eldest son Bahadır. Together with his sons, Ahmed left Crimea, settled on the lower Dnepr and behaved as an independent ruler, offering to serve the Moscow Grand Duke Vasili III as 'his serf', giving Muscovy details of the Crimean army and proposing a joint attack on Vilnius and Kiev. Ahmed then began raiding Lithuania's Ukrainian territory, which was embarrassing to Mehmed who had concluded a peace treaty with Poland-Lithuania. Fortunately, Vasili III despised Ahmed as 'an utterly useless cripple and fool'. Ahmed was lured back to Crimea, and was told by Mehmed and Bahadır to apologize to the Polish king Sigismund and surrender his youngest son to Poland as a hostage. But for the objections of Nurun-Sultan, his senior wife, who threatened to leave him, Mehmed would have sent his own two youngest sons as additional hostages to reinforce the apology to King Sigismund.[1]

Ahmed still resented his brother the khan and decided to slander him to Sultan Selim, who was sheltering two more of the khan's brothers in Istanbul. The conspiracy took three years to mature: in 1519 Ahmed sent his eldest son to Turkey to gather troops who might help overthrow Khan Mehmed. This was too much for Mehmed: he sent his sons Bahadır and Alp to intercept and kill Ahmed. Mehmed's unseemly patience with Ahmed, however, had encouraged dissident *bey*s of the Şirin clan, to whom Ahmed was connected by marriage. The Şirins felt that Mehmed was favouring the Mangıt-Mansur clan, whose ranks were swollen by Noğay settlers. The Şirins sheltered Ahmed's family and boycotted the khan's assembly. Worse, a Şirin *mirza*, Bahtıyar, invited Mehmed's brother to come from Turkey and claim the khanate; allegedly, Sultan Selim favoured the plot. No Turkish troops landed, however, for Selim, now conquering Egypt and Mecca, had lost interest in Crimea. All Selim would do was tell Mehmed Giray that Ahmed's family and the Şirins were under Ottoman protection.

That year the Noğays appealed for help again: they were being driven from their territory by Kazakhs who had migrated across Central Asia to the Caspian shores and the banks of the Volga. The need to protect the Noğays and stop the Kazakhs was another pretext for Mehmed Giray to refuse to serve in Sultan Selim's war against Poland. The Kazakhs, uneasy on European soil, soon retreated. Many more Noğay settled under Mehmed Giray's protection, leaving Mehmed stronger, with an even larger Mangıt clan to rely on. Russian chroniclers reported that Mehmed now preferred his Noğay subjects to his native Crimean Tatars.

By 1520 Mehmed was free to pursue his ambitions to restore the Golden Horde. The khan of Kazan had died childless in 1516; the candidate successor was Mehmed Giray's uncle by marriage (to Nurun-Sultan), Abd-ul Lâtif (Ğabdel-Lâtîf), now virtually a hostage in Moscow. Vasili III was anxious to choose from the puppet state of Kasimov a new puppet khan of Kazan, and would not release Abd-ul-Lâtîf, even if by Genghisid law he was legitimate heir to Kazan. Vasili III had Abd-ul-Lâtíf poisoned before he could leave Muscovy. This only strengthened Mehmed Giray's position: his own children were now next in line. Mehmed told Vasili that he would install his son Sahib Giray as khan of Kazan. Vasili quickly found an alternative candidate, Shah-Ali, whom the Holy Roman Empire ambassador Sigismund Herberstein described as 'arousing his subjects' deep hatred with his ugly weak body, enormous belly, thin beard and feminine face'. Nobody in Kazan (or in Muscovy) could take Shah-Ali seriously, especially as an accompanying Russian boyar took all the decisions for him. When these decisions led to executions, a delegation from Kazan travelled to Crimea, seeking help to overthrow the new khan. Sahib Giray duly arrived, exterminated the Russian garrison and Shah-Ali's guards, but refused to kill Shah-Ali, who was a Genghisid by blood. Shah-Ali was stripped of his clothes, mounted on an old nag and escorted out of town together with his Russian governor-general who was spared to act as a messenger. Such mercy was a mistake. Shah-Ali found shelter with Vasili III and became a dangerous enemy.

Apart from Crimea, Hacı Tarhan was now the last khanate remaining of the Golden Horde's domains – the so-called Throne Territory, *Tahta Eli*. Mehmed Giray proposed to Grand Duke Vasili III that they should invade together; Moscow should even station a garrison there, so that 'my brother the Grand Duke may have the fish, the salt, and every necessity . . . as long as the city is mine.' This, like every proposed conquest, in the eyes of the Crimean Khanate was not acquisition of new territory, but restoration of a rightful inheritance. Vasili, however, was not interested in acquiring more sturgeon, caviar and salt; he preferred to install his own puppet in Hacı Tarhan and to oust Sahib Giray from Kazan. Mehmed then offered Cani Beg, Khan of Hacı Tarhan, an alliance against Muscovy, but Cani Beg was risk-averse.

Around January 1523, perhaps unknown to Mehmed Giray, a group of Şirin *beys* wrote to Sultan Süleyman, asking him to send his hostage and friend, Mehmed's brother Sa'adet, as a replacement khan. They accused Mehmed of

> spending his days and nights in the company of heretics – gatherings that amount to depravity, drinking non-stop, neglecting affairs of state, letting his sons tyrannize the common people, conspiring with Persians, plotting to move the Crimean Tatars out onto the steppes to unite them with Noğays and Persians. We Şirins would never countenance such treachery against an Ottoman Sultan . . .

All Mehmed's plans had to be dropped when the new Ottoman Sultan Süleyman the Legislator (*Kanuni*, but known in the West as 'the Magnificent') forbade it. The Ottomans were conquering Hungary and Poland and needed friendly relations with Moscow. Even though swearing obedience, Mehmed gave Süleyman in early 1523 four strong excuses why the Crimea should make war not on Poland, but on Russia:

> The King of Poland has sent to Your humble servant an ambassador promising to pay annual tribute of 15,000 florins so as to spare his country and I have given him Evliya, a Şirin *mirza*, as hostage . . . Sheikh Ahmad Khan, our old enemy, sovereign of the Horde is still a prisoner of the Poles: if they set him free, the peace and order of our country will suffer . . . I have sent my younger brother Sahib to be Khan in Kazan: the Grand Duke of Muscovy was making Kazan's citizens pray in Christian churches, so we decided to go and help our brother conquer . . . If we undertake a campaign against Poland, Cossacks will ally themselves with the Khan of Hacı Tarhan and attack our country.

Süleyman told Mehmed Giray, 'Don't endanger your life and don't attack, for Vasili is my great friend. If you attack the Grand Duke of Moscow, I shall attack your country.' Süleyman knew the Crimean Khanate well: before succeeding to the Ottoman throne he had been, from 1504 to 1512, paşa of Kaffa. The rumour that he was a grandson of Mengli Giray is untrue, but he was a father figure for several Crimean khans to come. Certainly, he was treated with more reverence, and less fear, than his predecessor Selim the Inexorable. It was clear to Mehmed that, compared with Hungary and Poland, Crimea, its conflicts with the Horde and with Moscow, and the khan's fraternal quarrels were trivial matters. Süleyman did let Hemmet and Sa'adet Giray (the khan's nephew and brother) incite the nomads on the Dnepr to attack Crimea, but these two rebels were no match for Mehmed Giray's army.

Despite Süleyman's warning, that summer Mehmed invaded Russia. When he reached the Oka river, his brother Sahib came from Kazan and joined him at Kolomna, just outside Moscow. Vasili III fled Moscow in panic, at one point hiding in a haystack. The almost ludicrous chaos in Moscow was described by Sigismund Herberstein, who spent time in Moscow in 1517 and 1526:

> On 20 July the Tatars inspired the Muscovites with such terror that they felt unsafe even in a fortified city. During the panic women, children, anyone unable to fight, gathered in the Kremlin and round the gates with wagons, carts and all their belongings. The crowd was such that they were trampling one another. There was such a stench from the mob that if the enemy had besieged them for three or four days they would have died of disease, since everyone relieved himself where he stood. The cannon were so enormous that three days were not enough to drag them up and there wasn't enough powder ready for a single shot from the big cannon: that's the invariable Muscovite habit – keeping everything hidden and not getting anything ready, and then when the necessity arises, doing everything in a hurry. So people had to carry to the centre the cannons that had been hidden away. While they were doing this, news suddenly came that the Tatars were approaching: people dropped the cannon in the street and forgot about defending the walls. They all ran to the Kremlin, so a long chain of abandoned guns lined the street ... The defenders thought it best to appease Mehmed Giray by sending him lots of presents, especially [alcoholic] mead, to make him lift the siege. Mehmed promised to do so and leave the country if Vasili signed a document promising to be the Khan's tribute-payer for ever, as his forefathers were. When he received the document he wanted, Mehmed Giray retreated to Riazan where the Muscovites were allowed to ransom and exchange prisoners; everything else Mehmed put on sale.[2]

The governor-general of Riazan gave the Tatars provisions for their army, but, reneging on the Muscovite document, fired his cannons at the Crimean forces. Mehmed departed so quickly that he left Vasili III's document behind.

Mehmed Giray returned home to find that Khan Cani Beg, in support of Moscow, had invaded Crimea. Vasili III, back in Moscow, now challenged Mehmed to a new war, a challenge which the Crimeans would accept at a time of their own choosing. Meanwhile, Mehmed's army of Crimean and Noğay Tatars crossed the Volga in autumn 1522, conquered Hacı Tarhan and triumphantly installed Mehmed's son Bahadır Giray as khan. All three relict states of the Horde were now ruled by Giray brothers.

Mehmed's younger sons, however, were aggrieved when their father had no more prestigious posts to offer them. The Şirin *beys* thought Hacı Tarhan was too desolate a territory to bother with, and resented the half-Noğay Mangıt clan who felt at home there. One night in March 1523 the malcontents galloped back to Crimea. Some Noğay *beys* could no longer tolerate the dictates of the Crimean khan, even though he had taken them in when they were driven out by Kazakh invaders. The imposition of Mehmed's son Bahadır on Hacı Tarhan was to them an insult. They feared another Giray might be made khan of the Noğays, too. The Noğays only pretended to support Mehmed as he pursued his rebellious teenage sons. When the posse stopped for the night for a feast and a game of chess, a Noğay *bey* raised his sabre and beheaded both Mehmed and Bahadır, before killing all the chess-playing Crimean courtiers and attacking the horsemen.

This bloody coup undid all Mehmed's achievements: all over the steppe zone, Noğays exterminated fleeing Crimean horsemen. Many drowned in the half-frozen Don: all that year the steppes were covered with abandoned wagons and the rotting corpses of men, camels and horses. Much worse was coming: Mehmed's young sons, Ğazı and Baba Giray, took refuge in Or Qapı, but within a few days the Noğay managed to breach the defences and began looting and killing in all the northern and central zones of Crimea. The *beys* rounded up 12,000 men from the khanate's routed army and drove some Noğay back, only to find that the garrison at Or Qapı, manned largely by Ottoman Turks, refused to open the gates to either side. Crimea was utterly defenceless: only when the Noğay had rounded up more cattle, horses, slaves and other loot than they could take away did they depart eastwards.

The survivors compared this disaster to the devastation left by Timur Leng: the only Girays left to inherit the khanate were the two teenagers who had initiated this disaster. The *beys*, assuming that their seniority would make them the real rulers of the khanate, reluctantly placed Ğazi 1 Giray Khan and Baba Giray *qalğa* nominally in charge of the smoking ruins and weeping survivors of what had briefly been a restored Golden Horde. Khan Ğazi 1 Giray, however, blamed the *bey*s for the murder of his father and brother, while the *bey*s renewed their secret correspondence with a more amenable candidate, Sa'adet Giray, brother to the late Mehmed. Accordingly, the Şirin *beylerbey* travelled to Istanbul to formally ask Sultan Süleyman to send Sa'adet. This set a dangerous precedent: until 1523 no Ottoman sultan had meddled with the accession of a Crimean khan; hereafter various sultans would insist on choosing the Giray that suited them best.

On 3 June 1523, after twelve years in Turkey, Sa'adet, now aged 31, arrived in Kaffa on a Turkish ship accompanied by a force of janissaries. He had been thoroughly 'Ottomanized', believing in the joint mission of the Ottomans and the Tatars to conquer new territory and repress all dissent. A friend as well as an acolyte of Sultan Süleyman, and a pupil of the late Sultan Selim, Sa'adet Giray was highly cultured – he too could write verse in Persian. He disdained any limitations imposed by *bey*s on his absolute monarchic power, and had no regard to rank when he chose his servants and ministers. Sa'adet saw nothing wrong with the ruthlessness of Ottoman principles, such as the need on accession to kill all the new monarch's brothers and their male offspring. Sa'adet duly beheaded his nephew Ğazı, the interim khan, and shackled Ğazı's brothers.

To appease the shocked Şirin *bey*s, Sa'adet married the widow and adopted the sons of the rebellious Ahmed Giray. Sa'adet no longer depended on the clans for his military forces: Süleyman sent him 20,000 heavily armed cavalrymen. Within a fortnight, Sa'adet was in the north, at Or Qapı, where he expected Turkish reinforcements to defend the isthmus from Noğay attackers. The border fortress was rebuilt and cavalry reconnoitred the approaches. Very slowly, Crimeans who had fled the invasion returned home. The country was still desperately short of men and horses, but the Turkish artillery deterred invaders.

Sa'adet did not share the late Mehmed Giray's dream of resurrecting the Golden Horde, even though his brothers, he warned Moscow, still ruled Kazan and Hacı Tarhan. Sa'adet wanted to create a miniature Ottoman court at his capital Qırq-Yer, which he called 'Little Istanbul', and which he staffed with an elaborately hierarchical Turkish-style court. He made peace with his surviving nephew Islam, and with the Noğays who had conspired against Mehmed Giray. Sa'adet's refusal to take revenge annoyed the *bey*s and they boycotted the *divan*. This was a serious gesture, for when the *bey*s met separately without the khan they expressed dissent by assembling at a special place near Qırq-Yer, *Kaya altı*, 'the lower rock' where their clans' heraldic symbols were carved in stone. They did not realize that Sa'adet enjoyed taking decisions without their input. He was used to silent insolence as a response to his irrevocable decisions and knew he was disliked for deferring to Sultan Süleyman's wishes.

The new army obeyed Sa'adet Giray alone: they had artillery and muskets, they were chosen and promoted solely on merit, not birth, they paid no taxes and they rode roughshod over the Crimean nobility. This would be a new source of discord in the country. (Süleyman foresaw the consequences and urged Sa'adet to be lenient with his *qaraçı bey*s.)

In 1524 an old enemy surfaced: Sheikh Ahmad, the last khan of the Horde, for twenty years a prisoner of King Sigismund, was wanted by the Noğays to lead an attack on Crimea. The Noğays asked the Polish-Lithuanian king to let his elderly prisoner join them. Sigismund would receive Crimean forts on the Dnepr as a reward, and the river would be a border between Polish and Noğay territory, eliminating the Crimean Khanate. Polish-Lithuanian forces now came very near to Or Qapı.

Unfortunately for Poland, this two-pronged advance against Crimea and the Ottomans was just what Sultan Süleyman wanted in his war with Sigismund. Sa'adet sent out an army together with four of his sons. He also tried diplomacy, marrying a son to the daughter of a prominent Noğay to show he had no hard feelings against his brother's murderers. Sa'adet was dismayed, however, when he was joined by his powerful brother Sahib, khan of Kazan. Sahib had abandoned Kazan, inviting his thirteen-year-old nephew Safa to replace him. Sahib saw that Grand Duke Vasili III had not only the intention but the means of capturing the city. Sahib was now asking for artillery and Turkish soldiers to fight back. Sa'adet urged Vasili not to attack Kazan. Vasili III ignored him. Sahib then appealed directly to Istanbul, also in vain. The inhabitants of Kazan lost all sense: they abandoned their khans, began revering a *seyyid* (a descendant of the Prophet), then, on discovering that this holy man was an agent of Moscow, killed him. Sahib, seeking asylum in Crimea, and thought to be heading to Istanbul, if not Mecca, was accused of cowardice and incarcerated by his brother and fellow Khan Sa'adet in barracks at Balaklava. On his flight from Kazan Sahib had encountered and murdered one of the Noğays responsible for beheading Mehmed Giray two years earlier, but Sa'adet showed no gratitude. The Tatar proverbs, 'Two sheep's heads won't fit in one cauldron' and 'Two watermelons won't fit under one armpit' clearly applied to khans.

The boy-khan Safa coped remarkably well when Moscow attacked Kazan in 1524, for the Russians were thrown into disarray by guerrilla warfare waged by Finnic Cheremis peasants on the border of the Kazan khanate. A truce was agreed, and Vasili III recognized Safa Giray as ruler of Kazan. Sahib had no reason to return, and his elder brother Sa'adet soon freed him.

It was now Sa'adet's turn to flee: while crossing the Dnepr, he was badly defeated by Lithuanian and Cossack forces. The *beys*, seething at Sa'adet's Ottoman despotism, rebelled and urged Mehmed I Giray's surviving son, Sa'adet's nephew Islam, also retreating from this failed campaign, to overthrow him. Islam reproached Sa'adet for slaughtering his male relatives, and refused to enter the peninsula. Sa'adet, evidently afraid, hid all his treasures in the ramparts of Qırq-Yer. Islam Giray then attacked, rustling Sa'adet's horses and cattle. He kidnapped Sa'adet's mother Mahmut-Sultan and her servants, and made the Şirin clan town Eski Qırım his base. There Islam Giray was raised by the *beys* to the khanate's throne.

Sa'adet fled to Or Qapı; in November 1524 Islam began a siege of the frontier castle. Sa'adet held out for nearly three months. Sultan Süleyman would not come to his aid. Instead, it was Sa'adet's younger brother Sahib who cunningly intervened, hinting to their nephew Islam that he might be recognized as khan if he sent two *beys* to Qırq-Yer for discussions. The *beys* were duly taken hostage by Sahib until Islam's forces withdrew from Or Qapı. Islam left with them, and the two half-brother khans – of Crimea and Kazan – who owed one another their freedom, were joined by their elderly mothers, who made Sahib Giray forswear the status of khan and accept demotion to Sa'adet's *qalğa*. Sa'adet duly forgave the *beys* who had besieged him, and tried to make them attack Islam, who had no trouble escaping.

Sa'adet had no interest in the fate of the Kazan or Hacı Tarhan khanates, or even in Moscow's attempt to conquer them, whereas Sahib had come to Crimea not to save his half-brother Sa'adet, but to raise a force to defend Kazan from the Russians. Hoping for Turkish reinforcements, he raised an army of 50,000. As Sahib's army moved north, Islam took advantage, fought Sa'adet and once again, for a short time, became khan. He knew his victory was precarious and had already arranged for asylum in Poland. *Beys* supporting Sa'adet broke off their journey up the Volga, deserting Sahib; they drove Islam to hide in the North Caucasus. The following year Islam reappeared, fell at Sa'adet's feet, and was given Sahib's post of *qalğa*: the half-brothers' quarrel was partly settled when Sa'adet's mother Mahmud-Sultan issued a joint decree with Sahib's mother, each guaranteeing their sons' immunity. Thereafter Sahib and Islam Giray, uncle and nephew, lurked at frontier posts on the Dnepr, watching out for Polish and Lithuanian attackers and for fratricidal treachery.

To keep his enemy even further away, the next autumn Sa'adet sent his nephew on campaign to Circassia. Islam, however, was unwisely advised to turn north and attack Moscow, grab as much loot as he could and bribe Sultan Süleyman into making him khan. Meanwhile, Sa'adet was obeying Süleyman and keeping the peace with Moscow. When Grand Duke Vasili III heard of Islam's plans, he killed the Crimean envoys to Moscow and routed Islam's raiders. Sa'adet could hardly object, and vented his wrath on Islam's *beys*: Islam Giray himself escaped with a score of followers. This brought no peace: irate Şirin *beys* would not let the execution of their leaders go unavenged.

Islam was irrepressible: he reminded King Sigismund of Poland's promise of asylum. The Poles welcomed any enemy of Sa'adet Giray, who had caused such discord. The king let Islam Giray overwinter on the Dnepr, leasing him grazing lands near Cherkasy (the lord of Cherkasy, an Ostafi Dashkovych, a crony of Islam, joined him on his looting raids). Sigismund even sent Islam and his men warm sheepskin coats. Feeling safe in Islam's absence, in February 1527 Sa'adet Giray sent his brother Sahib on a raid against Lithuania. The raid failed. King Sigismund reacted: he permitted his aged prisoner Sheikh Ahmad, the last ruler and spiritual head of the Horde, to return to his people on the Volga, escorted by Lithuanians and Noğays. The Noğay Horde, Islam Giray and the Poles all planned to have river galleys equipped with cannon for a campaign next spring against the Crimean Khanate, though Sheikh Ahmad had no troops of his own. Sa'adet began negotiations with the Poles, who demanded a new Crimean hostage as a guarantor of peace. Sa'adet's *yarlıq* (sworn decree) sent to Kraków in summer 1527 argued that it was because of Poland-Lithuania's failure to recognize the power of the Crimean Khanate and ally with it that Muscovy had become so powerful; he boasted that he was now in sole control, having 'put a wooden bar over Islam Giray's neck', by giving him the post of *qalğa*. He justified his attacks on Poland as a way of enforcing payment of unpaid tribute and as retaliation for destruction of Crimean forts. Now he proposed friendship and an exchange of embassies. Nevertheless, the following year he wrote confidentially, in Russian lest the letter was intercepted by the Ottomans, to Grand Duke Vasili of Russia, handing his letter privately to the Muscovite diplomat Nikita Miasnoi:

I've written this letter in Russian, so nobody but you and I know, and if you, our brother, need to write to us, you should send a letter in Russian. I have a man who can read it. Don't trust the Tatars to tell the truth: the Tatars don't respect God and there is no truth in them . . . I became Khan by God's grace, yet you will have heard that they have raised armies three or four times against me. Thanks to God's mercy and Sultan Süleyman's good health, I first became Khan in my father's place.[3]

Islam immediately disputed Sa'adet's claims with his own embassy – 'I too am a son of the ruler in my state' – declared himself and the Şirin and Barın clans to be pro-Polish, and, like Sa'adet, claimed payment of tribute.

When the ice melted in 1528 Islam began an invasion of the Crimea, only to be let down by the nervous Sheikh Ahmad and therefore easily persuaded by Sa'adet to make peace and just accept the post of *qalğa*. (Sheikh Ahmad's demurral was punished by the younger *bey*s on the Volga: they killed him.) That year Sa'adet executed the Şirin *qaraçı* leaders: Islam rebelled yet again, and yet again made peace with his uncle.

This settled nothing: the Şirin clan wanted Sa'adet dead for killing their leaders. Only in 1531 could they act, when Sa'adet Giray was marrying a daughter of his to a *mirza* of the junior Siciut clan. The Şirin *beylerbey* invited the whole wedding party to their capital, Eski Qırım. Sa'adet must have been warned of a plot to depose him, for he travelled to Eski Qırım with a detachment of guards, and ordered Sahib Giray first to infiltrate the Şirin rearguard. When Sa'adet reached Eski Qırım, he had his hosts and potential usurpers executed. The survivors of the massacre appealed to Islam Giray for protection from a khan who, they feared, was going to exterminate the entire Şirin clan. Sa'adet feasted, then arrested his own wife Şirin-Bek (the widow of his elder brother Ahmed), sent her to the fortress of Qırq-Yer and executed her son Buçkak. They had been complicit in the plot. Sa'adet then massacred, with Sahib Giray's help, every clansman whom he distrusted. (It was awkward for Sa'adet that one of his victims, a *bey* called Bahtiyar, was the father of Maqul, whom he had just sent as an ambassador and a hostage to King Sigismund: the envoy's diplomatic status had to be hastily anulled.) The relatives of Sa'adet's victims, however, blamed Sahib Giray rather than his brother for this ruthlessness and, presumably to deflect hostility, Sa'adet sent Sahib off to Istanbul, where the sultan's court was now losing patience with the endless paranoic chaos afflicting the khanate.

In summer 1532, after Sa'adet had in vain laid siege to Dashkovych's fort, King Sigismund could no longer choose between the two claimants to the Crimean Khanate: he sent to Sa'adet and Islam separate embassies, separate tributes of 2,000 florins and separate demands for an oath to keep the peace, explaining to the Lithuanian chancellor and council, 'at present there are two khans in this Horde.' But before Sa'adet received the king's embassy, tired of constant antagonism, he abdicated and sailed off to Istanbul, leaving Islam, now dependent on Sigismund, to sign the oath as well as a 'grant' of old Horde territories to the Poles and Lithuanians. Not daring to visit the capital Qırq-Yer or use the official chancery, Islam's oath and grant were clumsily phrased.

Sahib Giray re-establishes order

Sultan Süleyman would never have endorsed a young khan as erratic and aggressive as Islam. Now that the Ottomans felt entitled to appoint and not just approve new Crimean khans, he preferred to install Sahib, the youngest son of Khan Mengli, who had lived for some time at the Istanbul court, had accompanied the sultan on a victorious campaign against Hungary and had already been khan of Kazan and *qalğa* in Crimea. Sahib Giray was now living in comfort and, like other Girays, had an estate in Yanbolu (Yambol in southeast Bulgaria, a former Genoese concession that the Ottomans had confiscated). He could not refuse the khanate. Islam had to accept demotion as *qalğa* and Sahib was sent to Akkerman, at the mouth of the Dnestr river, with fifty Turkish artillery men (manning impressive cannon like the *balyemez* ('doesn't eat honey')), 1,000 musketeers, 300 armoured cavalrymen and a personal guard of *sekban* (the Persian word originally meant 'dog-handler', but in the Ottoman army designated guards armed with rifles and loyal to the sovereign).[4] Once in Salacıq, Sahib received the Mangıt clan leader Bakı-bey, an encounter that would shape much of his reign. He started to turn Salacıq into a garden of Eden, starting with the 'garden palace', Bağçasaray. Sahib's joy was marred only by the death that year of his much-loved wife Fatma-Sultan (a year later he consoled himself, travelling to Kerç to marry a Circassian princess Khanyke-Sultan).

The Ottoman sultan and the king of Poland-Lithuania were now allies, with a common enemy: Habsburg Austria, which lay between their realms. Sigismund was prepared to let the Ottomans take over Hungary. Süleyman did not insist on Sigismund negotiating a permanent peace with Crimea, since its khan, in the sultan's eyes, was an Ottoman subject, not a sovereign ruler. This conclusion, ominous for the status and fate of the khanate, exists today only in an Italian version of the Ottoman decree (*ahdname*):

> The all-powerful ruler of Tatary, Sahib Giray, attached to our Threshold of Felicity . . . has now been told by us that he should be a friend to you; you need to maintain close friendship with him and see that his Tatar relatives, if disobedient or fugitive, are recaptured . . . disregarded, and expelled from your country and pursued.

When Sigismund demanded a rephrased decree that would bind Sahib Giray personally, the Ottoman vizier in 1533 dared to tell Süleyman that the khan, although indebted to Süleyman, was a sovereign monarch who could not be bound, but might be persuaded, by a Polish–Turkish bilateral agreement. In the end, all sides were content: Sahib Giray controlled the south of Crimea, where the Ottoman forces were strong; Islam Giray, as *qalğa*, effectively ruled the north, the border with Lithuanian territory. Furthermore, all Girays might well have been united when the Russians expelled Safa Giray from Kazan and Crimean Tatars had a pretext to attack Grand Duke Vasili (and, in 1533 after Vasili's death, Elena Glinskaya, the regent mother of the future Ivan IV, the 'Terrible'). Safa, no longer a teenager but now a mature, determined warrior, encouraged Islam Giray (Sahib remained a benevolent neutral) to attack Russian territory: their campaign failed for want of men. Devious as ever, hoping to please Safa and oust Sahib, Islam then explained to Moscow that the mood of the Crimean people had forced him to attack Russia. In 1534 Islam and his cousin Safa, together with other disaffected Girays and Şirins, rebelled against Sahib Giray, occupied Or Qapı, cut off the khan's escape from the peninsula and waited to see which of their two enemies – Poland-Lithuania or Muscovy – would support them. Compared with the south, the north of Crimea, Islam's Perekop district, was too poor in goods and men to bribe or intimidate anyone. Safa Giray suspected Islam of stealing his share of foreign tribute and left, hoping to reconquer Kazan. Islam foresaw his end and wrote to Süleyman, blaming Sahib. He asked either to be named khan or to have his old enemy Sa'adet brought back from Turkey, promising in either case to be a faithful servant of the Ottomans and, if Sa'adet were reinstated, to live in Hacı Tarhan (where in 1531 he had briefly reigned, and which he now promised to turn into an earthly paradise), and from there help the sultan make war on Persia.

Even the most rebellious *bey*s had now lost faith in Islam and Safa Giray: they were ready to accept Sahib's generous amnesty. Sahib did not, however, trust the former rebels, who still kept up a treasonable correspondence with Istanbul. His solution was to plot Islam's murder: he offered Bakı-bey, the ambitious *bey* of the Mangıt clan, advancement and enormous wealth if he would pretend to be an enemy of the khan, seek shelter with Islam and kill his host at the first opportunity. Bakı-bey, however, resented Sahib-Khan's failure to promote him earlier and promptly revealed the plot to an incredulous Islam Giray. Bakı-bey sought shelter with the Noğay Mangıt clan.

Islam Giray was not worried by his uncle's assumption of power: he had just received a valuable prisoner, the Muscovite prince Semion Belsky, a refugee who had fallen foul of the boyars advising Vasili III's widow Elena. Belsky wanted to lure both Poland and the Ottomans into making war on Muscovy. He was sent by Sultan Süleyman to Crimea with a recommendation that Sahib Giray and the governor of Kaffa help Belsky raise an army. Islam Giray captured Belsky and guaranteed Moscow that there would be no attack from either Belsky or the Turks. Discussing Belsky's defection, Islam wrote to the Grand Duke of Russia:

> If you want my advice, know that the Ottomans are evil people . . . They'll bang stones to get territory, they don't care if someone is the son of a serf or slave, as long as he brings territory. If they get to you, then they'll get to us.

The Moscow boyars sent Islam valuable presents and asked him to kill his prisoner, or send him in chains to Moscow. Sultan Süleyman was furious with Sahib for letting this happen: Sahib had to carry out a night raid on Or Qapı, from where Islam escaped with Belsky and then asked Sahib for forgiveness.

The exiled Bakı-bey now saw that Sahib had no intention of promoting him and had merely exploited him. But he saved the situation in August 1537: he emerged from the Noğay Horde, raided Islam Giray's camp, killed Islam and abducted not just Islam's family, servants and property, but also his prisoner Belsky, before fleeing back to Hacı Tarhan. Sahib thought that he now had just to appoint a new *qalğa* and hand over the castle at Or Qapı to be manned by a reliable Turkish garrison. In fact, he ignored the new danger of the newly united and fervently pious Noğay Horde, which had held a *qurultay* (parliament) under Bakı-bey's influence: the Noğays now demanded that Moscow pay tribute to them, not to the Crimean Khanate, on whom they intended to make war.

This was a dangerous time to leave the country, yet in 1538 Süleyman required Sahib Giray's help in a campaign to quell a revolt by the Moldavian prince Petru Rareş. Before leaving, Sahib reinforced Or Qapı and dug the moat deeper, before routing dissident *mirza* forces on the Dnepr river and heading for the Moldavian front.

That winter Bakı-bey led an attack, first confronting Sahib's son and *qalğa* Emin Giray, who was on his way home from a campaign against Lithuania. The weather was exceptionally cold and snowy, enabling the Noğay to ravage the Crimean forces in the steppes, before Emin Giray finally repelled the attackers. Sahib then had Bakı-bey's younger brothers shackled: a year passed before Bakı-bey approached Crimea again, holding out at Azov. Sahib sent his brothers, one by one, to persuade Bakı-bey to return, accept appointment as leader of the Mansur-Mangıt clan and see one of his brothers married to a daughter of the khan. Sahib's principle was now to keep his enemies closer than his friends. The lure worked: Bakı was received with honour, given the lands and command of the Mansur clan. In exchange, Bakı handed over Semion Belsky, whom Sultan Süleyman wanted as a hostage against Moscow. Bakı did not, however, hand over another hostage, a son of Islam Giray, whom he may have planned to use as a puppet Crimean khan and thus revive the Great Horde.

It is from this time that we have the first coherent diplomat's account of life in the Crimean Khanate: Michael the Lithuanian (real name Więcesław Mykolaewicz or Michajlo Tyszkiewicz) reported in Latin to his master King Sigismund what he had learned in two years of the mores of the Tatars (and of the Russians, whom he knew only by hearsay):

We consider the Tatars barbarians and paupers, but they are proud of their modest lives ... The whole country is very fertile, producing lots of grain, wine, meat and salt ... the descendants of the indigenous Greeks have submitted to the yoke of the Turks and pay them poll tax: they produce grain and wine, and farm cattle and are rather prosperous ... The Tatars have multiplied so much that they can recruit up to 30,000 horsemen for war ... equipped as usual, almost without weapons. Only one in ten or twenty had a sabre or a quiver, armour was even rarer – they just had bludgeons of bone or wood, others had empty scabbards ... But they all set off with several new leather straps, especially if the raid is towards Lithuania, then they bother more with means of tying us up, than with weapons of self-defence ... They excel in their ability to endure hunger, thirst, hard work, lack of sleep, heat, cold … These unbelievers treat judges with gratitude, judges are like clergy and take special oaths, and are elected by people disinterested in worldly affairs. Justice does not put up with procrastinators or listen to slanderers … At home they offer any guest, even strangers, board and lodging gratis … In other ways Tatars are less civilized, they think it utterly obscene to show their womenfolk to guests, friends, even much loved collocutors … and make their wives do all the tailoring and shoe-making. They are not content with monogamy … They have more prisoner-of-war slaves than cattle … so many that they use slaves as pledges, gifts, payment to creditors … They sell them at auction by the dozen under the supervision of a valuer, who shouts out praise, 'New slaves, not yet spoilt, not underhand, from Poland-Lithuania, not Moscow.' (The Muscovite slaves are considered dishonest and cunning and have a low market price.)

Sahib Giray finally lured Bakı-bey back to Crimea, together with the latter's hostage, Semion Belsky, but Bakı-bey still held back a son of Islam Giray. Sahib was more bothered by the intentions of Moscow's boyars. They had held power since 1533, while the future Tsar Ivan IV was still an infant, and plotted to seize Kazan and overthrow its khan Safa Giray.

Crimean–Muscovite peace negotiations were held and embassies were exchanged in 1540. Urged, however, by the turncoat Prince Belsky, the khanate was tempted to invade Russia. As a precaution, an envoy was sent to restore the alliance with King Sigismund of Poland, and a thirteen-clause treaty and oath were signed. The Tatars would help recover Lithuanian territory lost to Moscow, Polish merchants would have trade privileges in Crimea, Sigismund would send bolts of cloth worth 30,000 florins, but would not receive frequent or large Crimean delegations, because they cost him too much to entertain.

Sahib warned Moscow that he was planning a campaign. In 1541, after a Tatar envoy swore yet another oath to Sigismund and to his son and co-ruler Sigismund Augustus in Vilnius, Sahib assembled an army, reputedly of 100,000 men, at Or Qapı. The only obstacle on a rapid advance was the Oka river, where the Crimeans faced salvos from Russian artillery on the northern bank. Prince Belsky chose a well-concealed crossing point on the southern bank, where only a few Russian musketeers manned the opposite bank. The Crimeans assembled rafts. Then they were betrayed. Sahib's biographer, Remmal (the Geomancer), describes what followed:

Ali Kılınç Bey sent the Khan a message: 'Watch out,' Bakı-bey said. 'When the Khan gets on the raft, let's grab his treasures and kill him. Then let's take Islam Giray's son, and the whole country.' Khan Sahib said to himself, 'If I don't cross today, he'll certainly have me killed . . . Let him cross the river first. If he takes the raft and crosses, the message is just a lie, but if he won't cross, look out.' Then the Khan sent an urgent message to Bakı-bey: 'If we delay, the Russian soldiers will gather with musketeers and stop us.' Bakı-bey replied, 'We won't cross unless the Khan crosses first. The Russians may have laid us a trap.' The next morning they saw that the opposite shore was swarming with Russians, who had their cannon ready and were barking like dogs. The Tatar army was worried and retreated.

On the way back to Crimean territory, Bakı-bey and his brother, afraid of the khan's suspicions, asked permission, once they arrived in Crimea, to leave the army and rest. Sahib wrote letters to his relatives, promising revenge if he survived his enemy's plot. He also wrote to the boy Tsar Ivan IV a furious warning, whose abusive tone prejudiced Russia's attitude to the Crimean Tatars forever. The message ran, the Geomancer records:

Accursed infidel without faith or law, so-called Muscovite, slave who pulls my plough. Know that my plan is to pillage your provinces and harness you to a plough as my forefathers did yours. I consider you to be an inheritance from my forefathers. I shall weigh down your feet with chains and make you dig a well, and you will realize what you are. I shall make the peoples of the world laugh at you. Go, thank God that your hour has not yet come, and thank Bakı because we couldn't cross the Oka. First I have to kill that wolf in my sheepfold and cleanse my garden of thistles and brambles. Then I shall conquer you.

In early 1542, after further raids on Russsian territory, the Crimean Tatar army reached the Dnepr. Sahib Giray wrote letters to his mother, his wives and his daughters, ostensibly arranging the wedding of Ak-Bibi, Bakı-bey's brother, in Bağçasaray. Bakı was too terrified to face the khan surrounded by his loyal *sekban* guard. He claimed he was ill and on his way to rejoin his Noğay clan. Meanwhile he waited on the river bank until his men and his great herds of horses were rounded up. He was surprised to encounter the khan on the river bank, dressed for hunting, with thirty falcons and hawks, fifty dogs and just a hundred huntsmen. Bakı did not realize that these huntsmen were guards and marksmen and that the khan's wagons hid four cannon, as well as shackles and chains. Sahib Giray remarked that Bakı-bey seemed to have recovered his health, and offered him a banquet. There he reproached Bakı for making the army spend an extra night on the banks of the Oka, letting thousands of them freeze to death. When Sahib Giray left the tent, his guardsmen shackled Bakı-bey and escorted him to Bağçasaray, where he was dropped into icy water and left to freeze to death. (Ak-Bibi, who was merely complicit in his brother's plot, was humanely strangled.)

Khan Sahib Giray's decisive actions had quelled any incipient rebellion and intimidated the Mansur clansmen (integrated with the Noğay tribes' Mangıt clan). The senior Şirin clan were the only *qaraçı* who retained the khan's respect, although neither side could forget a Şirin plot to kill him in a hunting 'accident' during the Moldavian campaign of 1542, when the Crimean Tatars were operating jointly with Sultan Süleyman's forces. In any case, no *bey* could be sure of returning home alive after visiting the khan.

On that campaign Sultan Süleyman treated Sahib Giray like a brother: he seemed not to mind that the previous year's invasion of Russia had ignored the Ottomans' wish to coexist peacefully with Moscow, and had prolonged the dispute with Poland. Sahib's close relationship with the sultan, however, aroused the resentment of the Istanbul courtiers, who began to blacken his name. When Sahib Giray forbade his men to enslave their prisoners of war, he incurred the anger of his own army, which, unlike the Ottomans, fought more for loot than for the faith. In campaigns that did not involve the Ottomans, for instance Tatar ventures against the Circassians of the Caucasus, Sahib did encourage looting and enslavement. There he was personally admired for his military talents.

From 1542 Sahib Giray had long-term peace treaties with both Sigismund and the Moscow boyars. In peaceful intervals between campaigns Sahib Giray could tame his dissident nomad subjects, who might defect to the Noğays and take with them cattle and horses, by decreeing compulsory settlement and house-building: those that disobeyed had their yurts and carts smashed. He further expanded his armed forces. He already had the *sekban*, riflemen paid for by the Ottomans. Now he copied the Turkish janissaries by instituting a monarch's army, the *qapıqulu* (slaves of the gate). They were largely cavalrymen, some former prisoners of war, and, at least in Sahib's reign, they, too, were generously funded by Sultan Süleyman. The khan now relied less on the armies of the *qaraçı beys*. Like the janissaries, however, the Crimean *qapıqulu* soon expanded into a political force as recalcitrant and powerful as hostile clans of *beys*.

Sahib Giray now looked eastwards for conquest. Disputes with Poland, for instance over grazing rights on the lower Dnestr, were belittled in Sahib's letters to the Polish king: 'This land is neither yours, nor mine, but God's: whoever is stronger, keeps it.' Sahib attacked instead Astrakhan's Noğay Tatars and their khan Yamgurça who threatened to invade Crimea and, as a foretaste, executed a caravan of merchants making their way there from Kazan. To defeat the Noğays required an unprecedented mobilization of every adult Crimean Tatar male. The Noğays took fright, and, with a mere score of cannon and 1,000 horsemen, Sahib defeated Yamgurça, who fled across the Volga. The Crimean khan captured Yamgurça's family, took them to Crimea and sent a message to Yamgurça offering peace and settlement in the Crimea. He also captured his own nephew Bölük Giray. But Sahib could not install one of his own sons as khan of Astrakhan until he had defeated the Noğays, which he tried to do by deporting as many as he could back to the Crimea to reinforce the population with yet more warriors. In autumn 1548 Sahib Giray made a second attempt to defeat the Noğays, this time at the very gates to the Crimea, at Or Qapı, where there was no room to shoot arrows: the Crimeans slaughtered the Noğay with sabres. Fifty Noğay were spared to take the news back to Astrakhan.

In 1549 the khan of Kazan, Sahib Giray's brother Safa, died (apparently striking his head on a washbasin) after years of resisting Russian subversion and attack. Safa left only an infant son (his older sons were in Crimea). Sahib Giray tried to install a son of his own to rule the city. He dared to disobey Sultan Süleyman, who instructed the Crimean Tatars to move around the Black Sea and over the Caucasus as a second prong in the Turkish war against Persia. Sahib, however, doomed himself by idle talk of annexing the Ottoman-controlled port of Kaffa, where on a lightning visit he imprisoned an Ottoman military officer who had been taxing local Tatars and seizing land in the khanate's territory.

Sultan Süleyman was angry because Sahib had made no move against Iran's formidable *kızılbaş* soldiers. Sahib offered a mere thousand men to appease the sultan. Listening to his viziers' denunciations, the sultan was inclined to replace Sahib with a more compliant Giray, who would not antagonize the sultan's courtiers. Süleyman's obvious choice from the Girays still alive in Yambol and Istanbul was Devlet, the late Sa'adet Giray's son and former *qalğa*.

Sahib Giray's nemesis came in 1551, when he was dealing yet again with his Circassian neighbours on the mainland opposite Kerç. Like two of his nephews, Sahib Giray had a Circassian wife; the Crimean Tatars had a long-standing custom of sending boys to Circassia to be brought up and given military training by a Circassian *atalyk* and *analyk* (foster-parents), and then returned as accomplished cavalrymen. This created alliances among the leadership of both nations, but did not prevent frequent clashes, sometimes raids, as far as Kaffa, after which defeated Circassian chieftains would apologize. The notoriously aggressive Zhané tribe of Adyge Circassians controlled the area around Taman. The Ottomans conceded that these Circassians should be subject to Crimean sovereignty (an arrangement that would bring the khanate into conflict with Moscow when Ivan the Terrible took a Circassian bride), but the Ottomans expected order to be maintained, so that they could move their army across the North Caucasus when at war with Iran. In 1551 two Circassian princes, Aleguk and Antonuk, attacked Ottoman subjects near Azov. Sahib was supposed to punish and pacify the aggressors.

Sahib knew that his absence from Crimea would be an excuse for Istanbul to get rid of him: his refusal to fight in Iran and his land-grab of part of Ottoman Kaffa convinced Sultan Süleyman that his viziers were right, and that Sahib was undermining Turkish power. Before setting out to deal with the Circassian princes, Sahib at first sent his sons Emin and Adil to Or Qapı to stop his nephew Devlet, the replacement khan that the Ottomans had chosen, from entering the country. He wrote to Süleyman, telling him the Crimean *beys* thought it best for Devlet to become khan of Kazan. The sultan and his viziers responded with equal cunning: they announced that Devlet would indeed be going to Kazan, not Crimea, with a large military escort to see him safely up the Volga. The viziers and sultan assumed that Sahib would fall for this and would not stop the Turkish contingent and new khan from crossing Crimean territory. The sultan told Devlet in private that he would in fact be the new khan of Crimea and warned him against being as disobedient as his uncle Sahib. A thousand warriors and sixty cannon accompanied Devlet to the western boundaries of the khanate. When they were sure that Sahib had left for Circassia, they moved to the isthmus at Or Qapı, where Sahib's sons gave them a reception and generous gifts, but blocked their army's access to the peninsula. This made Devlet fear that he was to be assassinated. Devlet was allowed to cross the Crimea to Kerç, where he was met by Sahib who urged him to carry on to Kazan and to send a message to Bağçasaray when he arrived there.

Convinced that he could not conquer Crimea by land, Devlet went back to his military escort at Or Qapı, and sent to Akkerman on the Dnestr for two fleets of ships. One fleet disembarked at Balaklava, ostensibly to load wood; instead the sailors rustled local herds of horses, before proceeding to Inkerman and liberating the Giray princes, Sahib's great-nephews, whom he had captured in Astrakhan. The other fleet took Devlet to Gözleve and disembarked at night: the local Tatars greeted Devlet and, looting all the way, rode with him to Bağçasaray. In Bağçasaray, Devlet produced Sultan Süleyman's decree appointing him khan and took possession of the khanate's treasury. The treasury's contents were more effective than force of arms in winning over Sahib's courtiers.

Emin Giray, the *qalğa*, tried to intervene, but when he headed for the capital found that all but seventeen men of his army had deserted him. Worse happened. Two Mansur clansmen now decided to avenge all the Noğays whom Sahib had killed: they personally strangled all Sahib Giray's sons, except for one who had accompanied him to Circassia, and then slaughtered his three infant grandsons.

As in previous Circassian campaigns, the Crimeans were lured into the mountain gorges north of Mt Elbrus to where their opponents had retreated. With some difficulty the Crimean forces pursued the enemy into an impasse and took an enormous number of slaves, the youngest and most beautiful of whom were destined for the sultan's pleasure in Istanbul. A Circassian warrior who had boasted of his ability to take on a hundred Crimean Tatars was horribly tortured with a red-hot branding iron thrust between his buttocks. After humiliating the Zhané Circassians, Sahib made for home.

When Sahib reached the coast and learned what had happened in Bağçasaray, he stoically announced that his martyred sons would be in paradise. He cared little about the loss of his treasury: he was convinced that Devlet Giray was too 'soft' and that in his hands the country would fall apart. Sahib decided to sail to Istanbul, but his *mirza*s and servants deserted him and Sahib got no further than the fortress of Taman, where he asked for asylum from the Ottoman commandant, who had been forewarned by Devlet and the Turks, only to be confronted in a bedroom by the liberated Bölük Giray, who hacked the khan to death with a sabre, while his thirteen-year-old son Ğazı was murdered by a Şirin *mirza*. The bodies were loaded onto a cart and taken to Eski Qırım. The procession encountered Devlet Khan, on his way to Kaffa to consult with the Ottomans. Devlet shed tears, put on a black gown, justified the murders as 'in the interests of law and order' and, no doubt, recalled that his uncle Mehmed I Giray had likewise connived at Sultan Selim's murder of his brother. Devlet gave Sahib's widows and twelve daughters generous allowances, and paid lavishly for Sahib Giray's funeral. He commissioned the shocked Geomancer, the late khan's closest adviser, to supervise the burial, and then had the khan's and his son's remains taken to Hacı Giray's mausoleum in Salacıq. At the interment, Devlet Giray, following Mongol custom, wore the bloodstained garments in which his murdered uncle had died. Posterity was kind to Sahib: Seyyid Muhammed Riza named him the 'second planet' for his achievement in making the Crimean Khanate a formidable and autonomous entity. The magnificent new mosques and medrese that Sahib had endowed in Bağçasaray must have given Devlet cause for reflection. Sahib's great-nephew and murderer Bölük did not prosper: Devlet at first appointed him *qalğa*, but, when he heard Bölük boasting of what he had done, personally stabbed him to death with his dagger. How guilty Devlet felt is hard to assess: some Crimean historians blamed Istanbul's viziers for commissioning the murders of Sahib and his family, some believe the initiative was Devlet's. Apparently, Devlet hanged a certain It-Hoca who had proudly brought him the body of Sahib's son Emin.

4

MILITANT KHANS

Devlet was not as soft as Sahib Giray feared: his reign lasted some 27 years, as long as his grandfather Mengli Giray's. True, there were few male Girays still alive who might challenge him for the khanate. Throughout his reign, however, Devlet Giray faced a worse threat, that of a new power, imperial Russia, which was ruled after 1547 and the enthronement of Ivan IV, not by a grand duke, but by a tsar. The Russian Orthodox Church now saw itself as the guardian of a new 'third Rome, and there shall be no fourth'. Tsar and church began a rapid and violent expansion of power, both territorial and spiritual. What was left of the Horde was threatened by a crusade, as well as incorporation into Muscovy, and forcible conversion from Islam to Orthodox Christianity. The khanate of Kazan had enjoyed a decade of relief while Ivan IV was a child and Russia was ruled by his mother and then by a council of boyars. Now, in 1550, Kazan itself had an infant ruler with his mother (Süyün-bike, the widow of Safa Giray) as regent. Although rumours that Devlet was to be their khan had proved false, many Kazan Tatars decided that a pro-Moscow orientation was safer. Tsar Ivan IV quickly cut off access to Kazan from the south via the Volga. A small army of Crimean guardsmen was intercepted, sent to Moscow and executed. The Russian blockade of Kazan was devastating: the city accepted as its khan the Russian puppet Shah-Ali. Süyük-bike, despite her own and her father's pleas to be allowed to join her family in Noğay territory, was taken prisoner by Ivan IV. Shah-Ali and his Russian guards began a series of executions so horrible that they were expelled by the angry Kazan citizens. Shah-Ali abducted Süyük-bike and went to live in the puppet khanate of Kasimov. The infant khan of Kazan, Ötemiş Giray, was converted to Christianity and named tsar of Kazan, before being deported to Moscow, where he mysteriously died ten years later (it was suspected that he was poisoned).

The failure of his politics in Kazan and the turmoil in Crimea persuaded Ivan IV that only violent force could subdue the remnants of the Horde. In 1552 he set an entire army on Kazan. Devlet Giray, determined to fight back, sought support from the Noğay tribes in Astrakhan, which was next in Ivan IV's programme of conquest. First, Devlet had to release the Noğay he had held captive in Crimea for the past four years. Younger Noğays were in favour of resisting Moscow, but the influential senior Noğay Yusuf-Bey, whose daughter and grandson were hostages in Moscow, did not want to fight on the grounds, as the Tatar proverb puts it, that 'A lot of friends are like one friend, but one enemy is like a lot of enemies.' The khan of Astrakhan, Yamgurça, also vacillated.

Devlet was encouraged, and at the same time left in the lurch, by Sultan Süleyman, who assured the Crimean Tatars they could defend Kazan on their own. Devlet sent a son with just 7,000 men, followed by Turkish janissaries and artillery – the first time that Ottoman forces had accompanied Tatars against the Russians. They got as far as Riazan, to find that the Russian army had not yet moved from Moscow, a battlefield where Devlet would have been overwhelmed by all Ivan IV's forces. Devlet returned home, his rearguard harassed by Moscow's troops. Ivan overwhelmed Kazan, looting everything of value, massacring the male inhabitants, carrying away the women and children, while his puppet khan Shah-Ali congratulated the tsar amid the smoking ruins.

It was important for the khanate to reaffirm its peaceful intentions to Poland-Lithuania. In doing so Devlet was helped by his wives: four of the five are mentioned in Polish-Lithuanian government records. The most influential of these was the senior wife Aişa-Fatma Sultan (mother of the *qalğa* Mehmed), whom Devlet always consulted before acting. Unlike the khan's step-grandmother Nurun-Sultan, who generally sympathized with Moscow, Aişa-Fatma was strongly pro-Polish. Russian records note that 'the Khan defers to his empress Aişa-Fatma, mulls things over with her and listens to her.' In 1552 (and again in 1560) Devlet sent a long missive to King Sigismund August, renewing the 'lease' granted by the Horde to much of Poland-Lithuania's territory, and giving reassurances (in exchange for annual gifts of 13,000 florins' worth of cloth) of cooperation and restraint from extortion:

> And – God willing – also in the future, according to our letter of agreement, we will send the sultans, ulans, beys, and mirzas along with our great army to the land of our Muscovian enemy, and against

other enemies, wherever our brother, King Sigismund Augustus, needs it . . . And we should not send more envoys and couriers but only the number that used to be heretofore . . . If more envoys and couriers were to come, you may send them back without giving them anything, and I will not reproach you, our brother, for this, because as you lavish gifts on envoys and couriers who come to you, on seeing this, they do not want to stop going, but if you send them back empty-handed, you will see yourself whether they will come again.

Devlet spent the following year trying to forge another alliance: he gave thirteen cannon to the khan of Astrakhan, Yamgurça, who now feared the Russians. But the Noğay nobility sought protection first from Istanbul and, when rejected, from Moscow, with whom they agreed jointly to attack the khanate of Astrakhan (or, more exactly, its capital, Hacı Tarhan). In 1554 30,000 Russians came down the Volga and were puzzled by the absence of the Noğay leaders (who were engaged in fratricidal battle). This invasion by Ivan IV is recorded by the Ottoman historian Peçevi:

> Khan Devlet Giray then notified Istanbul that the Russian lord Ivan had gathered sixty thousand warriors whom he planned in spring to use to ravage Islamic lands. When this became known, immediately a skilled commander named Mehmed was appointed as general in charge of thousands of Tatars. When they realized that the Tatars were approaching, the infidels came out to meet them. At noon a furious deadly battle flared up and the two sides fought until the next morning. By dawn the battle was at its climax and before noon the wind of victory blew towards the Muslims, and the infidels sought salvation in flight. The Islamic warriors pursued and struck them. God knows that in this war of sixty thousand infidels very few survived.

Khan Yamgurça offered no resistance; he and many citizens fled, so that the Russians managed to detain only a boat carrying Yamgurça's wives. A puppet khan was installed, thus splitting the Noğay Horde: those who fled south to the Kuban steppes would be known as the Little Horde, *kiçi Noğay*, and this Horde quickly integrated with Devlet Giray's forces. Eventually the puppet khan and his master decided that Tsar Ivan was too dangerous a patron: they expelled from Astrakhan the Russian viceroy whom Moscow had installed. Devlet sent the insurgents more cannon and men, infuriating the remaining pro-Moscow Noğay, who now begged Ivan IV to destroy Astrakhan and exterminate its inhabitants. In 1556 Ivan effectively did so and, despite the reproaches of his Noğay allies, turned the once prosperous centre of the Horde into a Russian garrison city. Just a very few Tatars, deciding that Ivan IV must be descended from Genghis Khan, revered him as the White Shah of Shahs, in which case the Crimean Khanate could expect to be absorbed into this revived empire. The Crimeans were not aware that in 1555 Ivan IV's military advisers, Prince Kurbsky and Daniel Adashev, urged him to join Poland in a war to reduce the Crimean Khanate to a vassal state.

Such an invasion was already planned by Ivan IV: he was waiting for an opportunity, which appeared when Devlet set off for Circassia to quell a revolt with pro-Russian implications – in 1561 Ivan IV would marry the daughter of the Circassian prince Temrük. He sent Prince Sheremetev and 13,000 men south, forcing Devlet to abandon his Circassian expedition: in an encounter with Sheremetev's army two of Devlet's sons perished; a third son, Mehmed, left to guard the approach to Crimea, intervened and defeated the Russian force. Devlet boasted to Sultan Süleyman of a glorious victory over the Russian 'Ban' (Ivan). Crimean historians, however, conceded that the 'accursed' Sheremetev was exceptionally skilful and brave for a *giaour* and concluded that Sheremetev was really an Armenian Persian, not a Russian, and his name was in fact *Shir-Merd*, Persian for 'Lion Man'. The following spring Devlet's army attempted a comeback, but the Russians were warned in time to repel it. A resumption of Devlet's Circassian campaign also failed when fleets of Cossack boats came down both the Dnepr and the Don. Eventually, however, Cossacks were enemies only from time to time: the Western Cossack *hetman* ('chieftain') Dmitri Vishnevetsky so resented his Polish overlords that he was the first Cossack leader to seek protection, first from the Ottoman sultan, and then from the Crimean khan. Only when protection was refused did Vishnevetsky declare for the Russians. Until the end of 1558 it seemed possible that Ivan IV would win Crimea thanks to a two-pronged Cossack attack, extended to a prolonged raid on Crimea's western ports and on Kerç. Noğay Tatars took the opportunity of invading the steppe zone of the peninsula. Refugees fleeing the Cossacks flooded into central Crimea, bringing famine and plague.

Devlet tried a fourth time to attack Moscow, and failed again. Sultan Süleyman had sent his blessings, but no artillery. The Russians took care not to anger the Ottomans: when they took prisoners from the Tatar army, they weeded out Ottoman citizens and freed them, saying they were making war not on the Ottoman empire, but on the remnants of the Horde. Crimea was saved, however, from destruction: the Cossacks deserted the Russian army, and Ivan IV now had to focus on the Livonian War, a struggle with Sweden far more of a threat to the future of Russia than the Crimean conflict. So crucial was this northern conflict that Ivan IV offered Devlet Giray peace, even an alliance. Devlet was relieved, even glad, but responded a little surlily, reminding Ivan IV that previous alliances with Russia had only helped Muscovy expand its territory and had brought Crimea nothing. Yet Devlet badly needed peace, for his Crimean Tatars had begun to think that their 'unlucky Khan' was under a curse.

A ray of hope came from Poland: opposed to Russia in the Livonian war, the Poles looked to Crimea for support. The tributes and gifts that both Russia and Poland were offering could be a salvation for the Crimean economy, at least of the nobility. The *qaraçı beys*, however, opposed any reconciliation with Russia that might make it more powerful: Devlet therefore demanded exorbitant tribute, unacceptable to the notoriously parsimonious Ivan, who required one of Devlet's sons as a pledge.

Devlet Giray had another lever to pull. He knew that Sultan Süleyman was now interested in acquiring Astrakhan, partly because southern trade routes across Central Asia were cut by the almost perpetual war between Turkey and Iran, and northern routes by Ivan IV's attempts to expand across the Urals into Siberia and further east. A Russian conquest of the mouths of the Don and the Volga would give them access to the Black Sea. Devlet himself was more worried that the sultan would be apprehensive enough to abolish Crimean autonomy and Crimea's exclusive access to the Volga, in order to integrate the whole northern Black Sea coast with the Ottoman empire.

One reason why Astrakhan now attracted Ottoman interest was the idea that, by gaining access to the Volga, Ottoman warships could cross the Caspian and invade Iran from the north, instead of marching overland through Anatolia and across the Tigris and Euphrates. To reach the Volga it was thought that ships could row up the Don and then a canal could be dug across the short stretch of steppe land to the Volga. (A similar plan was then being hatched to dig a canal in Egypt from the Nile to the Red Sea.) It was not until 1568, when Süleyman had died, that the new sultan, Selim II 'the Drunk', went ahead, sending the viceroy of Kaffa with Crimean and Turkish soldiers and labourers to dig. They had only a local nomad's advice to go on, and did not know that the Volga flowed 44 metres (144 ft) lower than the Don, that the canal would first have to climb 44 metres and then descend 88 metres (288 ft), which would demand a series of locks beyond even the technology at the time of the Dutch, Venetians or Chinese, let alone the Ottomans. Had the canal been built, it would have drained the Don into the Volga and made the Sea of Azov too shallow to navigate. In any case, when digging started, the ground began to freeze: exaggerated tales of steppe winters and endless northern nights aborted the project, to Devlet Giray's relief. (Eventually Peter the Great attempted to build, with Dutch and British help, a canal between small tributaries of the Don and Volga, a waterway so shallow and easily frozen that it would have been useless. Not until 1950 was today's Volga–Don canal built, and even now it is too cumbersome to be a trade route from the Caspian to the Black Sea.)

Disease, cold and starvation on the canal project killed most of its 30,000 workmen. Equipment, including some 16,000 spades, was abandoned in Azov. The skirmishes with Russian Cossacks and troops, because the Ottoman forces lacked artillery, caused enormous casualties to both Crimeans and Turks. Quite apart from the canal project, any hopes of wrenching Astrakhan from Russian occupation perished. Devlet reproached Sultan Selim, 'If we fail to take Hacı Tarhan, the dishonour will be yours, not mine.'

Every year from 1562 to 1565, in spring, summer or autumn, Devlet sent his army north towards Russia's borders, destroying settlements and capturing slaves, but never going further than Riazan, not risking defeat from a serious Russian armed force. There were attempts to make peace, but in 1564 Devlet Giray told the Russian tsar that he would not accept any Russian promises unless the tsar first kissed a cross in the metropolitan bishop's presence. Ivan IV duly did so.[1] For Ivan and his army, the prolonged Livonian War was more crucial than conflict with Crimea, although at this period the fighting was at its least intense.

In 1571 Devlet Giray humiliated Russia and Tsar Ivan IV personally, even more so than had Sahib's insolent abuse in the 1540s. A year earlier Devlet had sent his two sons with 50,000 horsemen to devastate Riazan and Kashira. A year later he had the approval of both Poland-Lithuania and the Ottomans (the Ottoman historian Peçevi says that Devlet had not just permission, but orders from Sultan Selim) to mount the Crimean Khanate's most devastating invasion. Guided by a Russian turncoat, the Crimean army avoided interception as it crossed the Oka and approached the walls of Moscow. Tsar Ivan fled the city northeastward to Rostov Veliki. After a brief retreat, Devlet camped outside Moscow and set fire to the suburbs. Within three hours the city itself was ablaze. Foreigners in Moscow at the time give an unbelievably high estimate of the number of civilians who perished. The crowd of refugees and soldiers packed for shelter into the Kremlin died when gunpowder stores exploded. The very next day Devlet, who had spent two weeks ransacking Moscow's ruins, turned back, taking as many Russian prisoners – his contemporaries estimate 150,000 – as his men could herd. He sent the Russian tsar a message, demanding that Kazan and Astrakhan be ceded to the Crimean Khanate. Ivan IV offered him just Astrakhan, which Devlet refused, assuming he could now conquer all of Russia. Devlet was awarded by his people the title *taht-algan*, 'Throne Snatcher'. For Sultan Selim the news of Devlet's victory came on the same October day as a counterbalance to the news of the annihilation of the Ottoman fleet at the battle of Lepanto. Selim disliked Devlet Giray's ambition to seize both Kazan and Astrakhan: the sultan wanted Astrakhan for his own empire, and would cede only Kazan.

Devlet's real gain was the annual financial contribution that he forced Ivan IV to make: called *tış* in Tatar, *vykhod* in Russian, it was payment for exemption from further attacks. Crimean historians commented that the Russians had to pay by a due date a tribute, *tış*, for Crimea's rulers; the equivalent of a poll tax, it consisted of sable and ermine skins and fur coats and other gifts, according to the designated recipient's rank. When payment was due, a clerk would come from Moscow and compile a list of persons benefiting from this tax (*tış-sahıbları*). An imperfect command of language and accountancy led to errors: the Russian clerk compiling this list ended it *şul evq*, 'so much the total', so that a non-existent recipient 'so much the total' was included.

Devlet (whom Ivan called 'the Ismailite cur') was not paid the tribute he expected. Tsar Ivan, whose sense of humour was as grim as his cruelty or meanness, put on a coarse-cloth shirt and old sheepskin coat to greet Tatar envoys. He told them, 'You see how I am. The Khan did this to me. He seized all my realm, burnt my treasury: I have nothing to give the Khan.' Devlet took countermeasures. First, he asked the sultan for permission to detain the Russian ambassador in Crimea's Mangup fortress until the campaign against Moscow was over: Sultan Selim was now so confident of victory that he assumed responsibility for the war as imperial and religious leader of both Turks and Tatars. 'To take part', Devlet was told, 'is a sacred duty of religion and the State.' In July 1572 Devlet's enormous army was reinforced with 40,000 Turks. This time, however, the Russians were ready and cut the Tatar–Turkish force off from Moscow. Devlet suffered a terrible defeat, losing two of his sons and a leading Crimean general. One fiasco followed another in Devlet Giray's retreat; at most 10,000 Crimeans and Turks survived the retreat. In 1574 Devlet captured the injured Russian commander Vasili Griaznoi and asked for a generous ransom. Ivan IV refused, however, to pay ransom or to exchange him for a Tatar leader: 'There is no advantage to Christianity [in such an exchange], you're not worth more than 50 roubles,' he wrote to Griaznoi. Devlet undertook no more anti-Russian campaigns and his disappointed elder sons, Mehmed the *qalğa* and Adil, turned against him. On 29 June 1577 Devlet Giray died of plague, aged 65. Even though his defeat at the hands of the Russians in 1572 had forever shattered the Crimean Khanate's hope of restoring the Horde and reconquering Kazan and Astrakhan, the Crimean historian Seyyid Muhammed Riza named Devlet as the third of his 'seven planets' who had determined the historical orbit of the khanate.

Devlet bequeathed to his country, apart from further development of the garden city capital, a magnificent mosque, the Han-Cami, in the port city of Gözleve. Like many other khans, Devlet wrote verse, although only one couplet of his survives:

The reason that a rose leaf tears your collar
Is the nightingale lamenting in the rose-garden.[2]

Khan Mehmed II Giray the Fat[3]

Of Devlet's ten sons, three died in battles with Russia; the eldest survivor, Mehmed, had twenty years' experience as *qalğa* and as a successful military leader. In the eyes of the people, the *bey*s, the Ottoman sultan and both Mongol and Turkish tradition, Mehmed was the obvious and legitimate successor to the khanate. His problem was that his brothers, particularly the next youngest, Alp Giray, were ambitious (four of them would have a spell, a few months or two decades, on the throne). On the death of Devlet, Alp left the peninsula in a huff, to settle in a palace surrounded by Noğay followers on the Kalmius river. Devlet, just before his death, had reconciled him with Mehmed, but relations remained fraught.

The 45-year-old Mehmed was notoriously obese. No horse could carry him for long, yet, contrary to Tatar custom, but to general admiration, he rode everywhere – whether in Russia, the Balkans or Azerbaijan, to battle or in retreat – in a cart harnessed to six or eight horses.

Mehmed II Giray's political stance was intransigent and tense. Both Russia and Poland-Lithuania, at war with each other, curried favour with him. Ivan IV sent generous gifts and emollient letters, to which Mehmed responded that the Russians had to cede Kazan and Astrakhan to the Crimean Khanate if they wanted to become allies. Mehmed knew this was out of the question; he then concluded a separate treaty with the new Polish king Stefan Batory, who was anxious to live in peace with the Ottomans and the Crimeans and to secure their help in repressing rebellious Cossacks. This was mutually advantageous: Batory would try to stop Cossacks raiding Crimea, and Mehmed would try to stop his Tatars raiding Polish Ukrainian territory, although the Cossacks had minds of their own and sometimes attacked with Russian complicity.

For the beginning of Mehmed II Giray's reign we have an extensive and credible survey of the Crimean Khanate by the Polish ambassador Marcyn Broniewski, who spent three periods on the peninsula, the last one a prolonged period from 1578 that was more detention than residence. Broniewski's report to the Polish king was written in Latin, and soon became widely known in Europe. Broniewski noted the transition of the steppe Crimeans from a nomadic pastoral to a settled agricultural existence, in which a carnivorous life in yurts and on two-wheeled ox-carts gave way to eating grain, ploughing and haymaking. After observing the steppe life, Broniewski found that there was only one land entry to Crimea itself, via Or Qapı with its seventeen towers and a deep moat across the isthmus, and that no foreigner could leave without written authorization from the khan. He also inspected the castle of Mangup, the capital of the Goths, its dungeon for political prisoners being all that was left after Turkish invasion and a fire. Bağçasaray struck Broniewski as 'small', but the adjoining town of Salaçıq with the khan's court impressed him, as did the orchards, vineyards, forests and clear streams. The area was full of game – boar, hares, goats and birds – that were hunted by the khan with dogs, but only foreigners took an interest in the plentiful river fish.

Broniewski noted that the khan employed Christians of Genoese descent, and that these civil servants had their own Catholic church, with a Franciscan monk, once a prisoner of war, now an intermediary who visited, with a Tatar escort, Papal legates in Europe. In Broniewski's time Eski Qırım was the largest Tatar city, with strong walls and a Greek community. Its church, where allegedly 1,000 Christians' bodies had lain unburied for a hundred years, was closed.[4] Once in Ottoman-controlled Kaffa, Broniewski could taste fine wine and contemplate the city's decline since the expulsion of the Genoese. With a good wind, Kaffa could be reached from Istanbul in just two days.

Impressed by the country's fertility, Broniewski was dismayed by its politics, particularly by the fratricidal chaos at each new accession, when younger brothers and their male relatives had to flee for their lives, and rebellious *beys* were slaughtered or shackled. But once a khan had secured his throne, then the court was well administered, with younger men trained for higher rank, and non-Tatars – Circassians and Noğays – promoted by merit and well paid. The wealth created by capturing, ransoming and enslaving foreign prisoners was not squandered on luxury, but spent wisely, often on the maintenance of several wives. Children, even of concubines, whether sons or daughters, were taught to read and write. Like other foreign observers, Broniewski was most impressed by the civil and criminal courts, where there were no lawyers, but just a religiously trained judge, reputed for honesty and fairness; often the khan would hear and decide cases personally, for which he was trusted, even revered. Over nine months Broniewski encountered no criminality or denunciations, except for horse-theft.

The rich, Broniewski observed, ate bread and beef, and drank wine and mead; the poor had ground millet with milk. Fields were cultivated mainly by captive Hungarians, Russians and Romanians, who were 'treated like cattle'. For Greek Christians, farm labour was close to serfdom. Trade, crafts and manufacture were largely the preserve of Greeks, Armenians and Jews. As a foreign diplomat, Broniewski was given a modest allowance of food and accommodation. He noted an extensive, but, he thought, bearable taxation system and the tight control of foreign exchange, which enforced the usage of money minted by the khanate. Like those attacked by a Tatar army abroad, Broniewski was impressed with the Tatar military organization, their horses, their fine weapons, their modest logistics, and he appreciated that the motive for the khanate's militancy was the income from looting and slave-trading, not extending territory, or promoting religion.

Only when examining the fate of prisoners and slaves did Broniewski become indignant: 'This barbarous, dishonest, greedy, hungry and cruel nation, trying to raise every day the ransom price by deceit and torture, shackles prisoners and keeps them in very cruel conditions.' Foreign agents who brought ransoms to free prisoners had equally devious means of lowering the price of freedom, but if no bargain was struck, a prisoner of war might be enslaved for years or, worse, sold to work in Ottoman galleys.

In spring 1578 a new field of operations, far from Poland, opened for the Crimean Khanate: an invasion of Iranian territory in Shirvan in eastern Transcaucasia, today's Azerbaijan. Previous Crimean khans had annoyed Istanbul by their reluctance to attack Iran, a country and culture the Tatars admired. It was, for them, too far away, across difficult mountains, and with an enormous army that would in twenty years' time be trained by the British and equipped with the latest firearms. Apart from new sources of slaves, however, Iran offered Mehmed an opportunity to give his power-hungry brothers (and his eldest sons) a chance to show their prowess. It ensured, in particular, that Mehmed's brother Adil and his uncontrollable Noğay tribesmen could be sent 1,000 kilometres (620 mi.) away from Crimea.

For this first anti-Iranian campaign, Mehmed excused himself on the grounds of illness, but he satisfied the new Sultan Murad III by dispatching his brothers Adil, Mubarek and Ğazı. It took them three months to cross the Caucasus mountain chain and join the Ottoman Osman Paşa in Dagestan. At first the Tatars triumphed, totally destroying an Iranian army (Iran's soldiers in Dagestan were *kızılbaş*, 'red-heads', Turkmens related to Tatars, not to Persians). Peçevi described the battle:

> At a moment when the Ottoman army was biding its time and watching, three young, brave brothers of the Tatar Khan – Adil, Ğazı and Sa'adet Giray and his glorious son Mubarek – at the head of the whole Tatar army of 40 to 50 thousand warriors, suddenly fell on the enemy. With the help of Allah the All-Highest there was such a battle as even the heavenly angels' eyes had not seen. Not only were many khans and sultans killed, but there was a count of 7,760 severed human heads.[5]

The main Iranian army was more formidable: when Adil Giray tried to break through and save the surrounded Turks, he was thrown back out of Dagestan. Heavy rain made the going hard and soaked the Tatar arrow feathers. In the defeat that followed, Adil was wounded and unhorsed. He would have been killed, had he not been recognized as a Genghisid prince. He was taken to Qazvin palace and treated as a guest by the blind and retiring Shah Khudabanda, who thought of making Adil his son-in-law. Unfortunately for Adil, it was the shah's wife Khayr-an-Nisa who actually ruled the country (to the fury of the Iranian army). Peçevi relates the consequences a year later:

> The Shah's wife and sister fell in love with Adil Giray, they had close relationships, drinking sessions and gatherings that led to desire. People in charge became suspicious and their suspicions were confirmed. They said, 'How fickle and wretched our Shah is! Don't we

have our honour?' One day a group of soldiers went to the Shah's bedroom. The Shah's wife was hiding behind an easy-chair by the bed, and the Shah tried to save her, but failed. They dragged her from the Shah's easy-chair and killed her straight away. Then they went to the Shah's sister's room and killed her. They joined the men at the gates and on the roof guarding Adil. When they came down and entered Adil's room, a terrible fight broke out. Adil cut down seven men, but was wounded, and had no strength left: he was shot, then died a martyr.

Adil perished when his mother was halfway to Qazvin, bearing gifts in the hope of ransoming her son.

That same year, 1579, Sultan Murad III insisted on Mehmed Giray personally leading a second campaign in Transcaucasia. Mehmed reluctantly obeyed. While his son Ğazı conquered the port of Baku, Mehmed stayed in the city of Shemakha, rewarding his soldiers with tax exemptions on their loot. He was anxious to get back to Crimea, where Cossack incursions and his brothers' plots undermined his authority. Mehmed proposed to leave his son Ğazı to overwinter, while the Turkish commander Osman Paşa went home to a warmer climate, only to be told that he, Mehmed, was forbidden to leave the front. He wrote an angry letter to Sultan Murad III: 'Are we not better than Ottoman *beys*?' Then he left with his son Sa'adet.

Peace in Bağçasaray was disturbed when Mehmed Giray replaced his late brother Adil with his own son Sa'adet as *qalğa*. Mehmed's brother Alp objected to the choice. Alp and his brother Selâmet galloped off to Istanbul to complain to Murad III, but were intercepted and imprisoned in Cherkasy by Cossacks. The brothers appealed to the king of Poland first to redeem them, and then jointly to invade Crimea. Mehmed bribed the Cossacks with 7,000 gold coins and four hundred satin kaftans to hand Alp and Selâmet over to his *mirzas*, who had instructions to kill the two rebels. Şirin *beys*, however, intervened and forced Mehmed not just to spare Alp, but to make him *qalğa*. The khan's situation was now unendurable.

Mehmed defused the situation with a new political appointment, second only to the *qalğa*, of a *nureddin* (literally, 'light of the faith'). The title had been used for military commanders in some Turkic tribes of the Golden Horde. Under Mehmed and his successors this would be not just the provision of an 'heir and a spare'. The *nureddin*, like the *qalğa*, was given extensive lands and a share of the Crimean army: the *qalğa* controlled the west, the *nureddin* the east of the country. Alp became *qalğa*, and Mehmed's son Sa'adet *nureddin*. If the Şirins and the khan's brother Alp became too overbearing, Mehmed could rely on his son Sa'adet and the Noğays, who cherished their new importance, to counter them. A wary balance of power had been struck.

Sultan Murad III called for a third attack on Iran. Ğazı Giray had been taken prisoner, and the small Tatar detachment there was leaderless. Mehmed's *divan* agreed with the khan that this war was senseless and that the Crimean Khanate should withdraw from further campaigns, especially in autumn rains and in the extreme cold of a Caucasian winter. Murad III decided to force the Crimeans and sent a fleet of ships to Kaffa. Mehmed started bargaining: he would send troops to Shirvan if the Ottomans gave him the tribute they received from Moldavia and the customs revenues of Kaffa. In the end, the viceroy of Kaffa had to lead the army to the Caucasus without the Crimean khan. Murad III suspected Mehmed Giray of treasonable dealings with the shah of Iran. Punishment would follow.

In October 1583 the Ottoman troops returned from Iran not to Istanbul, but to Kaffa, to arrest Khan Mehmed II Giray and bring him to the sultan's court. Mehmed brought 40,000 men to Kaffa's walls, manned by Turkish artillery. There was a stand-off for a month. Alp Giray, the *qalğa*, secretly met the Turkish commander Osman Paşa and offered to make the Crimean army lay down its arms if he, Alp, were installed as the new khan. Mehmed laughed this proposition off, declaring that nobody had the right to depose or appoint a Crimean khan whose name was proclaimed at Friday prayers and whose face was on the coins. The *bey*s agreed with him. The *mufti* of Kaffa was consulted. To Mehmed's consternation, the *mufti* sided with the Ottomans. Osman Paşa waited until spring 1584 for naval reinforcements to come and enact the *mufti*'s decision.

When the Turkish galleys arrived, they brought not just janissaries and guns, but Mehmed's brother Islam Giray who, as an honoured hostage in a Konya dervish house, had not seen or perhaps even thought about his homeland for three decades. Islam was now clutching a sultan's decree enthroning him as the new Khan Islam II Giray. This sudden promotion was, to Mehmed's surprise, accepted by the Şirin *bey*s as legitimate. Mehmed's Noğay supporters felt outnumbered. Three brothers and three sons of Mehmed all galloped away from Kaffa. The obese Mehmed could not move so quickly, and got only as far as the isthmus at Or Qapı. Here his brother Alp had him strangled. The well-informed historian Peçevi was sure that Sultan Murad III had ordered Mehmed II Giray's brothers to kill him; Peçevi describes Mehmed's fate:

For so many years Mehmed had made generous pledges to the Tatars, saying that nobody could depose him, but this did him no good. In the end, he tried to flee across the mouth of the River Or, cursing 'Whoever deposes me, may God pay him back.' As he was extraordinarily corpulent and bulky, he realized that he wouldn't manage to get away. Suddenly he spread out a prayer mat and bowed his neck. Then some of the Khan's sons caught up with him and finished the job.

As Tatar custom dictated, after the murder the victim's body was treated with reverence. Mehmed was buried in a special mausoleum at Eski Yurt near Bağçasaray.

Islam II Giray, Mehmed's oldest surviving brother, was a legitimate replacement. Sultan Murad III may have felt that Islam's life as a submissive Sufi would make him more compliant with Istanbul's commands. Islam's nephews, however, did not welcome his enthronement: Sa'adet and his brothers returned to Crimea, whose borders were now unguarded, with an army of Noğays and a couple of hundred Don Cossacks. The *beys* and army chiefs were taken by surprise. Within a week they fled, hiding the new khan in the Ottoman fort at Balaklava. By then Sa'adet had confiscated the Crimean treasury and was himself crowned khan in Eski Qırım, before besieging Kaffa for ten weeks with the help of Zaporozhian Cossacks. Islam Giray sent an appeal to the sultan. When Turkish artillery eventually arrived, Sa'adet and his two brothers once more fled. They tried to invade in spring 1585, but the sultan had put a price on their heads. Sa'adet defected to the shah of Iran, his brother Murad Giray to the new ruler of Russia, the meek and mild Tsar Fiodor. The tsar's advisers housed Murad in Astrakhan as a potential Russian puppet to be installed in Crimea. Murad anticipated sharing his future khanate with Sa'adet, as 'rulers of the four rivers [the Don, Volga, Yaik and Terek]'.

Mehmed's sons were just as hostile as his brothers were to Islam II Giray, who was widely hated because his Turkish guards were shedding the blood of anyone suspected to be a malcontent. Moscow exploited the situation, knowing that the Crimean Khanate was now incapable of attacking Russia. Meanwhile Russia used Murad to send an army around the northern Caucasus and persuade Circassians, Noğays and Kumyk Tatars to reject Turkey and Crimea in favour of Russian protection. Islam's brothers Alp and Selâmet reacted by forcing Islam to agree to an attack on Moscow. Islam refused personally to leave the khanate. At the same time, Alp and Selâmet told the Poles that when Moscow installed its puppet Sa'adet in Crimea, they would make peace with Poland. Meanwhile, Zaporozhian Cossacks rowed down the Dnepr, raiding coastal villages in western Crimea and preventing Turkish relief forces from protecting Islam's khanate.

Sultan Murad III blamed Islam for the chaos: 'Thanks to your lack of care, Lithuanian Cossacks are seizing my towns and ravaging Crimea. Earlier khans did not let this happen, and if it is repeated, then you shall no longer be Khan in Crimea,' he wrote, telling him to prepare for war on Poland, which the Ottomans held responsible for the Zaporozhian Cossack raids. Islam was also ordered to prepare for a war on the Volga to recapture Astrakhan. Strangely enough, Islam's nephew Sa'adet Giray, the first Russian candidate for khan of Crimea, suddenly died at the age of forty. It was widely believed that the Russians had poisoned him to prevent him welcoming the Ottomans to Astrakhan. Moreover, Sa'adet's brother Murad was reported to have deserted his Russian sponsors once he realized that an Ottoman army might be on its way. Suspicions grew that Ğazı Giray, who had escaped from the Iranian shah's prison, was organizing for his brothers a triumphant return to Crimea under Ottoman protection.

Islam II Giray in March 1588 obeyed the Ottoman sultan and slowly led his forces in the direction of Poland. He had never been to war before. His army was so lackadaisical that he had to order janissaries to punish his deserters. The Dnepr had not yet frozen: the army waited for a month before the ice formed. By the time the Crimean Tatars crossed the river, their Turkish allies had given up waiting. Here, at Akkerman, Islam II Giray died and was buried. His brother Alp was acclaimed as the new khan and a *bey* was sent to Istanbul to have their choice confirmed by the sultan. But Alp, however ambitious, was unpopular. The Crimean people wanted to have as khan his brother Ğazı, hero of the Iranian campaign ten years earlier, a much-admired adventurer and poet. The sultan, too, felt that the Ottoman empire now needed not a loser, but a Giray with a record of repeated successes.

Ğazı II Giray

Ğazı, left by his brother Mehmed to guard the new Ottoman–Iranian frontier in Azerbaijan, was surprised by an Iranian night raid in spring 1581. He escaped on horseback into the forest, but was unhorsed and captured when he rode into a tree. He was held by Shah Abbas I in Iran's infamous Alamut mountain prison, a former Assassins' hideout, now used for

ALEHIERE SVLTAN, RE DI TARTARI

Franco Forma.   *Cum priuilegio.*

Khan Ğazı II Giray, *c.* 1596, engraving.

high-value prisoners and reputed to be impossible to escape from. Some of Alamut's famous library may have survived the Mongol invasion, and the deposed scholarly Shah Khudabanda was also locked up in Alamut: Ğazı therefore had scholarly resources and was able to develop his skills in Farsi and in writing poetry while a prisoner. Ğazı Giray proved to be the most broadly talented of all Crimean princes. Born in 1554, he was sent as a boy to Circassian foster-parents to become an accomplished horseman and archer. He then spent some years in Istanbul, at the Enderun Academy in Topkapı palace, an institution founded in the fifteenth century and resembling a modern Parisian *école normale*, where sons of the aristocracy and promising youths from non-Turkish and non-Muslim backgrounds received a wide-ranging education. By 1575, aged 21, Ğazı was in the Crimean Tatar army, fighting rebellious Moldavians and Cossacks. Ğazı developed two sides of his character: the 'nightingale' that wrote poetry and composed music, and the 'steppe eagle' that preyed ruthlessly. His prowess as a military leader earned him the nickname 'Bora', the stormy cold northern wind that hits Crimea in winter; the name contrasts strangely with his reputation as a considerate, friendly companion, with Sufic inclinations, to Ottoman viziers and intellectuals. Although Ğazı's *divan* (complete works) have been lost, some forty poems, long and short, many of real originality and genius, are preserved, largely in others' anthologies. His instrumental chamber music, typically preludes in 8/8 time (*mahur peşrev*), is today part of Turkey's classical music heritage.[6]

Iranian captivity from 1581 to 1585 did not stunt Ğazı's development. When the Iranians heard of Khan Mehmed II Giray's clash with the Ottomans, they hoped to induce the Crimeans to desert Istanbul's protection for Shiraz's. The new shah, Abbas I, ferocious and paranoic, but boldly decisive, offered Ğazı freedom, his daughter in marriage, command of the army and the governorship of Shiraz, if the Crimean prince would serve Iran. Despite rumours to the contrary (and the tomb of an unknown Iranian princess in Bağçasaray), it is probable that Ğazı rejected the offer both of Abbas's daughter and of command of the Iranian army. The prisoner's response was a four-line poem in perfect Farsi:

> There was grief, there was joy, and deprivation:
> Whole ages passed in dreariness.
> What we took to heart was that in your kingdom
> Any relief was to be found in a fortress or dungeon.

Some four years later Shah Abbas, who meekly accepted Ğazı's rejection of his offer, moved his hostage westwards to Tabriz (perhaps Ğazı had in fact pretended to accept the offer, which would explain why Abbas moved him so close to the Ottoman–Iranian front). After bribing two guards, Ğazı escaped, disguised as a dervish, to Erzurum in Turkish-held territory. He fought on the Anatolian front for a short while under an Ottoman paşa who resented the Crimean prince's superior status and reputation. In Istanbul Sultan Murad III received Ğazı as a hero and gave him a large estate in Thrace near Yambol, close to other Girays. The sultan promised to make Ğazı Khan and to reserve the Crimean throne for Ğazı's descendants. Here another two or three years were spent on poetry, music and conversation.

At the end of April 1588 Khan Ğazı II, after his investiture by the sultan, disembarked at Balaklava. He was not met by any of his brothers or nephews: his nephews Murad and Safa were in Russia, while Sa'adet had just died; his brothers Alp and Fetih were with the army in Akkerman, Selâmet was guarding the isthmus at Or Qapı, and Mubarek was at Kerç. Ğazı summoned all the living to Bağçasaray. He ordered Alp, who had murdered Khan Mehmed II, to be executed. Alp fled to Turkey, while Mubarek, his co-conspirator, stayed in the Caucasus. Ğazı made Fetih *qalğa* and appointed as *nureddin* Vaht Giray, the son of Adil, who had been shot dead in Iran. Ğazı also created a new post, *baş ağa*, effectively a prime minister, and appointed a trusted assistant, Ahmed-ağa.

Women played an important part in Ğazı's diplomacy: he changed the meaning of *anabegim*, 'dowager mother', to 'senior wife *or* sister'. His older sister Kutlu-Sultan-hanım, who was married to a leading Şirin *bey*, was Ğazı's chief Crimean diplomatic correspondent with Moscow: she explained that the khan had 'ordered her to take charge of every matter', and Crimea's Moscow envoy advised Tsar Fiodor that she was a person he needed, that 'she was like a mother to the Khan'. The oldest of Ğazı's several wives, Ferhan, was thought by Moscow to be a mother or stepmother: she, too, was important enough to be listed as entitled to receive the Russian salary paid to Crimean emissaries. Moscow's foreign 'ministry' lists Ğazı's four other wives, presumably junior, entitled to gifts or payments: Fatma-Sultan, Karim-Shah, Mehrivafa and Zeinab. Only Girays among the Crimea's aristocratic women were entitled to have official communications with foreign countries. Their friendly, albeit formal letters to the tsar and his officials, even when both countries were at war, mitigated the harshness of the threatening missives that Crimean khans were inclined to send. In Mengli Giray's times, the khan's female relatives would personally receive Russian or Polish ambassadors; later in the sixteenth century the ambassadors were told that 'this is not customary,' and Crimean male intermediaries had to be used.[7]

In the eyes of certain *bey*s Ğazı was not legitimate: Ğazı's elder brothers, Alp and Mubarek, however fratricidal, were more entitled by traditional law to the khanate. Sultan Murad III wrote a remonstration: 'You must recognize Ğazı Giray as your Khan and never disobey him. Do not let yourself get involved in disorders and do not become traitors to your faith by listening to the words of robbers and plotters.' The *bey*s gave in: they realized that to support Alp or Mubarek and their foreign masters might mean the end of the khanate. Ğazı encouraged this reconciliation by repatriating the dissidents, welcoming the Noğay of the Mansur clan, marrying his nephew to Safa's mother and adopting the young man. Ğazı sent an envoy with a message to Tsar Fiodor in Moscow asking him to repatriate from Astrakhan his nephew Murad and promising to forgive him. In Crimea there was ill feeling between the returning exiles and those whose families had been their victims. Ğazı's brother Selâmet had killed and robbed too many people under Khan Islam's rule: he fled to Kaffa. Ğazı immediately dismissed him as *qalğa* and appointed another brother, Fetih. Of Ğazı's nephews, only Murad remained: he was willing to return in exchange for forgiveness, but had to wait for the Russian tsar's permission to leave Astrakhan.

Ğazı's show of strength made the Russian boyars abandon their plans of conquest. In summer 1589 it was the Zaporozhian Cossacks who persisted in raiding the khanate's ports. The Cossacks attacked a major trade fair in Gözleve: eight hundred Cossacks ravaged three hundred shops and killed or enslaved the merchants, Turks and Karaim, before being driven off by Ğazı's brother Fetih. Ğazı led an army deep into Poland, as far as Lwów. Although they were ambushed on the way home, the Cossack and Polish losses were enough to deter further Cossack raids and for the king of Poland to promise to restrain his subjects.

Moscow was happier with the new regime in Crimea, once it saw that Poland, not Russia, was the khan's target and that Ğazı was discouraging both his own forces and the Ottomans from attempting to capture Astrakhan. (Sultan Murad III was, in any case, wholly occupied with wars against Iran and in the Balkans against the Habsburgs.) But Russia was not yet prepared to release Murad Giray, possibly because this self-proclaimed 'ruler of four rivers' knew too much. The solution was typically Russian: in 1591 Murad was given permission to leave, but he, his wife and his son died suddenly, as had his brother Sa'adet three years earlier. The Astrakhan doctors and Russian governor-general declared that Sa'adet had died of

Tatar witchcraft: two Arabs were arrested and tortured until they confessed to drinking Sa'adet's blood. They were forced to regurgitate it, and were finally burnt at the stake. Chances of friendship between Bağçasaray and Moscow were nullified when Tsar Fiodor then sent Russian forces into the Caucasus, cutting Crimea off not only from its military route to Dagestan, but from its vassals in Circassia.

Ğazı II Giray responded in summer 1591 with a large army, crossing the Oka river and setting up camp on a hill on the western outskirts of Moscow. Boris Godunov, now tsar in all but name, was well prepared with artillery, riflemen and a stockade (and skilled German military advisers), to prevent a repeat of the siege and fire that Devlet Giray had inflicted on Moscow twenty years earlier. Crimean arrows and sabres were useless against cannon-balls and rifles. Tsar Fiodor stayed in a Kremlin tower, praying and then observing the battle with a confidence that amazed his boyars, but he proved clairvoyant. Ğazı and his *beys* agreed that a rapid retreat was their only option. In the Russian pursuit Ğazı was wounded in the arm, and Crimean stragglers were slaughtered as the army reached Tula. On 5 August Fetih Giray was back in Bağçasaray; only after a week did Ğazı reappear, prostrate in a cart. This was the Crimean Khanate's last attempt to reach Moscow.

Ğazı did not lose face: he summoned Bibikov, the Russian ambassador, and complained, 'I went to Moscow and was not received well: they don't like guests.' Bibikov replied, 'Khan, you didn't stay very long. If you'd stayed a bit longer our Emperor would have known how to receive you.' Ğazı gave the ambassador a dinner and a silk brocade kaftan. At dinner the conversa-tion was more serious: the *beys* asked the ambassador why Russia was building new towns along its southern frontier with Crimea, reminding him that Crimea was, unlike Kazan, not vulnerable to these tactics. Mean-while, Ğazı Giray assured the king of Poland: 'I did not accept the Muscovian envoy and his words, neither did I look at his gifts favorably; in the sight of [your] interpreter, Hocam Berdi, I ordered the Muscovian envoy arrested, rushed to the dungeon, and imprisoned.'[8]

In 1592 Fetih and Vaht Giray raided the Russian cities of Riazan, Kashira and Tula, purely for slaves and loot. Ğazı told the Russians that his brother and nephew had set off without his permission.

Ğazı's brothers Alp and Mubarek actively undermined Ğazı from abroad. Mubarek, married to a prominent Circassian princess, had a base in the Caucasus, from which he lobbied Sultan Murad III, demanding that Alp, as senior brother, be made khan instead of Ğazı, and himself as *qalğa*. Mubarek tried and failed to enter Crimea when Ğazı was away attacking

Poland; he then tried to ingratiate himself with the Ottomans by opposing
the Cossacks' building of forts in the Caucasus. Rumours from Istanbul of
a positive response to Alp's treacherous proposals alerted Ğazı ıı Giray: he
abandoned his inland capital at Bağçasaray for a fort on the banks of the
Dnepr, from where he could prevent invasion. The khan's ambassador hinted
to Moscow that Ğazı Giray was breaking away from Ottoman suzerainty
to form an independent country in the steppes where his army and his population could settle. The ambassador asked for 30,000 roubles to pay for
new forts and a joint war on Turkey. To convince the Russians, Ğazı offered
to send his four-year-old son Toqtamış to Moscow as a hostage. Before words
could be translated into action, however, Ğazı lost interest: his brother
Mubarek had died, and Sultan Murad ııı's suspicions had been allayed. Still
preferring to move to a haven from which escape would be easy, Ğazı
deserted Bağçasaray and chose as his new capital the port of Gözleve, a
miniature Istanbul with its harbour and the magnificent mosque that
Devlet Giray, Ğazı's father, had built. Four years earlier Ğazı had moved the
mint to Gözleve and Crimean coins bore that city's name.

Sultan Murad now found himself in urgent need of Ğazı Giray's military
genius. Fully stretched, fighting Iran for domination in Transcaucasia, the
Ottomans were losing their grip on Balkan territories thanks to an aggressive Habsburg drive to secure the freedom of Christian Hungary. Although
the Ottomans were gaining the upper hand over Iran, in the Balkans they
needed the skilled Crimean Tatar archers and horsemen to push back
Austrian and Hungarian forces.

Ğazı Giray, unlike his brothers Mehmed and Islam, was happy to show
gratitude to the sultan for his enthronement and, after his failure outside
Moscow, to taste victory again. First, he had to assuage Moscow, still vengeful after the unauthorized raid by Fetih and Vaht Giray. Ğazı generously
renounced all Crimea's antiquated claims to the Horde's Volga territories.
He then formally recognized Fiodor as a tsar who owed no tribute to the
heirs of Genghis Khan. Thoroughly realistic, Ğazı saw that his khanate
could expand only by tightening its grip on the North Caucasus and by
crossing the Dnepr to take charge of Moldavia and Wallachia. In summer
1594, on a bridge over the frontier Sosna river, the Crimean and Russian
ambassadors exchanged copies of a peace treaty. Ğazı himself with 80,000
Crimean and Noğay Tatars was well on his way to Hungary, his nickname
Bora, 'north wind', already inspiring fear.

It could well be at this time that Ğazı composed his best-known poem
Bayraq ('The Flag'), which became almost a national anthem for the

khanate, expressing the motto underlying not just Ğazı's, but his people's mindset: 'Make war, not love!'⁹ It begins:

> Instead of our straight-backed beloved we revere the flag,
> Instead of fragrant tresses, our hearts are entangled with banners,
>
> Instead of the arrow-like wink of your eyes or brow
> The bow's arrow of desire never leaves the heart . . .

and ends:

> Instead of an angel-shaped, gazelle-eyed idol,
> We love a well-schooled, well-paced horse
>
> Instead of an appealing moon-shaped houri's cheek,
> We give our soul to martyrdom and glorious jihad.
>
> Our devotion is not to a lively teasing slut
> But to guarding Islam's perfection: the campaign is very hard.
>
> We now long with our souls and God for holy war:
> Instead of water we drink the blood of foes of the faith.

After a difficult journey through unfamiliar country, Ğazı II Giray's army found a Tatar guide whose competence seemed due to supernatural powers. The khan was met in Hungary by the Ottoman commander-in-chief, Osman Paşa, who greeted Ğazı without dismounting, and then seated him on his right in the banqueting tent, offered him a golden bowl to wash his hands and gave him a fine warhorse, a sabre and 5,000 gold coins: this was, in fact, an insultingly paltry reception for a commoner to give to a Genghisid Khan. After the banquet, the paşa and the khan planned the siege of the city of Raab. The Crimeans had striking success in the sieges that followed: this stung Osman Paşa's pride. He responded by strictly forbidding Tatar soldiers to loot Hungarian towns and by hanging looters. Ğazı Giray was so indignant that he withdrew his men, except for 10,000 Noğays, to Crimea: in any case, a harsh Hungarian winter was approaching, in which the ill-equipped Crimean Tatars would have rebelled. The route home took Ğazı through Moldavia, once a tribute-payer to the khanate: Ğazı considered that the Ottomans should appoint a Giray to rule this province.

While passing through Moldavia, the Crimean army suppressed an anti-Ottoman rebellion by the Wallachian and Moldavian rulers, and hoped for the sultan's approval. This enterprise was disastrous: Ğazı was badly wounded by a bullet; his army was forced to retreat to the Danube. Both khan and army had to wait until autumn 1595 before they recovered enough to continue the fight, now with the king of Poland, who had invaded Moldavia and taken control. This time Ğazı Giray's army succeeded in restoring Moldavia to the Ottoman empire. Ğazı was given merely an annual tribute from the new Moldavian prince: the new Sultan Mehmed III refused to cede control to the khanate. The death of Murad III had dismayed Ğazı, because he had now lost imperial favour – all promises were 'thrown into the bin of oblivion'. The new sultan proved his ruthlessness by immediately having his nineteen brothers strangled.

Sultan Mehmed III invited Ğazı Giray to join him at the front in the endless war against the Habsburgs. Ğazı Giray felt fury at the indifference of the sultan's court to the army's suffering. When the Austrian army was besieging Sombor, he wrote a denunciation:

> Here we weep, spill our blood in furious battle:
> While you drink chalices of fine wine and play with
>   one another.
> An infidel enemy ravages Islamic peoples' lands.
> You, who fear no God, just sit there taking bribes!

He advised the sultan 'See for yourself . . . Don't run away from the sword and battleaxe.' Khan Ğazı II Giray was now being treated not as an ally, but as an insubordinate general. Murad III's promises were annulled by Mehmed III. Ğazı decided to desert the Turks and plan an anti-Ottoman alliance. (But he still left his brother and *qalğa* Fetih with 10,000 men on the Hungarian front; they pleased both the army's paşa and the sultan so much that the Ottomans contemplated making Fetih the khan of Crimea.) In November 1595 Ğazı sent an envoy, Can Ahmed Çelebi, from his camp to Kraków, ostensibly to collect 'gifts', but probably to prepare a peace treaty. In furious letters to the prince of Moldavia and other potential allies, Ğazı reminded everyone of what he had suffered while serving the Ottomans: two bullet wounds, while his ankles were permanently scarred by the shackles that he had worn in Iran. Ğazı Giray denounced Sultan Mehmed III as 'A contemptible liar, an infidel, the son of a slave girl.' (Mehmed III was in fact the son of a Venetian captive, Cecilia Baffo, who had converted to Islam;

the Girays, unlike the Ottomans, married almost exclusively the daughters of Muslim, preferably Tatar or Circassian aristocrats, and shunned slaves and captives, Christians or Europeans.)

A son of the influential Sinan Paşa, Çigala-zade, had managed by intrigues to secure the dismissal of Ibrahim Paşa from the post of chief vizier, despite the latter's brilliant victory, together with Fetih Giray, over the Austrians. Çigala-zade immediately made trouble, killing 30,000 soldiers who had deserted: as a result Muslim prisoners of war refused to return to Ottoman territory. Worst of all, Çigala-zade, who preferred Fetih Giray to his brother the khan, stirred up the court's suspicions of Ğazı Giray. Mehmed III was induced to announce that Ğazı Giray was deposed and replaced by his brother Fetih. (Fetih, according to the historian Na'ima, tried in vain to reject the promotion: 'he would be infringing the rights of his brother, who had been kind to him.') Too late, Çigala-zade was replaced by the former vizier, Ibrahim Paşa, an admirer of Ğazı Giray's prowess, who protested that the resulting outrage in Crimea would be disastrous for Ottoman campaigns. Mehmed III's preposterous reaction was to appoint both Ğazı and Fetih as khans, then dispatch the official documents of investiture and wait to see which of the two brothers was first to receive and enact the sultan's appointment. A courtier was sent to Crimea to assess which khan was acceptable and then quietly to destroy the losing candidate's document.

The courtier who had this commission was a Circassian warrior, Handan-ağa, an old friend of Ğazı Giray. His ship to Crimea was blown by crosswinds to Sinop on the Anatolian coast, and there, by coincidence, he met Ğazı Giray, also on his way to Crimea. Ğazı had been forewarned of the coming contest with his brother. Fetih already knew that he had originally been proclaimed by Sultan Mehmed III as the new khan, and hastened to Kaffa, where he produced a copy of the sultan's decree. When Ğazı also arrived, the chief Tatar judge in Kaffa studied the documents and found that Fetih's was more valid, since it bore the sultan's signature. Ğazı disagreed, and the political matter was referred, perhaps for the first time, to a higher, religious court, the judgement of the *mufti*, Azaki Muhammad-efendi. The *mufti* in his fatwa found that Ğazı's document bore the sultan's *tuğra*, a calligraphic seal, superior to a simple signature. Ğazı was therefore declared khan, and Fetih an enemy of the state. Fetih realized his short reign was over, since a *mufti*'s decision was final, and he decided to leave, not for Istanbul, but for his wife's homeland, Circassia, where he might gather an army and regain the khanate.

In summer 1597 Ğazı Giray left Crimea with his army. Fetih presumed his brother was returning to the Hungarian front and duly invaded the peninsula, aiming to capture Bağçasaray. In fact, Ğazı had moved no further than the mouth of the Dnepr and quickly returned. Fetih decided to make peace (and then, perhaps, seek refuge in Moscow). He entered Ğazı's tent near Kaffa, threw off his hat, kneeled and recited, 'Oh, from the shame you put me to, by throwing stones of rejection, You have gone and sundered my head in two.'[10] As Fetih kissed the hem of Ğazı's gown, a Mansur *mirza* picked up an iron mace and killed Fetih with a blow to the head. Fetih's death was followed by the murder of his *qalğa* and of all his nine sons, including an infant at the breast. Ğazı, though hardly penitent, apparently reacted with a quatrain, 'The heavens have dealt cruelly with Fetih today – But it is right for mankind on earth and angels in heaven to weep.'[11]

Sultan Mehmed III was displeased. He blamed not himself but his vizier Ibrahim Paşa, who was now temporarily dismissed, for the 'death of Fatih Giray and all its consequent evils'. He dared not seek another replacement for Ğazı Giray, even though Ğazı's brother Alp was still alive and, technically, as his senior, had a claim. Only in 1598 did Ğazı reluctantly return to the Balkan war, making it clear to the enemy (but not to his own army) that he would be willing to desert the Ottomans and join forces with the Christian countries. On arriving in Transylvania, Ğazı Giray had a dispute with the Ottoman general. The Ottomans, with their heavy artillery and baggage wagons, preferred to take main roads that were vulnerable to attack; the Tatars stuck to forest paths where they were unlikely to be intercepted. In any case, the Tatars' late arrival and arguments on tactics took up most of the fighting season. When autumn began, forty days of freezing rain, high winds and a dearth of provisions precluded military action. The Ottomans forbade the khan's army to loot. Bread had to be paid for in gold. Turkish soldiers mutinied, trying to kill their commander-in-chief, who retired, traumatized, to Belgrade. The Tatars decided to overwinter in Silistra on the lower Danube, where a sympathetic paşa, Satırcı, allowed Ğazı Giray to act as local ruler. Satırcı's sympathy for a suspect khan, unfortunately, earned him a death warrant from the army's chief. Ğazı had warned Satırcı, and after the latter's murder, took Satırcı's close friend to safety in Crimea. After this murder, warned that he might be the next victim, Ğazı Giray would meet an Ottoman vizier only when he was surrounded by his own bodyguards. In the Hungarian campaign, when the Turks desperately held on to Buda, Ğazı Giray left the worst of the fighting to his brother and *qalğa* Selâmet.

By autumn 1599, after a year in Hungary, Ğazı ('strongly inclined', says Na'ima, 'to retire to his own country lest he should be incarcerated and meet Satırcı's fate') was safely back in Crimea. He was not tempted by the gift of a beautiful horse and ornamental dagger from the Hungarian battlefields. Nor was he enthusiastic when in April 1601 Ławryn Piaseczyński, ambassador of Poland's King Sigismund III, offered a ceasefire, which was unacceptable given Sigismund's conditions, the ambassador's failure to bring gifts and the unabated raids by Cossacks and Tatars. Ğazı was dealing once more with internal strife between the Şirin and Mansur clans. All the clans resented increasing centralization, in which the khan's *kapı-ağası*, 'master of the gate' (or 'prime minister'), enforced his will, especially as this *kapı-ağası* was a Circassian, Ahmed-ağa, who directed military and foreign affairs. Ğazı Giray also formed a personal guard of five hundred Circassian riflemen. Unlike Sahib Giray's *sekban* they were paid from a tax of 24,000 sheep paid by the population, not from the sultan's grant. The khan could trust these men.

In Ğazı Giray's year-long absence, his *nureddin* Devlet had enjoyed autocratic powers: he plotted with Kutlu Giray, a Şirin *bey*, to kill Ğazı Khan and usurp power. On 12 June 1601 Ğazı Giray invited the nobility, including his would-be killers, to a Bayram feast; too late, the conspirators realized that they were being served not by waiters, but by riflemen. Devlet and Kutlu Giray were killed and their male relatives fled to Turkey. Ğazı suspected his brother Selâmet, the *qalğa*, of complicity. Ahmed-ağa agreed, telling the khan, 'My lord, if you gave me the opportunity, I would cut his throat like a tame ox's and you would then be freed of these worries and reflections.' Selâmet sensed danger: he moved away from his usual quarters, claiming that he was avoiding an epidemic there. Later he fled secretly to Istanbul, to be yet another candidate in the sultan's holding pen for future khans. Ğazı demanded that the sultan return him to Crimea, reminding the Ottomans that they still needed Tatar help in their Balkan wars. Selâmet rashly joined the Jelalist rebellion led by Mad Hassan in Anatolia, thus ensuring that the sultan and the khan both took against him.

When Ğazı Giray, again brushing off Piaseczyński's renewed offers of a ceasefire, decided in autumn 1602 to go back to the Ottoman army, he could be sure that all his rebellious brothers were now either dead or in exile. He appointed his thirteen-year-old son Toqtamış as *qalğa*. In Hungary the Ottoman army was preparing to overwinter in and around the town of Pécs. Here Ğazı Giray found an unexpected friend, admirer and intellectual companion, Ibrahim Peçevi, an ethnic Hungarian, distinguished Ottoman historian and senior official. Peçevi recalls their friendship in his *History*:

That winter his Excellency the Khan spent in Pécs. I spent most of the day in his noble company. Sometimes we would go for walks together, or hunting, or on springtime picnics. Sometimes we spent time writing or on other pleasant and laudable activities. He worked on getting your humble servant to learn *ta'liq* [a Persian pendant script], to prepare the quill properly and he taught me the rules of calligraphy. However, the seed of this skill seems to have fallen on barren ground ... He said, 'I achieved so much in Pécs.'

It was probably in Pécs that winter that Ğazı wrote his best works. Two long poems, however, have been lost: a dispute between 'Coffee and Wine' (a pastiche of the Azeri poet Fuzuli's 'Hashish and Wine')[12] and a conventional poem in Persian style, 'The Nightingale and the Rose'. Ğazı Giray's best surviving long poem is 'The Water Mill', in which he compares himself, as his strength wanes, to a willow tree that has been sawn up and dried to make a mill: the poem concludes with resignation to the fact that everything comes from God. It could have been written by an eighteenth-century English country parson: there is no trace in the poem of the warrior or the man who could kill nine innocent nephews.

In spring 1603 the Balkan war resumed. Now, however, the Jelalist revolutionary movement had infected the Ottoman army. The sultan and his vizier did all they could to placate the rebel soldiers, even offering amnesties. Ğazı Giray was indignant that rebels should be treated as well as loyal soldiers, and that the dissident Selâmet was therefore likely to be restored to favour. In fact Selâmet and other amnestied rebel Girays were plotting a return to Crimea. Ğazı Giray wanted to get back to the khanate before the rebels came back. As an inducement to stay in the Balkans, he was offered 30,000 *akçe* (to be handed over by Peçevi). He refused and, to the Ottoman sultan's anger, left.

To shield himself from Sultan Mehmed III's wrath, Ğazı Giray rapidly concluded a treaty with King Sigismund III of Poland, asking for forts to be built and artillery to be provided, even hinting he would accept Polish instead of Ottoman suzerainty. (He was reverting to the strategy of the first Crimean khan Hacı Giray.) The stroke that killed Mehmed III in 1603 defused the crisis. The thirteen-year-old new sultan Ahmed I was encouragingly mild and abolished the Ottoman custom of slaughtering on accession a new sultan's younger brothers. Istanbul's viziers were too concerned with political manoeuvring to be bothered with Crimean affairs. Ğazı merely had to send the young Toqtamış to serve in the armies still fighting in Hungary, a useful education for the heir to the khanate, and a source of income to the treasury of Crimea, which was now suffering from famine. The khan was even glad that tens of thousands of his men were now receiving army rations in the Balkans at Ottoman expense.

Disillusioned by his European prospects, Ğazı sought to expand his territory in the Caucasus, where Moscow was consolidating its forts and Cossack stations. Cossacks were forcing Noğay Tatars to take refuge in Azov 'like mice in their nest', and Adyge Circassians loyal to Crimea were being attacked by aristocratic Kabarda Circassians allied to Moscow. At the head of the Kuban river, the khan established his own fortress, named Ğazı-Kerman after himself, a base from which he could rescue his Circassian allies. Despite the mutual antagonism of the 1590s, Ğazı persuaded the Ottomans' enemy, Shah Abbas I of Iran, that Iran's interests in the Caucasus and its defence against Turkey and Russia were best served by friendship with the Crimean Khanate. Relieved that no Tatar army would now attack, Iran also offered Ğazı the prospect of refuge from any Ottoman vengeance that his fugitive brother Selâmet might spearhead. Ğazı also had a Noğay ally, Batır-Shah. They had fought together in Hungary, where Batır-Shah had been wounded, and thereafter sought recuperation and asylum in Circassia. Batır-Shah was privy to Ğazı Giray's plans to flee to Iran or even to Russia, should the Ottomans hound him.

In 1603 Ğazı Giray refused an Ottoman invitation to join the war against Iran, especially as Çigala-zade, the vizier who had tried to overthrow him, was now commander-in-chief. Eventually, in 1605, Crimean forces supported a Dagestani rebellion against Russian occupation, an uprising which looked likely to make the Crimean Khanate, instead of Russia, the sovereign power in the North Caucasus. Two years later the khan arrived in Ğazı-Kerman to receive oaths of loyalty from Kabarda Circassians and Dagestanis and to found another Crimean fort. As the winter of 1607 approached, Ğazı Giray set off home, but got only as far as Temrük, on the mainland opposite Kerç, when he was struck down by plague and died within a few days. His funeral procession crossed the Crimean peninsula to a mausoleum in Bağçasaray. Shortly before his death he appears to have written an elegy for himself, comparing his life to a fast-burning candle, flickering and melting. He would be remembered by his people and by Ottomans not only as the 'fourth planet' in Crimean history and as an extraordinary warrior and politician, but as the composer, musician and, above all, superb poet Ğazayı.

Jean de Contaut, Baron de Salignac, eulogized the late Ğazı Giray in his memoirs of his time as French ambassador to the Ottoman court: 'For the owners of Crimea and Perekop he had acquired so much glory and reputation by his praiseworthy generous gestures that among his subjects he was held by all to be a second Marcus Aurelius.' Ridvan Zade, the Ottoman court historian, wrote in his *History of the Deşt-i-Qıpçaq*:

> Ğazı Giray was the most accomplished prince the Tatars ever had, the Sultan who gave him this principality esteemed him and, to bear real witness, presented him with several banners and a musical orchestra. He really was a prince more worthy to reign than any who preceded him . . . In combat with the enemy he was like a lion whose roar makes forests resound and deserts tremble . . . he had in addition to these rare qualities an affability and generosity which won everyone's heart . . . Before he was made Khan his principal occupation was instructing himself in religion and defending it by action and words.

5

KHANS WHO WOULD
BE MONARCHS

The death of Ğazı Giray from plague left his Caucasian projects in abeyance, but the country's traditional enemies still fearful. For the coming century the Crimean Khanate would be in a state of political tension, for many of the khans, brought up, imprisoned or just serving in Turkey, fancied becoming an absolute monarch like the sultan, able to take quick, irrevocable decisions, not having to juggle the interests and views of a hereditary nobility, such as the powerful *qaraçı* clans, particularly the conservative Şirins and the aggressive Mansurs with their wild Noğay backers. On the other hand, Ottoman sultans were wary of a khan who might exercise absolute power in Crimea. They preferred to exploit dissident *beys* when Ottoman interests required. The *beys*, meanwhile, resented the occasions when an Ottoman sultan, rather than the Crimean nobility, chose a new Crimean khan, just as they disliked the growing centralized authority of the khan's guardsmen and civil servants. Meanwhile, the balance of clans was disturbed in the first three decades of the seventeenth century by the increasing power of the Mansurs, now that the Noğay tribes that grazed the plains of Bucak (Bessarabia, between the Dnestr and Danube rivers) were united under a powerful *mirza* Kan-Temir and considered as subjects of the khanate.

In the first three decades of the seventeenth century, the Crimean Tatars' northern neighbours began to populate the empty steppe lands, the cordon sanitaire that separated them. Russia was pushing south from the forested zone into the fertile Black Earth plains. Both Russia and Poland-Lithuania (the latter now united under a single monarch and parliament as a Commonwealth) had populations of Ukrainians – Zaporozhian and Don Cossacks – sometimes loyal, sometimes rebellious. New state boundaries, however fuzzy, complicated future conflicts and agreements with the Crimean Khanate and the Ottoman empire.

The era after Ğazı Giray's death began inauspiciously. For five years his only living brother, Selâmet, had been in Istanbul's Yedi Küle prison together with his great-nephew Mehmed, with no prospect of release. Ğazı himself had designated and trained his son Toqtamış to succeed him, and in early spring 1608, without consulting Istanbul, the nobility in Bağçasaray placed Toqtamış on a white felt carpet and crowned him khan before sending a delegation to ask Sultan Ahmed I to confirm their choice. But the sultan, impressed more by Ğazı's insubordination than by his military brilliance, did not want to see Ğazı's son as Crimean khan. Ğazı Giray would have been horrified by Sultan Ahmed I's decision: Selâmet, who had rebelled against Ğazı in Crimea and the sultan in Anatolia, was designated khan, with Mehmed as his *qalğa*; they were released, given appropriate attire and dispatched to Crimea, Selâmet by sea, Mehmed overland. Toqtamış and his younger brother Sefer set off to Istanbul to protest. About to cross the Bug river, they stumbled on Mehmed and his guard of janissaries. Responding to the janissaries' firearms with bows and arrows, Ğazı's two sons were killed. Selâmet could now feel secure on his new throne, but his *qalğa* Mehmed had not forgotten that it was Selâmet who helped murder Mehmed's father (Selâmet's nephew) Sa'adet II Giray in 1584, and vengeance was due.

Informed of Mehmed's murderous intentions by his nephew Canibek, Selâmet ordered the execution of the plotters. Mehmed and his brother Şahin fled to the North Caucasus; Selâmet asked Istanbul for help. An envoy from Istanbul defused the conflict, but before the two plotters returned to Bağçasaray, Selâmet died of illness in May 1610. (His consolation may have been that his dozen or so sons would be the forefathers of almost every future Crimean khan.) The two plotters' journey changed from a penitential return to a triumphant assumption of power. The new khan, they declared, was Mehmed III Giray. Mehmed immediately pursued Canibek Giray, who had denounced him to the late Selâmet. Canibek galloped off to Kaffa and put himself under Ottoman protection. Mehmed III Giray besieged Kaffa with a large army, threatening to destroy it unless the paşa handed over Canibek and his brother 'bound hand and foot' to be hanged. The paşa replied that the two refugees were under the sultan's protection and that Mehmed III's accession had not yet been recognized by the sultan.

Mehmed III Giray then announced, 'All power is in my hands,' and made his declaration of total independence: 'What powers do the Ottomans have over the ruler of the *Deşt-i-Qıpçaq* to make me receive my appointment from their hands? Does anyone's sword rise above my sword?'

The paşa in Kaffa would not let Canibek sail to safety in Istanbul: instead he sent to the sultan another Giray with a report. Mehmed III Giray, aware that he was not secure as khan until the sultan had confirmed him in post, also sent a mission to Istanbul, largely to bribe the appropriate officials. Unfortunately others, including the Istanbul commandant and the chief eunuch, had previously been bribed by Canibek, and Mehmed's envoys paid the bribes to them instead. Canibek was confirmed as khan by the sultan and sent to Kaffa, while Mehmed fled to the steppes, waited for the Turkish escort to sail back to Istanbul, and then attacked Canibek in Bağçasaray, only to be defeated by a large number of Turkish soldiers waiting for them there. He fled once again to the steppes to be given asylum by the Noğay Tatars of Bucak.

Strictly speaking, Canibek Giray was not entitled to become khan: unlike Mehmed III, he was not the son or brother, but merely a grandson, of a khan. Ottoman military support, however, outweighed native Crimean rules. Mehmed did have one supporter in Istanbul, the new grand vizier Nasuh Paşa, who arranged for Mehmed to meet Sultan Ahmed I when out hunting. Mehmed ruined the meeting by shooting his arrow at a roe deer that the sultan was targeting. Sultan Ahmed was led to believe that this breach of etiquette by a gatecrasher at his hunt was in fact an attempt to assassinate him: Mehmed was sent back to Yedi Küle prison, and Nasuh Paşa was executed.

Canibek Giray, now undisputed ruler of the khanate, had an easy start to his reign. A mild, highly educated and generous man, he was liked by his subjects. They only gently mocked his reliance on a Beki-ağa, once his tutor, now his inseparable adviser: 'Whatever he tells the Khan to do, the Khan does.' Very soon, however, the Crimea, like Bucak and other Ottoman provinces, was hit by a swarm of Zaporozhian Cossacks, who rowed down the Dnepr, looting, burning, rustling cattle and capturing children to sell as slaves. In the early 1600s many Cossacks had joined the Polish army that invaded Russia in the 'time of troubles', when two False Dimitris were installed by the Poles as puppet tsars. The cold and the lack of fodder, or any other benefit, eventually thwarted these Cossacks, who reverted to warmer and more lucrative hunting grounds. The king of Poland assured both sultan and khan that Cossacks, nominally his subjects, were beyond his control and complained that the Noğay of Bucak, incited by Kan-Temir, were the real instigators of this predation.

Still at large, Şahin Giray, Mehmed's brother, also took part in Noğay and Cossack raids, but his purpose was to gather an army big enough for him to usurp the khanate. Şahin, the polar opposite of Canibek, was admired in Crimea by those who resented the khan's lack of interest in looting raids. On Beki-ağa's advice, in spring 1614 Canibek set off with an army to deal with Şahin and the Noğay and Cossack raiders. Şahin was at first nowhere to be found in Bucak. Only when the khan began to return was the rebel found at Akkerman. He deceived his pursuers: all they knew was that his Polish wife had divorced him and gone back to Poland. Eventually he was reliably reported to be in the Caucasus. While the Crimean army sought him in the steppes, a Cossack flotilla invaded Crimea for the third time in two years and ravaged Gözleve. Canibek in 1615 moved his army deeper into Poland, taking thousands of prisoners and many herds of cattle: his citizens were so enriched that they forgave him his former passivity and called him 'the Lucky Khan'. Canibek's main aim, however, was to persuade King Sigismund III to rein in his Cossacks. The Cossacks only grew bolder: in 1616 thousands of them crossed the Black Sea 'storming Trebizond and the entrance to the Bosphorus in frail home-made boats . . . returning home with a lot of loot and some slaves, usually small children, which they keep as servants, or sell to their lords . . . they devastated both Trabzon and the entrance to the Bosphorus'.[1] Canibek duly made peace with Poland, although his *qalğa* still aided Ottoman forces fighting on that front.

No sooner had Canibek achieved a truce in the north than the sultan ordered Crimean forces to fight their way across the Caucasus and join the war against Iran. On the way, Canibek wanted to support his son-in-law Iş-Terek, the *bey* of the independent Great Noğay Horde, who had sought to break free of Moscow's rule by seeking Ottoman sovereignty, but was refused, since the Ottomans were now united with Russia against the Poles. Iş-Terek then quarrelled with Canibek, who tried to fight his way through tribes allied to the Noğay in Kabarda and Dagestan. He failed to reach the front and returned to Crimea.

The sultan then told the khan to take his army across the Black Sea into Anatolia and fight on the western frontier of Iran. When Canibek arrived the grand vizier presented him, in the name of the sultan, with an ornamental sword, a fine steed and 5,000 pieces of gold, to cover his war expenses. Canibek complied, but many of his men deserted. On this front, in alien territory, the Crimean horsemen met their equals, the Iranian *kızılbaş*: worse, they found the Iranians led by the rebel Şahin Giray, whom the Crimeans had assumed was somewhere in the Caucasus, encouraging Noğays and Circassians to block Canibek Giray's progress. (Both Canibek and Şahin Giray had spent their boyhood with Caucasian foster-parents whose sons would treat the khan's offspring as brothers, but Canibek gained no advantage from these relationships.)

Şahin was still loyal to the khanate: he persuaded Shah Abbas to spare Crimean prisoners of war and release at least the lower-ranking horsemen. But the confrontation ended when both Turks and Crimeans were routed by the Iranians. The defeat of the Ottomans and Crimeans was a godsend to the king of Poland, who could now pursue his own expansionist plans and not fear reprisals.

In summer 1617 a new sultan, Osman II, the fourteen-year-old son of Ahmed, eventually took power: his viziers took a dim view of Canibek's military inadequacy. Canibek stayed in the Crimea to defend it from any attack by Şahin: he sent his brother Devlet via the Caucasus to carry on the fight with Iran and thus increased the Caucasian tribes' hostility to the Crimean Khanate. Turks and Crimeans were sobered by a grim omen when a comet with a tail like a curved sword appeared over the Black Sea.

By now Canibek could expect to be deposed, and the proven warrior Mehmed III Giray to be released from Yedi Küle to become once more khan of Crimea. Mehmed, however, jumped the gun. In February 1618 Mehmed Giray bribed his guards and escaped. In one day he got as far as Varna on the Black Sea, halting beneath a large tree in open country. Locals tried to surround him and called out the military. With an arrow from his bow Mehmed shot one of the janissaries. He was sent to Rhodes, and the *mirza* who helped him was executed. Canibek also came to Turkey: he won favour with the new sultan.

The citizens of the Polish-Lithuanian Commonwealth, whose territory then extended from the Baltic almost to the Black Sea, were desperate. After two centuries of paying tribute, concluding treaties that were breached, having their towns and villages raided and destroyed, their populations depleted by enslavement, they began to seek effective ways of resisting. Their army could not rival the speed of Tatar horsemen; unlike the Tatars they had not trained their men and horses to swim across great rivers (towing clothes and weapons on light rafts). Nor could the Poles match the Tatars' lethal archery (Tatar laminated short bows shot arrows faster and harder than any firearm of the time could fire bullets). Polish horsemen could not bring themselves to imitate the Crimean Tatars, who would in battle strip to the waist (to lighten the burden of their chargers and also, quite possibly, to shock the cavalry they were attacking). The Poles did learn, however, some tactics from the Tatars: their heavyweight cavalry was made lighter, and they dispensed with armour and with logistics reliant on slow-moving ox-carts. With the development of powerful artillery and infantry firearms, Polish forces were, in any case, becoming less vulnerable. More ominously, a new genocidal ideology was afoot in Poland: in 1618 the scholar Szymon Starowolski published *A Call to Arms, or Advice to Exterminate the Tatars of Perekop* (the name of the isthmus and moat that protected the Crimean peninsula from the north, a name often used to denote the Crimean Tatar nation):

> It is most urgent to free ourselves first of all from those pagan Tatars who have learnt without restraint to pinion the wings of the Polish eagle and wade through Christian blood, driving numberless throngs of our brothers into slavery . . . The locusts ravaging our fatherland . . . Poland unable to get rid of the Tatar louse . . . Let us exterminate the wild Tatars and multiply the invincible Poles by taking up the sword with both hands.[2]

The Frenchman Guillaume Levasseur de Beauplan, observing Noğay Tatars' enslavement of Poles and Russians in the 1640s, was horrified: 'Their brutality lets them commit an infinite amount of vile acts, raping young girls, wives in front of their fathers and husbands.'[3]

But Poland did not have the resources to rid itself of Tatar raids. The king promised the sultan to integrate Cossacks into the regular Polish army, but he lacked the funds to pay them. Poland could only relax when the Crimean Tatars were engaged elsewhere. Canibek made peace with his northern enemy only when Sultan Ahmed I ordered him south to the front in the never-ending war against Iran. West of the Dnepr, the fearsome Noğay leader Kan-Temir was still able to further Crimean interests by pushing Polish and Cossack forces back north. In autumn 1620, however, the tables were turned: the Cossack *hetman* Stanislav Zholkevsky came south to Moldavia and wrote a letter to Canibek Giray persuading him that the Cossacks' quarrel was purely with the Ottomans, not with the Crimean Khanate. The Crimeans held back, more because they were worried about an incursion into Crimea by the rebel Şahin than because of the Cossack's letter. The Ottomans and Noğays also seemed to be dissuading the khanate from aggression, but they were motivated by a desire not to share their anticipated booty of slaves and cattle with the Crimeans. Devlet Giray, the *qalğa*, was so aggrieved at being sidelined that he fought even harder: at the battle of Ţuţora (in Moldavia, on the Prut river) in October 1620 he saved the Ottoman army from defeat.

Victory inspired the young Sultan Osman II, likewise, to resume fighting, at one point forcing an evacuation of Warsaw and hoping to reach the Baltic. On 2 September 1621 the greatest and longest battle with Poland, in which 100,000 Muslims fought 60,000 Poles and Ukrainians for four weeks at Khotyn, resulted, after desperate fighting and disasters and apparent triumphs on both sides, in the Ottoman army running out of men, morale and supplies. Nevertheless, for his bravery and near-victory, Kan-Temir the Noğay leader took the credit: he was made an Ottoman vizier for his services. Canibek Giray had asked permission to let his men loot Ukraine and go home, rather than besiege Khotyn. Added to failure on the Persian front, his reluctance to fight, once the Ottomans had been decisively defeated, undid Canibek's reputation. Sultan Osman II demoted the khan to 'a slave of the Sultan whose state and head are at the Sultan's mercy', and crossed his name out of the ensuing peace treaty. The Crimeans went home to await the fruits of the sultan's wrath.

On the island of Rhodes Mehmed III Giray was visited by the chief eunuch Mustafa, who had been responsible for Mehmed's dismissal. The eunuch was now ordered to give Mehmed 90 kilograms (200 lb) of silver as 'coffee money'. Then Mere-Hüseyin Paşa called at Rhodes on his way back from Egypt. He promised, once he became vizier, to petition the sultan to reappoint Mehmed as khan. The next year Sultan Osman II began to modernize his army, which Khotyn had proved to be sluggish and ill-motivated, but he infuriated his janissaries and in the ensuing uproar was murdered. The Ottoman empire then chose as sultan the insane Mustafa, rather than one of Osman's two brothers, both still boys. Chaos ensued: Iran, Poland and Cossacks took advantage of the Ottomans' empty treasury, quarrelling viziers, demented sultan and internal uprisings.

Only in 1623 did Mere-Hüseyin Paşa become grand vizier. He made peace with Poland and promised to rein in the Noğay leader Kan-Temir. Then he restored Mehmed III Giray to the khanate of Crimea. Canibek arrived in Istanbul: no bribe or argument could help his case. Sultan Mustafa, literally tied, hands and feet, to his throne, was forced by his vizier to confirm Mehmed's reappointment. While a cowed Canibek retired to a Giray estate in Thrace, Mehmed III celebrated by going to the port to mock the Russian ambassadors and the Turkish governor of Azov who were embarking there. In May 1623, after his family, his suite, the sultan's agent and a large naval escort had gathered, Mehmed III sailed for Kaffa, where he was met by a welcoming crowd, a salvo of cannons and a lavish feast. Canibek's chaotic heritage, however, persisted.

For this period, with intervals until 1658, we glean how dire life could
be in Kaffa and the rest of the Crimea from the diary of an Armenian priest,
Khachatur Kafayetsi. He noted the arrival of Mehmed just after a terrible
famine, partly due to a Cossack invasion the previous year, and partly to
Canibek's last act before he was deposed in 1623: minting silver coins and
shutting down all commerce for months until the new currency was in
circulation. Khachatur recorded:

> Our city was visited by a deadly epidemic and famine: a bushel of
> wheat cost 600 silver coins, a lot of people set off to Taman and got
> provisions there ... On Friday 9 May Mehmed Khan Giray came to
> Kaffa ... In September the Cossacks came via Or Qapı, stormed the
> city, and the Christians butchered them; many Tatars killed them
> or took them prisoner. A lot of people were destituted ... There
> was a drought and we couldn't get any drinking water ... In April
> 1624 the Cossacks came to the upper town from Eski Qırım, took
> Christians prisoner, stole the Holy Cross ...
>
> On 3 May Şahin Giray came from Persia and people congrat-
> ulated one another on his arrival, for he was a just *qalğa* and we
> hoped he would bring us peace.[4]

The return of Şahin Giray was prompted by a request from his brother
Mehmed III to Shah Abbas to let the fugitive return as the Crimean *qalğa*:
Mehmed was convinced that Şahin, for all his reputation as a turncoat,
would help repress the *beys* who had got out of hand under Canibek's indecisive rule. (Mehmed told the clansmen, 'My courtiers are my slaves, not
my friends as they were to Canibek Giray.') Mehmed had already selected a
nureddin beholden to nobody but himself, a Mustafa, the offspring of the
late Fetih Giray and of a Polish captive who refused to convert to Islam and
who died in childbirth, fortunately before Fetih could have her killed. This
Mustafa, in childhood a shepherd, was raised up by Mehmed and renamed
Devlet Giray, although he and his offspring were never accepted by the
Crimean nobility and were called the Çoban ('shepherd') Girays.

Shah Abbas I saw the advantage of sending Şahin Giray back to Crimea
as a Persian agent. Reckoning that Şahin hated the Ottomans even more
than he distrusted the Persians, Abbas prepared to repatriate him and his
Persian wife, escorted by a regiment of *kızılbaş*. As they parted, the shah
asked, 'If the Sultan sends you, will you fight us?' to which Şahin replied,
'If a wolf sees a lamb, can it hold back?' When Şahin was welcomed back in

Crimea, this was by no means the end of the story: further betrayals were in store.

Khan Mehmed III, in his second reign, proved to be confident and intransigent. In 1623 the Ottomans disposed of the mad, easily manipulated Mustafa in favour of Sultan Murad IV, a ruler even more uncompromising than the Crimean khan. Mehmed, now in cahoots with Shah Abbas, refused to obey Murad's demand that the Crimean army should return to the war against Iran, on the grounds that he needed to defend Crimea against Cossack raiders. Crimean *beys* wrote to Istanbul, supporting the chief eunuch in his demands that Mehmed be deposed. Crimea could now expect an Ottoman invasion.

Experience in Iran had made Şahin Giray an expert in dealing with rebel nobles: he reorganized the Crimean army, subordinating the *beys* to the khan, and their sons to himself as *qalğa*. The slightest disloyalty shown by a father would be punished by hanging the son, and vice versa. Mehmed and Şahin brought to Crimea a number of Circassian, Kumyk and Noğay clan leaders. Şahin added several hundred shipwrecked Cossacks who had expected to be sold as galley slaves to the Ottomans, but were now recruited as soldiers, expert in firearms and artillery.

When his second deposition was announced, Mehmed III responded not by defiance or acceptance, but by sending a present of three hundred slaves, and his only son Ahmed as a hostage.[5] The Ottomans had already sent Canibek to Kaffa as the new khan, but the soldiers who came with him on twelve galleys were blocked by Şahin and Mehmed. More threats and proposals came from Istanbul. Şahin responded with a promise to turn Crimea into scorched earth and asked if the Ottomans really intended to destroy mosques and medreses. The stand-off lasted until the middle of 1624, when another Cossack flotilla took advantage of the situation, sailed into the Bosphorus and threatened those Turkish ships that had not yet gone to Crimea. All the sultan could do was to execute Hüseyin Paşa for the 'crime' of restoring Mehmed III to power.

Once in Crimea, Turkish troops took their cannon off the ships and, led by Canibek, marched into the interior, which was strangely deserted. At Qarasuvbazar, Crimean cavalry and Cossack gunners emerged and encircled the Turks, who, having no tools, could not even dig trenches for protection. Seeing that Canibek had no internal support, the Ottomans agreed to a truce and confirmed Mehmed in his post. Canibek fled back to Kaffa. As the Turks pursued him, they encountered the *nureddin* Devlet Çoban Giray and killed him. The Crimeans then broke the truce: most of the janissaries were slaughtered. The survivors set sail with Canibek for Varna. Şahin's men purged Kaffa of stray Turks, taking so many prisoners that a slave now fetched only the price of a barrel of beer.

By September an agreement was reached (Sultan Murad explained that the invasion of Crimea was not his idea, but a vizier's). Şahin would release surviving Turkish prisoners and their guns, and Kaffa would revert to Ottoman control. Crimeans who had accompanied Canibek, and the five sons of Khan Selâmet Giray, all submitted to Mehmed III. Only Şahin was dissatisfied: his idea was to unite all the Ottomans' enemies from the Baltic to the Indian Ocean under Crimean leadership. He wanted to found this empire by inducing the Zaporozhian Cossacks to join with both Sigismund III of Poland and Shah Abbas I of Iran in an anti-Ottoman coalition, offering to hand over to Poland not just Bucak but Muscovy. The letter to King Sigismund came with a bejewelled sword; in return Şahin Giray wanted only lead and gunpowder.

The fly in the ointment was the unruly Noğay Kan-Temir, who undermined the proposed alliance by his incessant raids deep into Polish territory. Şahin set off to Bucak to restrain Kan-Temir, and then to the unofficial customs point at the border between Polish- and Ottoman-controlled territories, taking with him the Cossacks whom he had recruited to fight the Ottomans and rewarding them so generously that he had to provide them with a baggage train of ox-carts to take away their loot and severance pay. The Poles, it turned out, could not agree whether or not to join Şahin Giray's grand alliance; but on 3 January 1625 Şahin and the Cossacks celebrated the first-ever Crimean–Cossack pact, Şahin personally serving the Cossacks with wine from his chalice. This persuaded the Noğay to join in and accompany Şahin back to Crimea: they even asked the Volga Noğay under Russian rule to follow suit.

The downside of this reconciliation was that Russia and the Ottoman empire had a common motive to resist Poland, to restrain Crimea and to end Cossack autonomy. A Russian embassy appeared in Crimea and had to listen to bitter reproaches for letting Don Cossacks raid Kaffa and for having seventy years earlier illegally annexed the old Horde lands of Kazan and Astrakhan. Şahin planned to follow up verbal protests with military action, but this was aborted when another Ottoman fleet appeared at Kaffa. In fact, the fleet was there to deter Cossack flotillas and to deliver an order from the sultan to make war on Poland. Mehmed III did not disobey outright: he merely procrastinated. He was saved by Poland's entry into a war with Sweden – this was an offshoot of the Thirty Years War, which had raged in

Western Europe since 1618 – making Poland seek peace with Turkey. Şahin's Cossack allies had, as they would several times, switched sides and were now exploiting this new situation to rebel against Roman Catholic Poland, which had for some time tried to suppress the Cossacks' Orthodoxy and deny Cossacks political rights equal to those of the Polish nobility.

Despite the war with Sweden, the Polish general Stanisław Koniecpolski was able to disband the Cossack troops that threatened southern Poland and drive the stragglers into Crimean territory. Şahin did not lose hope of re-forming his alliance; Mehmed III was merely glad not to have to fight the Poles on behalf of the Ottomans.

Khachatur Kafayetsi recorded the many miseries and brief joys of life in Kaffa in this turbulent period:

> Canibek's return closed all the shops in Kaffa and Turkish ships blockaded the port. Because of the civil war, the grain rotted in the fields, hungry cattle bellowed, children wept, until Canibek and the Turks sailed away in the summer of 1624, after hundreds of them were butchered in the streets and on the sea shore . . . In December that year a mighty wind came and blew down houses and walls and uprooted trees. In 1627 a heavy tax was demanded from the Christians: some Kaffa citizens had to pay 5 gold pieces . . . more gold and silver, men (wagoners, labourers) and 75 tonnes of rusks were requisitioned for the army from Kaffa's Armenians and Turks.

Despite plans for an alliance, in 1626 Khan Mehmed III, on the pretext of overdue tributes and misbehaviour by Cossacks, twice ravaged Poland while it was at war with Sweden (whose king Gustavus Adolphus was inciting the Crimean Tatars to attack). Mehmed III was willing to attack, but Şahin was not, nor was Sultan Murad, ostensibly, despite his orders encouraging Mehmed to fight. The Poles' victory over Cossacks and Crimeans at the battle of Bila Tserkva in central Ukraine brought Poland momentary relief. Meanwhile, between Poland and the Crimea the Zaporozhian Cossacks, the Poles' nominal subjects, were blocking any Polish counter-attack by rebelling against forced military service, taxes and incipient serfdom. They were particularly angered by the Polish kings' construction of two forts on the River Dnepr to preserve Poland's access to the river's estuary and fish stocks from Cossack incursions. Tatar raids continued: a Polish slave (between about 5,000 and 10,000 Poles a year were enslaved by Crimean Tatars) was highly valued.

So severe was the depopulation by Tatar raids that the bishop of Przemyśl allowed divorce and remarriage by members of his flock whose spouses had been kidnapped by the Tatars and were still alive in the Crimea or Turkey. Mehmed and Şahin for a while concentrated their forces on consolidating their rule in Circassia, but they fell foul of a Noğay blood feud when Mehmed III's Circassian son-in-law was murdered as he left Mehmed's quarters. As a Bucak Noğay *bey* was involved, Kan-Temir had to be called upon to arrest the man. Kan-Temir evaded Şahin, galloping off half-dressed and followed by his guards. Şahin rounded up every relative of Kan-Temir he could find, shaved their heads and sent a wagonload of their hair to where Kan-Temir might find it. There was a message saying that if Kan-Temir did not hand himself in, then the hostages would be tortured to death. Many of Kan-Temir's *mirza*s returned home, hoping to save their kith and kin. Kan-Temir did not, and Şahin had his wife and all the children he could find murdered. The blood feud now developed into a Crimean–Noğay war. Kan-Temir defected to the Ottomans and offered to capture both Mehmed and Şahin and hand them over to Sultan Murad, who now prepared Canibek for restoration and happily anticipated taking revenge on the brothers for humiliating the sultan's army at Qarasuvbazar. Kan-Temir became virtually the sultan's viceroy in Bucak, Dobruja and Silistra. He was waiting for the right weather to sail to Kaffa and take it by storm.

Şahin did not wait: he pursued Kan-Temir across Bucak to Dobruja. When the Crimeans camped by a small forest in the steppe, Kan-Temir's men came out of hiding and destroyed the Crimean force, allowing only Şahin and a few others to escape. Kan-Temir then pursued Şahin back to Crimea, with Şahin recruiting Cossacks as he fled (the Cossacks considered that fighting Kan-Temir would not be a breach of their peace agreement with the sultan). By 3 May 1628 Şahin was back in Bağçasaray, where there were very few armed men to support him; worse, Mansur clansmen were supporters of Kan-Temir. Mehmed and Şahin made a stand at the hilltop fortress of Qırq-Yer, while the Bucak Noğay overran the peninsula and besieged both khan and *qalğa*. The local Karaim provided food and water to the khan's men, but not enough. The siege was broken by the arrival of *hetman* Mikhail Doroshenko's 4,000 Cossacks, who camped behind a defensive circle of wagons. Kan-Temir was reinforced by Ottoman *sekban* riflemen. At the battle of the River Alma on 31 May the Cossacks triumphed, but lost their *hetman* to an enemy bullet. Kan-Temir was wounded; he led his men on a hasty retreat and persuaded the paşa at Kaffa to open the city gates and let him in. Meanwhile, Şahin Giray gave each Cossack 5 gold pieces. The Cossacks also surveyed Crimea for the first time and decided that they could one day conquer it for themselves.

The woeful results for Kaffa, however, were described by Khachatur Kafayetsi:

> The accursed Noğays devastated the region, they stole sheep and cattle and let the soldiers eat all the horses. They did a lot of evil beyond telling. Then God sent light: 12,000 Cossacks came from Poland – they started fighting the Noğays and put an end to the battle. Kan-Temir came himself with 1,000 of his people, wagons, horses, camels, buffalo and sheep, wives and children, slaves and servants. They filled Kaffa . . . all the Armenians and upper-city Turks fled to the citadel. The Noğays reduced many houses to rubble and took over villagers, sheep and cattle . . . [eventually] Mehmed III Giray Khan and Şahin *qalğa* came with 12,000 Cossacks . . . [the Noğays] pulled down the walls, dug up the ground, forced three churches open, took lights, incense burn-ers, curtains, books, bibles, the iron out of the window panes . . . they broke into mills and took mill wheels. For six weeks the city was closed, no buying or selling. There was no bread or alms, no hay, no water supply.

The situation worsened: a Turkish flotilla came to Kan-Temir's rescue. A civil war raged. Kan-Temir spent his nights not in Kaffa, but aboard a ship ready to sail. By day he insisted that all Şahin's supporters and all Christian priests in Kaffa should be executed. (The paşa of Kaffa took the priests under his protection.) A new flotilla from Istanbul now brought Canibek. Many Crimean clansmen, including all the khan's commanders in Kaffa, went over to the former khan's side – after the disasters caused by the mili-tant Mehmed III and Şahin, Canibek's passivity was attractive. Mehmed fled to the mountains, Şahin was protected by his Cossack guards. Both khan and *qalğa* escaped to Zaporozhian Cossack territory, where Mehmed vanished without trace. Şahin begged King Sigismund III of Poland to take the Crimean Khanate under his protection and to give him 12,000 Cossacks to fulfil this task. The king's advisers were enthusiastic, saying that even Julius Caesar never had an invitation that attractive, but they had not reck-oned on the certainty of war with the Ottomans, not to mention the Swedes, if they did take over Crimea. King Sigismund, in the hearing of Ottoman envoys, told Şahin that he could not accept Crimea as a subject nation without written confirmation from the sultan, but that Cossacks might help the Crimeans if Poland was not complicit. In secret, however, the king was eager to help.

Crimean refugees were emerging in Ukraine. Suddenly Mehmed III Giray materialized, having hidden in the forests for months and slipped past the guards on the isthmus. With Ukrainian cannons and a reconstituted army, the legitimate khan planned his return. He now had a very fragile alliance: a Polish king who wanted to stay offstage; Zaporozhian Cossacks who were arguing over an unpopular *hetman* and were more interested in rustling cattle than helping a deposed Crimean khan; Kan-Temir the Noğay leader who harboured ambitions of being himself a khan; and Crimean *mirza*s who could not accept either Canibek Khan's rule or Ottoman domination, but were not necessarily enamoured of Mehmed and his brother Şahin. Their first campaign in autumn, attacking Or Qapı, ended in farce when the Cossacks, reluctant to fight in cold weather, were diverted by a large herd of Noğay cattle which they had trouble, because of the lack of water, rustling and driving back home.

Mehmed held a ceremony in Bağçasaray in which his nobles, including those who had tried to kill or depose him, swore allegiance; even Kan-Temir, who was kept waiting five days to be received, was included in the amnesty. (He then fled from his enemies to safety in Bucak.) At last, it seemed, there was only one claimant to the khanate, and he was legitimate.

Peace came to the peninsula, but it had been depopulated by civil war, epidemics, famine, Ottoman and khanate taxation, floods and gales. Khachatur Kafayetsi's diary records little but extreme suffering from hunger, thirst, collapsed and looted houses, taxation: the worst problem affecting the north and the east of Crimea was lack of water. The bustards of the fields around Kerç were so desperate for water and food that they wandered into the kitchens in Kaffa: the only food relief that was recorded.

Mehmed III's first instinct was to punish Poland for its covert support of his enemies: he overcame his suspicions of Kan-Temir, and together they invaded Galicia, but were badly defeated; Kan-Temir lost a son and most of his men. On the isthmus, in early summer 1628, the battle with Canibek's forces and the Ottomans was so fierce that Mehmed III secretly sent a message offering to surrender in exchange for his own life. His Cossack supporters got wind of this treachery, however, and a fratricidal battle took place between Cossacks, Noğays and Crimean dissidents, while the defenders of Canibek just watched, their artillery aimed, waiting for the outcome. Mehmed III Giray beheaded a Cossack leader and was then killed (perhaps accidentally) by a Cossack bullet. The battle ended with a quarter of the Cossack force dead and Şahin Giray slipping away.

Mehmed III's body was solemnly taken to Bağçasaray and buried in his father's and grandfather's tombs: all three, Selâmet, Mehmed II and Mehmed III, had been deposed, exiled, murdered and then repatriated for burial. Canibek was now the undisputed khan for the next seven years.

In October 1629 the Poles forded the Dnestr river and captured many Crimean and Noğay Tatars. Among the Poles' prisoners was Mehmed III's cousin Islam Giray, who would not be released until 1634 and subsequently would become a khan with an understanding of, if not love for, Poles. There was, however, no reason to carry on a war with Poland. Russia under the new Romanov dynasty had recovered from the dominance that Poland enjoyed during the 'Time of Troubles' in the early seventeenth century, and was fighting to recover territory that Poland had taken.

The 1629 campaign was, for Russians, more promising: as well as attacking the isthmus, Cossacks sailed to Balaklava, and stormed and looted the fortress of Mangup, where Khan Canibek's treasures were stored. Local Tatars counter-attacked and the treasures were scattered in the forest. Regardless of what the Ottomans, now Russia's allies against Poland, felt, the Crimean Khanate now had to focus on a rapidly recuperating Russia as its main enemy. Tsar Mikhail was letting Don Cossacks under Russian protection row downriver and attack eastern Crimea, at the same time demanding that the Ottomans replace the Crimean khan with someone more amenable. Faced with Russian demands, from the 1630s on the Crimean Tatars, of all Poland's neighbours, would for much of the time be the most supportive. They had a common interest in preventing Russian expansion. All that Canibek Giray Khan asked of the new king Władisław IV was to free his cousin Islam Giray and hand over the former khan's brother Şahin, should he ever reappear. In 1633 Crimean forces under Canibek's eighteen-year-old son Mubarek joined the Poles in an attempt to reach Moscow. The Crimeans, however, stopped short at Serpukhov, about 160 kilometres (100 mi.) from Moscow. Rather than storm the capital's walls, they waited for Russian negotiators. The tsar sent his envoys and, after they promised to send an embassy to Bağçasaray with arrears of tribute, Mubarek Giray turned back. Never again would a Tatar army threaten Moscow itself. The khanate's underlying aim was, apparently, to make the Russians treat Crimea as a country totally independent of the Ottomans (the Russian ambassador in Istanbul, however, repeatedly asked the sultan to depose Canibek Giray).

Canibek was expecting payment from Poland for Crimean participation in the campaign against Moscow. First, he had to find ways to ignore the sultan's insistence that he attack Poland, in coordination with both Ottomans and Russians. Canibek had already refused to lead an army against Iran. Worse, Sultan Murad IV suspected the khan of siding with the Zaporozhian Cossacks. Murad IV had suppressed the mutinies raging in Istanbul and could now threaten Canibek with a Turkish fleet that would sail to Kaffa, bringing a more compliant khan. For a while, however, Turks and Crimeans had a problem requiring a joint solution: Kan-Temir's Noğays were ravaging the outer provinces not just of Poland and Crimea, but of the Ottoman empire itself. One solution was to make Kan-Temir the governor of an Ottoman province, but to remove his Noğay men to the Crimean peninsula – not an idea that appealed to peaceful Crimean farmers and townsmen. Eventually, Sultan Murad IV decided that the Noğays, however unruly, were best kept close by, as a deterrent to the khanate when needed.

As for replacing Canibek, the ideal and most feared candidate was Mehmed III's fugitive brother Şahin. In vain, Canibek sent killers, Crimean, Cossack or Russian agents, after him. Şahin slipped across the Caucasus and turned up yet again in Iranian service, under Shah Sefi. Rumour had it that Sefi would give Şahin 40,000 men to capture Crimea and put it under Iranian protection. Şahin already had secret supporters in his homeland. Canibek found out and invited them to a *bayram* feast, where most of the traitors, including their male relatives, were shot dead. This only raised Şahin Giray's prestige in Istanbul. Murad offered him an amnesty and invitation. In summer 1633, taking great precautions, Şahin sailed from Azov to Istanbul and proffered his apologies. After a very friendly reception, he was sent to Rhodes, the holding pen for potential khans. Canibek, in the end, sluggishly obeyed orders and set off for Iran, not realizing that this was the sultan's ploy to isolate and depose him, until an Ottoman official could intercept and unthrone him by decree. Canibek and his family were then also sent to Rhodes, living next door to his nemesis Şahin Giray. (Şahin exasperated the elderly Canibek by stealing his carpets and tormenting his servants.) In October 1636, aged seventy, Canibek died.

On reflection, Sultan Murad IV realized that Şahin would not be a reliable leader of a campaign against Iran. Instead, he appointed one of Khan Ğazı II Giray's sons, who had lived in Turkey for some thirty years and whose reputation for acquiring real estate, 'grabbing with their teeth like wolves', was proof of their toughness. The sultan chose Inayet Giray and told him to move to the Iranian front as soon as he had established himself with the Crimean *beys*. (Kan-Temir was also ordered to Iran, but showed no intention of leaving his fief on the Dnepr.) Inayet put on a show of obedience, but turned back to Crimea as soon as he reached the Caucasus. His excuse was a menacing migration of Noğays, fleeing from invading Mongol Kalmyks. The Noğay refugees were moving in enormous numbers from the Volga to Crimea, adding to the threat from the Noğay of Kan-Temir who was hovering around the isthmus. Inayet had to spread the Volga Noğays widely, five households per village, to avoid creating a state within a state, or reinforcing Kan-Temir's Horde.

Murad IV was frustrated by the failure of yet another Crimean khan to turn up on the Iranian front, all the more after Ottoman forces were defeated at Erevan. Inayet tried once more to move against Iran, but his *beys* dug their heels in. The sultan cut off the customary pension that a khan expected to receive from Kaffa's customs dues and for military expenses. Inayet's offer of a contingent far smaller than the 60,000 men demanded was rejected. The sultan threatened the Crimean Tatars with the *harac*, a tax on non-Muslims. Inayet pondered rebellion. First, he needed allies, and thought of Poland.

Even when a Crimean khan proposed friendship and alliance with the Poles, the offer was soured by the khan's exorbitant demands for money and his grotesque threats in case of non-compliance. On 29 June 1635 the young Inayet Khan, at the start of his short reign, sent a 'diplomatic' note to King Władysław IV:

> And if it so happens that gifts and money, due according to the ancient customs and agreement, are not sent by you, our brother ... I, Inayet Giray Khan, will send my troops to your state and raid it in summer as well as in winter; and if I breach your peace with a hundred thousand Tatars, raid it with fire and sword with the assistance of God and our Prophet, and capture commoners and nobles, assuming that each Tatar takes one captive and one head of cattle, you should consider whether this would not exceed the value of the gifts that you are to send.

Inayet means 'grace', but Khan Inayet's boyhood, in the shadow of death, had made him tough and remorseless. When he was nine years old, after the death of his father, Khan Ğazı 'Bora' (North Wind), the sultan had finally sent out from Istanbul not Ğazı's eldest son Toqtamış, but his brother Selâmet, who in accordance with Genghisid and Ottoman practice, murdered some of his rivals still residing in Crimea, notably Toqtamış and his brother Sefer. The khan's vizier had saved the younger brothers – Inayet, Husam and Aivaz – by shipping them to Turkey.

Inayet had his reasons for threatening the Poles and demanding tribute: he needed money to crush an incipient civil war in the Crimea. The Poles, on the other hand, were not to be intimidated: they sent an envoy with just enough money to assuage the Crimean Tatars, knowing that Inayet was too embroiled in conflict to attack Poland. The conflict involved the Mansur clan, including Noğay Tatars in the steppes beyond the ill-defined borders of the khanate, insubordinate and at daggers drawn with the dominant clan, the all-powerful Şirins, who had as strong a claim as Inayet to be descended from Genghis Khan. Kan-Temir, as *ağa* (chief) of the Mansur Noğays and virtually the sovereign of Bucak province, well placed for raiding Moldavia and Poland, still saw himself as a kingmaker. In the mid-1630s he planned to make Inayet a mere puppet khan. Kan-Temir had a lot of leeway from the Ottomans, thanks to his exploits in their wars against Poland. He never forgot the atrocious murder by Mehmed III and Şahin Giray of his children and of his pregnant wife, who was tied to a spit and slowly roasted to death, a sadistic torture typical not so much of Crimean Tatars as of Shah Abbas's Iranians, who had honed Şahin's survival skills.[6] Şahin would, however, survive Kan-Temir only by a year, for in 1641 Sultan Ibrahim would have Şahin strangled.

Kan-Temir could only act on his plans for revenge after Sultan Murad IV had deposed Canibek Giray. Inayet Giray, now enthroned as Crimean khan, was blamed for the Ottoman loss of Erevan to the Persians, a humiliation for which Sultan Murad IV would never forgive either Inayet or Kan-Temir.

Kan-Temir's prestigious victories over the Poles at Khotyn counted for nothing once his rebellion in Crimea made him Inayet's enemy. Khan Inayet began a campaign and threatened to exterminate Kan Temir and the Mansur clansmen of the steppes. The latter were dominated by Noğay fighters, refugees from the Don Cossack and Kalmyk Mongol settlers in eastern Ukraine. Inayet was backed by his brother Husam, the *qalğa*, a bloodthirsty enemy of Kan-Temir. Khan and *qalğa* crossed the Dnepr and attacked the Noğay, because, according to the king of Poland, the Noğay were in breach of treaties with Crimea. The Turkish authorities, however, forbade Kan-Temir to fight either Poles or Crimean Tatars. He was summoned to Istanbul. Kan-Temir's many brothers began to surrender to Inayet. They were pardoned, but Inayet deported Kan-Temir's men to the Crimean interior, confiscated

Kan-Temir's property and imprisoned his new wife and surviving children. In Istanbul Sultan Murad was in no mood to compromise with either side: he issued menaces when Inayet offered him only a small contingent to fight the Iranians. Inayet and his *beys* then threatened to declare independence from Istanbul. Castles were besieged: the conflict reached a climax when, ostensibly to forestall an Ottoman invasion, Inayet annexed the Ottoman-ruled port of Kaffa and executed the city's judge and chief *bey*, who had refused to give Inayet his share of customs revenues. Despite Inayet's promise of impunity if Kaffa handed over its judge and *bey*, the city was looted.

Inayet failed to make peace with Kan-Temir, although both sides knew civil war would lead to Ottoman intervention. Inayet demanded that the sultan hand over Kan-Temir as a proven enemy of the Crimean Khanate. He even threatened to march on Istanbul if extradition were refused. No Turkish sultan could tolerate such arrogance: it had to be neutralized. Meanwhile, Kan-Temir's brothers Süleyman-Shah and Orak took drastic action. One night, when Husam Giray and his brother Seadet Giray, the *nureddin*, were not just complacent but dead drunk, they and their men were murdered. On 30 April 1637 Kan-Temir's brothers happily informed the sultan of this Noğay 'victory'.

Inayet's first instinct was to hurry to Istanbul to give his side of the story, but he could only expect, after his defiance, a hostile reception. Although Inayet assumed that no sultan would ever execute a Giray, a descendant of Genghis Khan, he still sought, as earlier Crimean khans had done, Polish protection. Kan-Temir meanwhile extracted only lukewarm assurances from the Ottomans; his own sons joined other Bucak nobles in preferring Inayet's authority. Kan-Temir then fled to Istanbul, deploring Inayet's 'rebellion' and asking for protection.

Inayet had sent a letter, far too well-informed and arrogant for the sultan's taste, to the leading Ottoman religious official, Yahya-efendi, *Sheikh-ul-Islam*, denouncing the sultan's interference in the khanate. Now that his brothers were dead, Inayet had nobody to appoint as *qalğa* or *nureddin* and was totally isolated. King Władysław of Poland, himself afraid of provoking the Ottomans, would not come to Inayet's aid.

Summoning up courage worthy of his father, the formidable Khan Ğazı II 'Bora' Giray, on 13 June 1637 Inayet sailed to Istanbul and tried to justify himself to Sultan Murad IV, who had already sent to Crimea two large galleons with a replacement khan. Not for the first time, the formal term for the sultan's capital and palace, The Threshold of Felicity, proved wholly inappropriate. On 2 July 1637 Murad IV confronted Inayet with

Kan-Temir. The sultan listened to their mutual denunciations and rebuked Inayet for treasonably invading Bucak without permission. His temper no doubt exacerbated by his sciatica and arthritis, which no amount of massage with honey and vinegar could assuage, he declared: 'The death penalty for such an ungrateful evildoer can only be of enormous benefit for the faith and the state.' Murad immediately had Inayet strangled. (Murad recognized Inayet's merits, however, by giving his body a fine ceremonial funeral.) Inayet was only forty years old and had reigned for just over two years. He was replaced with another cousin of Khan Ğazı 'Bora', Bahadır Giray. Shortly afterwards Murad IV executed Kan-Temir in turn for his part in the disturbances and for daring to protest at the execution of his son for murder (the executioners brought the headless body to Kan-Temir's house and the father reacted with a torrent of invective against the sultan).

Murad IV now felt free to leave the capital and lead the fight with the Persians in person for the possession of Baghdad (another city over which Ottomans and Persians had fought for over a century). Murad IV's draconian actions quelled for a time the adventurous spirit both of the Crimean khans and of the Noğay. Kan-Temir's transformation of Bucak into a private fief was aborted, and the expelled Bucak Tatars either resumed nomadic life in steppes rendered barren by fire, or were forcibly integrated with the khan's Crimean subjects, or tried to negotiate protection and integration from the king of Poland, who vacillated and then demurred (for the Poles, Slavic Cossacks were bad enough, and taking on Noğay or Tatar Cossacks was a step too far). The Crimean Tatars, meanwhile, were traumatized by the unprecedented execution of Khan Inayet, whom they venerated for his fearlessness.

Why did Murad IV, given that some seven grandsons of the great 'planet' Khan Devlet I were eligible, now select Bahadır, one of the youngest? Bahadır, like many Giray, grew up in exile in Yambol in Thrace. He was a poet and scholar, using the pseudonym Rezmi ('struggling'), known for his good looks and eloquence, as well as his love lyrics dedicated to his cousin and future wife, Khanzade-Hanım. Her father, Bahadır's uncle, was the formidable Khan Ğazı 'Bora'. Khanzade-Hanım was herself a poet (but her works have been lost); she is remembered for her counsel of monogamy, when she quoted to Bahadır the Qur'anic *sura*: 'Marry women of your choice, two or three or four; but if you fear that you will not be able to deal justly, then only one: that will be more suitable, to prevent you from doing injustice.'[7]

Promotion to khan and the turmoil of the khanate's capital city Bağçasaray may have been traumatic for the 35-year-old Bahadır, after scholarly peace on the Giray estates in Yambol. Once in power, however, Bahadır proved ruthless in suppressing sedition. In his 1637 diary entry, the Kaffa priest Khachatur Kafayetsi approved: 'Now Bahadır Giray Khan has woken out of his dream and sworn blood revenge on the Noğays: he killed Salmaşa Mirza and other accursed *beys*, small or big, even babes in their cradles. He exterminated the Mansur race.' Bahadir obtained a fatwa from the *mufti* of Kaffa, the revered and austere Sufi Abdullah Afifeddin, to justify his execution of all the adult male Mansur-Noğay clansmen for sedition. Bahadır's revenge on the Mansur clan, whom he suspected of treasonable links to the Noğay, even to the Don Cossacks, was merciless. After a banquet he began slaughtering the suspect *mirzas*, even those who had taken no part in the murder of Khan Inayet's brothers, and their bodies were swept into latrine pits. The clans had now lost their political power. Bahadır's lyrical poetry shows that he had no illusions about his security:

Don't expect generosity from fate, so generous to commoners.
The treasures of knowledge bring only harm: expect no honour
    from them.
Your concupiscent eyes will be glazed by a curtain,

What does it matter that Rezmi's gloomy lines burn with fire?
The house is on fire, but you can't see the smoke.

Predatory bands of Cossacks were destabilizing Crimea. Hitherto Poland and the khanate had been inconstant enemies or allies; Crimean Tatar policy towards Muscovy and Poland had been generally to support the weaker side and thus redress the balance between these menaces. Now Cossack groups amounted to a third force that periodically and unpredictably attacked or supported Poland, Muscovy, Ottoman Turkey or the Crimean Khanate. Recovering from Polish invaders and usurpers, Russia under the Romanovs was by 1635 becoming the greater threat to the khanate. Despite the Ottoman desire for peace in the north, the Tatars were happy to be bribed by King Władysław to raid Muscovy. Yet Inayet's predecessor Khan Canibek had promised to help Tsar Mikhail fight Władysław (needlessly, since the Poles, unaided, defeated the tsar at the battle of Smolensk in February 1634).

Some forty years later, in the 1660s and 1670s, Juraj Križanić, a Croat priest who came to Russia in the guise of a Polish diplomat, and was exiled to Siberia for denouncing Russian sodomy and drunkenness, composed carefully considered advice to Tsar Aleksei. Russia, he said, should not expand towards the barren Arctic and Central Asia. Instead it should unite with Poland to conquer the fertile southern steppes and the Crimea, gain access to the Black Sea and liberate the southern Slavs from Ottoman rule: 'We should not wait for the Tatars to come to us, we must seek them out in their own country, destroy their settlements, seize their wives and children, so that they can no longer reproduce.'

Tsar Ivan IV 'The Terrible' had received similar advice in the 1550s, but despite Muscovy's successes – destroying in 1552 the khanate of Kazan, and replacing in 1556 the khanate of Hacı Tarhan (which blocked access from the lower Volga to the Caspian Sea) with a new settlement, Astrakhan – Ivan IV had realized that the Crimea was too much to bite off, let alone chew. In the late 1630s Tsar Mikhail Romanov put up with the new rapprochement, based on a promise of regular Polish tribute, between the Crimean khans and Poland. But he did attack the Crimean Tatars by proxy, using the pro-Muscovy Don Cossacks (east of the Zaporozhian Cossacks), who could easily row up and down the Don to the Sea of Azov.

This was by no means the first Don Cossack incursion on territory belonging to or bordering the khanate. On 18 August 1633, two hundred Don Cossacks had joined a flotilla of 1,300 Zaporozhian Cossacks (even though the Don Cossacks, Russian subjects, and the Polish Zaporozhians rarely collaborated), landing at the west Crimean port of Gözleve (today's Evpatoria) and forcing Khan Canibek's musketeers to retreat to Gözleve's impregnable castle. The Crimean main army, then on a raid in the steppes, was too far away to stop the Zaporozhian Cossacks from showing their notorious antisemitic barbarity, murdering the Karaim Jews of Belbek and Çufut Qale. Laden with plunder, the Cossacks left for the open sea a fortnight later.

In 1637 the Don Cossack menace, covertly encouraged and financed, although officially denounced by Tsar Mikhail of Muscovy, was worse. The migration of many Noğay – the *Kiçi* ('little') and Mangıt Hordes (warrior tribes), but not the main *Ulu* Horde that continued to roam the steppes by the Caspian Sea – had left a vacuum, now being filled by Don Cossacks and the Mongol Kalmyks, refugees from China. The Kalmyks, who were Buddhists and cattle rustlers, were even more hostile to Muslim Tatars than were the Cossacks, but it was the latter who restored to Muscovy, if only for a short while, what Kievan Russia had aspired to seven hundred years earlier: access to the Sea of Azov and thus the Black Sea. On the tsar's behalf, the Cossacks, fewer than 5,000 strong, mined and stormed the Ottoman coastal fort at Azak (now Azov), which guarded the Crimea's eastern coast. The Turkish garrison and nearly all Azak's inhabitants were slaughtered. Unlike the Crimean Tatars, Sultan Murad IV seemed complacent about the threat to his northeastern outpost. Khan Bahadır Giray, who was busy pacifying Bucak, was disgraced by this defeat; reluctantly, he turned east to Azak and helped the Turks in a counter-attack that failed. Yet the Turkish troops were armed with artillery, which the Tatars lacked, and out-numbered the Cossacks twenty to one (according to a witness, the patriotic Ottoman traveller Evliya Çelebi). This counter-attack, however, alarmed Moscow enough to force it to offer the Crimean Tatars a treaty, embassies and gifts, and, a year later, to order the Cossacks to retreat up the Don so that once more Azak was in Ottoman hands.

Crimean public opinion had come near to panic: there were predictions that the Russians were about to conquer Crimea and settle Mongol Kalmyks there. To prevent more Cossack incursions, Bahadır Giray's viceroy rebuilt fortifications at Bağçasaray and at Or Qapı.

Khan Bahadır, although reassured by Russian blandishments, still expected the Polish king Władysław to stop Zaporozhian Cossacks from attacking Muslims, and also to send annual 'gifts' worth 30,000 florins. Bahadır's *qalğa*, his brother Islam Giray, who in his twenties had been an honoured hostage of the Poles, was conciliatory, recalling the Tatars' alliance with the Poles and Lithuanians when the khanate was in its infancy. This did not prevent Islam from enslaving 8,000 Ukrainians (Polish subjects) and selling them to row Turkish galleys in perpetuity.

Bahadır, during his short tenure, proved to be resolute, even innovative: he arranged an exchange of ambassadors with Queen Christina of Sweden, his mother and his senior wife acting as correspondents, which Bahadır thought was appropriate when addressing a female monarch (one letter assured the queen that good relations, not manufactured goods, were all that the khanate wanted from Sweden). At the same time Bahadır concen-trated on writing poetry, under the pseudonym Rezmi. He devised witty puns, but his best Sufic lyrics deal with the unknowability of God, whose face is 'hidden by the shadow of His lock of hair', which is all that the poet-khan is allowed to contemplate.

The khan was, however, also preoccupied with money. To finance mili-tary expeditions to Bucak and then to Azak, he raised oppressive 'arsenal' taxes. At the same time an unexpected opportunity, or rather a chasm, opened up. Sultan Murad IV died. All his eleven children had perished in infancy. On his deathbed the sultan ordered the execution of his doctors and of his only surviving brother, Ibrahim, a shy, perhaps mentally disabled, youth who had lived all his life in terror of the executioner's bowstring. Murad's last orders were not carried out: his viziers were sure the sultan would never rise again. In any case, if Ibrahim were executed, there would be no Ottoman heir. The Polish ambassador in Istanbul wrote to his king, 'Ibrahim is the last of the Ottomans . . . The whole empire will fall to the Tatars, the Girays of Crimea, who have already boasted of their dominance and have stopped obeying the Turks.' (The Girays' claim to the Ottoman throne, if extinct, was also asserted by Emiddio d'Ascoli, head of the Franciscan mission to Kaffa from 1624 to 1634, but denied by at least one later Crimean khan.[8])

Ibrahim, however, survived; the empire's reins were managed in his lifetime by his and Murad's able mother, the Albanian Kösem Sultana, and by a competent vizier Kara-Mustafa Paşa. Ibrahim, for all his idiocy, proved as ruthless as his late brother. He was persuaded by his chief vizier that Şahin, the rebel brother of Khan Mehmed III, who had been exiled to the island of Rhodes, was identified in an astrologer's prophecy that the sultan of Turkey would one day be overthrown by a rebel with a bird's name: Şahin means 'falcon', and Şahin Giray was duly murdered. Indulged by his mother, who wanted him to become virile enough to beget an heir, Ibrahim typically spent his time trying to ravish virgins and in a palace carpeted with furs: diplomats called him 'Le fou de fourrures'. His perverse viciousness, however, grew so dangerous that in 1648 his mother agreed to, and witnessed, his execution.

In the Crimea, in 1640 Bahadır Giray, fearing that Russia might now encircle Crimea from the east, renewed the khanate's attempts to retake Azov from the Cossacks, with Turkish ships and a large army. Khachatur Kafayetsi was dismayed by the outcome: 'The Khan, the Paşa . . . Rumelian soldiers, Noğays . . . impossible to count them all . . . set off for Azov, caused a lot of mutinies, but were very much blamed for coming back without loot. They couldn't take Azov, so came back in disgrace. 40,000 assault troops fell . . . There was great distress.' Fortunately, Tsar Mikhail was anxious to avoid war with the Ottomans and therefore disowned the Don Cossacks' conquest of the port. In any case, the khan had little artillery and his *beys* preferred an increase in Russian tribute to a Russian withdrawal from Azov. In the end, with help from an Ottoman fleet, Russian access to Azov from the Don was cut. In October 1641 Bahadır died in Gözleve after a long illness.[9] He had abandoned the attack on Azov: attempting to unseat the Cossacks, even under determined Ottoman leadership, had cost Bahadır 1,000 infantry blown up by a Cossack mine. Despite the failures of his last years, Bahadır's versatility earned him the title of 'fifth planet' from the historian Seyyid Muhammad Riza.

Bahadır had a son (and a very promising grandson, the future Khan Selim), but it was his younger brother Mehmed IV Giray who was named as khan, even though Islam, Bahadır's *qalğa*, was senior and was a hardened warrior. Istanbul was then, more than ever, as the Crimean historian Seyyid Muhammed Riza puts it, 'a marketplace where a khan's garments could be had for money, effort and lobbying'. The choice of Mehmed was all the odder since he was generally ostracized in Crimea and then in Yambol for his conniving at the murder by his half-brother Khan Canibek Giray of their brother Azamat (despite this crime Mehmed had accepted from Canibek the posts of *qalğa* and then *nureddin*). Mehmed was a skilled lobbyist and won the post of khan for at least three years, even though none of his immediate kin would serve him as *qalğa* or as *nureddin*. (Instead he appointed as *qalğa* Fetih Giray, the son of the illegitimate 'shepherd' Mustafa Giray, and as *nureddin* a nephew, Ğazı.) When Mehmed arrived to take up his throne, he was met by surly, embarrassed looks. He defused the situation by a short speech, warning that the quarrels and envy besetting the peninsula threatened the very existence of the khanate. Meanwhile, Mehmed's better-qualified brother Islam had been exiled to the shores of the Dardanelles.

Khan Mehmed IV's three-year reign, his first, was cut short by his mistakes in Circassia: he failed to defend his Circassian vassals from a Kalmyk attack and ravaged Circassia instead. He made the wrong choice between two brothers aspiring to be prince of Circassia, a decision reversed by Sultan Ibrahim. Once deposed, Mehmed was lucky to be allowed to live in Rhodes. His brother Islam, helped by his wise and faithful counsellor (and, it appears, former tutor) Sefer-Ğazı Ağa, found and bribed the best patron in Istanbul, the chief *baltacı* (halberdier). These bribes proved futile when a complaint was lodged by the paşa of Kaffa that Islam was a troublemaker: he and the bribed *baltacı* were both exiled to Rhodes. Bigger bribes – slave boys and girls – were paid to the chief eunuch of the harem (a particularly influential figure in the court of the erotomaniac Sultan Ibrahim and his favourite 'Sugar Dumpling' (*şakar para*)). Bribes finally won the day: the paşa of Kaffa was executed for abuse of power, and Islam was enthroned as Crimean khan. The Ottoman historian Na'ima describes Islam's solemn inauguration by Sultan Ibrahim:

> The Sultan, wearing an ordinary hat, was happily enthroned, leaning on a gold-embroidered cushion at the edge of a pool. The Khan kissed

the ground and the Sultan, without moving or changing his position, spoke: 'You see, Islam! I've made you Khan. Watch out! You have to be the friend of my friend and the enemy of my enemy.' The Khan then kissed the ground again and stood. He responded, 'May Almighty God preserve the person of my fortunate master from errors. If God pleases, I shall make no omissions in service, as long as I have my Lord's blessing.' – 'You have my blessing. You, your children and forefathers have all had the bread and salt of the favour of my great forefathers ... Be careful, and look only to me, and listen to nobody else's words ... How old are you and what are you like on horseback?' ... Then the Khan, proud of the Sultan's kind words ... turned to the Chief Vizier and said, 'Since I've been made Tatar Khan, in future pay attention to what I write. Don't flood me with warning letters, telling me to disagree with one man, not to annoy another ... don't confuse me, as if I need to be told how to act. Friendship with infidels is unthinkable to me.'

This interview demonstrated that, however subordinate a Crimean khan might be to an Ottoman sultan, he still ranked higher in the court than even the grand vizier, let alone any provincial governor.

Two months later a ship took the new Khan Islam III Giray to the Crimea.

In the 1640s, in contrast to Ottoman corruption and weakness, Khan Islam Giray stood out as a firm, determined and efficient statesman, with the benefit of advice from Sefer-Ğazı Ağa and the latter's son Islam Ağa. The khan's bodyguards, the *qapıqulu*, were suspicious of these low-born counsellors of the khan, and the newcomers in turn were distrusted by the traditional aristocrats, the *mirzas*, in a clash that nearly killed Sefer-Ğazı Ağa. The counsellors sided with the *mirzas*, and the *qapıqulu* rebelled. Sefer-Ğazı retreated to Ottoman-controlled Kaffa. The rebels demanded that he be sent to Istanbul for execution: Khan Islam signed the death warrant, presumably hoping that his counsellor would, as in fact he did, leap the Kaffa moat on his fast Circassian horse to seek support in the north at Or Qapı. In the end, a frail truce (the terms are obscure) was negotiated between Sefer-Ğazı Ağa and the khan's guards and aristocratic counsellors. The matter was partly settled by Khan Islam's decree exempting commoners, *qara halqlar* ('the black people'), from Bahadır's much-hated war taxes.

If Khan Islam was a skilful peacemaker to his own people, to his northern neighbours he was a devious extortionist. Both Poles and Russians found themselves forced to pay the traditional Golden Horde tribute or endure looting. The income made up the deficits in Khan Islam's treasury. Islam was much helped by Kutlu Shah, chief *mirza* of the Şirin clan, who gave the khan a fifth of his raids' proceeds – slaves, gold and bolts of cloth. Islam several times resorted to war against Poland. For the time being, he sent Russia elaborate flattering diplomatic notes, reminding the Muscovites of their ancient pecuniary obligations towards the Golden Horde and its successors, the Crimean Tatars. Consequently the Crimean Khanate by the end of the 1640s was prosperous as never before and rarely afterwards.

Crimean economy and society in the mid-seventeenth century

The prosperity of the khanate under Khan Islam III and his successor, the restored Khan Mehmed IV, was of course largely due to slave-trafficking. Slaves were typically captured prisoners of war whose families were too poor to ransom them; many slaves were women and children rounded up in Tatar raids all over the Ukraine. Circassians, particularly young girls and youths, captured, bought or given in tribute, were even more desirable. Thousands, perhaps tens of thousands of slaves were kept at any one time in Crimea, handed out or sold as farm labourers, builders or servants. Many more were sold in the local market in Bağçasaray and the Turkish market at Kaffa, which supplied the harems and businesses of the Ottoman empire with concubines, eunuchs, labourers, peasants, educated men and musicians, and which drew overseas traders (some Jews, some Armenian Christians) from all over the Muslim world. No reliable total can be counted of the men, women and children enslaved: quite likely more than two million human beings, mostly Slavs, were enslaved during the three hundred years of the khanate's existence. The Poles themselves estimated that by the end of the seventeenth century they had lost a million people, predominantly children and young adults.

So many Crimean Tatar men spent their time as soldiers that foreign slaves were essential to keep the country's intensive agriculture and animal husbandry going. When Tatar forces fought as unpaid auxiliaries to an Ottoman army, they were compensated by permission to loot and take captives. The Tatar civil service also needed to enslave (and sometimes employ) literate and numerate foreigners to assist with translation, education, diplomacy and trade. The khan's and the *beys*' treasuries, with their enormous expenditure on arms and servicemen, could not survive without the income (tariffs and direct sales) from exporting slaves. Borders between Poland, Russia and the Cossack and Noğay steppe lands were fluid: not until the end of the seventeenth century did Russia manage to build a defensive line of stockades and outposts that might deter Tatar raiders, while Polish peasants in the vulnerable southern provinces had to take a musket as well as a hoe when they went out to cultivate their fields. In any case, neither Poland nor Russia always had the necessary funds or organization to ransom any but the most highly valued prisoners of war and other captives.

Traditionally, the khan taxed one-fifth of the price of any valuable captives when they crossed the border; the *qalğa* and *nureddin* were also entitled to a tithe. Four *akçe* (12 grams of silver) for every slave exported from Kaffa was given to a *vaqf* (a charitable organization). Slave traders and owners were also taxed. Typically, a khan had about 3,000 slaves (they, like his other possessions, were meticulously recorded for probate on his death). Periodically slaves were sent as presents or bribes to the Ottoman sultan – typically, good-looking boys and girls, as well as hefty Russian peasants who would man the Turkish galleys until they died of exhaustion or drowning. (One Cossack captured by Tatars served on a galley of the Kaffa *bey* for seven years. Freed by a Cossack raid, he later testified that 260 Russian slaves had served on his galley. Ivan Bolotnikov, the famous leader of a rebellion during the Time of Troubles in the early 1600s, had also been taken prisoner by Crimean Tatars: sold in the Ottoman empire, he served as a galley slave for some years and was freed only when a German ship captured his galley.)

Slaves 'gifted' to the sultan were accompanied by more prosaic tribute: sacks of salt (a valuable commodity in the Black Sea countries) and sheep fat.

The reports of foreign observers (and a few escaped slaves and prisoners of war) are contradictory. The English mercenary Captain John Smith, who escaped across the steppe to Russia around 1604 and then became a pioneer in Virginia, where he taught other colonists how to construct a Tatar yurt, reported violent treatment and freezing, starving conditions:

> [I] among the slaughtered dead bodies and many a gasping soule, with toile and wounds lay groaning among the rest, till being found by the Pillagers ... perceiving by my armor and habit, my ransome might be better than my death ... sold for slaves, like beasts in a market-place, where everie Merchant, viewing their limbs and wounds, caused other slaves to struggle with them, to trie their strength.

Baron von Sigismund Herberstein reports horrors that he heard about the Crimean Tatars in Moscow: 'The old and infirmed men, who will not fetch much at a sale, are given up to the Tatar youths, either to be stoned, or to be thrown into the sea, or to be killed by any sort of death they might please.' The French diplomat Charles Peysonnel claimed in the eighteenth century that elderly slaves were thrown out of the houses to beg or die in the street.

In the steppes slaves were easy to capture for a horseman who had a spare horse and a dozen lassos, but returning home with their captives was a much slower journey for the normally fast-moving Crimean Tatar cavalry, and they became vulnerable to vengeful pursuing Cossacks. Baron de Tott, the French emissary, describes in the mid-eighteenth century:

> Five or six slaves of various ages, about 60 sheep and 20 oxen – that was one man's usual plunder, and he coped easily. The children's heads poked out of a sack hung from the saddle-bow, a young girl was mounted in front, held by the rider's left hand, while the mother was on the horse's croup and the father on a spare horse, the son on a second one; the sheep and oxen were driven ahead, and all this moved, without straying, under the herdsman's watchful eye. He had no trouble gathering his herd, directing it, seeing it had fodder, while he would dismount and walk to relieve his slaves.

Mikhalon Litvin, the Lithuanian ambassador to the Crimean Khanate in the mid-sixteenth century, while pitying his enslaved countrymen, considered them better off than serfs in his own country: 'The Tatars take slaves only from other countries and treat them fairly and even though slaves are taken in battle or bought for money, they keep them no longer than seven years.' Frequently, the Crimean Tatars observed Ottoman customs and Qur'anic dictates: the manumission of slaves was encouraged, as was their treatment as household servants; it was forbidden to take a slave on a military campaign; if a slave converted to Islam, he had to be freed in a Muslim household (or could be sold on to a Jewish or Armenian owner); a slave's children were supposed to be (but rarely were) free citizens. There are examples of Crimean slaves being freed and becoming prosperous, and prisoners of war were often freed (some, particularly Russians, stayed in the Crimea, for fear, even in the seventeenth century, of being treated, as Soviet citizens would be centuries later, as agents of a foreign power). Prisoners from Austria and Hungary, particularly if unable to secure a ransom, preferred labouring in Crimea to the uncertainty and destitution that might await them at home.

Slaves were protected, in times of scarcity, by their high value: Circassians were the most highly prized (for their beauty), Italians the least (for their alleged laziness). They could be leased out or used as payment of debts. A Russian woman was sold for 40 gold coins (a good horse cost 15). Prisoners might establish families: an Arslan Ağa presented his young son with a family of eighteen Cossacks, of whom four were married with children who all bore Muslim names. Kınalızade's manual of ethics of 1564 gave recommendations on the pros and cons of enslaved prisoners of different nationalities: 'Hungarians are clever, sensible . . . at the same time malevolent and tend to kill, harm and escape . . .' High-ranking prisoners of war could be exchanged for Tatar prisoners in Central Europe, typically at a valuation of 380 thaler (up to 100,000 for a prince or an army commander). The Tatars were far more conscientious than their European enemies in ransoming their own countrymen in European captivity.

We must remember that some of the Crimean Tatars' enemies were also slave-traders. True, Crimean Tatar horsemen usually fought to the death and rarely surrendered, so that few ended up as prisoners and slaves. Nevertheless, Russian archives have reports, for instance, of more than three hundred Tatar slaves at the start of the eighteenth century freezing or starving to death at Pskov in northwest Russia.

In the mid-seventeenth century the Tatars developed a spy network in Central Europe. 'Pavel the Lithuanian', disguised as a priest, collected not only information on enemy fortifications, but also valuations of property belonging to families of prisoners enslaved in Crimea. He passed his intelligence on (until he was caught and executed by the Austrians) to a German colonel, known just as 'The Bald One', working for the Crimean Tatars. This covert Tatar service also sold passes to citizens of countries that the Crimean Tatars were invading, giving immunity from capture, robbery or murder. Thus the khanate had integrated an organization of intelligence-gathering, slave-trading, ransom and labour.

The Crimean Khanate was less of a major entrepôt than it had been when the Turco-Mongol empire controlled Central Asia and when the overland Silk Road terminated at Kaffa. But it still remained crucial to Black Sea trade, and during the interminable Turco-Persian wars, despite depredations of Turkic tribesmen around the Caspian, goods still flowed between the Balkans and Central Asia via the Black Sea, through Crimea, where custom duties were paid. Furthermore, the khan, his *qalğa* and *nureddin* received regular subsidies from the Ottoman court (except when Crimean policies were in conflict with the sultan's), and these subsidies, paid eleven times a year, were measured in 'bags' (*yük*) of 100,000 *akçe* (silver coins of about 3 grams), 300 kilograms (660 lb) being an acceptable load for a Bactrian camel. In addition there was 'boot' money for mobilization and 'honey' money for other expenses incurred in Ottoman service. Many exported commodities were the khan's monopoly. The energetic Ottoman traveller and prolific writer Evliya Çelebi testifies that in the mid-seventeenth century the annual export of the famed pink-tinged salt, cut into 'bricks' from the lagoons around the isthmus of Or Qapı, was worth about 15 tonnes of silver. (Salt was transported to Kaffa in gigantic wagons, carrying on average 10 tonnes, drawn by 16 oxen.)

In times of harmony the khanate was awash with silver. According to Hezârfen ('Polymath') Ahmed Çelebi, writing in the mid-seventeenth century, every year the khan himself received 10,000 camel-loads of silver coin from the custom revenues of Kaffa (this must be a gross exaggeration, for 3,000 tonnes of silver, worth 2 billion u.s. dollars at today's prices, was far more than the annual silver production of the Ottoman empire). The *qalğa* and *nureddin* each received 1.5 tonnes from the Gözleve and Balaklava customs. These revenues, admittedly, were largely spent on maintaining a civil service and charitable institutions, and on providing commensurate sums to the *beys* of the four noble clans and their assistants. But in many decades the private sector of the khanate was conspicuously wealthy. Witnesses and court registers in the mid-seventeenth and mid-eighteenth centuries testify to rich markets and cheap produce and labour. Ottoman coinage was not always preferred to the khan's Crimean coins, for both mints tended to debase their silver currency with copper and could be discounted by officials and merchants. Nevertheless, the *akçe* had the purchasing power in the Crimea of today's British pound: it would buy a dozen eggs or a kilo (2 lb) of mutton, while four *akçe* would buy a chicken, half a kilogram (1 lb) of caviar, or 15 kilograms (33 lb) of wheat flour. Mulberries were so plentiful that they were free; markets had a dozen varieties of grapes (some local, some imported), and renowned Crimean figs, including a variety named after Devlet Ğazı Giray. Crimean honey sold for twice the price of imported honey. Horse flesh, from specially bred animals, was the most expensive meat, at 2 *akçe* a kilo. Crimean Tatars were tolerant *hanafi* Muslims, so a mild millet beer, *buza*, was freely available at 4 litres (7 pts) per *akçe*; wine, although supposedly legal only for Jews and Christians, was drunk by prosperous Muslims. A hundred years later, Charles Peysonnel, the knowledgeable French emissary, asserted that the Crimean white wine was 'better than our Chablis'. Some production, such as candles, was limited to non-Muslims;

other kinds, such as bread-baking, were overwhelmingly Muslim. Staple food prices were strictly regulated by the well-paid *mühtesib*, the local market inspector.

The French architect and mapmaker Guillaume Levasseur de Beauplan, a captain in the Polish army, was commissioned in the 1640s by King Jan Kazimierz to map Ukraine. Beauplan described the Crimean Khanate and its inhabitants in depth. He spares us no detail of the steppe Tatars' diet – in particular, bleeding to death any sick horse, then cooking the blood, slicing the rump meat to mature for three hours between the saddle and skin of their riding horse, before serving the meat with a coating of horse sweat. The horse fat was consumed, mixed with millet, groats or buckwheat. In the steppes honey was brewed unboiled into mead and caused terrible colic; in towns the mead was boiled, and as harmless as milk. The poor drank soured buttermilk.

Beauplan was a keen observer of the Crimean Tatars' clothing. It had already been noted by foreign dignitaries that even Tatar lords appeared to possess just one set of outer garments, which they replaced only when worn out. Beauplan noted that commoners wore a short cotton shirt, rough wool underpants and stockings under quilted cotton trousers and a sheepskin tunic, with the fleece outside in warm weather, so that 'they are frightening, for you could take them to be polar bears on horseback.' The better dressed wore cotton kaftans, a gown and headwear trimmed with fox or marten, and red morocco-leather shoes.

Wages were low, although many employees, from labourers to cooks and teachers, had free board and lodging: 4 *akçe* a day paid for a labourer or a regular soldier; 8 *akçe* for a refectory cook. Teachers in a medrese, however, were paid between 20 and 50 *akçe* per working day, depending on the medrese's prestige and the range of subjects taught (tuition, however, was free for the students, and medreses were funded by charitable foundations). Schoolteachers in the primary *mekteb*s were paid less, while their wives, who taught the girls separately from the boys, appear to have been unpaid. (The result, however, was that literacy, especially female, was higher in the khanate than in almost any other Muslim country.)

The most burdensome element of life in the Crimean Khanate was taxation: a number of Mongol taxes were still imposed, even though Ottoman taxes superseded many of them. The Mongol *tamğa* (originally a VAT on all transactions) and *qalan* (whose purpose is obscure) were abolished to appease the common people, but the sheep (or skewer) tax, *şişlik*, lower than its Ottoman equivalent, survived. There were taxes on the purchase of guns and wine, for the maintenance of musketeers and for warfare. The *öşr* was a tithe on agricultural produce, while *zakat* was a 'voluntary' wealth tax to help the poor. Non-Muslims paid the *ciziye* and also a bride tax.

Ships left Crimean ports largely for the southwest, to Istanbul and Rumelia, or the south, to Sinop or Trabzon in Anatolia. (The eastern Black Sea had few harbours, ports or centres of trade.) Custom tariffs and market fees, particularly in Kaffa, brought the khanate and the khan personally an annual income of millions of *akçe*. We have detailed records of shipping, imports, exports and prices for the mid-sixteenth century and the end of the seventeenth. For instance, the import or export duty on a slave varied, according to the market price, around 27 *akçe* (a horse cost 40, however), and a female slave sold at market incurred an 'embellishment' fee of 12 *akçe*. The range of imports – from Cossack cheese, to cheap Russian ironmongery, coffee, Dutch cloth – showed the Crimea to be thoroughly cosmopolitan in its trade. Most of that trade was in the hands of Muslims, but Greeks, Armenians and Jews participated (Kaffa's Armenians, for example, were more numerous than its Muslims, although a process of conversion to Islam or to Catholicism gradually reversed the proportions).

While the khan and his circle were responsible for military and foreign affairs, the *bey*s of the cities regulated commerce, and the *mufti* and imams ran the education system and the mosques. The organization that really held Crimean society together was a nationwide system of *qadi*s, the judges in the civil and criminal courts, who came under a *qadiasker* 'military', or superior judge. A *qadi* was appointed by the khan, but in the territory of an influential Şirin clan *bey*, the latter might determine the appointment. Only the khan's own judicial council could overrule a *qadi*'s court. The *qadi*, more often than not trained in the khanate, was required to be financially independent, incorruptible and to treat all plaintiffs equally, regardless of their wealth or social position: he was protected from temptation by a generous daily pay as high as 150 *akçe*. His powers of detention were limited only when a genuine *seyyid* (a descendant of the Prophet) was arrested. The *qadi* had a scribe (*katib*) and at least one *naib*, who was a clerk and, in remote areas, a deputy. The accused were brought to court by the *zabit*, a police officer (who was also responsible for apprehending runaway slaves, for which he was paid 2 *akçe* a day, recoverable from the slave-owner). A typical case is cited by Natalia Królikowska-Jedlińska:

> The Qarasu *zabit* brought a married woman named Saime, and
> Ibrahim, son of Hasan, to the local court. They were found together

at night in the woman's house while her husband was absent. Saime said that she had found Ibrahim in her house when she had returned home in the evening and had not invited him. Perhaps to avoid a more serious charge of robbery or rape, Ibrahim maintained that he had come at her invitation. He produced witnesses who confirmed his version. Both defendants were found guilty of illicit sex and the judge sentenced them to a discretionary punishment (*ta'zir ile hükm şod*, usually flogging, which would be carried out by the *zabit*).[10]

To judge by observant foreigners' comments, and by the surviving two hundred or so registers (*sicil*) of the seventeenth and eighteenth centuries (in St Petersburg's archives and still being studied), which give detailed, albeit edited accounts of plaintiffs' and defendants' cases, the system was free of the corruption that imbued Ottoman institutions. A *qadi* in conflict with the khan and his court, however, was liable to dismissal. Non-Muslims resorted to the *qadi*'s court as frequently as Muslims. Witnesses had to be male, unless, say, a woman witness saw a woman's body in a women's bathhouse. Women resorted to the courts primarily when initiating divorce proceedings. The *qadi* could investigate a crime scene if witnesses' testimony was insufficient. Court fees were set by decree, 8 *akçe* for recording a case, 32 for issuing a certified copy, 40 or 50 for a certificate of a slave's manumission, 2.5 per cent for probate of an inheritance. Judges were also responsible for supervising tax collection. We have less information about verdicts and, in criminal cases, sentences: many crimes against the person were outside the courts' jurisdiction, being dealt with under sharia law, leading to reconciliation, compensation or vengeance. Convicted murderers had to be executed, if not pardoned, by a kinsman of the victim.[11] (In one case, when a convicted murderer was a Jew, the Jewish community explained that they were forbidden to shed Jewish blood, so the *qadi* permitted the murderer to be stoned to death.) It is notable that observers of the Crimean Khanate noticed few amputations of thieves, corporal punishments or executions (except in military cases, or for treason), and there appeared to be few prisons. (Only when a new khan acceded and rival brothers or nephews had to be eliminated were there any atrocities comparable with Ottoman dynastic massacres.) Since quite a few Crimean Tatars, even some khans, were monogamous, there was limited demand for harem eunuchs, the curse of the Ottoman court. The khan's harem employed only a few African eunuchs, for castrating Muslims was taboo in Crimea. Torture was sporadic (notably of annoying Russian emissaries), but there were cases of witnesses and suspects being threatened with cutting off an ear or nose, a mutilation that actually happened on the Moldavian border, when a prisoner about to be freed failed to produce the agreed ransom.

6

RUSSIA STRIKES BACK

Securely enthroned, with the chief vizier Sefer-Ğazı Ağa managing internal and external affairs, Islam III Giray's position seemed safe. Around 1650 Sefer-Ğazı Aga commissioned a Hacı Mehmed, known as Sena'i, to write a history in stately old Ottoman Turkish of the khan's reign. Respectful to Crimean khans, Sena'i disparaged all other ranks and nations: *beys* were 'dogs', Russians 'accursed infidels'. It is at this period that Tatar folklore generates anti-Russian sayings (to which Russian folklore responded in kind): 'Friendship with a Russian is like expecting a sheepskin rug from a pig [*Urustan dost bolmaz domuzdan post*]' versus 'When the bowstring breaks, the Tatar stops fighting.'

In 1648 two events set Khan Islam III Giray's Crimea on a new and ultimately fatal trajectory. One was the onset of chaos in Istanbul: Sultan Ibrahim's extravagant orgies and his concubines' corruption resulted in his being incarcerated and then strangled. The new sultan Mehmed IV was just seven years old, and power was now disputed between Ibrahim's and Mehmed's mothers, their quarrel manipulated by avaricious eunuchs. The Ottoman empire was adrift until in 1651 Murad's and Ibrahim's mother Kösem Sultana was, despite her impressive political skills when she acted as regent, herself brutally murdered by janissaries, and a new paşa took over as regent to Mehmed. The Ottoman war effort was being expended on a long battle with the Venetians for possession of Crete, and in fighting in the North Balkans against Austrians and Hungarians. Meanwhile, in the Crimea, Khan Islam Giray felt free to ignore orders from Istanbul and to devise his own policy towards Poland and Russia.

In Poland a Cossack rebellion flared up, headed by the 51-year old *hetman* Bogdan Khmelnycky. He was either a Polish gentleman claiming to be a Cossack, or vice versa, from the small town of Chyhyryn. An Orthodox Christian (tolerated by the Catholic regime of Władysław IV) and an experienced soldier, Khmelnycky had been a captive of the Ottomans long enough to speak fluent Turkish and to pass for a Muslim (he read Arabic and knew how to pray). Khan Islam III Giray was sufficiently impressed by Khmelnycky to declare him a friend and a fellow Muslim (a conversion that the Cossack leader had to deny to avoid being assaulted by his own subjects). After a prisoner exchange, he became a leader of Cossacks more and more enraged by restrictions on their freedom and by the king's demands that they serve in Poland's wars. Under their *hetman* Koniecpolski, the Cossacks anticipated war with the Turks and Tatars, while King Władysław, instead, succumbed to blandishments from Khan Islam. On Koniecpolski's death, Khmelnycky moved south to the Dnepr, became the *hetman* of the Zaporozhian Cossacks and began a rebellion, ostensibly against Poland's arbitrary lords. For this revolt he secured (to every observer's surprise) the help of Khan Islam. On 26 May, at the battle of Korsun (100 kilometres (62 mi.) southeast of Kyïv), the Polish army was badly defeated, and four months later Cossacks and Crimean Tatars, led by Khmelnycky and Islam's *qalğa* Qırım Giray, took Lwów.

The 1648 joint campaign, led by Khan Islam III Giray's best general, the commander of Or Qapı Tuğay-bey, and by Bogdan Khmelnycky, marked the point at which Poland-Lithuania's power began to wane. For the Crimean Tatar poet Edip-efendi, it was an ideal subject. In his *Sefername* (Poem of the Campaign) he gave a classic portrayal of Tatar archers preparing for battle:

> The youth holds a whip, his voice is like steel,
> Hey, young men, gather round, we're off to war!
>
> Have the horses shod, get bow and arrows ready,
> Have the farewell dinners cooked.
>
> Take the sabre off the wall, sharpen it,
> If you are fighting for a just cause, you will win.
>
> Hang two nooses and a lassoo on your saddle-bow,
> A red leather amulet on the horse's neck.
>
> Don't feed a warhorse, then he won't get tired,
> A fat horse can't take the journey and will let you down in battle.

Tighten your tunic, pull your hat down hard,
Mother won't be there, think of everything.

The palace has ordered us to set off from Mamai,
Mother gave you a talisman, father – arrows.

Seventy sons led out restless horses by their bridles,
Seventy mothers sprinkled water from seventy bowls ...

Lord Bogdan is a famous lord, he gave to the Khan forty of
   everything,
Forty stallions, forty bulls, all the finest.
Adil Giray and Bogdan took counsel all night.

Next year, 1649, the new Polish king Jan Kazimierz had to meet Khan Islam III in his tent and make peace, marked by generous 'gifts' to the khan. The king was forced to confirm Cossack liberties. In a secret treaty article, the Crimean Tatars were allowed to keep the Polish prisoners they had enslaved, and a Polish magnate was taken hostage to the Crimea to ensure payment of yet another 200,000 thaler. Khan Islam advised Khmelnycky to be satisfied with an amnesty from Poland and with recognition of his *hetman's* authority over the palatinates of Kyïv, Chernihiv and Braclav, from which Jesuits and Jews would now be expelled. Nevertheless, just like his father Bahadır Giray, Islam III, as political insurance, had his mother and his senior wife write friendly letters to Queen Christina of Sweden, Poland's enemy, arranging an exchange of ambassadors.

A treaty between sworn enemies was bound to be broken at the first opportunity, and in a brutal battle of June 1651 between Poles and the combined Crimean and Cossack forces several leading Tatars perished and Khmelnycky was captured. In 1652 it was the Polish army's turn to be massacred: in the battle of Batih, the Cossacks began to kill all their prisoners. They had to be stopped by the Crimean Tatars, who were so aghast at the loss of potential ransom and slaves that they dressed their Polish prisoners up as Tatars. Khan Islam, together with Khmelnycky, invaded Moldavia, forcing its ruler to break with Poland and to marry his daughter to Khmelnycky's son Timofei. In 1653 the pendulum of war swung both ways again, until serious negotiations began in December. The Poles would not admit the Cossacks to the conference table, so they were represented by Khan Islam's Crimean Tatars. Again, the Crimeans kept both the money

Hacı Mustafa, Khan
Islam III's envoy to
Queen Christina of
Sweden, 1650.

and their prisoners. Although the new treaty was expressly kept oral and unwritten, it held for the next twelve years. Khmelnycky, however, was disgruntled by the Tatars' refusal to let him kill Ukrainian peasants; his notorious hatred of Jews (hundreds of thousands of whom he murdered) was also alien to the pro-semitic Crimean Tatars.

By early 1654 Khmelnycky's Zaporozhian Cossacks had decided on a new volte-face: they now swore allegiance to Tsar Aleksei of Russia, which led to what was the effective annexation of Ukraine by Russia, as well as to the union of Cossacks on both sides of the River Dnepr. The Crimean Tatars began to complain of Cossack depredations.

The Commonwealth (the first *Rzeczpospolita*) of Poland and Lithuania faced attack from both Muscovites and Cossacks. A new alliance had to be forged with the Crimean Tatars. Khan Islam excited his new allies by proposing an invasion not of Ukraine (still regarded as Polish), but of Muscovy itself, in conjunction with the Noğay, Volga and Kazan Tatars (those not yet fully cowed by Russian rule). Even the Mongol Kalmyks seemed eager to participate. Cossacks would be attacked if they refused to join in. Urged by a Muscovite emissary to attack Poland instead, Khan Islam refused and responded: 'Erasing a state like Poland from the world would be shameless and contrary to the will of God.'

Khan Islam III was not as deluded as he might seem: in June 1654, in his last letter to King Jan Kazimierz, he wondered, 'From where has Moscow drawn so much strength and power that it is no longer in its natural condition?' The balance had to be restored, and the weaker side supported, but it was too late. In June the khan held a party to celebrate the circumcision of his young sons. He fell ill with carbuncles; the doctors' ministrations only hastened his death.

Istanbul reacted within two months: the Threshold of Felicity retrieved the former Khan Mehmed IV from forced retirement on Rhodes, and his namesake, the teenager Sultan Mehmed IV, dispatched him by boat from Istanbul to the Crimea, with an injunction to do even better than his brother Islam had done in serving 'straightforwardly and sincerely'. Khan Mehmed IV had to disembark, however, and travel by land when news reached the ship that gangs of Cossacks or Russians were descending the Dnepr by boat to intercept him. Arriving in Crimea, he had to quell a brawl between two sons of Khan Bahadır who had hoped to inherit the throne. Mehmed IV was no longer the polite, deferent khan he had been up to 1644. His inaugural greetings to the king of a now enfeebled Poland were lavish, but they reminded the king of his promises:

> If it ever falls to our lot that we conquer Astrakhan, Kazan, Terek, Tura, or any [other] Muslim provinces, or [any provinces] inhabited by Tatars or Noğays, neither you, our brother, nor any of the Polish lords shall interfere, as [these conquests] will belong to us; and each year you shall punctually send your ancient gift.

In July 1655 Charles X Gustavus of Sweden invaded Poland to snatch the crown from his cousin Jan Kazimierz. Khan Mehmed backed Poland: he besieged his former ally Khmelnycky, enabling Jan Kazimierz to hold on to Lwów; he taught the king's loyal troops to utter the Tatar war cry *hall* to intimidate the Swedish invaders. In this initial instalment ('The Swedish Deluge') of the First Northern War of 1655–60, Crimean Tatar auxiliaries defeated Charles Gustavus's ally, Friedrich Wilhelm I of Brandenburg, seized Prince Radziwiłł, and left an indelible impression – partly by relentlessly looting both enemy and allied territory. In 1657 Friedrich Wilhelm saw the folly of his alliance with Sweden and adopted a neutral, almost pro-Polish and pro-Tatar stance: in July 1656 he wrote from Vienna to Khan Mehmed IV:

To preserve our friendship and good relations, we shall definitely do what we promised . . . After establishing relations with his Majesty the Khan, who has a clear view of the future and whose name is known to the whole world, we see that he is a man of his word.

Now György Rákóczi of Transylvania joined the war, plotting a division of Poland whose crown he might snatch. An underhand attack by Khan Mehmed's forces took a great number of Hungarian prisoners. Rákóczi was reluctant to pay ransom: only after ten years' negotiations were the prisoners freed. Khan Mehmed IV pocketed a sum equal to his income from half a year's trade in slaves and prisoners.

The war expanded. Danes and Ottomans supported Jan Kazimierz. By 1657 a brilliant Ottoman chief vizier, Mehmed Köprülü (who in 1661 would be succeeded by his even greater son Fazıl Ahmed), was conducting affairs: he decided that only by helping the Poles and Crimean Tatars could Rákóczi be stopped from taking over Central Europe.

Crimean Tatar envoys were now received at the courts of Vienna and Copenhagen, where Khan Mehmed's diplomats urged the Danes to attack Muscovy as well as Sweden: 'Our friend the Polish King Jan Kazimierz is under attack from Moscow and Sweden and Transylvania.' The Crimeans also tried to persuade the Danes not to send ships into the Mediterranean to aid the Venetians in their war with Turkey. The Danes were defeated by the Swedes, and Catholic Europe was perturbed by that Protestant nation's success. The Poles secured, for a while, the reintegration of their Cossacks by making them a third component of the Polish-Lithuanian Commonwealth. For the Crimean Tatars, however, the end of the war was ominous. Russia could now resume its war on Poland.

The missives that Khan Mehmed IV now sent to the newly emboldened Russian tsar were not as craven or apologetic as they had been in his previous reign. This time he told the tsar that the Russian failure to restrain Cossack looting was unworthy of a tsar; he demanded that the murderers of a Crimean interpreter in Moscow be caught and punished. He also contrasted his tolerance of Christians with the tsar's persecution of Muslims. He reproached the tsar for ignoring previous promises to grant the Cossacks autonomy and, instead, subjecting them to Russian rule. He denounced Russian interference in Polish affairs. When Tsar Aleksei, newly crowned, listed his titles, Khan Mehmed responded with a 23-point remonstration: 'Are you putting yourself above your forebears?' As for the tsar's claim to rule the West and the East, Mehmed retorted, 'There are rather a lot of great rulers and states between the West and the East, aren't there?' He concluded, 'If you don't stop it and if you stick to your errors, you'll make the whole world your enemy.' To the Cossacks Mehmed wrote simply, 'Break with Moscow, then you'll be favoured by us.'

The Cossacks were by 1656 no longer well disposed to the khanate, which had to break a Cossack siege of the port of Azak. Nor did the Ottomans have any faith in Khmelnycky's protestations of alliance. In 1659 Khmelnycky died and was replaced by a new dissident *hetman*, Ivan Vyhovsky, who led a Cossack faction resentful of Moscow's usurpation of their rights. Now Khan Mehmed IV could once more unite with Cossack forces, this time planning an invasion of Russia designed to forestall Russia's attack on Ukrainian Cossacks. He showed his grudge against Russia in 1659 by imprisoning two shackled Russian envoys in a pit.

In early summer 1659 Moscow prepared for a campaign that aimed to destroy Bağçasaray. The Russians faced a larger force of Tatars, Cossacks and even a few thousand Poles. In June 1659, at the battle of Konotop, these unlikely allies crept up on the Russian army in pre-dawn darkness, slaughtering soldiers and rustling horses, and then, by pretending to retreat, destroying their pursuers, taking 5,000 prisoners and, according to a Cossack chronicle, disabling the Russian army for years to come. The khan authorized a mass slaughter of Russian prisoners, so horrific that as far away as Moscow the panicking authorities started building ramparts and digging trenches. A second battle routed the last Russian forces in October 1660.

However glorious the victory, this was the last major battle that the Crimean Khanate would stage abroad on its own behalf. The Crimean peninsula now had to be defended against Moscow's forthcoming revenge; Moscow held Tatar prisoners whose release had to be negotiated. The khanate's neighbours noted a shift in Tatar psychology: their desire to conquer was yielding to a desperate longing to be left in peace and to be treated respectfully as a sovereign nation. The seventeenth-century Russian historian Andrei Lyzlov noted with approval, 'The Tatars are now abandoning their many coarse habits, are becoming more human, and, without saying so, putting up with hard labour and poverty.'

In the Crimean Tatars' struggle to stop Russian expansion, diplomacy began to replace war. Khan Mehmed refused in 1663 to obey the vizier Fazıl Ahmed Köprülü's orders to join in person the Ottoman campaign in Hungary. Mehmed claimed that quelling internal unrest in the Crimea demanded his presence (bands of Mongol Kalmyks were, in fact, threatening Azak). In any case, Tatar troops disliked fighting in Hungary, where they would be expected to suffer the winter's cold and hunger, and where their prisoners (and any ransom money) might be appropriated by the Ottomans.

In 1664 Khan Mehmed IV Giray made himself hated: he sent two Circassians to skewer to death his talented vizier and chief diplomat Sefer-Ğazı Ağa, who had served his brother Khan Islam and himself so astutely, sometimes risking his own life. Mehmed confiscated all Sefer-Ğazı Ağa's property. The reason for this atrocious ingratitude was that Sefer-Ğazı, though liked by the Crimean people, had stirred up the wrath of the Mansur clan *bey*s. The unfortunate vizier's son, an equally capable diplomat and vizier, Islam-Ğazı Ağa, would survive into the reign of the next khan, but within a year he too fell victim to the Mansur clan. The Ottomans were already indignant at the khan's insubordination, his reluctance to fight in Central Europe, his attempts to restore diplomatic relations with Russia and his hostile treatment of his Noğay Tatar subjects. They deposed Mehmed in 1666. Khan Mehmed IV had little support from his nobility and he faced imprisonment, perhaps death, at the hands of the sultan. But, instead of making a penitent journey to Istanbul, the disgraced khan chose to retire to Dagestan where he had relatives. Possibly Mehmed was not just thinking how to survive: the khan was more and more interested in Sufism. The people gave him the title of *Sofu*, 'the Sufi'. In his old age he was admiringly observed by Evliya Çelebi, who clearly overlooked the khan's murder of his vizier Sefer-Ğazı Ağa:

> A radiant old man, dignified, pious, gentle, calm, avoids all things forbidden, shy and shunning empty desires, knowledgeable and always ready to help, welcoming the truth at all councils, inclined to be active in education, taking part in many conversations with the great and the just, witty . . . has travelled a lot by land and sea to see enquirers and sages of his time, known to talk to people one-to-one in his chamber about the *shari'at*, learned discussions in Arabic and Persian. Although a poet . . . he has been constantly keeping Allah in mind, all his deeds and strength are devoted to *jihad* in the name of Allah. I have never seen such a famous man, a leader doing good, a crown-wearing, moderate great Khan . . . All his life he has been making everybody, the servants, slaves around him, happy.

As his reign came to an end, Mehmed IV built mosques and a *tekiye* for Sufi dervishes. Under the name of Kâmil ('Irreproachable'), he wrote poetry of resignation:

Koşma [literally, a prayer-rug poem]

I have grasped the essence of the world and known its measure.
Praise God, I understand You in myself.
At the portal of knowledge I found out a secret.
Even as a gift, I wouldn't accept all the possessions of the Ottomans.
The All-Highest turns the wheels of fate.
Their secret motions are invisible to the eye,
As is the secret sense beyond human minds
Of the creator of the world from particles of mist.

Some of Mehmed IV's Sufic poems were set to music:

I pour out my grief and pain to You.
What has this involuntary groan turned me into?
I pour out yearning and affliction to You.
Save and preserve me, ravish me.

Kâmil said, 'I sought you and found you.
I desired You, the source of bliss and obtained You.
I fell to Your feet, I entered Your door.
I ask You, Lord, give me refuge.'

Exiling himself with just thirty servants to live among the Kumyk Tatars of Dagestan, Mehmed IV was allotted by the *Shamkhal*, the Kumyk leader, a small estate near the Caspian Sea at today's Makhachkala, and was allowed to rename it Bağçasaray. Once the richest of Crimean khans, Mehmed now distributed his wealth to his sons. Dressed as a pauper, an indigent 'Sofu', he was mocked by the public, who called out to him '*Miskin, neçine? Miskin, haldasin!*' ('How are you, wretch? The state you're in, wretch!'). In nine years of exile (he was now in his seventies) he became a silent recluse. A year after he died, one of his sons retrieved his body for burial in the family tomb outside the Grand Mosque in Bağçasaray.

The Crimean Khanate at the end of Mehmed IV Giray's second reign is comprehensively and sympathetically described by Evliya Çelebi in his *Siyasetname* (Book of Travels). Çelebi travelled the length and breadth of the khanate in 1666–7; a cousin of a grand vizier and favoured by Sultan Mehmed IV, Çelebi was befriended by the khan and given a sable coat and 100 gold ducats, as well as access to every part of and every influential figure in the khanate. Distances, Çelebi found, were here measured by the hours spent on horseback – one hour equal to 6.5 kilometres (4 mi.) in flat country, five in hilly terrain. Çelebi began his tour with the Or fortress on the isthmus, which Mehmed IV had renovated and extended to a long defensive line protected by artillery and a deep moat. The treeless steppe had few houses and little fresh water and, because the hovels were heated by dried dung, everyone 'smelt of cow manure'. Çelebi was impressed by the strong millet beer, so viscous that it could be carried in a cloth bag, and by a village of bow-makers who lived in stone houses. Crossing a four-span bridge, Çelebi arrived at the port of Gözleve (briefly Ğazı II Giray's capital), able to harbour 1,000 ships, a fine city with many shops, one Armenian and two gypsy quarters, beer houses and brothels, medreses and Sufi houses, bathhouses and hotels for merchants, and six inns for single male foreigners manufacturing hats and shoes. Only the Tatar habit of simultaneously drinking and urinating disturbed Çelebi. The city, like the rest of the khanate, had no doctors or hospitals,[1] but wounded soldiers were attended by a team of Hungarian surgeons.

Passing the ruins of ancient Chersonesus (now Salmia), Çelebi reached the hilltop fort of Mangup, once the capital of the Gothic–Greek principality of Theodoro: there was only a mosque and a well left intact, but below the ruined castle were Jewish Karaim villages, where fair-skinned, blue-eyed children betrayed their Gothic origins (Çelebi thought they were Jewish). Çelebi was disappointed that the Karaim knew no Hebrew, and shocked when he heard a local couplet that showed how the children were exploited by predatory paedophiles:

Against all religion, I stuck it up a little Jewish rascal,
Satan gave his approval by singing his praises.[2]

Çelebi then turned inland towards Bağçasaray. He noted that the 1,500 Jews in the stone houses of nearby Çufut Qale, their mountain-top settlement, shunned firearms and could defend themselves only by throwing down rocks. He then inspected Qırq-Yer's 'hellish' prison, where the khan's enemies stayed until they died. After this, Bağçasaray, the River Aşlama, the old capital of Salacıq, with their orchards, parks, palaces and parliamentary assembly halls, seemed like paradise. Women, Çelebi noted, were seen on the streets only if on their way to and from bathhouses (restricted to Muslims, for Christians had a separate washing area). Slaves were recognizable by their earrings, Jews by a patch of yellow silk on their garments, Greeks and Armenians by blue or purple patches on their headgear.

From Bağçasaray Çelebi travelled to Aqmescit (today's Simferopol, then the *qalğa*'s capital), and eastwards to Qarasuvbazar, famous for its slave market, controlled by deceitful Ottomans from Kayseri in Anatolia, who specialized in taking middle-aged Cossacks to the baths, shaving them, massaging their skin with ointments and auctioning them off as youths; likewise, the Kayseri slave traders took mature female captives and, after elaborate treatment with quince seed oil, sold them as young virgins.[3] On the other hand, Çelebi was impressed by the hospitality offered to strangers: a sheep would be slaughtered, rendered into kebabs and, if no firewood was available, the host would break a wheel off his only cart and use the spokes to grill the kebabs for his guest. The tour ended in Kerç, where Khan Mehmed IV's replacement Adil Giray, of dubious legitimacy, was arriving from Istanbul.

One of Çelebi's most interesting enquiries is into language. He notes that Noğay Tatar was so different from Crimean Tatar that Noğays had trouble making themselves understood. Çelebi collected Tatar vocabulary: Russian words (largely connected with the slave trade) were already penetrating, so that 'girl' was *devke* and 'woman' *mariya*. (The Noğays had begun to call captured Russian boys *Ivan* and girls *Natasha*.)

Fazıl Ahmed Paşa Köprülü, vizier to Sultan Mehmed IV, had decided to replace Khan Mehmed IV with the candidate most unlike him, most repulsive to the Crimean Khanate's people, aristocrats and commoners, and the least qualified (but, the vizier hoped, most easily manipulated). Adil (the name means 'just') Giray was fifty years old and had lived in Yambol, near Edirne, ever since he was a child. He was recommended by Islam-Ğazı Ağa, son of the murdered Crimean vizier Sefer-Ğazı Ağa: Islam rashly presumed that Adil was unlikely to pursue Mehmed IV Khan's vendetta against the Sefer-Ğazı family. He had been lobbying for the dethroning of Mehmed IV Khan, and the enthronement of Adil was a way of avenging his father's death. There were no objections in Istanbul, where the saying was, 'Any small fry can turn the mill wheel of state.' The main objection to Adil was that he was the first (and last) khan who was not a completely legitimate Giray. His father Mustafa was allegedly born to a Maria Potocka, a Polish prisoner and concubine of Khan Fetih Giray, who sent Maria back to Poland when she refused to convert to Islam. Maria was escorted by a Hacı Ahmed. At the time, Maria was pregnant. Despite an order from Khan Fetih that she and her alleged lover should be killed, Maria escaped, only to die in

Khan Adil Giray, c. 1670, engraving.

childbirth. She gave birth too soon for the child to be anyone's except Fetih Giray's, yet the latter was so furious at the news of the birth of a son by his infidel concubine that he kicked the valet who informed him in the face. The orphaned son Mustafa, thanks to Hacı Ahmed's intervention, grew up as a shepherd boy, but was singled out by Khan Mehmed III, who made him *nureddin* and allowed him to take the name Devlet Giray. Mustafa (who died fighting Ottoman authorities in Kaffa) had two sons by a former servant girl. The sons were legitimate, but widely despised as half-commoners and illegitimate Çoban ('shepherd') Girays (Adil was nicknamed *Çulboldı* 'wearing horsecloth' and his brother Fetih *Qulboldı* 'become a slave'). Khan Mehmed IV is said to have asked the sultan to exterminate the entire Çoban

Giray clan, a request that was ignored. Instead, the Çoban Girays were sent to Rhodes, the holding pen for past and future Crimean khans, a sign that they were regarded by the Ottomans as eligible future khans. (In fact, the details of their origin are dubious: the Potockis were a distinguished Polish family who would have ransomed any enslaved daughter, and no Maria was ever reported missing, captive or dead.)

In March 1666 Adil was sent to the Crimea with an escort, whether for protection or prestige, of 25 galleys. (At the same time, the sultan confiscated from Adil some Crimean territory on the Dnestr, in order to accommodate Noğays displaced by Cossacks.) In Adil Giray's favour, it is notable that, for the first time in history, the Crimean Khanate enjoyed (or, in its warriors' view, endured) five years of peace.

According to Evliya Çelebi, who was present when Mehmed IV left Crimea for Dagestan and Adil was installed in his place, there was an uproar, verging on rebellion, when Adil organized a census of the population and imposed heavy taxes, ostensibly to finance future campaigns, on the owners of slaves and of prisoners of war, including, for the first time, taxation on women and girls. (There were, Çelebi estimates with his customary exaggeration, some 400,000 male slaves and prisoners, and 100,000 female slaves.) At Bağçasaray the disaffected and disrespectful Şirins assembled, wearing armour, and refusing to dismount, forcing Adil to exempt the clan from the new taxes. Adil's oppressive actions, it was believed, were inspired by his vizier Islam-Ğazı Ağa, who wanted revenge on the Şirins for the murder of his father.

Peace reigned in Crimea and elsewhere for some six years after Poland and Russia signed the truce of Andrusovo in 1667. Adil favoured the Poles, and signed agreements for the repatriation of prisoners and the suppression of anti-Polish Cossacks. In the mid-1660s Adil's envoy to Warsaw, Dedeş Ağa, was an unusually urbane and obliging diplomat, even though his visits and gifts cost the Polish exchequer ruinous sums: Dedeş Ağa was accompanied by his family and was magnificently portrayed by the court painter Daniel Schultz, looking very European, without a Tatar's customary hat, in the Polish *szlachticz* style, with a dog, a monkey and his elder son kitted up as a falconer.

Adil was reluctant, despite the Ottomans' insistence, to support the renegade Zaporozhian Cossacks of *hetman* Piotr Doroshenko, who had accepted the Ottomans' religion as well as their military command. Adil cultivated an alternative *hetman*, the Zaporozhian secretary Piotr Sukhovei, and thus won for the khanate a small army of 6,000 dissident Cossacks.

This irritated the sultan so deeply that Adil was deposed in 1671. Adil had early in his reign murdered his chief supporter Islam-Ğazı Ağa, simply in order to quell panic among the *qaraçı* (the clansmen eligible for ministerial rank), who were already complaining of exorbitant taxation and confiscations. They also suspected that Adil, this 'bastard's spawn', planned to cull their number. Adil refused to reimburse taxes paid by the *qaraçı*: this was another pretext for deposing him. He was sent to Rumelia, and in 1673 he died, not necessarily of natural causes.

During his short rule Adil sought new allies, writing to the emperor of Austria, even sending an embassy to the king of Denmark. With Islam-Ğazı Ağa's help, Adil had written to Tsar Aleksei, as he had to the king of Poland, in the most deferential terms, even using the tsar's arrogant title of 'Lord of the West and the East', and deploring unnecessary bloodshed. He denounced the depredations of the Cossacks whom Tsar Aleksei was now subjugating, and he did not protest at the forcible conversion of Russian Muslims. In 1670 Adil sent a peace mission to Moscow, taking on the impossible role of being a friend to both Warsaw and Moscow. The Russian text of the agreement with the khan ran: 'And you, our brother Your Majesty Adil Giray, are to be with both of us great rulers in mutual neighbourly friendship, as with our third friend and closest neighbour.' Adil's avoidance of conflict led him to ignore the sultan's orders to make war on Poland in alliance with Doroshenko's Cossacks. The more he frustrated the sultan, the more he pleased the tsar. Russian historians praise Adil; Crimean historians denounce him. Seyyid Muhammed Riza wondered if he was mad, or merely stupid. The Crimean historian Halim Giray, fifty years later, damned him:

> Adil Giray was an ignorant man who knew nothing about how to rule. He was a naïve fool, with vile habits, indifferent to human dignity. None of his offspring was appointed to any high post in Crimea: all they got was the addition of 'Giray' to their names. Just a few of them had the honour of marrying a Khan's daughter.

In the Danish archives there is a description of life at Adil Giray's court from March 1669.[4] Written in German, it seems to derive from an interrogation of Adil's envoy (a *çapqun*, a roving ambassador, or army reconnaissance commander) to Denmark, Mustafa Ağa. The information was recorded by an anonymous speaker of Turkish who confused names of persons and places and who may have distorted some of what he was told.

We learn that Adil had four wives, the senior being Aişa Qadın, by whom he had two sons and a daughter. He had a choice of fifteen concubines, sent annually to the khanate from Circassia. Each time he went to bed, he selected one by throwing a silk cloth over her: she was then brought to him by a negro eunuch. The khan's and *qalğa*'s and *nureddin*'s total of twelve harem eunuchs were so fully castrated that they had to urinate through silver cannulas: because their operation had a very high death rate, they were expensive slaves, bought from Istanbul at 1,000 thaler each. The Circassian concubines, usually after one night, were given a dowry and married off to a minor nobleman.

Served by Circassian maidens in the harem, Adil Giray took his morning coffee, especially brewed by an apothecary. Then he gave his orders of the day to a meeting with *beys* and his military. Dinner, served by Russian slave girls, came on fifty silver platters, arranged in a tall pyramid. The khan sat alone on his throne, communicating with the serving maids through his eunuchs. Dinner was followed by prayers, attended by Abaza Circassian maidens standing 18 metres (59 ft) away from the khan: none of them were concubines.

According to this account, the khan's *beys* could mobilize 10,000 fully armed men in twelve hours and provide an even bigger force when Adil went hunting. His palace in Bağçasaray was closely guarded by 32 men, of whom eight were deaf mutes. His carriage was upholstered in red satin and pulled by eight white horses with manes dyed red.

Typically, after the inauspicious choice of Adil as Crimean khan, the Ottoman viziers swung to the other extreme and in May 1671 chose the forty-year-old Selim, loved and lauded by those Girays who had been persecuted by Adil and who were living in Yambol. The historian Seyyid Muhammed Riza singles out Selim I Giray, using red ink in his manuscript, as the sixth of his 'planets' determining the course of the khanate's history All Selim's contemporaries affirm that he was as legitimate, militant, thoughtful, highly educated, thrifty, unambitious and (apparently) as loyal to the Ottomans as the 'shepherd Giray' Adil had been illegitimate, pacifist, impulsive, ignorant, profligate, power-hungry and flagrantly insubordinate. Selim was the son of the heroic Khan Bahadır. His father died when he was only ten years old and he was raised by a foster-father in Circassia. When he came of age, he was attacked by a rival Circassian clan's small army, apparently on behalf of rival Girays. Selim was saved only by the patronage of the Şirin *beys* and by his uncle Khan Islam III Giray, before he fled to the Giray estates at Yambol.

After returning to Crimea, Selim went straight to Circassia to quash a tribal feud. Within a year of his inauguration Selim had to join the sultan, together with the renegade Cossack Doroshenko, in a campaign against the Poles, to force them to observe the conditions of the Treaty of Buczacz of October 1672. Selim, however, took care not to antagonize his Polish contacts any more than he had to. At the end of 1671, in his camp outside Bağçasaray, when he had received in secret a Polish envoy, Stanisław Karwowski, Selim told him:

> I must keep our meeting secret from the [Ottoman] *kapıcı başı* ['head gatekeeper']. After all, the Turks have already branded you Poles as an enemy ... I regret the loss of your friendship, because the former king showed me a lot of kindness. I know all your dignitaries very well, especially the Marshal [Jan Sobieski] with whom I spent so much time during the war in Ukraine. But what can I do? It is not my will, but the will of my Lord, the Caesar [sultan], by whose grace I ascended this throne of mine. And I will tell you something in secret, but do not repeat it. If I saw that you were as strong as before, I would support you and I would say [to the sultan]: 'Hold on [my] Caesar, the Poles are not guilty, they are our friends who stand by us whether in good or in bad times.' The whole of Crimea could repeat these words, because many of their rights, too, are violated by the Porte. But when I see you so impoverished, weak and friendless, what can I do? I would ruin myself, and yet I could not save you.

As the campaign began in 1672, Selim was awarded 15,000 gold thaler as 'road money'. The combined Ottoman and Crimean forces assembled outside the Polish fortress of Kamenets-Podolsky. Selim was seated in the place of honour at the right hand of the chief vizier; he and the Tatar nobles were greeted with a deafening salvo of cannon and muskets. A banquet was held in a series of marquees, the Tatar nobles grouped by rank: for Selim's 1,000 *qapıqulu* bodyguards 500 bowls of food and 150 carcases of sheep and cows, half boiled, were set outside the tents. The Ottoman caterers looked aghast as the Tatar soldiers devoured the bowls of food with their hands and then clambered like hyenas over the carcases, tearing at the meat until only bones were left. After the campaign, in 1674, an acceptable truce was agreed, and Selim was given further rewards.

Two years later the talented and principled Ottoman vizier Fazıl Ahmed Köprülü died (he was in his early forties, but a heavy drinker):

without Köprülü's consent, Selim would never have been enthroned. After his death the sultan's bureaucratic apparatus became treacherous and corrupt. Köprülü's successor Kara Mustafa would systematically undermine Selim's work as commander-in-chief of the Ottoman forces and slander the khan at the sultan's court. The punitive operation against Poland took a more serious turn, eventually fatal for the Crimean Khanate, when the Cossack *hetman* Doroshenko suddenly declared fealty to Russia and the tsar, and handed them the Cossack capital of Chyhyryn. A combined army of Selim's Tatars and the Ottoman general 'Satan' Ibrahim failed to capture Chyhyryn.

Effectively, the first Russo-Turkish war had begun. For Russia the Crimean Khanate was now an enemy combatant. Selim recognized that the Ottoman armies could not match Russian and Cossack forces: he advised Ibrahim Paşa to save their artillery and men from capture and withdraw, in the hope of returning with fresh forces. Inevitably, in 1678 both Selim and Ibrahim were dismissed. Selim resigned himself to dethronement (he had earlier asked to be relieved of his khanate because of illness). After a journey to Kaffa, he accepted compulsory exile in Rhodes with his harem, family and servants. 'Satan' Ibrahim, at first sure that he was to be executed, was relieved just to be imprisoned in Yedi Küle, the 'Seven Towers Fortress' on the southern city walls of Istanbul, which was usually reserved for dethroned princes and honoured prisoners of war.

Selim was replaced by his cousin Khan Murad Giray, whom the sultan felt capable of retaking Chyhyryn, where the Russian army fired stakes at the Tatar and Ottoman cavalry. Vizier and khan both despaired, but by the end of 1678 they had taken the ruined town. The war continued until a peace treaty was concluded at Bağçasaray in January 1681. The capture of Chyhyryn was celebrated in Istanbul for a week, but both sides were exhausted. Khan Murad became not so much an ally as an intermediary and concluded a truce with Russia: supposed to last twenty years, it established the Dnepr river as the boundary between Ottoman and Muscovite territory, giving Russia full control over the Zaporozhian Cossacks and the city of Kiev.

Despite the deplorable state of the Crimean army, the sultan insisted that Khan Murad bring his forces to the Balkans to help besiege Belgrade. Murad, very aware of the futility of this siege, especially after the Turks had been defeated by an Austrian–Polish army outside Vienna, resisted and argued with the sultan's vizier Kara Mustafa. The Turks nevertheless conducted a desultory war. The 1680s were a turning point in the Ottomans' wars of conquest: on the approach to Vienna, their armies found themselves outgunned and demoralized. The Crimean Tatar forces left a mixed impression on Austrian civilians. We have reports, some direct, some collected, from a priest, Balthasar Kleinschrot, and a lawyer, Kristian Lünig. The Tatar horses amazed them: thin, unsightly, unshod, with minimal tack, yet capable of galloping all day and going without fodder for four days at a time.[5] One not untypical civilian got on with the Tatars, saying, 'They're well brought up, like Hungarians, and their entire being is that of a Christian, they drank wine and ate any sort of meat. I spent all day with them and slept under the stars.' Others contrasted them unfavourably with the Turks: 'They gave no sign of respect for God or decency.' One Austrian was forcibly shaved and dressed as a Tatar. Some Tatars bathed naked in the river and then chased after the village girls who spotted them. There was worse:

> Their behaviour to females was something no Christian or decent listener can bear to hear about. They don't spare the weak, the under-age, the pregnant, the sick, the half-dead or even the dead from their bestial desires, so that the poor victims are overjoyed if they are afterwards sold to the Turks.[6]

Kara Mustafa wrote letters to Istanbul, blaming the Ottomans' failure on Murad. When the Crimean army heard that Murad was out of favour with the sultan and his vizier, the clans declared that they would not accept any replacement khan, that they had no complaints about Murad. Indeed, Murad was a talented general and in the Crimea proved himself an astute diplomat and ruler.

Living in the khanate was still easy, and produce, whether bread or fur coats, was cheaper than ever. In 1680 and 1681 Murad handled the Russian envoys so astutely that they paid the khanate its usual annual tribute and even the arrears, and agreed a twenty-year non-aggression pact on condition that neither side would allow Cossack incursions. The relationship was damaged in autumn 1682, however, when two Russian envoys, Nikita Tarakanov and Piotr Burtsov, brought gifts less valuable than anticipated. A Russian *voevoda* (a military general with a governor-general's powers), arranging an exchange of prisoners, witnessed the envoys' punishment: they were flogged on the *nureddin*'s orders; Burtsov was then publicly tortured and almost killed, strapped to a 'wooden mare' with a sharp spine, while heavy rocks were tied to his legs. Fearing even worse torture back in Muscovy if they agreed to increase tribute to the khanate, the two men held out (they were released a year later). Other Russian envoys, Tiapkin and

Army camp in the form of a double wagon complex (cannon-equipped
battle wagons as the outer ring and transport wagons inside), from the
Medieval Housebook of Wolfegg Castle, c. 1486.

Ottoman victory at Haçova, 26 October 1596.

Sultan Bayezid II (on throne), Khan Mengli I Giray (seated), his son
Mehmed, the future khan (standing), c. 1510.

Devlet I Giray (bowing) and Sultan Süleyman I (on throne), 1551.

Defeat of *qalğa* Islam Giray by
Muscovites on the Oka river, 1527.

Devlet I Giray (top right) and Tsar
Ivan IV (bottom left), 1568.

General Ahmed Giray, *nureddin* and eldest son of Khan Islam III, mid-17th century.

Sefer-Ğazı Ağa, chief vizier to khans Islam III and Mehmed IV, mid-17th century.

Daniel Schultz II, *Dedeş Ağa, a Crimean Envoy to Poland, along with His Retinue,* 1664, oil on canvas.

Carlo Bossoli, *View of the Khan's Palace of Bağçasaray on the Crimean Peninsula,* 1857, mixed media on paper.

Tatar children's school, colour lithograph by Carlo Bossoli, 1856.

Tatars travelling on the plains, colour lithograph by Carlo Bossoli, 1856.

Balaklava seen from the shore, colour lithograph by Carlo Bossoli, 1856.

Ruins of a Genoese fortress at Sudaq, colour lithograph by Carlo Bossoli, 1856.

Zotov, found this hard to believe: they reported that the fearsome red-haired *nureddin* Sa'adet Giray was 'kindly-looking, one-eyed, reasonable and nice to talk to'. Nevertheless, the Muscovy regent Sofia announced that henceforth no more envoys would visit Crimea, that she would deal with the Ottomans through their governors at Bendery, not via the khanate, and that exchanges of gifts with the Crimean Tatars would take place only at the border crossing. Meanwhile Murad became more pro-Cossack and pro-Polish as Russia tightened its hold on the Ukraine.

Murad's mood, like the reputed temperament of many Crimean Tatars, could switch at the drop of a hat from geniality to vicious fury. He was plausibly said to indulge in wild drinking binges with the common people, which made him only more popular, though not with Ottoman officials or Islamic clerics who remonstrated with him. Despite the prosperity of the 1680s, there was at the time, to judge by court records, a striking increase in severe personal violence in the khanate. In Khan Murad's five-year reign the *qadiasker's* court dealt with over 160 cases of murder and grievous bodily harm, and local courts must have dealt with many more. Typically, alcohol and a quarrel over a horse would lead to homicide.

Murad Khan alarmed Turkish viziers by his attempt to reintroduce some old Genghisid *töre* laws to supersede Islamic *shariat* (the *töre* code largely regulated succession and family: no compilation of it is extant). For example, *töre* forbade washing in running water or cutting an animal's throat, whereas Islam insisted on both; *töre* recommended marriage to a brother's widow, whereas Islam forbade it. *Töre* also prescribed that leading *beys* should be consulted on the accession of a new khan. Above all, as the Tatar historian Muhammad Giray insisted, the *töre* prescribed that succession or promotion to a higher status should depend entirely on seniority, even if there was just an hour's difference in birth time between two twins – a rule which Tatar aspirants and the khanate's populace often ignored, and which perplexed Ottoman sultans who sometimes wished to promote an energetic young princeling over the heads of his idle elder brothers. Murad also tolerated *shi'a* practices such as pilgrimages to the tombs of saints.

The real reason why the sultan decided to be rid of Murad, however, was his diplomatic correspondence, in which he recited in full his titles as ruler of the Golden Horde and its successor states: he assured the Russian envoys Tiapkin and Zotov that he was his own master and had no need of Ottoman ratification. There were also financial reasons for the sultan to intervene: the Ottoman treasury needed more income, and had begun to reassess the Crimea's taxable resources. Murad had no illusions about the durability of his popularity: once his funds began to dry up and his army realized they were destined to fight on the freezing plains of Hungary, enthusiasm for his leadership evaporated. He predicted, 'You Crimeans have never yet been known for keeping your oaths and agreements: you'd do best to leave me to my fate.'

In autumn 1683 the sultan dethroned Murad, who spent the next thirteen years on his Turkish estate, dying at the age of 69 in 1696. In his stead, the sultan appointed Khan Hacı II Giray, who had earned respect by saving the Ottoman standards from falling into enemy hands at Pécs. On his way back to Crimea as khan, Hacı triumphantly drove a Polish army out of Bucak. But Khan Hacı II Giray refused to fight for the Turkish sultan in Hungary. He merely sent his *nureddin* with a small force. Khan Hacı II was disliked in Crimea for what his opponents called his miserliness and mocked for his short stature (he was nicknamed *üzengisi uzun*, 'his stirrups are too long'). Those who pined for Khan Selim's benign rule, particularly the Şirin clan, hated Hacı II as Selim's long-standing antagonist. He was even suspected of plotting with the Ottoman vizier Kara Mustafa to exterminate malcontent Crimean aristocrats. Khan Hacı II's careful husbandry of Crimean finances meant that he sold government posts, withdrew the khan's discretionary pensions and salaries, taxed his well-paid judges and revoked his officials' traditional share of Russian tribute. The *beys* finally dared to ask the sultan summarily to depose Hacı II. Selim, although a semi-prisoner in Rhodes, may have manipulated Hacı's fall, and he was well placed to do so, as two of his sons, Devlet and Azamat, were *qalğa* and *nureddin* to Hacı II.

Once the *beys* knew that the sultan was about to restore Selim to the khanate they confronted Khan Hacı and told him that they would make war on him if he did not go. A mob was incited to loot the khan's palace and treasury, even his harem; Hacı's *qalğa* refused to intervene. Hacı had to flee with a dozen followers to Mangup castle. The Bosnian Rejeb Ağa, master of the sultan's horses, was then ordered to escort Khan Selim first to be invested at Edirne, and then to Crimea. Hacı II sailed to Istanbul, and thence to Rhodes, where he died five years later, at the age of 41, after a mere nine months in power.

There was turbulence in Crimea, famine in the Ottoman Balkan provinces, fury in Istanbul over Sultan Mehmed IV's obsession with hunting, over the *Sheikh-al-Islam*'s failure to speak truth to power, and the prospect of a new war with a much mightier Russia, allied to a hostile Austria. The Ottomans were greatly relieved to have Selim back, not just as a vassal, but as a wise and experienced ally, adviser and leader, almost on a par with the sultan. The crisis was so desperate that an assembly of Turkish military and religious leaders in Aya Sofia discussed overthrowing Sultan Mehmed IV in favour of a ruler who would take his duties more seriously. In 1687 Mehmed IV was replaced (but allowed to continue hunting around Edirne until his natural death in 1693) by his younger half-brother Süleyman II. After 36 years under house arrest in Topkapı, Sultan Süleyman II enjoyed a very short reign, but managed to reconquer Belgrade. The appointment of another Köprülü as vizier led to the Ottomans reversing several other defeats in the Balkans.

In his second reign as khan, however, Selim had to face, unaided, deep distrust from Poland and much more aggression from Russia, where the boy-tsar Peter was becoming an innovative and determined conquistador. Both Poland and Russia were contemplating drastic solutions to the Crimean Tatar problem.

The first serious Russian attempt to invade the Crimean Khanate was undertaken by the regent Sofia's minister and lover, Prince Vasili Golitsyn, in spring 1687. A total absence of planning by the Russian army, and the desultory progress of their Polish allies along the banks of the Dnepr, led to farcical failure. The armies, totalling 100,000 men, found no water or fodder for themselves or their horses. Half the army perished from hunger, thirst and disease as they advanced, before they stopped halfway and turned back at a point 200 kilometres (124 mi.) from Or Qapı, where the Tatar forces had dug themselves in. Russia had felt safe going to war with the Crimean Tatars, given that it had in 1686 signed a treaty of eternal peace with Poland, allowing it to 'protect' Poland by attacking the Crimean Khanate. The regent Sofia was eager for Golitsyn to make a name for himself. But Golitsyn's invasion force was typically Russian in its ignorance, incompetence and complacency. According to Russian accounts, Tatar attacks were the least of the army's problems. According to Crimean historians, however, the outnumbered Crimean Tatars mounted a three-pronged attack and in two days took thirty cannons and 1,000 prisoners. Golitsyn apparently tried to build a fort, but had to abandon the project and flee. His generals feared they would die of thirst before they reached Muscovy again. Selim tried to cut off the Russians' retreat. Under the pretext of negotiating a truce, many Russian soldiers escaped, although others were intercepted by Selim's advance from Bessarabia. There were more negotiations and Golitsyn reduced his demands from surrender of Crimea to a mere suspension of Russia's annual tribute. Even this was refused (after 1686, however, Russia sent no more money, furs or falcons). On his return, Golitsyn's fiasco was covered up by regent Sofia's public acclaim of his 'heroism'.

In the winter of 1688–9 Golitsyn tried again, establishing a base near to the Crimea, where the Samara river joins the Dnepr. The Russian emissary, Prokofi Voznitsyn, now ambassador to Constantinople, had negotiated with Austrian help the Russo-Polish treaty of Andrusovo. He was now urging both Poles and Austrians to support Golitsyn's attack on the Crimean Khanate. He could at best persuade Cossacks, Poles and Austrians to act as friendly neutrals, rather than allies. The boy-tsars Ivan and Peter sent a letter to Constantinople, urging Voznitsyn, 'Let's put all the Tatars, like chickens, into a sack, and eat them, so that their name be no longer heard in the world';[7] while a Russian adviser wanted to deport the entire Crimean Tatar population to Anatolia. Poles and Austrians were in two minds, however, and recommended watered-down alternatives to extermination: 'the deportation of all "enemies of the Holy Cross" from the Crimea' and, if this proved impossible, an undertaking by the Ottomans to stop the Crimean Tatars raiding their neighbours. By June 1689 Golitsyn realized he had failed once more. He limited his demands on the khanate to a renunciation of tribute from Moscow and of raids on Russian and Polish territory. The khan's vizier Batır Ağa declared victory. Golitsyn's defeat persuaded Russia's generals to engineer the fall of the regent Sofia and to enthrone a far more dangerous ruler, Tsar Peter (for a few years together with his epileptic half-brother Ivan).

Public opinion in Istanbul was alarmed, aware that the Crimea was but a stepping stone in the Russian plan to conquer Constantinople itself. Reluctantly the Ottomans conceded that Khan Selim need not release his army, despite its now enormous size, to join the sultan's campaign in Hungary: he had to protect his homeland. Some reproached Selim for deserting the sultan, his superior, in favour of his own fief, but Selim vigorously defended himself, saying he was a brother to the sultan and to the Ottomans, but that it was imperative for him to stand his own ground and stop Russia taking all Muslim territory north of the Black Sea.

Cossacks and some Russian diplomats could not see the point of Russia's invasion of the steppes: the *hetman* Samoilovich pointed out, 'There's nothing worth possessing until you reach the Danube, and crossing it is a step too far.' Furthermore, the Crimean Khanate might be a useful ally to Russia, should Poland decide to reconquer Ukraine.

The consequences of Golitsyn's invasion were discussions among the Cossacks, uncertain whether to support Russia, or to act as peacemakers and revive the 1681 peace treaty of Bağçasaray. Moscow quashed that intervention.

In 1689 Sultan Süleyman II invited Selim to Istanbul. Despite fears that this might herald his removal from power, Selim made the journey. He was treated as a saviour and was asked to speak, rather than listen, at Ottoman state councils. Khan Selim spared nobody, telling the sultan that without major reforms there was no point asking for a Crimean khan's help. Selim then went home to face a second invasion by Golitsyn, whose forces had supposedly been enlarged to 300,000 men. With help from the Giray in charge of Azak, Selim's army repelled this invasion, too. Lack of water and food forced Golitsyn to flee yet again, this time leaving behind more Russian prisoners than Crimea could accommodate. On the plain of Keniş-Oba the Tatar army then conferred: they agreed to inform the Ottoman sultan of their brilliant victory by a state visit, taking with them eight prominent Muscovite prisoners. This rash decision implied, also, a willingness to throw Crimean Tatar forces into the Ottoman war in Bosnia against the Austrians. Selim then moved against an Austrian army threatening Bessarabia. His victory was so alarming that Austria joined Russia in a plan to eliminate the Crimean Tatars. In the winter of 1689 Selim's forces were the key to the capture of Skopje (then Üsküb). In the battle the Turks and Tatars captured the commander of a Hungarian *hajduk* (Balkan guerrilla) band, who claimed aristocratic rank: his self-appointed ducal title, *Herzog*, was unfortunately overlooked, as it was transcribed into Turkish as *her sik* ('any prick'), and he was summarily executed at the stake in Skopje.

In his success Selim was the author of the khanate's eventual doom. Selim's reputation made the Turks determined to use Crimean cavalry to conquer Transylvania in the exceptionally cold winter of 1691. The Crimeans camped outside Belgrade in sub-zero temperatures with no fodder or provisions, except for some maize flour and cartloads of stale rusks left over from earlier campaigns. The Ottoman commander Halil Paşa had pocketed the funds for feeding the Tatar soldiers, saying, 'These people can eat whatever they find.' The Tatars had to eat their own horses and fight as infantry; some fell ill and even died after eating the old rusks. They began to mutiny against the Turks. The historian Fındıklılı records a furious deputation of Şirin and Noğay *beys* who harangued the *qalğa* (Selim was then in Istanbul, 'licking the Sultan's dishes'), and accused the khan and his family of deliberately trying to exterminate them by starvation and cold. They demanded that Selim abdicate. In vain, Selim pleaded that he was bound to obey the sultan; the *beys* then announced that they would withdraw their men from the army. Selim had to choose between disloyalty to the sultan or letting his soldiers starve and thus leaving the Crimea vulnerable to a new Russian attack. Worse, his son Azamat, acclaimed as a hero for driving the Austrians out of Bucharest, was killed in battle. Selim was devastated by personal and political disaster: he abdicated, and sought consolation in religion.

Unable to persuade Selim to stay, the sultan suggested replacing the khan with his oldest surviving son, the *qalğa* Devlet. Selim argued that Devlet was too young. Instead, he recommended his cousin, the elderly Sa'adet Giray, who had been Khan Murad's *nureddin*. While Sa'adet made his way overland to Crimea, Selim undertook the *hajj*. He had long been a Sufi and a *hafiz* (someone who memorizes the entire Qur'an), and he was fluent in Arabic and Persian. Before leaving Arabia for home, Selim settled a conflict between Syrian pilgrims and the authorities at Mecca, thus earning the gratitude of Sultan Ahmed II, who took the throne when Süleyman II fell into a coma and died.

Khan Sa'adet III Giray was disastrously stubborn and severe. His nephew, the historian Mehmed Giray, described him as 'a one-eyed, red-bearded man of fiery temperament, martial appearance, never approving any opinion except his own, proud and merciless'. Yet he was apparently loved by people for his military prowess, even though he may never have visited Crimea itself during his short reign. Despite his prowess, Khan Sa'adet III found it hard to assemble an army of disillusioned Noğay Tatars on the Danube to continue the war in Transylvania. They arrived late (possibly because Sa'adet's officers had been bribed by the Wallachian *voevoda* Konstantin) and therefore could not save the Ottoman army from defeat. Sa'adet's sacking of his popular *qalğa* Devlet (Selim's son), and his vicious punitive mutilation of soldiers who looted Wallachia as they passed through, made him odious to his men. When the Crimean forces finally arrived, they rebelled and began to desert. Before the year was out, the Crimean Tatar grandees denounced Sa'adet to the Ottomans. Sa'adet was deposed and incarcerated for the remaining fourteen years of his life. He was replaced by another cousin, Safa Giray, who had given the vizier Ali Paşa Arabacı (the 'wagoner') an enormous bribe to be recommended as khan. After the grand vizier Köprülü had been killed in battle, he was succeeded by this corrupt and cunning 'wagoner' (so-called because he once insulted an important official by providing only a humble wagon as transport).

Safa had been named after his father, who died forty days before his birth, and who had become infamous as *nureddin* for torturing Tsar

Mikhail's emissaries. Khan Safa was a chip off the old block: he quickly lost all authority as khan by using his post to enrich himself by trade and extortion. His own nephew, the historian Mehmed Giray, called him 'greedy, covetous, foul . . . Several times he started trading: either soap from Trabzon, or buying and selling fish . . . On arrival in Bağçasaray he straight away had a drinking orgy.' The Crimean *beys* refused to campaign in the Balkans under the leadership of a 'bribe-taker and oppressor'. Even the Turks declared Safa unfit to lead an army: he was recalled to Rhodes, as was his guarantor the 'wagoner' vizier (with the sultan's words, 'Clear off to Rhodes, enjoy the company of your favourite Khan!' ringing in his ears). In Rhodes Safa went on trading until he died in 1703.

In 1692 it took considerable persuasion to make Sultan Ahmed see that Safa would be unable to gather any loyal soldiers. The sultan had to use great tact to tear Selim, now in his sixties and ailing, away from his religious preoccupations and return him to the khanate. Selim was assigned a permanent doctor. In the Crimea he found a new and probably unwanted ally. In May 1692 Piotr Ivanenko, an egalitarian relative of the great Cossack leader Kochubei, arrived in Crimea, representing Cossacks who were indignant at the paltry subsidy Moscow had given all Cossacks (just 500 gold roubles and a score of sable skins for the entire nation) in exchange for all the forced labour, fodder and wood that Russia demanded. Ivanenko's argument was that the Cossacks and Crimeans, unable to withstand Moscow singly, could hold out if they joined forces. Khan (now *hajji*) Selim Giray and representatives of all Ukraine's Cossacks signed a treaty to defend Ukraine and Crimea 'against Poles, Muscovites and all enemies for ever'. The outcome of the treaty, however, was disappointing: a four-year war of the dissidents against the 'loyal' Cossacks of Mazepa, who preferred Moscow's tyranny and Orthodox Christianity to complicity with the khanate and Islam. The conflict ended only when Mazepa hired a killer to spear Ivanenko to death.

Inevitably, Khan Selim was summoned to the sultan's court at Istanbul, first of all for consultations on how to continue the Ottomans' war (the front was now at Belgrade) against an alliance of Austria, Poland and Russia. A few months later the khan was again called back, at the very moment that three Russian armies, of perhaps half a million men, were heading towards the sea forts of Dugan (the future Taganrog) and Azak, and, it was feared, Crimea itself. Selim dared not leave Crimea and sent the sultan his son Şehbaz in command of just 10,000 Crimean Tatars. This small force managed in early 1695 to drive the Turks' enemies as far back as Lwów, capturing standards, two enormous cannon and a useful 'tongue' (an informer): the sultan wanted to make Şehbaz khan of Crimea, but the latter persuaded the Ottomans that this would be an insult to his father.

Far more ominous news came in 1695: Peter the Great was planning an invasion that would seize Crimea and the northern Black Sea coast. The crucial point was that Peter was preparing a naval invasion: he had a Dutch galley some 40 metres (130 ft) long, with a draft of 1.8 metres (6 ft) (shallow enough to pass down the treacherous sandbanks of the Don and Sea of Azov), which he dismantled and brought from Arkhangelsk to Voronezh on the Don, the gateway to the steppes. The galley, with twenty banks of oars, each manned by five men, was reassembled. Further downriver another twenty galleys were built to the same design under the supervision of Peter and a Dutch naval architect. They also built a large galleass with sails to supplement the oarsmen's efforts. All the ships were equipped with artillery, as well as each carrying fifty musketeers. At last the Russians had a fleet capable of outgunning the Ottoman navy and breaking the blockade around Azak. Peter could have recited to the Crimean Tatars a version of the British imperialists' mantra:

Whatever happens, we have got
Battleships, and they have not.

In summer 1695 Peter himself, with a Russian army, was sighted near Or Qapı, the only overland entry to Crimea. The reaction was panic: some Tatars proposed slaughtering all their Cossack and Russian prisoners. Instead, the Tatar army threw itself at the enemy: they were lucky that Russian cannon, soaked by heavy rain, could not fire, and the Russians therefore moved eastwards to Taganrog. Selim warned the sultan that once Taganrog and Azak fell, the rest of the Ottomans' provinces would be defenceless. Meanwhile, the khan insisted, he had to stay in the Crimea to protect the khanate's women and children from the Russians. The Ottomans sent ships to the Sea of Azov, but their bombardment was too haphazard to have any effect. (It may be that the Ottoman naval gunners, who were Greeks, had no interest in killing fellow Christian Russians.) The Taganrog garrison surrendered and, while Ottoman naval officers looked on impassively, drinking coffee and sherbet, the Turkish soldiers were shackled and dispatched to Moscow. At this point Khan Selim despaired and left for Istanbul.

The Tatar army in Hungary was unruly, demanding to be allowed home to defend Crimea: one rebel grabbed Khan Selim by the beard and had to be slapped down by Selim's *qalğa*. Selim saw no point in returning home. With a few bodyguards, he continued his journey to the sultan's headquarters near Temesvár (today's Timişoara), although he was now sick with gout and had to travel the Balkan roads in a sprung carriage. The battle in Hungary was quick and victorious, marked by the killing of the Austrian general Friedrich von Veterani. Sultan Mustafa then allowed Selim a year's leave. Meanwhile the Russians were suffering heavy losses as they besieged Azak yet again: they retreated a short distance and built bases from which to renew their assault in spring 1696. The Crimean Tatars offered Cossacks fighting in the Russian army a peace treaty, but the offer came to nought, since none of the Cossack delegates could read Turkish. Noğays and Crimeans in Selim's army failed to agree a plan of action and their only achievement was to slaughter the herd of pigs which the Russian army had brought as provisions, that battle being recorded as the *donguz qirani*, 'the pig slaughter'.

Selim had little hope of any help from Istanbul, but he assembled a delegation of *beys*, clerics, leading civil servants and merchants and dispatched them to lobby the sultan's court and explain that the Crimean Tatars needed to fight the Russians on the Crimea's borders, not the Austrians in the Balkans. Meanwhile, to raise funds for defence, Selim forced reluctant rich farmers to sell their livestock. He was desperate enough to ask the shah of Persia for support against what he supposed to be their common enemy, but his envoy to Isfahan was scorned in favour of the Russian emissary to the shah, and returned empty-handed. The sultan understood the situation well enough to accept Selim's absence. In June 1696 Selim, in lieu of himself, sent three of his sons and a small force to relieve Azak, but by August the Russians had taken the fortress. Two other sons, Şehbaz and Seadet, compensated for the disgrace at Azak by success in leading the sultan's army into Poland. But their pleas to be allowed to return to Crimea, with a cargo of firearms and extra troops, were rejected. Worse, the Mongol Kalmyks, after some dithering, had decided to join forces with the Russians. Even mobilization of every fit adult male in Crimea would not have been enough to mount a successful resistance. Uninvited, Selim set off in autumn 1697 with a suite of twenty men to Edirne to urge the sultan to make peace with Russia and thus relieve Crimea. The Ottoman empire was on the brink of collapse, as, bit by bit, its Balkan empire fell away into the hands of Christian enemies. Sultan Mustafa II began negotiating the Karlowitz Treaty that would initiate the Ottoman empire's two hundred years' path towards extinction. Selim reconciled himself to the dominance of Russia, once the Crimea's tributary, and now its nemesis. If the Crimean Khanate was to survive, however, the Ottoman empire had to continue existing. Meanwhile, Selim was so exhausted and ill that in 1699 he abdicated.

Selim's sons, like many young Crimean Tatars, were horrified at the peace discussions at Karlowitz (then in Austria, now in Serbia): the Tatars had not even been invited to attend. Şehbaz retreated to the mountains of Circassia. Selim's son Ğazı Giray ignored the treaty and went on ravaging Polish territory: he was irate when the terms of the treaty forced him to free all his prisoners. The Noğay Tatars of Bucak also rebelled. Selim was replaced, effectively, by three of his other sons: the new Khan Devlet II Giray, with Şahin, and then on the latter's death, Şehbaz as *qalğa*, and Seadet as *nureddin*. The trio, however, did not get on with one another. Şehbaz was a military hero and resented taking orders from his older brother, while Seadet, being older, felt he was senior to Şehbaz. In December 1699 Seadet hired a group of Circassians to murder Şehbaz in the house of a Circassian emir. Ğazı Giray was warned by a leading member of the Şirin clan that the fratricide would not stop there, that Khan Devlet II Giray would kill Ğazı. Ğazı crossed the Dnepr in a fishing boat and made himself the leader of the Noğay Tatars, who once more outraged the khan and all the signatories of the Karlowitz treaty not only by looting Poland, but by bribing Turkish viziers in order to have a Noğay khanate recognized, separate from Crimea and protected by Istanbul. The Ottomans duplicitously told the Noğay that Khan Devlet II Giray would be removed, but secretly ordered Khan Devlet to crush the Noğay rebels. By the end of 1700 civil war had broken out in Crimea: the rebels, who had to face a Circassian army as well as the khan's forces, began to desert Ğazı Giray, to whom they had just sworn loyalty. Selim failed to make Ğazı see sense, and Sultan Mustafa, suspecting that Selim, although retired, was complicit in the rebellion, had him sent to Rhodes. The handwritten sentence was altered in Selim's favour by the sympathetic grand vizier (probably at the suggestion of Khan Devlet, who did not want his father to cause trouble in Turkey), so that Selim was exiled to a nearby Crimean village, Seres.

Isolated and deserted, Ğazı Giray moved to the Cossack capital at Chyhyryn for a while, before asking his brother Khan Devlet for forgiveness, threatening to convert to Christianity if he was not forgiven. In the end Ğazı was lured, as were the Noğay rebels, to Istanbul and Edirne, where the sultan promised to spare their lives, while Ğazı was sent to Rhodes, eventually to become khan for a few years.

The Treaty of Karlowitz brought peace to Eastern Europe, but not to the Crimean Khanate, where suspicions about Russian intentions grew after damning testimony given by captured Russians and, in 1699, by an official letter brought to Bağçasaray by a Russian priest on his way to Istanbul. The letter warned Khan Devlet II: 'I am the King of the East, you are the Khan of Crimea . . . When our chief ambassador comes for certain discussions on his way to Constantinople, do not hinder him.' At the end of 1699 a Russian emissary was intercepted in the Sea of Azov by a Turkish 32-gun battleship and forced to continue his journey overland, avoiding the Crimea. As Seyyid Muhammed Riza puts it, by now 'the inhabitants of Crimea had begun to look at the events of their times through the doors of fear and expectation.' After the Noğay rebellion, new feuds began: an influential Şirin *bey* thrashed the nephew of Khan Selim so badly that he nearly died. Both Selim and Khan Devlet II Giray would have shackled the *bey*, had he not fled to Noğay protection, and then to Istanbul to demand that Devlet be overthrown for dispossessing the Noğay of their lands. While the sultan pondered whether to replace Khan Devlet, who had allowed this rebellion to threaten the Ottomans themselves, Devlet took drastic measures, inviting members of the untamed *ulu* Noğay Horde to come from Circassia and crush their fellow Noğays: these men were described as 'nasty-looking, like trolls, not human, strangely dressed, utter panthers or tigers, seven-headed dragons'. The rebel Noğays slipped away across the Bug river, while the Circassian Noğays looted their lands and raped their wives and daughters, committing atrocities 'not seen since the times of Genghis Khan'.

Accounts vary as to the outcome of the Noğay rebellion: the sultan's authority apparently quelled them, and many Noğay were resettled in Moldavia, where they had to promise not to attack the inhabitants, to pay taxes (their arrears from Bucak were forgiven), to obey appointed judges and to observe *shariat*, not the old Golden Horde *töre* in family law. Khan Devlet II found it hard to cede control over the Noğay to an article of an international treaty, especially one where he was expected to desist from hostile actions against the Russians. Khan Devlet had other conflicts, too. There was pressure from Khan Selim's former concubine to appoint her son Qaplan, Devlet's half-brother, as *nureddin*, and the idea was supported by Devlet's vizier Merdan-Ali Ağa. Devlet suspected that his half-brother and his vizier had provoked the Noğay rebellion and were responsible for all the distress that the elderly Selim was suffering. After Devlet's angry tirade, Qaplan and the vizier fled on horseback at midnight and sought asylum from the paşa of Kaffa, who refused to hand them back to the khan. The refugees made their way to Istanbul, where Qaplan, like Ğazı, was deprived of his pension. Qaplan was housed in a Bosphorus palace; the vizier was sent to Lemnos. Selim was now allowed to leave Seres, and began to seek somewhere in the Crimea with the right climate for his gout: as a favour, the sultan also released his son Qaplan.

The sultan was fed up with Khan Devlet's querulousness, and the whole Ottoman government was nostalgic for Selim's calm wisdom, especially at a time when the Russian army was fortifying its position just fifteen hours' ride away from the Crimean border. A Turkish official, who had been sent to confirm the unwarranted presence of a Russian invasion force, was bribed with a sable coat and duly reported that the Russian base was just a small fishermen's settlement. (Russian bribery and Turkish venality were outrageous: at the Karlowitz negotiations the Ottoman diplomat Mavrocordatos received from Peter the Great's envoy Voznitsyn a sable coat, then a grey thoroughbred, five camels and some mules – in exchange for ceding considerable territory to Russia.) The Russian ambassador assured the sultan's viziers that any fortress Russia had built was well behind Russian borders and was meant only to protect Russian merchants, and that Russia had just twelve ships in the Sea of Azov, in such poor condition that Russia was willing to sell them to the Turks. Russian bribes induced Turkish officials to feed these reassurances to the Crimean Tatars. Khan Devlet II felt outraged by trivial complaints: the Ottomans complained that his *qalğa* Seadet was riding out with large hunting parties, so heavily armed that they frightened the peasants of the Danube and made the Russians, who alleged that Tatars were kidnapping women and children, suspect that the peace treaty was being violated.

Regardless of all this disinformation, Khan Devlet II planned a first strike against the Russians, even though his clerics told him that this would infringe the peace treaty and would require special permission from Istanbul. A Crimean delegation went to Istanbul to point out that the presence of the Russian navy and army proved that Tsar Peter had evil intentions. The response from the sultan and his vizier was to depose Devlet and reappoint the now invalid Selim.

Devlet II would not accept removal: he stirred up a new Noğay rebellion, supported by many Crimean Tatars, and threatened to march on Istanbul. Fortunately in 1702 the Danube failed to freeze over, and the Ottoman army easily repelled the attacking Noğay. The sultan had his vizier executed for mismanaging the Crimean problem. Devlet II Giray fled to Circassia, pursued by troops loyal to his brothers Kaplan and Seadet. Unwilling to cause uproar in Circassia, Devlet begged Khan Selim to pardon him, returned first to Balaklava and thence to Istanbul, from where he was sent to Rhodes. (Other disgraced Girays were restricted to Yambol in Bulgaria, a milder form of exile.)

There was brief rejoicing in 1703 in Crimea: cattle were slaughtered, new officials were appointed and slaves were emancipated to celebrate Khan Selim's fourth reign. After a clerical rebellion against Mustafa's ill-tempered and disorganized rule, Istanbul had a new sultan, the would-be reformer Ahmed III. Khan Selim was too ill and too disillusioned in the face of the Russian threat to achieve anything in Crimea but a temporary lull. He managed only to settle a bitter dispute between the Muslim clergy and the Jews in Qarasuvbazar over the ownership of the land on which a synagogue had been built centuries before. The Turks had now begun to build forts at the Straits of Kerç to prevent Russian ships moving out of the Sea of Azov into the Black Sea. They were naive enough to send an official to Azak to buy the twelve ships the ambassador had said the Russian fleet no longer needed: the official was laughed at by the Russian commandant and sent away empty-handed. On 22 December 1704 Khan Selim 'gathered his skirts from the path of life and set off for the paradise of the ethereal Eden'.

Selim, despite his reputation for austerity, left a considerable fortune, even after generous bequests to his Jewish doctor, to the organizers of his funeral and wake, and to his many heirs: he was survived by ten sons and seven daughters, from whom all future khans descended, though few inherited his virtues. Of Selim's writings, notably his historical study of the Genghisids, nothing survives.

Selim's heritage, through no fault of his own, left the Crimean Tatars with a bleak economic and political future. The Treaty of Constantinople banned any raids or slave-trading; the Crimeans had no fortifications, and no right to independent relations with either Poland or Russia, nor to annual tribute from foreign powers. The Ottomans from now on would strictly control the Crimean Tatars, for fear of European anger. Khans would be recalled and new ones installed by the sultan's *qapıbaşı*, 'chief gatekeeper', without consulting the clans.

Compared with the threat of Tsar Peter, these changes mattered little. Peter's Russia was determined to become, like the English, Dutch and French realms, an oceanic empire. For that, not only did ships have to be built, but all-year ice-free ports and coastlines had to be founded or conquered. By 1700 Russia had begun a two-decade long Great Northern War with Sweden to gain full access to the Baltic, and, after the Treaty of Constantinople, access to the Black Sea was imminent. It would be easy for Danes and Swedes to block Russian ships from escaping the Baltic Sea into the Atlantic; but the Ottomans were now weak enough for Russia eventually to negotiate passage for their ships into the Mediterranean through the Bosphorus and the Dardanelles. This made crushing, if not abolishing, the Crimean Khanate a desirable aim.

7

DISINTEGRATION
AND RESTORATION

Long after his death in 1704, Selim I Giray determined the fate of his khanate: each successive khan was his son, grandson or great-grandson. The later khans, however, rarely held power for more than three or four years. They reflected the destabilization of the Ottoman empire, where, despite the firm grip of most sultans, court intrigues and army rebellions led to constant changes of policy and patronage. The dethronement or enthronement of khans depended more and more on Istanbul's whims. This lack of consistent policies, the embroilment of the Ottomans in wars on several fronts (against Venice and the Persians), the rapidly increasing might of Peter the Great's Russia, and the inferior abilities of most of Selim's descendants would rapidly weaken and isolate the Crimean Khanate, as would its drastically reduced income now that looting and slave-trading in Poland, Ukraine and Russia had stopped.

Sultan Ahmed III chose as Selim's successor his son Ğazi III Giray, who had been offended when fobbed off with the humble post of Devlet II Giray's *nureddin* and had joined rebel Noğays in Bucak, a crime for which the sultan had imprisoned and exiled him. Now forgiven, Ğazi III Giray tried to continue his father's and his elder brother Devlet II's anti-Russian alliance with the dissident Zaporozhian Cossacks, many of them now residents of Crimea, and a joint hostility with King Charles XII of Sweden against Moscow. The Ottomans, happy with the peace treaty of Karlowitz, forbade, however, attacks on their northern neighbours, even if they turned a blind eye to Tatar incursions that were minor enough to disown.

With his brothers Qaplan and Mengli as his *qalğa* and *nureddin* (and eventual successors as khans), Ğazi III had an initially quiet year, although a foray to quell rebellious Circassians had no success. In spring 1706 an epidemic of plague in Bağçasaray drove Ğazi III to seek refuge in Gözleve; he then had to deal with a Noğay demand for independence, and called a *qurultay* (parliament) near Aqmescit (today's Simferopol), while his ambitious brother Qaplan stirred up trouble in Bağçasaray. Despite Ğazi's intervention, the paşa whose bribe-taking had angered the Noğay was allowed to keep his post. The Ottoman administrator in Crimea and Ğazi III's own vizier both denounced Ğazi III, and he was removed from office early in 1707, dying of plague on his estate in Thrace in summer 1708, aged only 36. He was remembered by his subjects for his spurts of generosity and for a piercing 'leonine' stare, his eyes flashing under thick joined eyebrows.

Like his elder brother, Qaplan failed to subdue the independently minded Kabarda Circassians, who retreated from the accessible hot springs of Beshtau ('five mountains') into the high Caucasus, from where they parleyed with a force led first by Qaplan's younger brother Mengli and eventually by the khan himself. Qaplan had pioneered a technique later adopted by Russian generals in their conquest of the Caucasus: he felled whole forests to create wide roads into the mountains with a clear line of fire. The Circassians agreed to submit (but not to descend from the peaks). At night they treacherously attacked the Crimean Tatar camp with rifle fire. After his army had suffered heavy casualties, Qaplan Giray went home briefly. He hoped to raise a new army that would take revenge on the Circassians, but, as the Krymchak rabbi David Lekhno records, 'the entire people remained silent and did not answer a thing, since they did not want to fight against them [Circassians] any more.' By January 1709 Qaplan was removed by Sultan Ahmed III and exiled via Istanbul to Rhodes. At Ismail, on his way to the Ottoman capital, Qaplan crossed paths with his successor Devlet, who was travelling in the opposite direction: the two men loathed each other, but politeness compelled them to exchange greetings. (Four years later Qaplan would be reinstalled by Sultan Ahmed III, but his second reign was just as unsuccessful.)

Devlet II Giray, Qaplan's older brother, was restored as khan: he was much loved by the grand vizier Çorlulu Ali Paşa, who tried to neutralize the dislike felt for Devlet by Sultan Ahmed and by the dowager Valide Sultan: they blamed Devlet for his part in the loss of Hungary and the consequent downfall and death of Sultan Mustafa II. Reinstated after nearly seven years' exile, Devlet II Giray immediately had to take part in a new war that had broken out with Russia. For the first time in nearly a decade, Crimean Tatars captured thousands of Russian prisoners, even though Devlet's army was relatively small (40,000 men) and the winter was the coldest in five hundred years – so atrocious that soldiers burned straw to keep warm (the war was named *toban çaqqan aqını*, 'straw-burning raid'). Devlet's army also captured a number of forts and persuaded more Zaporozhian Cossacks to join the Crimean Tatars, some as permanent settlers. In particular, Devlet II Giray's Tatar cavalrymen admired their new allies, Cossack followers of *ataman* Ignat Nekrasov, Old Believers who fought Peter the Great because of his determination to impose reformed Orthodoxy on them. Ignat became in Tatar *Inat* (stubborn) and was nicknamed *meshur cihânî*, 'bewitched man' (their enemy the tsar was called *deli Petro*, 'mad Peter').

'Mad Peter' in 1709 was triumphant: at the battle of Poltava he had effectively crushed Mazepa, who led Cossack resistance to Moscow's rule, and at the same time inflicted a crushing defeat on King Charles XII of Sweden. Only a few hundred Swedes and Cossacks escaped death from hunger, cold, firearms, arrows and swords, or capture; Mazepa and the physically and morally wounded King Charles fled to Moldavia, then Ottoman territory, where they were given a grudging welcome by the Turks, who still hoped to renew their peace treaty with Russia for the next thirty years. Russia, however, insisted that Mazepa be handed over, although the Swedish king was no longer important to them. Turkish spies reported Russian preparations on the Ottoman border.

In November 1710 the sultan invited Khan Devlet II Giray to advise him in person. The cautious and wise Sultan Ahmed III, listening first to King Charles XII, then to Devlet Giray, was persuaded that he had to declare war on Russia. Devlet eloquently predicted the loss of Crimea and the eastern Balkans if Peter the Great's aggression went unchecked. Ottoman viziers and religious authorities, like the sultan, now despaired of peace. Before war began, Devlet Giray had first to overcome the scepticism of the rulers of Moldavia and of the paşa in charge of the frontier zone at Bendery.

The outcome in August 1711 was a battle in a narrow valley on the Prut river in which the Russian army was hit by Turkish artillery – the notoriously effective heavy wrought-iron *balyemez* ('doesn't eat honey') cannon[1] – from both sides. The Russians' retreat was blocked by Devlet Giray's 40,000-strong cavalry, not to mention detachments of Swedes and 3,000 Cossacks. Outnumbered, trapped, short of water, food and forage, Peter the Great faced death or captivity. White flags appeared: the major part of the Russian army, Peter the Great himself and his consort Ekaterina, their treasury, plus hundreds of fine horses and heavy guns, surrendered.[2]

Every Muslim in the empire celebrated, with five days of salvos and awards, the Ottomans' greatest victory since the fall of Constantinople. Most European commentators credited this victory to Devlet Giray's lobbying and his son Mehmed the *qalğa*'s military cunning. Then, out of the jaws of victory, corrupt viziers snatched defeat. It is widely accepted that the Ottoman commander on the Prut, Baltacı ('halberdier') Muhammad Paşa, after a few days' bargaining with Peter the Great's representatives, negotiated an unimaginable bribe: he would let the Russians go in exchange for their treasury (including Ekaterina's jewels), tens of thousands of cavalry horses and artillery, and, it is alleged, to clinch the deal, a night spent by Ekaterina in Baltacı's tent.[3] Peter, paralysed with shock, left negotiations to his consort. As a result of her selfless efforts, seven wagons of treasures were seen by the Polish ambassador Poniatowski being hauled from the Russian camp to Baltacı's quarters. Then the Russian army was allowed to withdraw. On 23 July 1711, on a still uncleared battlefield, a treaty was hurriedly drawn up: all Peter had to do was to abandon Taganrog, Azov and a couple of minor forts, and promise not to interfere in Poland's internal affairs, nor demand the repatriation of Cossack refugees from the Crimea. Turkey, on the other hand, promised to expel King Charles XII of Sweden from its territory (Charles was, in any case, safely ensconced in Bağçasaray). Gratified, Baltacı then sent the Russian headquarters sacks of rice, coffee, sugar and bread.

Khan Devlet II Giray was humiliatingly excluded from negotiations: Baltacı told him, 'You deal with your Tatar business: the decisions of the Sultan's Court have been entrusted to me and you have no right to interfere with them.' Devlet was enraged by this gross and corrupt failure to exploit victory. The Ottomans had thrown away their last chance of redrawing the map of Europe in their favour. Crimean hopes of regaining the power that the Golden Horde once had over Muscovy were dashed.

According to the nineteenth-century German historian and observer of Russia August von Haxthausen, Devlet had an angry interview with Sultan Ahmed III (who, after signing the treaty regretted that Peter had not been made to surrender all the Baltic territory he had captured from the Swedes). Devlet did not think that the abandonment of Azov made Crimea any safer from Russian attacks: he wanted to pursue the war until Russia could be bound by an international treaty. Devlet is said to have demanded Baltacı Mehmed Paşa's head for corruption and treason. In any case, Baltacı was exiled to the island of Lemnos, where he died a year later, aged fifty, of illness or by execution.

Devlet II Giray himself paid dearly for his opposition to Ottoman passivity (Ahmed III had his reasons not to pursue war with Russia: he was about to renew wars with both Iran and Venice). Devlet had been negotiating with Sweden on a Crimean alliance that would restore Charles XII to his throne; the sultan threatened violent intervention if this alliance went ahead. Moreover, Devlet was plotting to unseat Dimitri Kantemir, a Moldavian prince (and distant relative of the Noğay Kan-Temirs), who would soon defect to Russia and become Russia's first modern poet.

So anxious were the Ottomans to be rid of the exiled Swedish king that they tried to remove him by force. Charles was naively, if not insanely determined to oppose Russia until Peter signed a peace treaty with all his opponents. Devlet now took the Ottoman side, offering to help repatriate Charles only so that he could rejoin his native country's army. Unlike the sultan, Devlet was prepared to give Charles an escort of several thousand Tatars to ensure his safe passage home through Polish territory, still occupied by Russian troops. A Polish emissary to Crimea, however, proposed shackling Charles and handing him over to the Polish or Russian sovereigns. Charles suspected Devlet of complicity in this plot and refused Devlet's armed escort. The sultan then authorized Devlet to kill the king and his suite if they resisted deportation. Devlet tried to take over the process of removal and secure Charles's immunity from Polish arrest. Charles had all his own horses slaughtered to prevent removal; Devlet II Giray's Tatars feasted on the meat. The janissaries, reluctant to kill a king, refused to carry out the sultan's death sentence on Charles XII. Devlet Giray then blockaded the Swedes for eighteen days; the starving Swedes attacked, killing over 150 Tatars. The Tatars responded by killing twice as many Swedes. Charles and fifteen surviving officers then surrendered. This absurd clash of two of Russia's opponents was called the *kalabalık* ('crowding out', from the Arabic for 'overwhelming by superior numbers'). Charles, severely wounded, was allowed to recuperate in Edirne and in 1714 was sent via northern Germany to rejoin his army.

Devlet was promptly dethroned by Sultan Ahmed III in 1713. The *kalabalık* was seen by the sultan as an embarrassing provocation, and it was then discovered that Devlet enjoyed friendly relations with Dimitri Kantemir, who he should have known had converted to Christianity and was plotting to defect to Russia, together with his principality of Moldavia. It was all the more insulting for Devlet that he had recently been lobbying for his replacement, the former khan Qaplan Giray, to be exiled to a yet more remote Aegean island. In vain Devlet protested to the grand vizier that he was building a bridge across the Prut in order to evacuate the Noğay population of Bucak from any imminent Russian attack. He tried to warn the vizier that his brother Qaplan was too young and out of touch to lead an army, and advised the Turks to be firm and not let Russia have access to the Black Sea and thus imperil the whole Ottoman empire.

Qaplan's second reign began in 1713 with a wasted winter on the long-disputed Ottoman–Polish–Cossack–Russian border at Khotyn: Sultan Ahmed had decided to restore the fortifications, even though the new peace treaty seemed to make the expense unnecessary. After the paşa in charge gave an exorbitant estimate of the cost, Qaplan Giray was ordered to bring a Tatar detachment to carry out the work more cheaply. By 1714 Qaplan had made Khotyn fit for an Ottoman garrison; he was recalled to help with Turkey's war against Venice. Qaplan sent his younger brother Selâmet to command Turkey's troops in Bosnia.

In the khan's absence from Crimea, Baht Giray, a son of the dismissed Devlet II, was stirring up a rebellion in the khanate's Circassian and Noğay territories. Thanks to the vigorous intervention of the khan's brother and *qalğa* Mengli, the rebellion was crushed. Further trouble erupted immediately: the peace treaty with Russia was breached by unauthorized Tatar raids on the roads leading to Astrakhan. Cossacks fought back, but the Turkish janissary garrison at Azov refused to restore the peace, claiming that they relied on Tatar looting in order to subsist. Janissaries and paşas fought one other: when the conflict was resolved, just one janissary officer was executed. Qaplan's passivity was found by Istanbul to be deplorable, even more so in 1716, when he was summoned to Temesvár, and his brothers to Bucak and Transylvania, to fight the Austrian army. Temesvár and Belgrade were both lost to the Austrians while the Crimean contingents were still crossing the Balkans at a leisurely pace. Qaplan had been advised by his own leaders not to be too obliging.

The sultan's council feared that the sons of Selim Khan, reacting to orders in such a desultory fashion, now felt free of any obligation to Istanbul. They rightly sensed that the khan and his brothers were angry at the Ottomans' refusal to make war on Russia, a refusal which severely reduced their income from slave-trading and looting. The sultan then agreed to appoint a new Giray Khan from the holding pen in Thrace.

For a few months in the winter of 1716–17 the Ottomans tried a now forgotten branch of the khanate's rulers, the barely legitimate Çoban ('shepherd') Girays: they appointed as khan the seventy-year-old Qara-Devlet Çoban Giray, in the hope that he could recruit a Crimean army to supplement the depleted Ottoman forces. The Crimean nobility spurned Qara Devlet because he was not a descendant of Khan Selim Giray, and his great-grandmother (the legendary Maria Potocka) was a mere captured

Christian slave. Qara-Devlet could not even recruit a servant in Crimea: he relied on a few Ottomans he had brought with him. The upstart khan was duly dethroned. Unlike any previous dismissed khan, he was stripped of the insignia and gown that he had been given just months earlier. He died shortly afterwards, it is said of humiliation. The sultan's council, sobered by its lost battles in Hungary, understood that, to avoid bloodshed in Crimea, it had to designate khans who were sons of Selim Giray.

Sa'adet, the son of Selim whom the Ottomans chose as Crimean khan in 1717, had at least lived much of his life in Yambol and proved his military talents in the Balkans. He spent his first year as khan with the Turkish army in Bucak and Bulgaria, until October, when, thanks to the intervention of foreign ambassadors and negotiations by Sa'adet's *qadiasker* (military judge), a truce with the Austrians was declared. The Ottoman army was in such disarray from mutinies and defeats that it had no proper plan of campaign for the 60,000 Tatars brought over by Sa'adet.

When Sa'adet IV Giray eventually reached Crimea, he had to deal first with unauthorized raids on Russian territory led by 'mad' Baht Giray, and then with a continuation of the Circassian rebellion that had troubled his brother Qaplan's reign. Fortunately, Sa'adet's son Salih had, like many Crimean boys, been brought up by a Circassian foster-father and could win over not only his foster-brothers, but many other Circassian clansmen: all the same, Salih asked for troops to strengthen his position.

It was in Sa'adet IV Giray's reign that Catholic missionaries and a pro-French orientation reappeared in Crimea. The original French aim was for missionaries to convert Crimea's 6,000 or so Orthodox and Armenian monophysite families, and possibly a number of Jews and Karaim, to Roman Catholicism. In the early 1700s Crimea had fewer than 1,000 Roman Catholics, none of them with a church, and all of them suspect to Muslims and oriental Christians. The Jesuit Père Duban, the first missionary in Crimea for centuries to survive its epidemics, noted in the early 1700s that Catholic slaves suffered badly, not just from physical cruelty, but from the absence of priests. Dr Ferrand, who attended Khans Selim and Ğazı III Giray, lobbied not only for a more aggressive stance against Russia, but for medicines and for humane treatment of Christian slaves. As a result, the French ambassador in Istanbul, Comte de Ferriol, gave Duban 1,000 écus with which to redeem a few Christian slaves in Crimea. (Children, at 20 écus each, were the cheapest to redeem.) Duban also maintained hospices for the old and refuges for the young: he had too little money to achieve more than a few token successses. When Devlet Giray came to power, Duban attracted hostility by trying to convert Protestant slaves, typically Swedes captured in Hungary or Danzig. The Armenian community was angered when some of its members defected to Rome: Duban needed support, which Qaplan Giray, a Francophile, and another Jesuit provided. What proved impossible was to get permission to build a church. Even when Duban was made consul, which he dared not tell Devlet II Giray Khan, there was no hope of a building permit: in 1718 Duban returned to France, leaving two priests in Crimea.

Sa'adet IV had inherited from Selim Giray a doctor and spiritual and commercial adviser, Saverio Glavani, an Ottoman citizen. A convert to Islam, Glavani was a strange choice by France to protect Catholic converts in the khanate. Glavani was a versatile polymath, described by the French ambassador, the vicomte d'Andrézel, in 1725 as 'intelligent, active, tough, knowing the language of a country where he is much loved and is zealous about religion'. He was born in 1680 on the island of Chios to an Italian father and French mother. He would prove faithful to the khan, and followed him to Yambol when a Şirin revolt put an end to Sa'adet's reign.

Pacifying Circassians had negative consequences: the Şirin clan leaders and other Crimean aristocrats, already suffering, thanks to peace with Poland and Russia, from the lack of tribute and loot, now felt deprived of their expected shares of the slaves, boys and girls, that Circassians sent to Crimea. The normal quota was 300 a year, but when a new khan was installed, 3,000 were sometimes expected. Since the death of Selim Giray, new khans now appeared every other year, instead of once in fifteen years: the toll of slaves was depopulating Circassia. Sa'adet did not relent: he sent the 'mad' Baht Giray to Circassia to enforce the payment of tribute by devastating large areas. The Ottomans turned a blind eye to these raids: they understood that Crimea had to recover the income it lost thanks to treaties with its northern neighbours. The search for new sources of income, however, brought the Crimeans only a small number of Circassian slaves. The nobility were so aggrieved that they petitioned for the overthrow of Khan Sa'adet IV Giray. Their complaints were semi-literate, even absurd: they accused the khan of stealing a bride for one of his relatives, they complained that Sa'adet killed too many young birds when hunting, that he 'had just got fat on over-eating and drinking'.[4] The petitioners told the sultan that they would accept as khan any other son of Selim Giray. Although Sa'adet's son urged him to repress these arrogant lords, Sa'adet was distracted by a quarrel between clansmen over a bride. Sa'adet tried a Solomonic tactic by awarding the bride to a third party. The fury that ensued was directed more at removing Sa'adet than at recuperating the lost bride. The *nureddin* proposed killing youths who were rioting over the affair. Sa'adet, however, was merely disgusted by his ungrateful subjects and by the Şirin *bey* Kantemir. In 1724, at the age of 63, he abdicated voluntarily and retired to Turkey where he lived for another seven years, bequeathing his estate to his impoverished sons. The Ottomans had only two feasible candidates to replace Sa'adet: either they forgave his brother Qaplan for failing to subordinate the Circassians and reinstated him, or they chose another brother, Mengli, Qaplan's former *qalğa*. On the pretext of a hunting party, the two were brought to Siyavuş estate near Istanbul and interrogated by senior officials on their proposed solutions to anarchy in the khanate. The grand vizier, impressed by Mengli's eloquence, commended him to Sultan Ahmed. (Qaplan, it is said, refused the post on the grounds of advanced age and a reluctance 'to stain my Muslim's garments of virtue'.)

Khan from October 1724, Mengli used cunning in lieu of force to subdue his unruly noblemen: he confirmed all the leading officials in their posts before arriving on the peninsula, smiling more at his enemies than at his friends. His next step was typically Ottoman: as war with Persia had flared up again, he sent 6,000 men under Safa Giray, thus removing a potential army of hostile plotters. Then he made appointments to make one Şirin *bey* jealous of another, and therefore unlikely to conspire together; he encouraged others to sue each other in the courts; he summoned those who expected his vengeance and assured them of his respect and desire for peace. In July 1726, with the support of the Crimean *mufti*, Mengli called all the emirs to his *divan* in Bağçasaray: several of them, in particular the Mansur clansmen with their Noğay members, led by Hacı Can-Timur, an intransigent rebel for forty years, may have plotted to kill Mengli. Now, seeing lines of riflemen along the route to Mengli's palace, they suspected that they were the intended victims. Mengli wanted, however, to avoid a bloody showdown in the narrow valley of his capital. He waited for the rebels to reach open country. They fled to the banks of the Don and, despite the khan's express orders, sympathetic janissaries ferried them to safety. But they were pursued and caught by two of Mengli Giray's cousins, Salih and Azamat Giray. After the *mufti* had reluctantly issued a fatwa, Salih hanged a dozen of them, including the blind Kutlu Giray: the rest fled to the protection of the Circassians. (One rebel, the *qadiasker* (chief judge) was too senior to be killed on the spot, and had to be sent to Istanbul for trial and execution.) Mengli sent his *qalğa* and *nureddin* across the Straits of Azov to deal with the survivors, exiled Safa Giray his *qalğa* and replaced him by another brother, Adil. Within two years Adil also betrayed the khan, petitioning the sultan to remove Mengli.

Adil fled to Rumelia, leaving Mengli to appoint new ministers in the capital, to mop up Noğay resistance in the steppes and to tame turbulent Circassian tribes. Mengli won popularity by abolishing the 'sheep tax' and by increasing pay for the *ulema* (scholars and imams). For his own security he established a chain of post stations. The population accepted the khan's determination to be an absolute monarch in the khanate; so did Sultan Ahmed. In 1729 Mengli received a jubilant imperial reception with fireworks and a banquet in Istanbul. It was here that Mengli, who had inherited as his French personal doctor the Jesuit de facto consul Saverio Glavani, was seen to share the Ottomans' friendliness towards French diplomats. The French ambassador noted that Mengli 'smiled at the sight of all the Frenchmen he saw and greeted them with a nod'. Before he left for Crimea, Mengli congratulated the French ambassador on the birth of a son and gave him a note for King Louis XV asking for Sr Glavani to be allowed an extended stay and additional medical supplies. Mengli's wounded arm was treated by the Jesuit priest de La Tour, who was rewarded by a daily pension of a kilogram of meat, three loaves of bread and two candles, and invited to ask a favour: de La Tour asked for protection for his Catholic mission, and for Glavani to be invited back to Crimea. Meanwhile the French treated Glavani as the French consul at Bağçasaray. Glavani helped Mengli to extinguish the Şirins' rebellion. At the same time, Glavani, risking exposure as a double agent, earned Russian gratitude by helping Russian merchants recover confiscated property. Glavani could be disturbingly proactive. In 1730, when two Noğay Tatars were arrested on suspicion of being agents of the pro-Austrian Polish faction, the French consul lobbied Mengli's vizier and his *mufti* to have the suspects, against all custom, executed. Glavani bribed the *mufti* with a watch to issue a fatwa, then bearded the khan in his harem. After the women had left the room and the Crimean *divan* had discussed the matter, Mengli Giray reached a compromise: at first, only the elder Noğay suspect was hanged; the younger suffered the same fate a week or two later. Mengli's vizier complained that this death had cost him several hundred piastres promised by King Augustus II of Poland if the Noğay were saved, and asked the French to compensate him with a gold repeater watch. Presents of watches, fine cloth or gunpowder, Glavani told his superiors, were the best way of maintaining a Crimean alliance.

Mengli had another new factor to deal with in Crimea's explosive ethnic mix. The Kalmyk Mongols, themselves driven to the Volga by hostile Central

Asian Turkic tribes, were pushing Noğays west to new pastures in the Crimean steppes; the Circassians, too, suffered from Kalmyk aggression. Worse, the Russians saw the Buddhist Kalmyks, who detested Muslims even more than did Russian and Cossack Christians, as a God-given force to help Russia tame the North Caucasus and the steppes around the Volga and Caspian. Buddhism did not prevent the Kalmyks from being ferocious warriors. Kalmyk loyalties, however, were fickle. In 1731 a Kalmyk leader, Donduk Ombo, overthrew his father and put himself and 15,000 households under the protection of the Crimean khan, yet in 1735 secretly held negotiations with the Russian empress Anna and swore allegiance to the Russian governor of Astrakhan.

Mengli did not foresee that a year later an uprising by Istanbul's janissaries would result in the death of the grand vizier and in Sultan Ahmed's abdication in favour of his nephew Mahmud I. Mahmud had no bone to pick with Mengli, but the latter's overweening pride and the advice of jealous viziers inspired Mahmud to exile Mengli II Giray to Rhodes for the next seven years and to restore the less fiery Qaplan Giray for a third reign. The viziers debated how to replace a popular khan without provoking civil unrest: some advised appointing Qaplan in secret, not telling Mengli of his removal from power until he accepted an invitation to Istanbul for discussions. A large rowing boat was sent across the Sea of Marmara to fetch Qaplan from the old Ottoman capital of Bursa; Qaplan felt too ill for a sea crossing, and slowly made his way overland to the Bosphorus to receive his investiture and insignia. Mengli also made his way overland from Crimea to Istanbul, evading attempts by Noğay tribesmen to wreak revenge on him: he chose exile on Rhodes, rather than in Rumelia, where there were too many angry Girays for him to feel safe.

Under Qaplan those whom Mengli had dismissed came back from exile in Poland, Kalmykia or Circassia and resumed their former posts. Qaplan himself was preoccupied with persuading the Ottoman government not to renew the war with Persia, because the Persians were now Russia's allies. In any case, Qaplan, unlike Mengli II Giray, had no need to send dissident opponents to war on the Persian front. The sultan's *divan*, however, was eager for war, believing that they could still keep the peace with Russia. Qaplan's ambiguity staved off a bloodbath between the pro- and anti-war viziers. Ivan Nepliuev, the Russian ambassador in Constantinople, although oblivious to the situation in Crimea, assured St Petersburg that the Crimean khan was now barred by the sultan from anti-Russian activity. When still in Istanbul, however, to Russian annoyance, Qaplan told the French embassy's dragoman, 'We Tatars value the French for their bravery, power and friendship, and we almost have a common religion.' The French ambassador welcomed Qaplan's support for French policy in Poland; he was worried only by Qaplan's 'avarice and avidity'. Crimea would now be used by the French as the best route for communicating with Poland. The khan saw things differently: Glavani was used by Qaplan as a medical escort for the slaves he sent to Istanbul as presents to the sultan, while the French embassy in Constantinople, when Glavani travelled back to Bağçasaray, asked Glavani to take presents for the khan and stir him to anti-Russian military action.

Qaplan was told by Istanbul to send Crimean reinforcements to the Iranian front. Russian forces tried to block this expedition, but a Chechen *bey* gave the Crimean army free passage over the Caucasus. In 1733 Qaplan himself joined an Ottoman expedition to Poland, an attempt to prop up Stanisław Leszczyński, the pro-Ottoman candidate who had been elected king. (This election sparked the five-year War of the Polish Succession.) Leszczyński was pro-French (his daughter was married to King Louis xv), a connection acceptable to the Ottomans, but not to Russia, whose government installed King Augustus III as their puppet ruler of Poland.[5] Qaplan, cautious as ever, despite Sr Glavani's urgings, would not cross the Polish border except on Ottoman orders. Glavani's superiors, disappointed that he could not make Qaplan disobey Istanbul, suspected their consul of treachery and corruption, 'a rogue we cannot do without', and sent him off to Anatolia. When, however, Russia captured the port of Danzig, the Crimean Tatars finally tried to relieve the Poles by attacking Russian bases in Circassia and Dagestan, but it was too late. The French no longer hoped that Khan Qaplan would help them determine who became king of Poland.

What Qaplan had tried to avoid followed in spring 1736: war between the Ottomans and the Russians, with a series of devastating Russian invasions of Crimea. Between the death of Peter the Great in 1725 and the accession of Empress Anna in 1730, Russia had for the first time in centuries reduced its army and cut its military expenditure, to the relief of its neighbours. With the advent to power of Empress Anna's lover and all-powerful minister Ernst Biron (Bühren), a corrupt, cruel and highly intelligent dictator, both Poland and the Ottoman empire were liable to suffer persistent aggression.

The 1736 invasion was led by Baron Münnich, a German officer originally invited to Russia as a hydraulic engineer by Peter the Great, but who was rapidly promoted for his organizational and engineering talents. As the leader of an invading force, however, he was notable only for destruction and the high mortality of both the enemy's and his own men.

With 80,000 men on the Polish border, and the rest of the Crimean army stuck in the Caucasus, the khanate was vulnerable. Qaplan himself was nearly sixty and frail. (Adil Giray, left to guard Crimea as best he could, was moribund.) Now, when the Ottomans had been badly defeated by the Persians, Khan Qaplan perversely sent his cavalry to the Iranian front. General Münnich took the opportunity to strike. El Haj Abdul Ğaffara Efendi records the preliminary incursion of November 1735:

> Adil sent criers to every town and village, calling on the population to defend the homeland ... The heart-rending cries echoed in everyone's ears. Young and old flocked to Or Qapı. Even I, who write this, coming back ill from the Haj, confined to my bed, was forced to forget my illness and rush to Or Qapı. Alas, all who had gathered there were weak and bedridden like me, for the Khan had set off on the Iranian campaign taking with him all the soldiers capable of fighting a war. When the Russians came, there was heavy snowfall, up to the horses' bellies. The Russians were forced to go home.

In spring 1736 Münnich led his men to besiege Azov and by mid-June 30,000 Russians and Cossacks reached Or Qapı, where Qaplan (fetched hurriedly from Istanbul) had his army. The Russians had heavy artillery, the Crimean Tatars almost no firearms at all. There were no Ottoman reinforcements. On the fourth day Russian mines and artillery blew up the Or Qapı fort. Qaplan's horse was killed under him. Münnich ordered minimal civilian casualties to be inflicted, in the hope of earning the Crimean Tatars' gratitude, but when he moved to Gözleve his troops burnt the port down and then looted it, loading up enough sheep and grain to feed the army for a month (their own supplies had been purloined by Russian quartermasters). The army turned inland to destroy Bağçasaray, which had no walls to protect it. The khan's palace, library and archives were levelled to the ground: only the tombs and baths survived (a hundred or so judicial record books and 350 books from the khan's library were retrieved much later). The capital city and the country's historical records, as well as thousands of manuscripts, some unique, dealing with Islamic, Mongol and Turkic history and literature, had been obliterated. Two thousand houses, many owned by Christians, were reduced to rubble. Münnich's own son admitted that only the carved and decorated roofs were spared, and sent as salvage to Petersburg. As for the French Jesuit library, a note in the Russian archives reads: 'Most of it burnt down, or was drowned in wine and damaged, because the Jesuits, when they retreated, put the books for safety in a cellar, which our Cossacks entered and where they got drunk; in that state they spilled the wine and thus ruined these books.'[6]

A holocaust was avoided only by epidemics of plague, cholera and typhus, which in that exceptionally hot summer killed at least half of Münnich's soldiers. In the towns there were too many corpses to bury, which made the epidemics worse. Despite the looting, the survivors were hungry and thirsty. Townsmen fled to the mountains. Those who could not flee died from the same diseases that killed off perhaps 90 per cent of the Russian invaders. The Russians who escaped survived by killing Noğay Tatars' cattle as they passed Or Qapı on their way home. Russia, however, considered the depopulation of Crimea and the damage to its agriculture a victory for the invaders. (The British ambassador in St Petersburg realized the extent of Münnich's casualties when he learnt that 60,000 men were being newly conscripted, without forming any new regiments, the following year.) The conclusion reached by the Russian government was that the next invasion should concentrate on closing the khanate's borders, so that the Crimean Tatars would suffer economic collapse and either accept Russian rule, or die.

In February 1737 Münnich persuaded the chancellor Ernst Biron to invade Crimea once more. Münnich did not head this second invasion; he avoided a court martial only thanks to the death of his main enemy Count Gustav Levenvolde. Instead, he was given command of forces on the Danube.

The condemnation of Qaplan Giray by Turks and Crimeans for his failure to repel Russian forces was far harsher. Qaplan's army had left it too late to restore the moat protecting Or Qapı; they had refused a Turkish admiral's offers of help at Gözleve; soldiers fled when Qaplan failed to provide them with artillery; after a bomb struck Qaplan's carriage, troops had run off in panic; the Tatars had failed to fill in the wells, but they let the enemy dig new ones; they had hung around the fort at Or Qapı and taken no action, assuming the Russians would soon run out of water and fodder. In short, Qaplan was incompetent, cowardly and sick. He was arrogant and hostile to his own officials and officers. He was too paralytic to ride a horse, and had to travel from one of three fronts to another lying in a cart.

Qaplan was removed by the sultan in August 1736, sent to Chios (where he died two years later) and replaced by his nephew and *qalğa* Fetih II Giray, who had earned a reputation for bravery, even chivalry on the Iranian front, and had then in Istanbul effectively curried favour with a number of viziers. Fetih's first decision, however, was at first unpopular: he ordered the Crimean army on the Danube not to go home, but to carry out a devastating raid on Russian-dominated Ukraine. Thousands of Ukrainians were captured: at the time, Russian outposts were garrisoned by demoralized soldiers, which gave rise to the ironic Tatar saying, 'You sleep, Ivan, while I work hard tying you up.' The number of Russian soldiers enslaved reconciled the Tatar army to their unrelenting service away from home.

Not that there were homes to go to in 1736: the cities – Aqmescit, Gözleve, Bağçasaray – lay in ruins; plague and other diseases raged. Only Turkish-controlled ports, such as Kaffa and Kerç, had been left intact, and in the mountains refugees survived uninjured, although starving. The Tatars' military losses had been small (around 2,000) but disease and starvation must have carried away a hundred times that many. The Russian view was that so much damage had been done that a second invasion would totally disable the Crimean Tatars.

The results of this second invasion in early 1737, which involved war with Turkey as well as the Crimean Khanate, were mixed: Kalmyks and Russians approached via the Dnepr and Or Qapı and, although met by Turkish artillery, captured a large number of Tatars. A counteroffensive, however, liberated the captives and rustled enormous herds of cattle. The Russian and Kalmyk forces were now commanded by an expatriate Irishman, Peter Lacey (known in Russia as Lassi), as ruthless and reckless as Münnich. (Münnich was now leading an army that captured the key port of Ochakov from an Ottoman paşa who was beheaded for his incompetence.) Lassi had achieved the highest rank a decade earlier by a policy of scorched earth and total extermination in Sweden, and he intended to do the same in Crimea against a Tatar army that Fetih Giray had no time to reorganize.

Nevertheless, the isthmus and Or Qapı were now impregnable, and Lassi's army had to cross salt marshes and lagoons via a narrow platoon bridge into Crimea: they planned to follow the eastern coast down to Kerç and then Kaffa. The St Petersburg press belatedly reported Lassi's summer triumph in January 1738:

Don Cossacks then turned 50 kilometres inland up Qarasu river and burnt and looted 40 villages, capturing 47, and killing or bayoneting

Overleaf: Map of the Black Sea region, 1737.

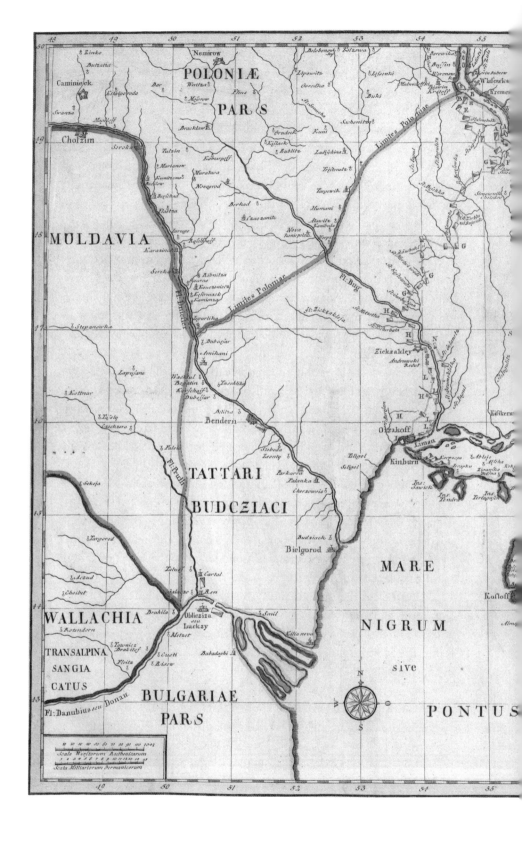

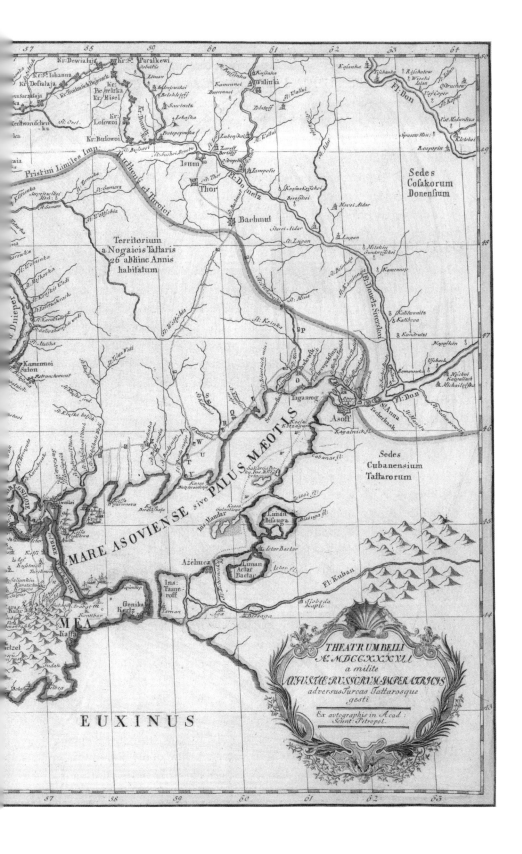

the rest, and taking away more than 20,000 camels, horned cattle and sheep . . . Kalmyks were particularly distinguished in looting and burning everywhere.

Qarasuvbazar surrendered. Any inhabitants encountered by the Kalmyk Mongols – 'predators with hearts of stone', the Crimean historians called them – were robbed, raped and killed. Some 1,800 wooden houses in Aqmescit (Simferopol) were burnt down, and those who had not fled were murdered, including the renowned Sufi healer Salğır-Baba, an elderly man praying at his sacred fountain. The Russian army went into the mountains, reducing a number of towns to ashes, before General Gustaf Otto Douglas's army was attacked by Tatar horsemen and Russians and Kalmyks retreated. The Kalmyks and Cossacks then returned as traders, selling captured women and children, as well as cattle, to Tatar officers. Lassi led his army out of Crimea over a bridge and trench that the Russians had dug to cover their retreat, east of Or Qapı. Fetih proved as hesitant as Qaplan: he dithered, and his force of 40,000 men failed to engage the Russians. Sultan Mahmud I dismissed Fetih II Giray and raised Mengli II Giray once more to the khanate, Mengli being, for all his faults, a much more intelligent strategist. Fetih spent the remaining nine years of his life in retirement in Bulgaria.

A Russian contemporary concluded that Lassi had finished what Münnich had begun, for 'all the eastern part of Crimea is covered in ashes and corpses'. Franz Wenzel Reisky Freiherr von Dubnitz, an Austrian captain in the Russian forces (where he was known as Paradies), counted a hundred wagons of loot and enormous herds of stolen cattle, as well as slaves, following the troops back to Russia. Reisky was appalled by Russian officers' late rising, which exposed their troops to long marches in scorching heat:

> The Russian army takes more than 30 hours for a stage that any other army would cover in four . . . When I left the army, there were more than 10,000 sick and wounded: they were transported in any old wagons, four or five in a wagon barely big enough for two. The care was poor: they had no skilled surgeons.

General Christoph von Manstein, a Prussian officer in Russian service, was equally horrified by the poor health of the Russian army, its soldiers as weakened by Orthodox fasts as by dysentery. A third of the sick – men, horses or draught oxen – died of diseases, hunger, sunstroke and exhaustion.

When the Russians repeated their raid in 1739, they found there was nothing left worth taking. They dared not attack Kaffa, which was under Ottoman control. The Polish historian Stanisław Jan Siestrzeńcewicz-Bohusz concluded, 'This war that lasted three years cost Russia several million roubles and 100,000 lives, to no purpose, except the ruination of a neighbouring country . . . Wretched Crimea had changed from being the most plentiful country to the most barren.'

By effectively destroying an Ottoman protectorate, Russia had waged an undeclared war with the Ottomans. A congress at Niemirów (Nemyriv), in virtually neutral territory between Poland and Moldavia, eventually resulted in separate peace treaties between Austria, the Ottomans and Russia. Austria was alarmed by Russia's demands for Ottoman territory, the liquidation of the Crimean Khanate and for unfettered Russian rights in the Black Sea: they became more supportive of both the Ottomans and the Giray Khans. Turkey, horrified by Russian extortion, broke off negotiations and resumed the war to forestall further depredations.

Mengli II Giray was so highly respected that the sultan's *divan* consulted him on how to deal with the enmity of both Austria and Russia. Mengli advised cautious secret negotiation; he reminded the Ottomans that Austria was now exhausted by war, and that it was not worth stopping the Russians from retaking Azov, even if the Crimean army wanted to fight on. Mengli wanted to establish firm borders and to build forts to control Russian access to the Black Sea from the Sea of Azov. Before he could persuade Crimea to move to a defensive strategy, Mengli fell ill. He died on 30 December 1739, satisfied to learn on his deathbed that a Russian fleet of 1,000 ships shelling Turkish ports south of the Sea of Azov had sunk in a terrible storm.[7] Mengli II Giray's main achievement was to instil into his subjects and his sovereign the sultan the idea that times had changed and that intelligent defence, not attack, was the best way to survive. This is why Seyyid Muhammed Riza named Mengli II the 'seventh planet' in the history of the khanate. Russia, however, had learnt one thing from its botched invasions under Münnich and Lassi: that the Crimean Tatars were as clueless and slow in defence as they were ingenious and quick in attack.

The year 1740 brought Crimea not just a new khan, Selâmet Giray, youngest brother of the late Mengli, but a new era. The Peace of Belgrade signed in September 1739 ended the war between the Ottomans and Austria and Russia: the Ottomans even regained territory, in particular Serbia, although the Russians kept a demilitarized Azov, and could sail the Black Sea, albeit ceding to Turkey a monopoly of civilian trade by sea. The

Ottomans, still embroiled in war with Iran, were conciliatory in Europe. In 1741 Russia had a new empress, Elizaveta, who dismissed Empress Anna's grim, ambitious German ministers in favour of Russian noblemen and a French cultural orientation; Elizaveta disliked executions and torture. Her war aims were directed not southwards, but westwards, to limit the expansion of Prussia under the young Frederick the Great, and to extract Russia from war with Sweden. Elizaveta was tolerant of small non-Russian minorities in her empires, for example granting the aggressive Chukchi of eastern Siberia autonomy. Crimea, in no state to raid its neighbours, let alone defend itself from more attacks, could begin to recover.

For the first time, Bağçasaray became a centre for political negotiations: first came the French diplomat Consul Jean-Michel Venture, representing the kings of France and Sweden.[8] His primary goal was to strengthen the links between the khanate and Sweden, in the now dwindling hope that Crimea would prove a Swedish ally if Sweden's struggle with Russia over Baltic territories was renewed. Selâmet was evasive: he consulted Istanbul, which was now friendly towards Russia and Poland, and demurred. For once the sultan was grateful for a Crimean khan who was not antagonizing Slavic neighbours.

A gentle and charitable man, Selâmet was provisionally appointed as acting khan by the Crimean religious and political elite: only after taking this step did they ask Sultan Mahmud I to confirm him as khan. Selâmet then appointed his nephews as *qalğa* and *nureddin*. He rebuilt the Bağçasaray palace and main mosque, to which the sultan was glad to contribute new books. Under Selâmet the Crimea acquired its first printing press, producing religious literature in Çufut Qale for the Karaim all over Crimea: for the rest of the century the Karaim, assisted by typographers from Turkey, printed Old Testaments and liturgies, using the Hebrew alphabet for both Hebrew and Karaim–Turkish texts – with great reverence, for worn books or misprinted sheets were given a religious burial.

Selâmet displeased Sultan Mahmud I by ignoring Russian requests for the repatriation of Russian children that the Crimean Tatars had captured in the wars of 1736 to 1739, a concession that the Crimean elite found humiliating and also unprofitable. Selâmet's ambitious *qalğa* and nephew Selim now used his connections in Istanbul to blacken Selâmet's reputation. Consequently, in 1743 he was exiled first to Rhodes, in the company of the sultan's head falconer, then, for his health, to Gallipoli, and finally to Thrace, where, after a life of piety and prayer, he died in 1751. Selâmet was mourned in Crimea, but not in Istanbul.

Selâmet was succeeded by his nephew Selim II Giray, who obligingly sent his son Qasim and his *nureddin*, also Selim, to travel overland through Anatolia and fight in Turkey's endless war with Iran (the *nureddin* was killed in battle). Selim raised an army for the Iranian front by demanding that every fifth household provide one fully equipped cavalryman (whereas Selâmet had conscripted only one warrior per fifteen households). The *qalğa* Şahin Giray did even better, recruiting one warrior from every third household for an invasion of Circassia that brought back some seven hundred prisoners (the sultan and his viziers were so pleased by the present of the best-looking boys and girls that they invited Selim to act as a consultant in Ottoman internal affairs). Selim II Giray then repatriated from Russia all the surviving Turkish and Tatar prisoners of war, for which he was rewarded by Istanbul with 5,000 gold ducats and, later, a solemn reception in Istanbul and an expensive watch. Ivan Nepliuev, the Russian ambassador in Istanbul, was worried by this lavish treatment of the Tatar khan, and by the fact that the khan's horses were grazing Bucak's rich pastures, usually a sign of an imminent Tatar raid: Nepliuev complained that Crimea was not repatriating fugitive Cossacks and Kalmyks who were Russian subjects. (The sultan responded reassuringly by sending workmen to build coastal forts near Azov that would protect Russian outposts from attacks by unruly Noğays and Circassians.)

Selim II Giray had great political skills, but he mismanaged his *qalğa* Şahin Giray, whom he dismissed, thus turning Şahin into a gadfly whose followers attacked and plotted against the khan from bases in Thrace, Poland and Bucak. Finally, Selim pretended to forgive Şahin, but ensured that the sultan exiled him to the island of Chios to render him harmless. Generally, Selim II Giray terrified his subjects, who called him Katı ('severe') Selim. In May 1748 he died, aged only forty, of dysentery.

So worried were the Ottoman viziers that, without a strict khan to restrain them, the Crimean Tatars might take up arms against Russia, they immediately sent an official with a full set of regalia to the city of Vize and had Selim's cousin Arslan Giray unceremoniously escorted to Crimea as khan. Arslan caused no disturbance: he spent the next four years supervising the reconstruction of mosques, courts and fortifications all over the peninsula. Above all, he maintained the peace. Four years later, Sultan Mahmud I gave Arslan a certificate and valuable gifts 'for superb behaviour and efforts to act in accordance with the Sultan's supreme will'. Moreover, Arslan resettled in Crimean Khanate territory, without a drop of blood being spilt, those Tatars living under Kalmyk rule.

Nevertheless, Aleksei Obreskov, the new Russian ambassador in Istanbul, had a bone to pick: he complained of armed clashes – looting raids, abductions, border disputes – between Noğay Tatars and Cossacks. The Ottomans responded that the Cossacks were as much to blame as the Tatars. Obreskov then suggested a solution: a Russian resident in Crimea, and an Ottoman resident in the Zaporozhian Host who would investigate and then punish these lawbreakers. The Ottomans resisted: such residents were too remote from the border and would not learn of any trouble earlier than the authorities in the capital. It took a decade to install a resident Russian in Crimea, and only after overruling the objections of the khan of the time, Qırım Giray. Meanwhile, Istanbul deflected Russian objections by ordering Arslan Giray to remove his sons from Kabarda Circassia, which Russia now claimed as its protectorate. Russia also protested about Turkish fortifications on the right bank of the Dnepr in a region known as 'New Serbia' (because it was settled by Bosnian and Serbian Muslims, refugees from Austrian rule).

It is hard to explain why a khan as obliging as Arslan was peremptorily removed from office and sent to the island of Chios in March 1756,[9] other than by the turbulence in Istanbul when Sultan Mahmud I, Arslan Giray's admirer, was in 1754 succeeded by his brother Osman III and the latter in 1757 by Mustafa III. The changes in viziers deprived Arslan Giray of support and led to his replacement by Halim Giray, son of Sa'adet IV Giray. Halim, however, made unfortunate appointments, for instance, a military governor utterly ignorant of Tatar customs, who caused uncontrollable rioting. Halim is reputed to have been 'scholarly, handsome and good-mannered, as well as nimble and courageous . . . but latterly he became addicted to hashish and opium and was beset by various illnesses, so that he became an old man incapable of managing his affairs.' The Turkish historian Vasif-efendi damned him:

> wan, immobile, he appointed his sons and grandsons to various posts and they were too young and inexperienced, and did a lot of stupid things and led the Noğays, always inclined to rebellion, to open insubordination, so that these Noğays looted part of Moldavia and there was no peace or security there.

In 1758 Istanbul hurriedly offered the khanate back to Arslan Giray, the man they had dismissed two years earlier. The Crimean Tatars, however, informed the sultan that they had already chosen Arslan's brother, Qırım

Giray. Sultan Mustafa III, anxious to avoid any interregnum, immediately assented. Qırım had already gone with his nephews to Bucak and quelled the Noğay disturbances. On the way, however, Qırım's men rustled Moldavian cattle herds: the complaints from the Moldavian prince were the reason why the sultan first wanted to restore Arslan as khan. Only afterwards did he realize that disgruntled Crimeans were a worse threat to peace than Moldavians, and thus overlooked Qırım's misdemeanour. In any case, the Turkish commandants at Ismail and Bendery urged Istanbul to appoint the decisive Qırım as khan.

We know more about Qırım Khan than about any of his predecessors, simply because he was studied (and courted) by two French and one Prussian diplomat: first by Charles de Peyssonel, also a French diplomat and orientalist, consul in Bağçasaray from 1753 to 1757, and author of the extremely informative *Traité sur le Commerce de la Mer Noire*; then by Alexander von der Golz, sent by Frederick the Great in 1761 to negotiate military assistance from the Crimean Khanate; finally by Baron François (Ferenc) de Tott, an orientalist of Hungarian–Slovak origin, speaking perfect Turkish and Greek, a roving French diplomat in the Levant, consul in Bağçasaray in 1767–9.[10] Even if we discount the partiality of these men towards Qırım Giray, his record as a wise, if severe, ruler and the sheer breadth of his interests mark him out as a khan who deserved to be the 'eighth planet', had Seyyid Muhammed Riza not died twenty years earlier. Qırım had what most Tatar khans, and the Crimean Tatar population, lacked: curiosity about the non-Turkic and non-Islamic world. Although he knew no Western languages and was an observant Muslim, Qırım (who slept only three hours a night) interrogated his visitors at length on mineralogy, geology, international politics, music (of which he was preternaturally fond), philosophy and literature (in particular, Montesquieu and Molière). Qırım had a strong sense of irony and humour (sometimes grotesque, as when he served his breakfasting foreign guests a Cossack's severed head under a silver platter, or tipped his concubines out of a pleasure boat into his pond).

Peysonnel was a French diplomat first and friend of Qırım Giray second. As a diplomat, he disapproved of his fellow Frenchmen, missionaries who refused to use modest houses as churches and thus risked expulsion, or worse. The French wanted to encourage Qırım to act as an implacable foe of Russia, whatever the Ottomans' reservations, and enthusiastically provided men, equipment and presents to further their cause. In the section 'Eclaircissement' of his *Traité* Peysonnel gives an encyclopaedic and plausible account of the social, political, economic and religious structure of

Qırım Giray's Crimea. He is critical of the ruthless arrogance of the nobility, the complexity and expense of the bureaucracy, but has only praise for Qırım, one of the youngest men to become khan:

> No ruler has ever been more loved by the Tatars or perhaps deserved to be. He is pleasingly tall, with agreeable features and a tough temperament that can be tested by anything; he has a lively intellect, solid judgement, delicate taste and rather extensive knowledge. He is eager for fame, wholly preoccupied with his reputation, a friend of the arts, seeking to educate himself, recognizing and protecting merit. He is prodigiously fond of luxury and would take it to excess if a Khan's duties permitted. His generosity is unlimited, so that even with revenues fit for a Sultan he is always in debt. He is very addicted to pleasure, but does not allow himself to drink and is ruthless with anyone who breaks the law in this respect, more out of religious zeal than love of order. He never goes back on his decisions, ignores any danger and exposes himself to anything in order to achieve his aims. His love of justice and his sternness would be virtues if they weren't excessive: he is always inclined to make big examples of little faults. He is affable, even familiar, with commoners, haughty to the point of arrogance with nobles, inflexible and pitiless to those who argue with him if he believes them to oppose his views, and he is magnanimous once he has overcome them. He has never shown any vindictiveness, but can be reproached for anger and being carried away, a great vice if it is accompanied with rancour and not followed by clemency . . . He restitutes all looted property with scrupulous precision, returning 20,000 slaves he had taken.

Peysonnel was perturbed by the role of women in the khanate: a khan's daughter, married to a minor nobleman, despite her dowry, could be a tyrant– Qırım's sister-in-law's bouts of fury forced her husband to wander the countryside like a tramp, and any nobleman who married the daughter of a khan had to come to the foot of the bed, kiss her feet and ask permission before lying down with her. In government, however, the only post open to a woman was limited to a wife of the khan, that of Treasurer of the Harem.

Later, when criticizing Baron Tott's memoir of Qırım Giray, Peysonnel, something of a gourmet, recalled how well he had eaten and drunk in Bağçasaray: baguettes from a Tatar baker, white wine as good as Chablis, an array of poultry that he fattened in the consulate yard, game, water melons better than those of Provence, asparagus so good that Peysonnel sent specimens back to Paris. Tott claimed that the Tatars didn't make butter: Peysonnel objected that it was one of Crimea's main exports.

Von der Golz's account is very different (and its love story should be taken with a pinch of salt). It begins with an envoy, Mustafa, arriving at Frederick the Great's camp in October 1760, when the Prussian king, faced with defeat by Russia and Austria, was desperate. Mustafa, Qırım's barber, was at one point a Russian slave, and then a refugee in Germany – a well-informed polyglot ambassador. What Qırım offered was an alliance with Prussia, which would enable him to participate in an attack on Russia without involving the Ottomans, and 16,000 Tatar horsemen in exchange for generous payments. Frederick was delighted to accept, and even contemplated resettling Tatars to eastern Prussia to reinforce his population and army. In the depths of winter, the young Lieutenant Alexander von der Golz was sent back with Mustafa, pretending to be a German buyer of horses, so as not to arouse Ottoman (or French) suspicions. Golz communicated only through an interpreter and, when he arrived, through an adventurer, M. de Boskamp, who had his own axes to grind in Bağçasaray.

Qırım invited Golz to smoke a hookah with him and expressed his admiration for Frederick of Prussia, especially for the latter's virtuoso skills on the flute: for Qırım a lead flautist in an orchestra was like a khan in Crimea, except that a khan not only had to play the tune, but use the flute as a cudgel on the heads of discordant musicians. Apparently Qırım habitually listened, as did members of his harem, behind a curtain to court cases, thus ensuring the impartiality of his judges. Golz was overwhelmed by the beauty of Qırım's private gardens and fountains.

The real business of the meeting began when Golz first presented a large sum of money and secondly laid out Frederick the Great's plan for a joint Tatar–Prussian attack on Russia, which would give Crimea scope to enrich and enlarge itself. Qırım demurred, insisting that any agreement required the sultan's consent, and reminded Golz that the khan's debts and expenses required a very great outlay. Qırım also complained of his illnesses and asked for a Prussian doctor. More presents – cloth, swords, gold watches – were dispatched from Breslau (Wrocław), together with the text of a treaty. Later an official interpeter, and eventually a Dr Frese from Berlin, arrived. Qırım would not sign, on the grounds that oral agreements were sufficient; he demanded time to think, to persuade his *beys* and the sultan's court. Qırım next demanded 100,000 piastres; Golz sent an Armenian to Constantinople to fetch this sum from the Prussian ambassador. Meanwhile Boskamp, apparently also working for Prussia, was jeopardizing the mission by conducting an affair with a Tatar girl whom Qırım was eyeing up for his harem.

The spring of 1762 brought disaster: Peter III, a fanatical admirer of Frederick the Great, became tsar of Russia and immediately proposed peace with Prussia. Frederick accepted and now suggested that Qırım send his men into Hungary against Austria, a campaign that would not profit Crimea, but would infuriate the sultan. Golz was meant to bring the Tatar forces to Causeni in Moldavia. Qırım arrived with Boskamp and Dr Frese, whose pills had apparently cured the khan. Qırım would fight in Hungary if Frederick secured Russian neutrality, if Russia demolished its forts on the Crimean frontier and withdrew Cossack forces, and if Frederick paid an additional 450 purses (equal to some 40 tonnes of silver). As Qırım well knew, these conditions were impossible to meet. The conversation turned to science, opera and theatre, with Qırım making notes in a book carried by a servant.

Soon the mood changed and Qırım Giray expressed his distrust of all written treaties with Europeans. He would now consult the sultan and treat Golz and Boskamp as mere guests. A third Prussian envoy sent by Frederick somehow persuaded Qırım to mobilize his men at Causeni. Again, everything stopped. Sultan Mustafa III suddenly took against the prospect of war and opposed the Prussian offer of a treaty. Worse, Qırım found out about Boskamp's intrigue with the Tatar girl and told him to leave instantly, or be beheaded. Golz, however, was given two fine Circassian horses and a friendly farewell.

The Prussian intrigue is probably the reason why in 1764 Sultan Mustafa III sent a messenger and a decree without the usual regalia, thus signifying Qırım's dismissal. Nikiforov, the tactless and offensive Russian consul whose presence in Bağçasaray Qırım had tried to make as uncomfortable as he could, reported that Qırım had been deposed for many offences against all the inhabitants of Crimea, and for extorting large sums of money from Greeks, Armenians and Jews. Rumours of Qırım's ruthless ploys for making money proliferated. Qırım's heavy taxation apparently required the help of a crooked dealer, Tütüncü ('tobacco dealer') Hasan-paşa, who was promptly beheaded once Qırım had been removed. Anecdotes circulated in Istanbul that Qırım had profited by helping a hat trader and making it compulsory for men in Crimea to wear his model of hat. The Russian consul claimed that there was much rejoicing at the removal of Qırım, which in the case of Armenians, Greeks and Jews may have been true. Three days later Qırım Giray set off for Rumelia, perhaps first escorted to Chios under arrest by court officials. Like other deposed khans, Qırım, exiled to the islands, acted as if he were a viceroy: the Greek islanders loathed the corrupt governors sent by Istanbul and appealed to Qırım's charismatic authority to see that justice was meted out to them, there, or in the courts of Istanbul.

To Nikiforov's dismay, once designated as khan of Crimea, Selim III Giray's first act in 1765 was to demand the expulsion of the Russian consul, explaining to the sultan that 'ever since ancient times no consul has been appointed here by the Russian state . . . in my predecessor's reign, when the consul was appointed he was responsible for improper actions incompatible with peaceful relations.' In Istanbul ambassador Obreskov confirmed that the Bağçasaray people and the clergy were hostile to any Russian consul. Despite his agreement with Ottoman policy, Selim III Giray failed to repress a group of *beys* who contemplated bringing Crimea under Russian protection: he was judged to be inadequate, and in 1767 he was deposed.

Selim III was succeeded by Maqsud I Giray, whose reign was so short and uneventful that little is remembered, except that he was useless as a warrior, was obsessed with magic and astrology, and left a bridge as his sole monument. From March to May Arslan Giray, Qırım's brother, functioned as khan, but he died of illness, possibly murdered, in Causeni, before he got to Crimea from exile in Chios. The emergencies of war made it imperative to restore Qırım.

The Ottomans could no longer remain at peace. The death of King Augustus III of Poland led to the election of a Russian favourite, Stanisław Poniatowski, now supported by Prussia, England and Denmark, even as Russian troops took over Poland. War, predicted in 1767 when the Russian embassy in Istanbul burnt down, was inevitable: Sultan Mustafa III was determined to halt Russia's annexation of Georgia and Poland. The Russian ambassador Obreskov was sent to Yedi Küle prison (where he lived in great comfort), the peace-loving grand vizier Muhsin-zade was dismissed, and in October 1768 war was declared. M. de Boskamp, who had surfaced again in Ottoman lands as a pro-Russian Polish agent, had to vanish again. Khan Qırım Giray, replaced first by his nephew Selim III Giray and then by a cousin, Maqsud Giray, was reinstated.

In his brief retirement Qırım had not renounced politics. Russian and Turkish documents suggest that when in 1764 the Polish *sejm* had to elect a new king, and a pro-Muscovite majority and pro-Ottoman minority both lobbied Istanbul, Qırım was urging the Ottoman court to take action. In 1768 he tore himself away from his study and went to the seraglio, where the heads of forty rebel Montenegrins were displayed, to receive the customary khan's insignia and 40,000 ducats. Qırım left for Moldavia to confront the Russian Cossacks at Bendery. The French were particularly supportive, and sent their envoy Baron François de Tott, then consul in Bağçasaray, in pursuit. Qırım was delighted, and asked Tott, when they met on the Dnestr river, to cook him fish with a French sauce. Qırım held his inaugural session in full regalia in Causeni, and then supper, prepared by both the khan's and Tott's cooks, was served; Qırım declared that the French dish was superior and that sauces were the mark of civilization. The khan and the diplomat discussed Molière's *Tartuffe*. Qırım declared he knew Tatar versions of its hero, and asked for a Turkish translation of the play (which, though promised, was never made). Tott notes, 'He could not perceive how such a character as the Bourgeois Gentilhomme could exist in a society where difference of rank is so perfectly understood, and so invariably established.'

Very soon Qırım asked Tott to go on a mission to Khotyn, then on the border of Poland and the Ottoman empire, to coordinate the war effort at the anti-Russian Poles' headquarters, and then to return to the Tatar camp. As Tott put it, 'The activity of this Prince, for whom nothing was too arduous, made him require also a great share of it from others.'

The Tatar army that was now invading the Bessarabian region of 'New Serbia' (renamed by the Russians Elizavetgrad) was enormous. Qırım commanded all the forces north of the Danube. His recruitment was unprecedented: he conscripted three cavalrymen, most with three horses each, per eight households. While the *qalğa* and *nureddin* led large armies up the Dnepr, Qırım's forces of perhaps 80,000 concentrated around Dubossary. Captured mercenaries told the Russians, however, that the Tatar forces had no wagons, merely baggage camels and oxen, and were armed only with bows and arrows; only the janissaries accompanying them on horseback had firearms. Qırım's forces had no artillery.

At Khotyn the Tatars were helped by Albanian and Greek cavalry under Ottoman command. This time, however, the Zaporozhian Cossacks rejected the sultan's invitation to join the Ottoman forces: they declared loyalty to Catherine the Great. (Ottoman historians were puzzled that military men could show such devotion to a female monarch.) Three Russian targets were attacked that winter of 1768–9 in what was perhaps the largest and certainly the last Tatar invasion of territory claimed by Russia. Thirty years had passed since the last major Russian–Tatar conflict: the Russians, unlike the Tatars, had forgotten how to wage this war of dissimilar forces.

Russia declared war on 29 November 1768. They noted that the Tatar horses were poor, if tough specimens, and that few Tatars wore armour. An Austrian witness was struck by the number of callow youths and decrepit old men in the Tatar forces. A Georgian in the Ottoman army reported that the explicit goal of the Tatar army was to depopulate the territory by enslaving the civilian population. Even before clashing with the Russian army, Turks and Tatars had begun devastating Moldavia and Wallachia.

On 7 January 1769, banners flying, mounted on a fine Arab horse, Qırım Giray left Causeni, wearing a sable coat and sable-trimmed turban, holding a gold-topped sceptre and sabre. A lot of wine was drunk and alms were thrown to spectators. Three weeks later, the Tatars advanced 280 kilometres (175 mi.) and crossed the frozen Bug into Russian territory. Qırım's traditional Tatar tactics were to pretend to besiege St Elizabeth, the main Russian fortress, while splitting their own army into small raiding parties to roam far and wide, looting, burning and enslaving. Disaster struck after a brief thaw and severe frost. The Turkish troops were unaccustomed to a steppe winter, and 3,000 men and 30,000 horses perished. After torturing two Tatar prisoners for information, the Russians avoided a full-scale battle and defended themselves behind ramparts, while the land around them was ravaged. Using burning arrows for want of cannon, the Tatars incinerated a church full of refugees. The cold made Qırım's forces vulnerable, and three hundred suicide fighters, *enfants perdus*, attacked a Russian fortress in search of shelter.

By the end of February, burdened with too much loot and too many prisoners to move quickly, let alone advance, Qırım and his army were back in Causeni. They had burned so much grain, fodder and shelters that the Russian army, now without reserves, could no longer pursue them. One Russian complaint was that 'the enemy scum are so vicious that even at death's door, wounded or unhorsed, they fight back and won't surrender ... All these actions have happened during severe frosts and blizzards almost beyond human endurance.'[11]

Russia's generals held an inquest over their defeat, giving Catherine improbably low figures for military deaths and civilian losses, but unable to hide the fact that the survivors had fled and the new 'colony' of Elizavetgrad was now deserted. In March Constantinople celebrated Qırım Giray's victory. Qırım's great-nephew Halim estimated that Qırım had captured 15,000 Muscovites. Many Poles, even though Poland was a non-combatant country, also suffered from Tatar atrocities.

Qırım tried ferociously to maintain order. He had whipped to death one soldier who falsely claimed to have killed a Cossack and brought the head to show the khan. He executed a Noğay Tatar for looting cloth from a Polish village, the condemned man voluntarily inserting his head between bow and bowstring, holding on, while a horse dragged him at a gallop to his death.

Before March was over, while Russia was planning revenge, Qırım Giray died at Causeni at the height of his glory. Before he died, he offered Baron Tott six slave boys; Tott replied that his religion forbade him to accept, but that he might be tempted by slave girls. Qırım explained that no Muslim girl could be given to a Christian, since women were too fickle to stay faithful to Islam. Depressed by the loss of so many men from the cold, Qırım's mood and body sickened: Doctor Syropoulos, a Greek who treated the prince of Wallachia, was summoned. Despite Tott's anxieties about an enemy doctor, Qırım took the medicine prescribed for his haemorrhoids. There was just time to fetch Qırım's ministers, wives and six musicians, so that the khan could die listening to music and consoled by his favourite wife. Syropoulos took his passport and vanished. (Whether he had poisoned Qırım, or was just avoiding the comeback a doctor could expect when a royal patient suddenly died, we do not know.[12]) A coach draped in black, drawn by six horses, escorted by fifty men, made its way to Bağçasaray with the coffins of Qırım and, according to Tott, Zeinab, the woman whom Qırım had eight years earlier snatched from the arms of M. de Boskamp and who died in despair a few hours after the khan.

8

THE CENTRE CANNOT HOLD

Yıkılupdur bu cihan sanma ki bizde düzele
(This world has rotted, don't think that it will recover in our lifetime)
Sultan Mustafa III

At this hour of triumph and death, Qırım left Crimea more prosperous than it had been ever, or would be again. The population losses after the wars and epidemics of the 1730s had been made up: polygamy meant that womenfolk in twenty years replaced a lost generation of men. Under Qırım and his predecessors, restoration and new building had taken place at a miraculous pace, and the conversion of Noğay nomads and pastoralists into settled farmers allowed Crimea to export more food, salt and manufactured goods than ever. Even though the slave trade was largely restricted to Circassians, and neither Russia nor Poland paid tribute, Ottoman subsidies were supplemented by Qırım's highly efficient taxation of non-Muslims and his customs dues, so that he could build fine palaces: a Moorish fantasy of a country park just outside Bağçasaray at Aşlama (of which nothing now remains), a palace at Causeni in Bucak-Moldavia, a manor house at Pınarbaşı in Thrace. True, labourers went unpaid and money was borrowed from Armenian bankers, but there was little discontent. Non-Muslims were exploited: at Gözleve import taxes were 2 per cent for Muslims, 5 per cent for non-Muslims, and the customs director was notorious for his compulsory purchase at a low price of anything the khan's palace might need. Foreign merchants were, however, encouraged and protected; Russian traders, who dominated much of the market, even though political relations were frigid, were exempt from most dues and restrictions.

Qırım was an enthusiastic engineer: new aqueducts brought water from the mountains to the steppes and to the Black Sea ports, particularly Kerç, which had no rivers. He began construction of a modern port to rival Gözleve and to load foreign ships with the grain that former cattle-herders, now arable farmers, were growing in the steppes. The peninsula's roads were improved and a modern postal system set up, odd in that the offices charged only whatever the sender was willing to pay. Greek geologists explored the mountains in search of valuable metals. The khan himself was fanatically interested in instruments, tools, electric batteries, as much as in philosophy, theatre and music. Information was freely available, even though the Muslims of Crimea, like those in Istanbul, still abhorred the printing press. (Turkish works were printed by Armenians, sometimes using the Armenian alphabet.) Peysonnel's *Traité sur le Commerce de la Mer Noire* (Treatise on the Black Sea Trade) sets out in great detail the range and prices of goods, the amounts imported and exported, and thus gives a picture of a khanate comparable with a prosperous Western European state.

All this was doomed to collapse within a decade. First, as far as the Crimean Khanate was concerned, one reason was the mediocrity, even unfitness, military, intellectual and moral, of Qırım Giray's successors, few of whom hung onto power for even one year. (Consequently, some Crimean subjects, particularly the Noğay, speculated that they might be better off siding with the Russian empire, now the likely victor of the still raging Russo-Turkish War.) Second, the Ottoman empire, still exsanguinated and impoverished by war with Persia, riddled with corruption and internal dissent, only nominally supported by France, proved incapable of standing up to Catherine the Great's Russia, even with an army three times larger. Third, Russia by the early 1770s had acquired formidable military power and generals whose genius was matched by their belief in Russia's mission to rule Eastern Europe and the Black Sea. And fourth, Russia could act unhindered: its forces effectively occupied most of Poland, and it was at peace with Prussia and with Austria– all three countries were now sharpening their knives for a lucrative series of 'divisions' of Poland. Few outsiders, not even the British, were yet worried by Russia's becoming a major naval and colonial power.

When Qırım Giray died, the Ottoman and Crimean viziers and *beys* agreed that his nephew Devlet iv Giray, then in Rumelia, should take his place. Devlet appointed his brothers as his deputies, *qalğa* and *nureddin*. On his arrival at the headquarters in Causeni, he immediately confirmed his reputation for fecklessness and incompetence (although his relative Halim Giray recalls his 'pleasant appearance and character, full of nobility and kindness'). Certainly, Devlet took no interest in his subjects or in the disastrous war, which became full-scale in autumn 1769. Devlet merely demanded more titles, honours and subsidies from the Ottomans. He watched complacently as the Ottoman cavalry fled across the flooded Dnestr, where a newly built bridge had been swept away, men and horses drowning if they couldn't pay mercenary Tatar ferrymen. Khotyn was lost to the Russians, as were the army's provisions and munitions. On his retreat to Iaşi, Devlet's men looted Wallachians and Moldavians, Ottoman subjects, but avoided clashes with Russian Cossacks or hussars.

For losing the key city of Khotyn, Sultan Mustafa III deposed Devlet IV Giray a few months after appointing him. He replaced him with Qaplan II Giray, son of Khan Selim II. (Devlet IV withdrew to Crimea, where he fought the Russians for three years.) Qaplan II could not make his mark now that the Ottoman campaign, overwhelmed by Russian artillery, was degenerating into a series of fiascos: at military councils Qaplan just pleaded for non-existent reinforcements and asked for Noğay Tatar families to be re-settled south of the Danube (consequently, the Noğay menfolk left the war zone). In any case, there was no time and there were no boats to evacuate the Noğay. Chaos followed: the Noğay seized what boats they could find, a panicking crowd drowned, and the next day a Russian force captured the fleeing Turks and Crimeans and then occupied the key port of Ismail. (General Aleksandr Suvorov sent Catherine the Great a triumphant couplet: 'Glory to God, glory to you/ The town is taken, and I'm there too.')

The Noğay were now negotiating with the Russians, who occupied Bucak unopposed. After a few skirmishes with Russian forces, initially successful with his two cannon, Qaplan lost most of his three hundred men to an ambush, and fled to Crimea. Catherine the Great now revealed her plans: 'We have considered it right to see if it is possible to undermine the fidelity of Crimea and all Tatar peoples to the Ottomans by instilling in them ideas of forming their own independent government.' Using Tatar prisoners of war as couriers, Catherine sent letters not only to Qaplan II Giray, but to many influential Crimean Tatars, outlining her cunning plan. By March 1770 the Russian government was debating whether Crimean Tatars could become reliable citizens of the Russian empire.

Catherine's letters had a very limited effect: a few *beys* were persuaded, but Qaplan either spurned or pretended to approve her approach (contemporary historians disagree).[1] While in Crimea Qaplan appears to have tried to persuade the Kalmyk Mongols of Kuban to desert the Russians and support the Ottomans. Qaplan II's desertion from the Danubian battlefields, however, was judged to be an error, attributable to his youth and lackadaisical character (he was only 31). On his return to the Danube, he threatened to abdicate, unless he was given more money than the army treasury held. The blackmail failed. In November 1770 Qaplan II (who would die of plague in August of the following year) was replaced by Selim III, restored to the khanate after nearly three years.

The year 1771 began with new disasters: the Ottoman commander-in-chief Ibrahim Paşa was captured and sent to St Petersburg, where he felt free to write an account of the disintegration of the Crimean Khanate. The new khan Selim III Giray extorted a large sum from the destitute Ottoman treasury in order to spend the winter in comfort near the Danube, waiting for the river to freeze, but that winter it did not and the expenditure on the Tatar army and its khan was wasted. Moreover, Selim insisted on the reinstatement of a dismissed vizier, Abazeh-Muhammad, who later had to be executed for treason. Selim left it to his brother and *qalğa* Mehmed to negotiate with the Russian prince Yuri Vladimirovich Dolgorukov, but first Mehmed imprisoned the Russian interpreter and threatened to have him burnt alive. The Ottoman command wanted to send Selim III Giray to Crimea to put an end to the anarchy. Selim III refused to go unless he received a larger subsidy than the treasury could raise. Corruption in the army was absurd: money sent to supply the Crimean army with provisions was spent on slave boys and girls, which the registrar in charge sent back to his own estate, and provisions were replaced with rough flour, ground from stale and rotten army rusks. Selim and his suite, avoiding the embattled Moldavian coast, sailed to Kaffa, where the *qalğa* refused, until he was paid, to provide wagons to take them to Bağçasaray. When Selim III Giray arrived at his capital, news came that some 30,000 Russians and Noğays were attacking the Or Qapı fortress. Selim's men were terrified by Russian artillery fire; Turkish officers mocked them, 'Make way, make way, a cannonball's coming!' The isthmus fortress, the key to the peninsula, was captured, probably thanks to treasonable Şirin *bey*s, and all Qırım Giray's renovations were turned to dust and rubble by Prince Dolgorukov. At the same time, news came that the Taman fort, just opposite Kerç, was also lost to the enemy. *Mirza*s and *bey*s panicked and scattered; Selim fled first to Bağçasaray, which was encircled by Russian forces. After offering to send two sons as hostages to St Petersburg, he took to the mountains, where he found no support. He fled to Gözleve and saw Russian ships moored offshore, but found a ship in Kaffa. Kaffa was still in Ottoman hands; a group of Christians led by a priest, who had assured the Russians that no Muslims were left there, had just been executed by the Ottoman commander. Selim sailed back to Istanbul. Many of the Crimean nobility also took to the sea. Abazeh-paşa deserted his command and crossed the Black Sea to Sinop, where he was executed. The remaining Ottoman forces in the Crimea reached a truce with the Russians. Those aboard ships preparing to flee became prisoners of war. Selim arrived in the Bosphorus in August 1771 and explained his return: the

Crimean Tatars, he said, had come to an agreement with the enemy. The sultan's court was so distressed by the destruction of the Ottoman fleet at Çesme by Russian ships guided by the English captain John Elphinstone that they reacted to Selim's desertion with tears, rather than recriminations. Although, the French orientalist Louis-Mathieu Langlès reports, he was 'hated by his subjects', Selim was allowed to live, building bridges and fountains at his Rumelian estate.

Once Prince Dolgorukov, now the senior general in the Russian forces, had captured Kaffa and the Ottoman commander Ibrahim Paşa, the Crimean *beys* took matters into their own hands. Without waiting for the sultan to carry out the formalities, they unanimously proclaimed Selim deposed, and acclaimed as their ruler *Topal* ('lame') Sahib II Giray Khan with his young brother Şahin Giray as *qalğa* (the latter would play a crucial part in the last decade of the Crimean Khanate's existence).

Military activity became sporadic and indecisive, now that Russia had taken the steppe lands between western Crimea and the Prut river and between eastern Crimea and the Kuban. With the support of Austria and Prussia, to consolidate their gains, Catherine and her ministers began negotiations. Catherine had her Tatar and Ottoman pawns, and with her skill at political chess, one or two of them would become queens.

On 16 December 1771 Catherine wrote to Heinrich, prince of Prussia:

> Şahin, brother of the Crimean Khan is our only entertainment at the moment ... He turns out to be a charming Tatar ... he has wit and more knowledge at 25 than all of Crimea. He writes verse and flirtatious notes to the ladies. The ways this Tatar phenomenon astounds one! Moreover, he is aware of the effect he has.

In April 1772 she wrote to Voltaire about Şahin Giray's interest in watching the dance classes at her boarding school for girls: 'He is allowed to come in for two hours after dinner on Sundays. You'll say this is letting a wolf into a sheep fold.'

Şahin Giray did, indeed, seem to represent a modernized Giray dynasty. He was a nephew of Khan Qırım Giray. Born in Edirne, brought up by his widowed mother in Saloniki, he had contact with Greek and European education; from Greece he was sent to Venice. After an exposure to Western science and thinking unique among the Crimean khans, his uncle Khan Qırım Giray summoned him to Crimea and promoted him, barely twenty years old, to command the Noğay. When war broke out, Şahin went to Bağçasaray.

As the Russian army began to take over Crimea and a pro-Russian movement among some *beys*, particularly Noğays, led to violence, Şahin intervened and stopped the hanging of pro-Russian mediators. He suggested a non-committal, procrastinating response to Russian proposals of surrender. Crimean magnates presented Şahin as the only popular and viable leader of the Girays who might also be acceptable to the Russians; Şahin, supported by the Noğay, could bring all Crimea round to a pro-Russian view. He persuaded a Crimean council not to execute, but to release Captain Mavroeni, the Russian army's interpeter, thus earning the trust of both allies and enemies. By the end of May 1771 Dolgorukov's army controlled the peninsula. Şahin's elder brother Khan Sahib II Giray, now elected by an assembly of the people, headed the negotiations with Russia, the young Şahin acting as paşa and travelling to St Petersburg to swear a formal oath of loyalty to Catherine the Great.

Şahin, whom the Russians now considered a candidate to rule the pro-Russian Noğays, was awarded spacious quarters and a daily allowance of 100 roubles; he behaved like a plenipotentiary, superior even to a Russian foreign minister, refusing to doff his hat during an audience, and demanding money and expensive tokens of respect. By the end of 1771 Şahin had charmed the St Petersburg public with his inquisitiveness about everything the capital had to offer; government ministers were appalled, however, by the debts Şahin incurred as he bought fur coats and silver dinner services on credit. When his suite of Noğay and Crimean deputies left St Petersburg in February 1772, Şahin stayed on, arguing with the Russians over a proposed treaty that conceded independence to Crimea, but handed to Russia the key ports and forts of Kerç and Yenikale.

At this point the Ottomans broke off negotiations with Russia, arguing that Crimea did not want independence from Turkey, let alone the loss of its ports. Russia responded by bribing the Noğays to stay pro-Russian, and by using the army to subdue the Crimeans by exemplary massacres of unpacified civilians. By September, Crimean rebellions were repressed; the Russian representative Shcherbinin was 'invited' to the town of Qarasuvbazar to sign a treaty conceding Kerç and Yenikale to Russia. Şahin finally left St Petersburg with letters addressed to Dolgorukov and Shcherbinin, and an investiture as khan of his brother Sahib II Giray. After Şahin's eight months in the capital, self-esteem convinced him that he, however, was the real khan, the creator of an independent khanate.

At the end of 1771, in the hope of discrediting the pro-Russian Sahib II Giray, the Ottomans chose a rival khan from the Girays still living south of the Danube. The choice fell on Maqsud Giray, with Khan Qırım Giray's son Baht as *qalğa*. Both turned out to be useless, feasting at the sultan's expense in Bulgaria and Anatolia, unable to take any action, even to cross the Black Sea, except for some desultory looting. Baht Giray had been a promising child, daring to shoot an arrow at his father's armpit, but now he and Maqsud were mere tokens of Ottoman irrelevance.

In November 1772 the Qarasuvbazar Treaty was signed. Drafted by Russian professional diplomats, and signed by Tatar amateurs, it was a trap for the Crimean Khanate. The Russians declared that submission to the Ottomans was 'unnatural and prejudicial' for all Tatars; they 'did not seek to take vengeance on' the Crimean Tatars for their raids 'because these were done against the Tatars' will and to their detriment'; the Crimea would be free to elect its khans without outside interference, but would inform the Russian government of its choice; Circassian and Cossack subjects of the khanate would now be Russian subjects; Crimeans must never take part in any hostilities against Russia, and Russia would defend their rights; Crimean forts would be occupied by Russian forces during war with the Ottomans, but without burdening Crimeans; Russia would keep Kerç and Yenikale and the rivers that provided their water supply, while Crimeans could only fish in waters not used by the Russian navy; Russia would cease occupying other Crimean areas when peace with the Ottomans was concluded; Noğays would be Crimean subjects, but their pact with Russia would remain in force; all Russians in Crimea, whether they had been converted to Islam or not, must be repatriated; Russia would not give refuge to non-Russian slaves, unless first voluntarily emancipated; trade with Russia had to be unhindered and subject only to agreed tariffs; Russia would have at the khan's court its 'resident' diplomat, immune from any harassment, which would be severely punished.

In 1773, even though the Ottomans at first breached the Qarasuvbazar pact between Crimea and Russia, announced at the end of January, a fragile peace was sustained. Catherine even handed back Moldavia and Wallachia to the Ottomans to avoid antagonizing Austria. Russia was occupied with the first partition of Poland and dealing with a new aggressive king of Sweden. Russia's navy, however, was threatening the Dardanelles, and Turkey was now fighting a long war with its former subject Egypt. Sultan Mustafa III died in January 1774 and the inexperienced Abdul Hamid I succeeded him, but even Mustafa's intelligence and experience could not have staved off the inevitable. In summer 1774 General Suvorov totally routed the Ottoman army. At the same time, Şahin assured Prince Dolgorukov, the commander, that in an independent Crimea he would guarantee friendship with Russia. Within weeks the Ottomans were forced to sign the Küçük-Kaynarca treaty, which sealed the fate of the Crimean Khanate (not represented at these negotiations, since the khanate had withdrawn from the war in 1772) and permanently disabled the Ottoman empire, which had to cede territory, pay reparations and recognize Russia as 'protector' of Christians in the Ottoman empire. The articles reinforced and extended those of the Qarasuvbazar accords with the khanate. Once again, Russia recognized the khanate's total political and economic independence, but Russia's right to 'protect' Christians included the Armenians and Greeks of Crimea and would provide a strong pretext for further interventions. All that the Ottomans retained in this treaty was the sultan's right to act as the Caliph with spiritual jurisdiction in Crimea. Even at the time it was signed, the more thoughtful European commentators saw the Küçük-Kaynarca treaty as a death sentence for the Crimean Khanate and, eventually, for the Ottoman empire.

Şahin Giray was foolish in some respects, telling Catherine the Great how much he disliked his subjects who were 'so ungratefully hostile' to himself and to Russia. In other respects he was perceptive: he distrusted the Küçük-Kaynarca treaty. He and Khan Sahib II agreed that, given Russia's dominance over the now 'independent' khanate, where an Ottoman sultan could no longer mediate between factions, and whence the Russian army had agreed to withdraw, rebellions would be inevitable 'given the fickleness and bestial morals' of their people.

Reactions to the Küçük-Kaynarca treaty were surprising. A few prominent Turks expressed relief that the Russian terms were so mild; some blamed the Tatars for having lured the Ottomans over the centuries into needless conflict with Russia, and were glad to be rid of the Crimean Khanate; others predicted that Şahin's baleful influence would make Crimea ungovernable for the Russians. Ahmed Resmi-efendi, the senior diplomat and adviser who negotiated the treaty for the Ottomans, was one Ottoman statesman glad to be rid of the Crimean Tatars. He feared only the Girays exiled in Turkey, who joined Ottoman clerics in protesting that handing over Muslim Crimea to Christian Russia would be an offence against God. Resmi-efendi (who died in 1783, before he could see how right or wrong he had been) wrote in his memoirs:

As knowledgeable historians have demonstrated, every time the Russians broke the articles of peace, the cause lay with the Tatars, who for four hundred years had oppressed them, burning their houses and killing their families . . . The Tatars have become weak and lazy, addicted to tea, coffee and opium . . . the Ottomans have mismanaged the Tatar Khan and his entourage by letting them ruin the treasury by taking 40 to 50 bags of *akçe* per month and exhausting six months' rations of barley, sugar and cinnamon in 40 days . . . they were to defend the banks of the Danube with 3,000 to 4,000 men . . . but recruited the riff-raff of Rumelia and were useless . . . The Crimean Tatars have since ancient times been a burden to the Porte. They are a seditious [*fitne-engîz*] and sinister [*şum*] tribe.[2] They themselves originally solicited the Russians to be made independent: they brought upon themselves a whole world of sufferings . . . When they saw the banquet table spread for them, they wouldn't go home until Judgment Day and passed the time with endless proposals.[3]

Conversely, Şahin Giray expressed displeasure that Russia had conceded to the Ottomans the right to interfere in spiritual matters. Şahin refused to protect the Russian resident Veselitsky when a Turkish commander landed troops and arrested the resident. Şahin hinted strongly that he was the only candidate qualified to be khan, that Sahib II was incapable, like 'a man riding an unbroken horse when someone else is holding the reins', of keeping order with such an unruly nation. Any khan had to have a free hand, otherwise he was 'like someone with a precariously fixed heavy rock hanging over his head'. To make his point, on Catherine the Great's advice, Şahin resigned as *qalğa* and left Crimea for Poltava in Ukraine, still pocketing 1,000 roubles a month.

Devlet IV Giray, with a small Turkish force and a few Giray princelings, set out in 1773, first to Ottoman-controlled Taman. He began by rousing Noğays and Circassians against Russian rule but, ignoring the sultan's instructions to confront Russian forces, operated underground, before moving west along the coast to land at Aluşta. He won a few clashes with Russian forces, and moved on to Kaffa, but was then compelled to observe the Küçük-Kainarca treaty and desist. Meanwhile, Şahin moved to Kuban, to rule the Noğays as a khan under Russian sovereignty. The new commander of Russian forces in the Crimea, Count Piotr Rumiantsev (now suffixed Zadunaisky 'Trans-Danubian' for his victories) despaired of peace in the Crimea, even after the treaty was ratified. Devlet IV Giray withdrew from Kaffa.

A Tatar delegation sailed to Istanbul in 1775, begging the sultan to restore Ottoman sovereignty; Abdul Hamid assured them that he would never recognize Sahib II Giray as khan. In spring 1775 Sahib II Giray was overthrown, unable to win over the Crimean *bey*s and not daring to ask for Russian support. The *bey*s' choice to replace him was Devlet IV Giray, who had been the Ottomans' agent in Crimea for the past two years. Sahib sailed to Istanbul, explaining that the Crimeans wanted neither independence, nor him as khan. He spent the next thirty years secluded in his country house. He spoke a strange mix of Crimean Tatar, Ottoman Turkish and Circassian – his brother Şahin was probably right to denounce him as useless.

In March 1775 the Russian ambassador in Istanbul apparently persuaded a friendly vizier that Devlet IV Giray was unacceptable because of his anti-Russian stance and should be recalled. Devlet, however, hung on for nearly two years: he cultivated the Russian agent, the Moldavian Captain Mavroeni, and the interpreter Konstantinov, apologized for Sahib II Giray's arrest of the Russian resident Veselitsky, and continued to stir up Noğay resistance. In Bağçasaray a decree was drafted to bring Crimea back under Ottoman sovereignty. The sultan, aware that Russia was now beset with problems involving Sweden and Poland, encouraged and subsidized this subversion, and went ahead formally investing Devlet IV Giray as khan. Rumiantsev reacted by bring a Russian army up to Or Qapı.

Devlet politely expressed his puzzlement to the Russian commander, but secretly called his *mirza*s and populace to armed resistance, while himself preparing to flee by loading a ship with his most treasured possessions. The Ottomans decided to send to Crimea a small fleet; if their denial of responsibility were disbelieved, they would claim it was a justified intervention to protect religion, by stopping Russia from installing its infidel protégé Şahin Giray.

Russia did precisely that, making Şahin first of all khan of Kuban; Circassians in neighbouring Temriuk declared they preferred death to Şahin, who had trouble storming the town. The Russian authorities knew how unpopular Şahin was, and their tactic turned to a pretence in necessary correspondence with the khanate's Tatars that Devlet IV Giray did not exist, or was merely a 'delegate' of the Ottomans. The Russian commander Aleksandr Prozorovsky then decided to engineer Şahin's 'election' as khan from behind the scenes. He ordered his army to stop mistreating Tatar civilians, he began addressing Devlet as 'your radiance', and professed total disinterest in the choice of khan, excluding Devlet only because the latter was Istanbul's candidate. In fact, the Russian army continued taking fuel and food from the population and viciously punishing any resistance to Cossack raids, threatening 'complete destitution and deaths which can be expected only from war'.

By 1777 Turkey was again embroiled in war with Iran and had lost interest in Crimean affairs. Russia took advantage and forced Devlet IV Giray to withdraw from Crimea. He had, in any case, lost popularity, partly because of the vengeance he took on *mirza*s who had sided with the Russians and with their Tatar appointees, partly because of his ineffective resistance tactics. Piotr Rumiantsev now not only demanded that Şahin Giray be recognized as khan, but that the succession in future should be simply hereditary, as in Russia, and as Şahin was insisting, thus depriving the *bey*s of their consultative role in the appointment of khans, turning the khanate into an autocracy with a centralized bureaucracy. (General Aleksandr Prozorovsky, however, considered that such a change would infringe the Küçük-Kainarca treaty.)

Tatars protested to Şahin and to Prozorovsky against Şahin's reforms and European habits: they threatened to boycott the new regime and any ships importing goods for this pretender to the khanate. Boycott breakers were robbed, even murdered on the highways. Russian merchants were given bastinadoes. Şahin was rumoured to have become a Christian and renamed himself Ivan Pavlov. In actual fact, he sat in chairs, wore a tricorne with the uniform of a Russian lieutenant, trimmed his beard to fit under his collar and, worst of all, did not roam on horseback to meet his people, as did previous khans, but rode in an English carriage (which the Tatars called his 'metal cage'), pulled by horses in single file along the peninsula's narrow roads. Şahin gathered round him a motley collection of well-paid bureaucrats. He was desperately short of money, but had no skilled officials, so farmed out taxes to rapacious extortionists. Captain Mavroeni leased the lucrative salt tax for a mere 215,000 roubles. A Zaporozhian Cossack leased fishing rights on the Dnepr for 1,000 roubles. The alcohol monopoly was sold for 16,500 roubles. The customary 10 per cent on all transactions doubled; people were forbidden to slaughter their own animals, but had to buy meat, as they bought bread, at exorbitant prices from monopolists. The only persons benefiting from Şahin's 'reforms' (some enacted with Russian advice, some against) were the Christians, who now paid the same taxes as Muslims. The khanate had earlier raised armies through the *bey*s, who conscripted one warrior from every nine, five or even three households, according to the needs of a campaign. Now Şahin wanted a regular standing army, subordinate to himself, mixing Muslims and Christians, wearing Russian uniforms, subject to brutal and humiliating Russian corporal punishment.

In Istanbul in 1777 the question arose whether 'this dog and pig' Şahin Giray was really a Muslim. Devlet IV Giray asked all Crimeans to prepare to take up arms, but failed to recruit any of the dispirited populace. They knew, in any case, that he was likely to flee, for he had packed his possessions on board a ship. They also accused Devlet of adultery and debauchery. The *mufti* would not issue a fatwa against Şahin. The sultan refused to see a Crimean delegation asking for Devlet to be supported and Şahin denounced. In April, dispatched by Prozorovsky, Devlet IV Giray left Bağçasaray, picked up his harem in Sinop and retreated to Istanbul, where he alleged that 40,000 Russians had removed him, and that Şahin in his carriage looked as much like a woman as like a man.

At the end of April the *bey*s agreed to sign an oath of allegiance to Şahin, as long as no Russian troops were present. (The oath of allegiance reads as if translated from a Russian original text.) Weeks earlier, Russian troops in Kaffa fired a salvo to celebrate Şahin's inauguration. Istanbul failed to make Sahib Giray reprove his turncoat young brother; the Ottomans declared the 'election' illegal and promptly annexed from Crimea all the Bessarabian lands up to the Bug river, driving out all officials and landowners who were citizens of the khanate. Şahin sent a delegation seeking recognition: it was received frostily and had to dismount and make its way on foot to the sultan's palace; they were served coffee without sweets.

Nothing deterred Şahin, however. He was mulling over the possibility of founding an empire along the northeast Black Sea coast, even though Russia was now consolidating its possessions all over Circassia. He built barracks and arsenals, he hired cannon makers and asked the Russians to sell him rifles, sabres, pistols and pikes. Bağçasaray had its roads paved with stone. Şahin abolished the *bey*s' control of much of the khanate and organized the country into six provinces (*kaimakan*) and 44 counties (*qadılık*), each with three grades of well-paid bureaucrats. (Loyal *bey*s received ministerial appointments with generous, and unaffordable, salaries of up to 5,500 roubles annually.) Şahin moved the capital from Bağçasaray in the mountains to the port of Kaffa, where, under Russian military protection, he established, regardless of expense, a foundry, a gunpowder factory and a mint. Şahin's strict bookkeeping could not compensate for the lack of a proper budget. Absurd decrees were issued for Russian prisoners to be handed over to Şahin, and Christians to be converted to Islam. Newly recruited troops, fed up with exercises and parades, mutinied and deserted: Şahin asked Prozorovsky for artillery to crush the mutiny. Most controversial of all, however, was Şahin's proposal to hold a census: in Islamic theology, only Allah could count the population.

By December the entire khanate was in revolt. Russian 'advisers' felt horrified and powerless to prevent collapse. The Tatar cavalry began attacking Russian units, provoking horrible retaliations that destroyed whole villages and massacred not just rebels, but bystanders. Şahin himself just published more manifestos, occasionally cancelling his own reforms and forgiving his subjects. Nobody relented; the Ottoman government looked on with *Schadenfreude* and confined its reactions to diplomatic notes, while the Russian authorities accused Istanbul of fomenting the unrest. Some Tatars announced that they would re-elect as khan the elderly sybarite Selim II Giray Khan. It was now clear that Russia might be welcoming the chaos as a pretext to take over the khanate as a Russian province. Catherine the Great's correspondence with Voltaire reveals that a decade earlier she envisaged not just the incorporation of Crimea, but her future 'Greek project', which required the Turks as a nation to be expelled from Europe (an idea that Voltaire enthusiastically supported).

In March 1779 Russia took advantage of Ottoman disarray and forced them to sign a new pact, giving Russia more power than the 1774 Küçük-Kaynarca treaty. Now they not only insisted on the same rights as the British and French to transport cargo through the Bosphorus, but doubled down on their rights to interfere with the Ottoman administration of Christian provinces. They forced the sultan to recognize their puppet Şahin Giray as khan of Crimea, and to observe the prohibition on exerting any influence, other than purely religious, on Crimean affairs. For Crimeans, the only glimmer of light was an agreement to withdraw armed forces from Crimean territory, a false light, since Russia withdrew just a few kilometres north of Or Qapı and could instantly invade again.

In 1779 a Russian punitive detachment carried out a widespread slaughter. They then supervised a deportation, disguised as a 'rescue', of over 30,000 Greeks and Armenians in the middle of winter to the unpopulated northern shores of the Sea of Azov. (Just 288 Christians, missed by the soldiers, stayed behind in Crimea.) The deportation was achieved partly by force, partly by fraud: Christians were assured by Russian officers and by Archbishop Ignati that their lives were in danger from Muslim disorders, and that on the mainland they would settle in newly built towns and farms. They were promised compensation for abandoned property, freedom from taxation and from military service. The Crimean–Greek city of Mariampol thus became the Ukrainian settlement of Mariupol. Within a few months a quarter of the deportees died of hunger and cold, since few of the promised arrangements for the settlers were made. The survivors sometimes had to sell their children to save their lives. Even Archbishop Ignati was horrified by the callousness of the Russian authorities. British witnesses confirm the cynical brutality of this 'voluntary' migration:

> In September 1778 there passed 75,000 Christians obliged by the Russians to emigrate from Crimea . . . a great part of them had no other shelter from the cold than what was afforded them by holes dug in the ground . . . the greater part perished; 7,000 only were alive a few years ago.[4]

The purpose of this ethnic cleansing was to wreck whatever was left of the khanate's trade, manufacturing and revenues, in which Greeks and Armenians played such a crucial role. In the Russian tradition, a country about to be annexed should first be ruined. The first effect of deporting the Christians was to deprive Şahin of substantial tax income. Şahin imposed a graduated poll tax, so that gypsies and Jews, for example, in Crimea paid annually up to 7 roubles, instead of the previous 60 kopecks. The annual income of the khanate averaged around a mere third of a million roubles, of which a fifth at least was spent on Şahin's court, which aspired to be a microcosm of Catherine the Great's and which employed a large number of Russian servants. (Catherine herself complained that supporting the independent khanate had cost her 7 million roubles.)

Şahin's own younger brothers Bahadır and Arslan were so horrified by events that they rebelled: first they tried to expel Russian garrisons from Kerç and Yenikale and prevent them from turning Ahtiar into the naval base of Sevastopol' ('city of glory'); Bahadır and Arslan were at least financially independent of the Russian occupiers, and for a few months Bahadır could claim to be the real khan of Crimea.

By 1782 Şahin was manic. That summer Catherine the Great, and then her most senior ministers, including Grigori Potiomkin, ordered Şahin to put an end to the rebellions, in which by 1778 some 12,000 Tatars had been killed. The *mufti* issued a fatwa authorizing any Muslim to kill the renegade khan. Instead of conciliation, Şahin organized a purge, arrested all the dissidents and rebels he could round up and forced a crowd of onlookers to sentence them to death. Şahin wanted, however, to distance himself from the executions. He declared that he did not want to be khan of 'such a devious people'. (His brothers Bahadır and Arslan were saved when the Russians evacuated them to Kherson.) A Lithuanian Tatar, Rudzevich, or Yakub-Ağa, after assuring the Şirin *bey*s that no harm would come to them, organized the killings. The victims, many of them senior nobles and officials, were bound, but the mob was reluctant to stone them to death. The next day another attempt was made: the condemned tried to persuade the crowd to pardon them. Şahin had a Cossack detachment fire a salvo, and the stoning of eleven men began. The Russian observers pretended to be unaware and were instructed not to inform St Petersburg. More men were killed over the following days; others had their ears cut off. Some highly placed officials were taken away and killed secretly. In a crime unique in Muslim history, the *mufti* who had issued a fatwa against Şahin was hanged in the courtyard opposite the window of Şahin's own house. Rudzevich had his nephew report to the corps commander De Balmain, 'We've had an execution, your excellency, and the wastrels have been exterminated . . . the assembly itself sentenced them to death, stoned them with whatever came to hand and, believe me, your excellency, after this, the mob cheerfully dispersed, as if they'd been at a wedding.' More executions followed, including two prefects (*kaimakan*) that Şahin himself had appointed. Rudzevich had assured a few of those summoned that they would not be harmed: two were strangled on the journey to Bağçasaray. A Russian diplomat, appearing before Şahin, who was dressed in a sable coat adorned with diamonds, gave the khan's 'severity and just actions' his approval.

Catherine, however, was both informed and indignant: she sent instructions that there were to be no more hangings or atrocities, and in April 1783 arranged for Şahin Giray's 'voluntary' abdication. On 8 April Crimea was officially annexed as a province of Russia. A Russian fleet of seventeen ships came down the Dnepr to Ahtiar, and another eleven ships from Kerç. Şahin was given guarantees of safety, awarded a general's rank and an annual pension of 20,000 roubles and was directed to a temporary residence in Kherson. Şahin sent his possessions, his harem (now a modest three wives) and courtiers, however, eastwards to Eisk, opposite Azov, before himself setting off for Taman nearby. His megalomania was undiminished: for a while he believed assurances that he might be a favoured candidate for the vacant throne of Iran. He tried to send an officer to intercede with Catherine, but was stopped. Meanwhile the local Noğay rose up to support Şahin: they were repressed by the Russians, and Catherine's favourite Grigori Potiomkin secured imperial instructions to give Şahin his 20,000 roubles and send him inland to Voronezh, Oriol or Kaluga. In May 1784, leaving his harem and 2,000 followers in Taman, Şahin chose the city of Voronezh, where he spent that summer in comfort.

Catherine, however, wanted to be rid of her useless puppet. She told the governor of Kiev to prepare for Şahin's arrival, after which he could be dispatched to Ottoman territory. Şahin protested for a year, and at the end of 1785 was moved a little further west, to Kaluga, where in a country manor he was joined by some of his suite – two mullahs, his ship's captain and twenty servants – and the Russian agent in Crimea, Lashkariov, who spoke Tatar well and who had earned Şahin's affection. The ex-khan tried to engineer a meeting with Catherine by bribing her chancellor Aleksandr Bezborodko with a ring. Potiomkin, who disliked Şahin intensely and had told the British ambassador Lord Malmesbury that the khan was 'a ridiculous mediocrity claiming to imitate Peter the Great', put a stop to all Şahin's contacts with the court and had the ring returned with an insult from Potiomkin and a rebuke from the monarch. Şahin reacted with a long apology, denying that he meant to bribe anyone – it was 'according to our Asiatic custom to give a friendly present' – and hoped 'her Imperial Majesty, his most merciful Protector, would not think him capable of bribing her chancellor'. He begged to be allowed to leave for Turkey. Meanwhile, a list was drawn up of all the retainers, 71 horses and wagons that Şahin had left behind in Taman. (Many of Şahin's retainers were Girays – widowed aunts and their unmarried daughters living at his expense.)

In Taman the retainers were anxious: Şahin's brother Arslan complained, 'We are all perishing here,' and asked what fate was in store for them. If Şahin was not long for this world, how would they live? (They were told by Potiomkin that they now had either to take Russian citizenship, or to leave for Turkey: like the Noğays in Taman, they replied that they had sworn an oath to Şahin and would do only as he directed when he returned to Crimea.) In 1786 Potiomkin had Şahin's property in Taman confiscated, and Şahin's Jewish agent in Bağçasaray was barred from acting on the ex-khan's behalf. All Şahin's letters to Crimea were intercepted and their bearers arrested.

Şahin's chief wife and chamberlain hesitated whether to emigrate to Romania, still an Ottoman dominion, or to accept Russian citizenship. That summer some 1,200 of Şahin's servants were escorted across Russian Kuban to the Turkish fort of Anapa, where the paşa demanded a large bribe, and imprisoned Şahin's chamberlain, until an armed mob intervened.

Şahin was deeply offended by the humiliations his family and court were subjected to, and demanded that his departure via Kiev to Ottoman territory be expedited. For the Russians the obstacles were firstly Şahin's debts, 130,000 roubles, which he hoped to pay from the lease of Crimean salt tax and customs dues, and secondly Constantinople's failure to respond to Şahin's application for entry. Nevertheless, the ex-khan's property and 34 of his servants were forwarded to Kiev, and his wives were put on one of the khan's ships and sent to Turkey (in the end, two ships belonging to Şahin, carrying 57 men and 117 women and children, left Taman for Istanbul). Slowly, from various directions, Şahin and his property approached the Ottoman border. The paşa of Khotyn, however, would not let him cross the border until the sultan sent consent. By mid-December 1786 there was still no reply, and Şahin was running out of money (his pension would stop the moment he crossed the border).

On 24 January 1787 the official invitation came 'for the reception of your radiance according to our ancient customs in expectation of honours on crossing the border and escort from Khotyn to Bucharest and thence to Edirne . . . as you are a respected and agreeable guest of his Majesty the Sultan.' The Russian ambassador in Istanbul had no illusions about the honours and respect Abdul Hamid I was offering: 'I don't know the true reason for Şahin coming here, but he asked for it and will regret this stupid action a thousand times.'

Şahin Giray had about 150 armed men with him and lingered in Khotyn three days, trying to contact the Bucak Tatars. The Moldavian *voivode* reported to Istanbul that Şahin hoped to be appointed khan of Deşt-i-Qıpçaq and Bukhara. Rumours reached Istanbul that Şahin wanted to seize the Dnestr region on behalf of Russia. Şahin hesitated, unsure of Ottoman intentions. On 27 January he was escorted from Silistra to Edirne. Abdul Hamid I examined Şahin's papers and found 'no sense in them', perhaps because so many were written in languages other than Turkish. The sultan blamed Şahin above all for the irretrievable loss of Crimea, and that alone, apart from the khan's many other offences, justified a death sentence. The government apparently gave Ali Paşa, in charge of Şahin's escort, secret instructions to poison Şahin, but no convenient opportunity arose. Şahin Giray waited in Edirne for a week, while his property remained in Burgas. He was then taken to Gallipoli on the north coast of the Dardanelles and from there sent into exile on Rhodes, rowed by an Ottoman 'Swallow' light skiff. Closely guarded by his own men against assassination during the sea voyage, he was at Rhodes allowed to live in a house in a vineyard instead of inside the castle. But he sensed that his death sentence had been passed and began to look for ways to escape to Europe. For months nothing happened: local officials hesitated to execute a descendant of Genghis Khan. Eventually, Sultan Abdul Hamid lost patience and denounced the Rhodes officials for their dereliction of duty. The visit to Rhodes of a senior paşa returning from Egypt to Istanbul, where he reported the state of affairs, settled Şahin's fate. In July the Rhodes judge Sünbülzâde Vehbi and his guards raided Şahin's farmhouse and tried to take their victim into the castle (Abdul Hamid I wanted his prisoner for the time being securely imprisoned). The ex-khan ran to the French consulate and sought asylum: he was hoping that his supporters in Tekirdağ were coming to Rhodes on a boat to enable him to escape. Sünbülzâde Vehbi, however, surrounded the consulate with soldiers on 31 July 1787. Dutrouy, the consul, badly shaken, described in a long letter to his superior, Count Choiseul-Gouffier, ambassador in Constantinople, what happened:

I hasten to report to your Excellency the most unexpected event, the saddest for an officer whose heart is as sensitive as it is zealous. Yesterday, at dinner time, I saw thirty armed men coming onto my property; two of them, having inspected everything around, left and came back with a third man, who no sooner had he appeared, pressed my hands and asked me in Turkish for asylum and protection. He barely had the strength to articulate his name: he said he was Şahin Giray, Khan of Crimea. Tears were pouring down his face, and all his limbs were trembling convulsively . . . I said that, being alone and having only my rank to oppose armed force and the fury of a whole town, I couldn't promise to protect him against force, or a failure to respect my house. 'It will be respected,' he told me emphatically, taking my hands again. He added, 'I only ask you not to abandon me.' After promising not to, I left him to put on my dress uniform and attach my sword . . .

How surprised I was when, coming out of the house, I saw all the surroundings filled with a crowd of armed men. The ones nearest had their hands on their sabres and confronted me with pistols . . . 'Hand over the prisoner,' they shouted. 'Otherwise you and your interpreter will be the first to be slaughtered. Four cannons will smash down your house.' . . . Another hour passed. Finally the Prince, after making all the officers swear that they had no order to take his life, and that they would let him send a messenger to Constantinople, consented to leave and go back to his former lodgings . . . The Austrian consul is shouting everywhere that, if the Tatar Prince had sought shelter with him, he could have stayed on. I don't know if today, as in Samson's time, an ass's jaw would be enough to annihilate 4,000 armed men, but if you believe the Turks in Rhodes, one wouldn't even have had the time to capitulate . . . But my heart will groan for a long time over the sad fate of a prince whom I treated so shabbily thanks to the most cowardly and most despicable creatures.

A week later, Dutrouy added a postscript:

> The tragic end of Şahin Giray has finally put an end to the disturbance in the town of Rhodes; this King was strangled this morning, like the vilest of criminals; his body was immediately taken without ceremony or a cortège to the cemetery where the most despised corpses are put.

Şahin was executed by strangulation on 7 August 1787 in a special area inside the castle. His head was cut off and sent discreetly to Istanbul; his body was dumped in a ditch later used as a latrine.[5] Şahin's possessions passed to his heirs in Burgas, where they were allowed to live.

Şahin Giray had to abandon property in every city he passed on his way to Gallipoli – in Khotyn, Iaşi and Edirne. Two ships in Burgas harbour, carrying Şahin Giray's personal belongings, were taken over by the Black Sea chief admiral: these treasures were 24,345 *kuruş* worth of gold and silver sent from Edirne to the Crimean Mint. The ex-khan's papers were sent to the Ottoman secret archives. Sultan Abdul Hamid I ordered that Şahin's property be distributed to his heirs: otherwise 'it would harm the glory of the state.' A court treasurer named Giridî, in Şahin Giray's entourage, could now afford to build a castle in Cyprus.[6]

9

UNDER THE TSARS

As soon as Şahin Giray had left Crimea and the peninsula was declared to be a province of Russia, an unprecedented process of ethnic cleansing, ecological and urban destruction and militarization began. The decline in population was precipitous: the civil war between supporters and opponents of the khan and Russian punitive expeditions killed tens of thousands; epidemics of plague and other diseases, hunger, cold and dislocation were just as lethal. Tatars who had money paid for a passage by ship to Anatolia; those who did not were given Russian passports and set off overland for the underpopulated steppes of Bucak or the Volga. The Christians had been deported almost in their entirety to the coast of the Sea of Azov. Perhaps, uniquely in Europe's history, the one ethnic group that was almost untouched were the Karaim and Jews of the hilltop town of Çufut Qale, who interested neither the Russian governors nor the Muslim Tatars.

Russia feared that Turkey might attempt a seaborne invasion in any future war and that the Tatars would rally to the Ottoman cause. They therefore encouraged emigration, sometimes driving herds of cattle and horses north of Or Qapı, so that the cattle-herders would follow their animals into the steppes. Then a ban was introduced: Tatars were forbidden to live in coastal towns where an invader might land, and the ban was extended to all Crimea's larger towns. Landholdings became deserted, the fruit rotted in orchards, houses crumbled or caught fire. The converse of this ethnic cleansing was an influx of Russian military, landowners and their serfs from the north: they had none of the skills or interests of the Tatars, so that the khanate's agriculture, once prodigious in quality and quantity, collapsed. Europe's largest ancient forest outside Scandinavia, an oval 100 by 60 kilometres (62 by 37 mi.) on the northern slopes of the peninsula's mountain range, was felled for shipbuilding timber and firewood, as were other forests, such as the blue hornbeams outside Balaklava (Kök Ağaç, renamed Mackenzie Heights after the Scottish architect who planned Sevastopol's construction). Russian officials who became landowners were granted, or bought cheaply, the absent Tatars' communal and individual holdings and squandered them. Tatars, meanwhile, were forbidden to take wood from their own forests.

Houses were set on fire; soldiers then plundered the burning or unburnt wood as fuel for cooking and heating. Cemeteries were dismantled, limestone tombstones used for floors and walls, mausolea (*türbe*) as pigsties and chicken houses. Monuments ancient and modern were broken up for rubble and building materials. Of the city of Kaffa, now renamed Feodosia, almost nothing was left standing, except for a couple of wooden buildings and the indestructible Genoese walls. Its thirty mosques were so utterly obliterated that Russian writers claimed that the Turks over the centuries had failed to build a single place of prayer.

Nevertheless, Grigori Potiomkin took steps from 1783 onwards to integrate 'reliable' noble Tatars into the Russian bureaucracy: Memetşa, a Şirin *bey*, was made *predvoditel* (lord lieutenant) of the gentry for the new province, although his civil service rank of collegiate assessor was humiliatingly low; seven others were made judges or counsellors. In March 1784 loyal young *mirza*s were recruited into three military divisions, each of two hundred men under a major.

In spring 1787 Catherine the Great, accompanied by her court and guests, Emperor Joseph II of Austria and other foreign nobles, made a grand tour of her new acquisition. Her travels were heavily publicized all through Europe, as the gracious acceptance of a new allegiance by Tatars relieved from Ottoman oppression. It had been secretly prepared (Catherine pretending that her destination was only Kyiv) at enormous expense for three years by Grigori Potiomkin, who restored roads, rebuilt a semblance of villages on the roadside, and formed a cavalry regiment of 1,000 Tatars to stand still in the hot sun while the imperial party picnicked. Worse happened: in Bağçasaray a muezzin was shot dead, lest his call to prayer waken the empress (the mosque was then abandoned by its congregation). The empress had, in fact, been kept awake, as she said in a poem she wrote for Potiomkin's amusement:

> I lay one evening in the Khan's summer house,
> In the midst of Muslims and the Islamic faith.
> In front of this summer house a mosque was built,

Where five times a day the Imam calls the people.
I thought of sleeping, but each time I closed my eyes,
He shut his ears and roared with all his might . . .
O, godly miracles! Who among my ancestors
Slept peacefully among the hordes and their khans?[1]

When Catherine and her court were entertained by a carefully groomed *mufti*, members of her suite prowled around the village and stole everything from the saddlery to the eggs.

Catherine's aristocratic companions were complicit in the hypocrisy, but Emperor Joseph II noted, 'Whatever the Empress does for the local population, every single Crimean, especially the old men, would be glad to escape the new authority.' Prince Nassau-Siegen was struck that, when they walked the streets of Bağçasaray, 'none of the craftsmen or traders got to their feet or bowed: some turned away in disgust.' The prince wondered, too, how Tatars who had desperately resisted Russian invasion could now be relied on: 'Are these the Tatars,' he asked in his memoirs, 'who were so outraged at the thought of discipline? Now they are being entrusted with guarding the Empress and she is quite calm among a thousand Tatars, meant to protect her.' (In fact, Catherine's Tatar guards were largely either *beys*, who benefited from Russian rule, or other nationalities dressed in Tatar clothes.) Foreign visitors, who under Russian auspices now came to admire the 'glories of ancient Greece' that Russia had acquired, were struck by the sparsity, or absence, of inhabitants in towns that obviously had once been populous.

Among the most perceptive was Gilbert Romme, the French mathematician, future politician, freemason and, at the time, devoted tutor and companion to the thirteen-year-old Paul ('Popo'), son of Count Aleksandr Stroganov. (Romme's tour, which he had planned for years, was an educational one, and it would make the adult 'Popo' one of Emperor Alexander I's most determined reforming generals.) Romme's copious correspondence with Russian and French friends and his journal reveal his shock on entering a country that looked 'like Eden after Adam and Eve had been expelled'. The horror began at the isthmus, the ruins of Or Qapı: it showed

the great capacity to bring death and horrors everywhere, as a result of glorified battles leading to the annihilation of industry and agriculture, destroying the happiness of many thousands of families who have become the sacrifice of an ambitious man . . . The *mufti* told us that Crimea used to be densely populated, with 150,000 houses and four families in each, not to mention Noğays in their tents, about 200,000 ... Now there are 30,000 soldiers and about 60,000 indigenous inhabitants.

Later, Romme calculated that there were only 40,000 native Tatars left.

The city of Kaffa used to be very extensive, with 20,000 houses ... at the moment there are 488 Tatars there, including 276 women, and 700 Armenians, and a few Greeks and Jews. Its trade used to be significant; now they trade only in salt ... The Russians, skilled at destruction, have destroyed the magnificent marble baths and built drinking dens. The greatest trading city in the east is now one of the poorest Russian towns.

Aqmescit, idiotically renamed Simferopol ('City of Benefit'), once the *qalğa*'s prosperous capital of 1,800 houses, was now 'devastated', a little village designated as a provincial capital. At Qarasuvbazar ('Blackwater Market'), renamed Belogorsk ('White Hill'), Romme saw that after Tatars, Greeks and Armenians had been expelled, the Russians were 'busy defending their conquest and unable to cultivate it'. German, British and French travellers, tourists, historians or missionaries, all record the same ruination of a nation and its genocidal consequences. Even during Catherine's 'procession', 7,000 Russian peasants were transported from Ukraine to Crimea to replace the human losses; so were a similar number of 'Arnauts' (Ottoman Christians, largely Greeks and Albanians).

During Catherine's tour Potiomkin began to create a new Tatar elite: he appointed a Moldavian Tatar as his adjutant; the Tatar military, however, was restricted to internal duties, guarding mail coaches, salt lakes and forests, pursuing fugitive peasants and highwaymen. Each of Crimea's four districts now had a supposedly elected Tatar leader of the gentry, a judge and a magistrate (the dreaded *ispravnik*): nearly all were *mirza*s, accustomed to rule villagers with rods of iron.

The departure of most of the indigenous Tatars in the 1780s and '90s (except for 1787–92, when a new war prevented movement) led to a labour shortage for the Russian settlers who came to Crimea for the cheap or even free land, and the mild climate. Russian serfs succumbed to the sultry summers and endemic diseases. The Crimean provincial government imported Christians from the Ottoman empire, predominantly Greeks, among whom the notorious *klefti*, bandits and rebels whose aims were not just political, dominated. The Crimean Tatars had few privileges: one was exemption from military service or billeting; the other was a delay in imposing Russian serfdom on them. At first they were tied to the land and its new 'owner' only for half the year; gradually, however, the terms became more severe, although landowners and officials rarely dared to split families or inflict corporal punishment, as they did with Russian serfs. Tatar 'gentry', like the nobility or gentry of other non-Russians in the empire, could achieve recognition as Russian *dvoriane* (gentry), and thus gain exemption from service, civil or military, from bankruptcy and corporal punishment, with the freedom to travel and to study in Russia or abroad. The catch was the need for documentary proof of noble ancestry, which few Tatars could produce. In the end, a system of mutual vouchsafing allowed a privileged caste of Crimean Tatars to enjoy the same freedom as, say, Kazan Tatars.

Another route to freedom for Crimean Tatars was through the army, where a Tatar *mirza* could obtain an officer's and thus a gentleman's rights. Regiments of only 1,000 or so Crimean Tatars were formed and stationed on the Polish or Prussian borders; they were valued not just for prowess and horsemanship, but as *amanat*, hostages ensuring the obedience of their relatives in Crimea.

From a Crimean khan's standpoint, the next Russo-Turkish war began promisingly: on 17 August 1787 the Ottomans imprisoned the Russian ambassador, and secured Prussian agreement that Russia was now in breach of the 1774 treaty and must hand Crimea back to Ottoman suzerainty. But Turkey's mobilization was sluggish, whereas Russia invaded Turkish territory both in the east (Anapa on the Circassian coast) and the west (Khotyn), massacring civilians as well as soldiers. Catherine's dream was to drive the Turks out of Europe and put her grandson Konstantin on the throne of a new Byzantium (under Russian protection). She had a rude awakening. Russia lost, to storms and incompetent navigation, every ship but one of its Sevastopol squadron. In Crimea, Russian officials stopped deporting as many Tatars as they could north of Or Qapı after Potiomkin decided that removing Tatars from the coast would be sufficient: 24 coastal villages were evacuated and their inhabitants dispersed all over the peninsula in the middle of winter. By spring more than 13,000 Tatars had been dispossessed. Human beings, horses and cattle died of hunger and cold. Only in summer 1791, when the war was grinding to a halt, were the surviving Tatars allowed back to their landholdings, ruined and barren after two years of neglect. Land whose owners had not survived went to Greek settlers, imported from

Ottoman territories the Russian army had invaded. Some Greek immigrants, fanatically anti-Muslim, robbed, raped and murdered Tatars: they were rewarded as 'colonists' with substantial landholdings, from 20 hectares (49 ac) for a soldier to 240 hectares (600 ac) for a battalion commander. There was not enough vacant land to meet the demand: more Tatars were dispossessed. Often they came back to their former farms as serfs of the new Greek owners. Two hundred rural Tatars were even moved into a new urban quarter in Kaffa (now renamed Feodosia). Once a fragile peace was established with Turkey in 1792, it became urgent to repopulate Crimea, and a priority to support Orthodox Greeks. In Feodosia they were given land, loans for setting up a household or business, and thirty years' exemption from taxation and service obligations.

In 1796, when Emperor Paul succeeded his mother, his chief obsession was to undo as much of Catherine's legacy as he could, albeit in the most petty way. The Tauridean province, as Crimea had been renamed, was abolished and became part of New Russia, the formerly Ottoman steppes from Bessarabia to the Don. Catherine's officials in the Crimea were dismissed, and reduced to preying on the land, making a living by demolishing mosques, aqueducts and bridges, felling mulberry and olive trees, dispossessing by force or fraud the remaining Tatar farmers. Even when the reputably open-minded Alexander I came to the throne in 1801, dispossession continued: Nikolai Mordvinov, Black Sea commander and marine minister, the richest Russian magnate in Crimea, denied the right of any Tatar, because of their hatred of Christians, to possess land; he declared to St Petersburg that 'Tatars are incapable of living and occupying lands fit for orchards ... We need foreigners who can value such fertile land.' Land-grabbing assumed monstrous proportions: Potiomkin himself took some 13,000 hectares (32,000 ac). While Mordvinov was content with just 5,500 hectares (13,500 ac), a leading Şirin *bey*, Mehmed-Shah, took a record 27,500 hectares (67,950 ac). The Tsaritsa's ladies in waiting, minor civil servants and army captains typically appropriated each about 1,000 hectares (2,500 ac) of Tatar land. Untilled, or tilled by inexperienced Russian serfs, many of these landholdings became unproductive forced-labour camps. By 1821 there were only 8,000 Tatar men and women who still actually owned the land they tilled. Common land was seized by Russian landowners and by 1833 failed harvests and landlessness were giving rise to famines. Whenever a Tatar family died of hunger, their land became crown property. The peninsula was deforested by the demand for shipbuilding materials: typically, the Russian government blamed the Tatars instead, and forbade them to graze their goats. The prohibition became permanent and goats, the source of dairy products and meat for many a Tatar household, disappeared from the country. If Crimean Tatars were allowed to graze any animals, each male farmer had to work an extra fifteen days a year for the landowner, and hand over up to half the hay they mowed. Officials profited from the peasantry as richly as landowners: one *ispravnik*, a magistrate, who was paid 250 roubles a year to maintain law and order among the peasantry, was found to have extorted another 10,000 from the Tatar farmers. No wonder that officials complained of Tatar laziness and unwillingness to work for the gentry.

By 1799 this process was already unstoppable: village Tatars could not become more destitute. Although the immigrant Arnauts and other colonists were bringing back a semblance of life to the towns, Russian serfs imported by ambitious new landowners were slow to adapt to a new climate and soil. In 1799, and again in 1801, a Russian civil servant, Pavel Sumarokov (nephew of the famous poet of Catherine the Great's era), travelled all over the Crimea and wrote a detailed description of all that he saw and heard. He was accompanied by an officer and a Tatar interpreter and was armed with a mandate from the governor-general entitling him to food, accommodation and horses from every community in Crimea. Sumarokov was a benevolent, conscientious, but naive observer. On the one hand, he took such a liking to the Tatars that he decided to live among them, and was appointed a judge to decide disputes over land possessions. He wrote, 'The Crimean Tatar's unselfishness and equally their sincere help can serve as an example to many enlightened nations.' On the other hand, all the terrible depopulation and destruction he witnessed did not dent his patriotism. He realized that there might be only 70,000 Tatars left in Crimea, as opposed to some 400,000 twenty years previously. Nevertheless, without any irony, he concluded: 'This kindly State [Russia], motivated by its philanthropic rules, preferred to have voluntary subjects, rather than prisoners . . . so that the Crimeans were granted the freedom either to stay, or to remove themselves.' Even when Sumarokov settled in Crimea, while praising the extraordinary quality of Crimean orchards and their muscat pears, he was blissfully unaware of his own contribution. He boasted of heating his house: 'We are burning quince, cornelian cherry and pear wood, and it is as cheap as ordinary firewood.'

Many of Sumarokov's impressions echo Romme's twelve years earlier:

Nowhere has war and internecine disorders left such depressing traces as in Kaffa. The town looks as if it had been turned upside down by an earthquake, nothing but piles of stone and brick. There are fewer than a hundred small, badly built houses, and the inhabitants are newly arrived Greeks, Armenians and Karaim Jews, there is not a single Tatar. It is a *porto franco* for trade all over Crimea, but not flourishing. [Thirty years earlier, Kaffa had 10,000 households.]

Kerç was no better: 'It used to be extensive, but now there are fewer than a hundred unprepossessing houses, and the inhabitants are Greeks.' Nor was Eski Qırım: 'fewer than 70 houses, or rather hovels.' Alupka 'seemed uninhabited', Balaklava 'destroyed to the foundations, with not a single house or inhabitant, with just a Greek battalion on the shore'. Only the new city of Akhtiar (Emperor Paul had reversed his mother's change of Ahtiar to Sevastopol) won praise for its modern European style and 741 houses built from the remains of ancient Chersonesus for the new Black Sea navy.

From the start of the nineteenth century foreign visitors began to tour Crimea, anxious to see this once inaccessible part of the ancient Hellenic world, to understand Russia's imperial plans, to convert Tatars and Armenians to Western Christianity, or to collect antiquities. Most were ecstatic about the Tatar heritage and horrified by Russia's rule. Edward Daniel Clarke wrote: 'If there exist upon earth a terrestrial paradise, it is to be found in the district intervening between Kutchuckoy and Sudaq, along the south coast of the Crimea.' He concluded that

should [Greece] ever fall under the dominion of Russia, the fine remains of Ancient Greece will be destroyed; Athens will be razed, and not a stone be left to mark where the city stood. Turks are men of taste and profound science in comparison with the Russians . . . If we were to detail half the cruelties, the extortions, the rapine, and the barbarity practised by the Russians upon the devoted inhabitants of the Crimea, and their deluded Khan, the narrative would exceed belief.

After 1801, under Alexander 1's quasi-liberal rule, landless Tatars were able to submit complaints to a Commission for Resolving Land Disputes. The Commission was too overwhelmed, and too dominated by Russian chauvinists, to do any good. In fact, the imposition of serfdom, nearly as brutal as that endured by the Russian peasantry, shackled Tatars and made their livestock and equipment the property of their 'owner'.

Many Crimean Tatars among the hundreds of thousands of émigrés and deportees found new careers in Ottoman territory: the poet and musician Ahmed Kâmil Qırımlı became music teacher and Imam to Sultan Selim III; the chief judge Feizila-efendi eventually held the same post in Istanbul. Other Crimean Tatars were recruited by Russia as spies: the Çelebi brothers penetrated Istanbul's bureaucracy with such striking success that they were sent back to Crimea as double agents with a mission to behead the Russian governor in Simferopol. They were betrayed by local Tatars who, like most of the surviving population, wanted only to be left alone. To the general astonishment of the authorities, Tsar Alexander I ordered that the Çelebi brothers be set free and returned to their original home in Evpatoria (the new name for Gözleve).

The most extraordinary result of Alexander I's policies was the freedom given to Scottish Protestant missionaries to roam Crimea and the North Caucasus, where they could spread the Gospel and convert, if possible, Muslims. In the Caucasus they ransomed captured adolescents and had limited success – in fact, they needed heavy armed protection from infuriated Noğays. Reverend Henry Brunton, who knew Arabic and tried to learn Turkish, published a New Testament for Crimean Tatars. Brunton's great success was the conversion, perhaps kidnapping, of a boy, Qatti Giray, possibly a nephew of the late Khan Şahin. Qatti Giray became a Russian officer and was chosen to present two elephants to the tsar. He was disinherited by his Giray relatives, and became himself a Protestant missionary and a friend of the tsar, who paid for him to travel to Edinburgh, where he presented a 'Sketch of an Institution in the Crimea to raise up Schoolmasters of the Word of God', with a printing press and a loom. Despite planning to marry a Crimean Tatar, in 1820 Qatti married a Scot, Anne Neilson (who was promptly disinherited by her father). Qatti's mission was based in Bağçasaray. It was not the mullahs, but the Greek Orthodox who violently objected. When four Crimean Tatars, including Qatti's former slave, had been converted, local Muslims also rebelled and handed the newly printed Gospels to the Russian police, who redirected Protestant converts to the Orthodox church. The death of Alexander I and accession of his brother Nicolas I as tsar put an end to Qatti Giray's and all other Christian missions. (The only Christian success was with a Tatar born in Iran, eventually Professor Aleksandr Kazem-Bek of Kazan University, who would become Russia's leading specialist in Tatar and Turkic historical writing.) Qatti stayed in Crimea, not making a single convert, and became an archaeologist in Simferopol, dying in 1847. His widow stayed in Crimea, and during the Crimean War their sons fought for Russia against the British. Both the British and Russian authorities offered Anne protection. Qatti and Anne's fourteen children formed a European and Russian Giray clan, some of whom became prominent in Germany, Russia and Britain, but none of whom, because of their links with the Russian establishment, was recognized by the Crimean Tatar community as 'real' Girays.

A few minor Girays stayed in the Caucasus. They were allowed by both Russians and Ottomans to keep their titles and, as military commanders, to maintain order over some Kabardian and Noğay tribes. The majority of the Giray dynasty, however, emigrated to Turkey, settling in Rumelia, from the coast to the borders of Macedonia. They proved to be a bellicose, disruptive and sometimes criminal network, exploiting peasants and fellow landowners, abusing their privileges (they were entitled to generous daily rations and accommodation from the sultan's court). Some took part in rebellions against Sultan Selim III. Selim had selected the elderly Sahib II Giray, khan from 1772 to 1774, who now lived only 30 kilometres (19 mi.) from Istanbul, as khan in exile and delegated to him civil authority over the family. Others, Şahbaz and Baht, became commanders of Tatar regiments in the 1789–92 war.

The Girays in Rumelia held their estates largely as *vaqf* (in trust), to avoid confiscation or inheritance tax, although this stopped them raising money from sale or rental. They often profited from tax farming, although, as aristocrats, they were discouraged from menial financial ventures. They were not, however, adept at preserving their wealth, which was vulnerable to the voracity of the sultan's treasury. In the chaos, revolts and fragmentation that arose all over Bulgaria and Macedonia after Selim III's attempts at reforms, some Girays effectively allied themselves with bandits, 'taxing' local communities.

Two brothers, Cengiz and Bahadır Giray, were particularly notorious. Both had been rewarded by the sultan for their military prowess in 1787, but they then threw in their lot with bandits. They were exiled to Russia for a while; Cengiz was pardoned, but then raised an army of 5,000 men, which controlled much of the Black Sea coastal region. Charles Maurice de Talleyrand, speaking for the French republic, offered to make Cengiz a provincial ruler if he assisted the French in partitioning the Ottoman empire. By the 1800s Selim III realized that amnesties only encouraged rebel Girays: he threatened 'to disrespect their ancestry and kill them all'. Cengiz Giray, however, died of natural causes and his brother Bahadır's estates were confiscated only posthumously. Their influence, however, waned: only one, Mesud Giray, would attempt during the Crimean War to stage a comeback.[2]

The rise of Napoleon spasmodically revived Turkey's prospect of retrieving Crimea from Russian annexation. Periodically, countries at war with Russia, such as Sweden, had made the return of Crimea to Ottoman control one of their demands. Immediately after the annexation, the French, nominally supporters of the Ottomans against Russia, had sent André-Joseph Lafitte-Clavé, a military engineer, to survey the Crimean coast, warning that a Russian fleet based at Ahtiar-Sevastopol would 'be a terrible threat' to the whole Ottoman empire, yet at the same time would benefit Franco-Russian trade. Napoleon was in two minds: at one point he thought of trading Egypt, which he had conquered, for Crimea, which he proposed to invade. After 1801 Napoleon strategically placed consuls on the northern coast of the Black Sea and sent more French specialists to reconnoitre Crimea. (In response, Russia closed Sevastopol to foreigners.) The appointment by Alexander I of Armand-Emmanuel du Plessis, duc de Richelieu as governor of 'New Russia' was, however, convenient for French espionage: it was planned to make Crimea a gateway for French influence as far as Central Asia and India. In Feodosia the diplomat Jean Reuilly made contact with the Crimean *mufti* Seid Murtaz-efendi and proposed to visit Paris with a Şirin *mirza* 'who adored Napoleon'. They believed Poland might invade the Crimean coast if its independence were restored. Negotiations went through two interpreters; it was not clear whether the *mufti* was pro-Bonaparte, or loyal to Tsar Alexander I. (Like the English traveller Elizabeth Craven, Reuilly suspected that Tatars had very vague ideas of European politics.) By the 1790s, in actual fact, Russians were so sure of Crimean Tatar loyalty that they were exiling rebellious Muslims from the North Caucasus to Crimea.

Napoleon continued to vacillate. In 1810 he wanted to hand Crimea back to the Ottomans in exchange for Crete and the Peloponnese, and to push Russia back beyond the Dnepr river. When the 1812 war began, Crimea was to become one of two new duchies on Russian territory, with preference for Crimea and its excellent ports. 'Crimea,' wrote Napoleon's adviser M. Rolandre (a retired employee of the Ministry of Foreign Affairs, and then an official in Nancy) in his anonymous *Projet de pacification générale et de paix perpétuelle* (Project for general pacification and perpetual peace), 'has good ports . . . and could be transformed into a European duchy . . . the Tatars can be allowed independence under Polish supervision and protection.' Napoleon's papers, captured after the war, showed that he had planned in detail a structure for his Crimean duchy under a French duke. Another adviser, the Polish general Michał Sokolnicki, proposed renaming an extended Crimea not Tauris, but Napoleonida, thus saving the Crimean Tatars from 'oppression and humiliation'. By the time he had invaded Russia, Napoleon changed his mind again, letting the Turks decide whether to land an army in Crimea (instead of which, the Ottomans made peace with Russia).[3]

In the 1812 Franco-Russian war four Crimean Tatar regiments fought for Russia: they had been formed four years earlier, when the head *mufti* had petitioned the tsar to accept Tatar cavalry: the motives probably included ingratiation and the prospect of loot. The Tatars were uniformed like Cossacks, only their black hats and curved daggers were Crimean. The Tatar officers included Şirin *mirza*s, as well as a Mengli and a Batır Giray. Some had been educated in Russia and spoke perfect Russian, French and Greek. One was promoted to a general's rank, and many, perhaps the first Crimean Tatars to do so, reached Paris, where they tethered their horses to the trees in Père Lachaise cemetery. Napoleon, too, had Tatars in his army, but these were Lithuanian *Lipka* Tatars, a branch that had split from the Crimean Tatars in the fifteenth century. Of the original 122 *Lipka* recruited, only fourteen survived.

Despite the Tatar contribution to the war against Napoleon, Russian landowners and officials never stopped ethnic cleansing and land-grabbing. Some Tatars felt that Crimea under Christian rule was unfit as a homeland for Muslims. They were encouraged to leave for Turkey from Gözleve (now Evpatoria) or Kaffa (now Feodosia). In autumn 1812 first a terrible storm, then a plague epidemic struck Feodosia. No provision was made for the migrants confined to Feodosia, waiting for quarantine to end so that they might embark. Many died, some were shot when they tried to break the cordon. Bodies were dragged to the seashore and burnt. The Crimean Tatar poet Ismeti, in his sole surviving (but still unpublished) work, *The Poem of Kaffa*, complains:

> Every morning a doctor comes to look at us,
> Stings us with the strange excuse:
> 'Clear off, fool!' he says, and instantly runs off
> Without further ado, the wretch, to Kaffa.[4]

Gradually Crimean Tatars attracted attention from the scholarly world: Western orientalists, preoccupied with Arabic and Persian, only later began to learn Ottoman Turkish, and by reading Ottoman historians, particularly Na'ima and Peçevi, they understood the cultural, as well as political importance of Crimea. Manuscripts of Seyyid Muhammed Riza's *Seven Planets*, an extremely difficult text written in 1730, concentrating on the seven most influential Crimean khans, and perhaps the finest piece of Ottoman Turkish historical writing, were found in Venice, Leiden and St Petersburg. Aleksandr Kazem-Bek, converted by Scottish Presbyterian missionaries, proved to be a linguistic genius and began a prodigiously productive career as a Turcologist in Kazan, turning Russia into a major centre of Turkic studies: Kazem-Bek published Seyyid Muhammed Riza's *Seven Planets* in 1832 (another 190 years passed before it was transliterated into the Latin alphabet). Meanwhile, in Ottoman Turkey, around 1810 Halim Giray (a khan's grandson) produced *The Khans' Rose Bush*, a concise, readable and quite accurate biography of all the khans. Peter Pallas, the polymath academician, spent 1793–4 in Crimea and produced the first ever authoritative, scientific monograph on the Crimean Khanate. Kazan, even after Kazem-Bek moved to St Petersburg, became once more a major centre for Crimean Tatars. The Kazan Tatars would long be the bellwethers of Russia's Muslim world – themselves relatively well respected by Slavs, they persuaded other Tatars that Russian domination had its advantages, largely in giving access to higher education and travel.

One of the most interesting accounts of life among Crimean Tatars between 1816 and 1820 came from Mary Holderness, who arrived with her husband and children to help farm an estate bought by an English pastor. Her books are critical of Russian settlers, but she portrayed everyday Tatar life in Karagöz near the coast in sometimes idyllic terms: the only horror she describes is the Russian introduction of the knout as a punishment for robbery and murder, in floggings that often proved fatal and which went against all Tatar customary law.

Anatole Demidoff's *Voyage dans la Russie Méridionale et la Crimée* (Voyage in Southern Russia and Crimea) of 1840 presented Crimea as a Mecca for tourists and botanists, especially now that it was served by a steamboat from Odessa: 'Italy has been superseded by Crimea, landscape painters have to admit.' Demidoff claimed, 'Russia has faithfully conserved the traditions of this poetic corner of the empire', although 'ravaged several times'.

Tsar Alexander I in 1825 visited Crimea, where he agreed to exempt Crimean Tatars from military conscription and to allow them, like Don Cossacks, to organize their own cavalry contribution to the Russian armed forces. He died suddenly that year. Tsar Nicolas I took a very different view of the Crimean Tatars, thinking them unfit to inhabit, let alone till, Crimean soil; he initiated a policy of Russification. Nicolas I's regime in the 1830s was merciless: he ignored warnings that famine made Tatar peasants unable to pay taxes or the annual levy of over 200 kilograms (440 lb) of grain per head of household. The major landowners, meanwhile, were each decade doubling their herds of sheep, and the resulting depopulation resembled that of the Scottish clearances. To repopulate the land with potential workers, the government now recruited dealers who brought in soldiers' widows and destitute Jewish and Polish girls to marry Russian soldiers stationed in Crimea. Germans and Swiss, driven by hunger or the persecution of Mennonites, were also settled (and subsidized) all over southern Russia and Crimea; two French sheep breeders were given 30,000 hectares (74,000 ac) and 100,000 roubles to increase the numbers of fine-wool sheep. German settlers and sheep bred so fast that Tatars were even more dispossessed. In the towns, where few Tatars lived, life was sordid: even in Simferopol pigs roamed the rubbish dumps, soldiers relieved themselves in the streets, civil servants were piggybacked by gypsies through the mud and filth to their offices, and the khans' public water system was never restored (only in Sevastopol, and only to official buildings, was water piped). Not until the British landed in 1855 was Balaklava given a European gloss, with cabs, shops and clean streets.

Population losses could be made up in a generation (though now more slowly, since polygamy was dying out in Crimea). Crimean Tatar women, exempted from field work, breastfed their babies and thus had a lower infant mortality (and better personal hygiene) than did Russian peasant mothers, who left their infants sucking on soaked bread while they tended the fields. While ruined Tatar houses could be rebuilt, Tsar Nicolas I's destruction, however, was irreparable, for his oppressive laws hit deep at Tatar culture. First came a restriction on the appointment of mullahs: those who were trained outside Russia or could not prove their political reliability were banned. The choice of a *mufti* was made by the Russian governor from three candidates put forward by the Tatars. The oppression was only partly relieved by the governorship of Mikhail Vorontsov. Brought up in England (he was the son of a Russian ambassador, and an uncle of Sidney Herbert, the British Secretary at War in the first years of the Crimean War, who resigned after being obliged to shell his uncle's Crimean palace), Vorontsov was liberal and innovative, if paternalistic: it was surprising that Nicolas I approved his appointment as a virtual viceroy in 1832. Vorontsov was devoted to his post, staying on in Crimea in 1829 to fight the plague epidemic: he was one of the few Russians trusted by the non-Russians of Crimea, and later of the Caucasus. He built new mosques for Tatars on his estates, introduced new cultivars (including, unfortunately, phylloxera-infested vines) and opposed Nicolas 1's efforts to deprive the Tatars of the freedoms Catherine had conceded. But, as a major landowner himself, Vorontsov would not stop the alienation of Crimean land from Tatars.

Not only Tatars, but Russians too, suffered from Tsar Nicolas 1's heartless and corrupt bureaucracy. In February 1830 the naval base at Sevastopol suffered outbreaks of both plague and typhus, both brought from war with the Ottoman forces in 1828–9. The port and the slum that was set aside for 1,000 members of sailors' families was quarantined for months, with no proper provision of medicines, food, blankets, firewood or drinking water. Spurred on by double pay, the naval doctors and officials diagnosed every case of sickness and death as plague and forced whole families (largely women and children, since the menfolk were on-board ships) into barracks, where they were dumped together with the sick, the dying and the dead, and deprived of care: typically, of eighty admitted, sixty would die within days. Some were 'treated' to fatal bathing in freezing seawater. In June, led by infuriated womenfolk, an armed insurrection broke out and the houses of officials and doctors were ransacked. The governor-general brought in the army: seven 'ringleaders' were shot, and some 423 women were flogged (up to 3,000 strokes of the cane, sometimes followed, if they survived, by hard labour in Siberia). The dead, whether from plague, typhus, starvation or cold, were buried in the ruins of Chersonesus just outside the town. The corrupt doctors escaped lightly.[5]

In 1833 Russia's navy made landings in the Bosphorus, ostensibly to help Sultan Mahmud II maintain order, but in fact to force him to sign a treaty of mutual defence so that Ottoman interference in Crimean affairs was disabled. In Crimea the Russian Interior Ministry and the puppet Tatar *mufti* and *qadiasker* (chief judge) began a very different operation: 'to relieve the Tatars of books and manuscripts that are harmful for them and for social peace, or are not in accordance with the laws and rules of good sense'. Everything, from the khans' surviving libraries and civil service registers to rare Mongolian and Chaǧatai manuscripts, the four-hundred-year heritage of Crimean Tatar historical and poetic writing, Qur'ans and private letters, was gathered by police officials into an enormous pile. The Russian invasions of 1735 to 1739 had already obliterated a great deal of Tatar material culture; after the Russian annexation, visitors had been sold, or just given, loose pages from the libraries of ruined mosques and medreses. This, how-ever, was a burning of books on a scale worse than Hitler's or Stalin's, for the Crimean manuscript heritage was unique. Eventually, civil servants and curious passers-by rescued from the pile a few volumes or loose pages, and over the next century or so some of these were handed to archives and librar-ies (where they are still being discovered and studied). Of all the crimes committed against the Crimean Tatars by Russia and its henchmen, this was the least redeemable. The *mufti* in charge of the operation, Seit Celil-efendi, was given a gold medal inscribed *For Diligence*.

The Tatar population was still low: the first thorough census in 1830 counted 130,000 Tatar adult males. Of these, only 13,000 lived in towns, and only 6,612 were clerics who could be assumed to have a more than rudimen-tary education. Before 1830 estimates of the population depended on the number of armed men a khan could raise for a campaign: if the army had 50,000 horsemen and the mobilization was one warrior per five households, an informed guess would put the peninsula's Muslim population at 1,250,000, to which we should add an unknown number of Armenians and Greeks, and a fluctuating number, depending on market demand and success in war, of slaves. At a guess, Crimea's Tatar population in 1830 was around one quarter of its population in, say, 1630. In 1858, after the losses following the Crimean War, the total population of the peninsula was less than 200,000; fifty years later it was over three times as many, but the increase came from immigrant Russians and other nationalities. Only 180,000 Tatars were counted in 1913, a number equal to those who had emigrated or been deported to Turkey: Tatar mothers had replaced a lost generation, but it in turn disappeared from the peninsula. The northern steppe zone was noticeably deserted: dozens of abandoned hamlets, and a population replaced by barely 10 per cent, largely Russian peasants. The major difference was that Crimeans, some 45 per cent now in towns (Simferopol, Sevastopol and the ports and resorts of the south-ern coast), were now among the most urbanized populations in Russia. In these towns Tatars were a small minority: only in the southwestern mountain range around Bağçasaray were they the dominant ethnos.

Particularly acute for the Crimean Tatars was the shortage of Muslim clerics, and of mosques, although some imams did return after completing their studies in Turkish medreses. Muslims and Christians in towns paid three types of local tax, amounting to over 2 roubles a head. Overwhelm-ingly, these taxes were spent on building and maintaining Orthodox churches. The Crimean *mufti* had five times as many believers to serve as had the metropolitan bishop of Gotthia, but was paid one-third less.

In the 1840s, a hungry period for all Russia's peasantry, bureaucratic corruption, the inspiration for Gogol's *Dead Souls*, became so intolerable that even the lord lieutenant of Or Qapı complained: the peasants' grain, collected taxes, settlers' subsidies and cattle were being stolen, Tatars were being forced to work unpaid in the forests, to repair roads, to transport prisoners and mail, to borrow money to pay illegal taxes, to act as guides for surveyors. Islam had strong restrictions on such exploitation: Crimean Tatars suffered morally, as well as economically. Their choice was between emigration or total isolation in remote villages too inaccessible for Russian bureaucrats. Although Russian law forbade peasants to leave their community for more than two weeks, the administration encouraged Crimean Tatars to leave for good.

When in September 1854 the Russo-Turkish War (known to Westerners as the Crimean War) broke out, ostensibly over an Orthodox–Catholic quarrel about access to a Jerusalem church, 7,000 Turkish infantry, led by Ömer Paşa, landed at Evpatoria with an even larger contingent of French and British troops. The French, under Napoleon III, had specific war aims, among them to detach Crimea and Poland from Russia, while the British were more interested in not letting the wheat exported from the Balkans fall into Russian hands; the Turks were desperate to prevent their European possessions and vassals from gaining independence under Russian tutelage. None of the allies thought of restoring the Crimean Khanate, even though a Mesud Giray had been sent to spy out the land. Many Russians in Crimea fled north, leaving the Tatars to administer their own affairs as they thought fit. The Muslim clergy, fearing that Tatars would suffer revenge if Russia lost the war, were willing to help the Russian war effort. Tatars in Simferopol offered their houses and bedding for billeting, at a time when the Russian headmaster of Simferopol's secondary school refused to take in the wounded. Wounded Russian soldiers were abandoned by their officers to die in sheds or barns, if no French or British doctor found them. After the battle on the River Alma, a Tatar army major saved several hundred abandoned Russian soldiers. The winter of 1854–5 was so severe that roads were impassable and Russia could not supply its cavalry with fodder: several Tatar farmers sacrificed their own haystacks. There was, however, some collaboration with the 'enemy'. At Balaklava, which the British over a few months turned into a European port, Tatars provided the allies with some 350 carts and all the horses they could round up. According to unreliable Russian sources, they collected 100,000 roubles for the Turkish leader Ibrahim Paşa and called him 'khan'. They did, in fact, provide guides for the allied landings at Yalta.

But the Tatars were generally treated no better by the allies than by the Russians: they were forced to rebuild fortress walls, they were forbidden to leave Evpatoria when Russians besieged it, and at Kerç they were fired on by Scots when they began looting Scythian burial mounds. Some Tatars ransacked deserted Russian estates, others sold 'certificates of exemption' to Russians who had stayed, and then, allegedly, drove non-Tatar citizens out of at least one town. They did not participate in the fighting, although thirteen were killed 'observing' the great artillery duel at Evpatoria. Behind the lines, Russian soldiers ravaged Tatar villages: Fiodor Stulli (who later became Anton Chekhov's geography teacher) recalled:

> A detachment only had to spend the night in a village and the next morning most of the cottages, abandoned by their owners, lost their doors and roofs, used for bonfires, even though there was plenty of brushwood about. The destruction was not out of need, but often just out of boredom. After a month stationed anywhere the Tatar villages were totally empty, not a single sheep, or ox, or any grain, or hay or straw was left ... No other nationality would have been so unresentful, given the means they had for vengeance.[6]

The reason, perhaps, that the return of Ottoman forces after eighty years' absence met with little response was that the Turkish army was no longer a Muslim one: since 1850 the Ottomans had conscripted Christians as soldiers and employed many Christian officers, many of whom did not even speak Turkish. Ömer Paşa, the commander, was a schoolteacher from Serbia who had risen to be Sultan Abdül Mecid's tutor and then commander-in-chief. The Ottoman army had fine artillery, but dreadful logistics, with no medical aid or fresh food, so that three hundred died every day from cold, hunger and typhus. In Evpatoria the French kept the Turks back as 'reserves', allowing them to fire their guns only on holidays. The Turkish contingent suffered spectacular defeats, losing 1,000 men, but the British and French, in the end, wore down the Russians besieged in Sevastopol and in 1856 declared victory. The peace terms left Crimea's status unchanged, but for the next two decades the Black Sea was demilitarized and Sevastopol lost its strategic importance.

Surprisingly, the Russian army sent one of its two Tatar cavalry squadrons to defend Sevastopol: the fact that the squadron consisted of aristocratic Şirin and Mansur *beys* must have been reassuring. Under Russian command they fought the allies on the Black River[7] and the Mackenzie Heights[8] over

Evpatoria and received medals for capturing one British dragoon and five soldiers. Nevertheless, in the Crimean War the Tatars were generally neither allied nor enemy combatants: they were bystanders who suffered collateral damage, and, whatever the outcome of the war, it did little to improve or worsen their situation.

Once peace was declared, Russian officials returned to Simferopol and were amazed to find their offices intact and even due taxes paid. Nevertheless, some Russian officials blamed Tatar 'treachery' for the country's defeat and recommended further ethnic cleansing of the peninsula. Fortunately Tsar Nicolas died of cholera shortly before the end of the war, and Alexander II, planning major reforms, decided to 'forgive' the Tatars (although for the next sixty years Tatar soldiers were forbidden to take part in any Russian conflict with Muslims). Tatars began to farm again; some scrambled through the ruins of Sevastopol, gathering shells and shrapnel to sell as scrap metal. Fearing further oppression, however, Crimean Tatars began a mass evacuation, at first encouraged by the Russian authorities. Alexander II himself ordered in December 1857 Crimean Tatars on crown lands to be resettled on privately owned land, and the crown lands to be tilled by Russian peasants. Most Tatars chose a new life in Ottoman Anatolia. Several thousand Russian peasants, hearing rumours of emancipation and of ethnic cleansing, gathered around Or Qapı waiting for land grants in Crimea. So many Tatars now prepared to leave of their own will that the Russian authorities found there was no need for deportation. They assumed that the Crimean Tatars, afraid of reprisals for collaboration with the allies, were lured by the sultan's offers of fertile land in Anatolia. The real reasons are simpler: war left Crimean Tatars even more destitute, and, despite the proclamation of emancipation from serfdom, their suffering from forced labour, taxation in produce and money, cultural suppression and ethnic discrimination, by Greeks as well as Russians, by soldiers and Cossacks, as well as officials and landowners, was unendurable. Complaints from those deprived of their land were no longer accepted, and tax was now levied in roubles, not produce, which for an economy based on bargaining, not money, was burdensome. Vorontsov retired and died during the Crimean War. The new governors of Crimea were far less sympathetic.

Seven thousand Tatars left Evpatoria by boat as soon as peace was declared in April 1856; they were followed by others from Kerç and Sevastopol. When Tsar Alexander II was informed, he approved the 'liberation of the area from these people': the governor of New Russia, Aleksandr Stroganov, agreed. Even loyal Crimean Tatars despaired of their future. The flight abroad intensified when Tsar Alexander began an ethnic cleansing of the Caucasus, where Russia's war against Circassians and Chechens was coming to a successful end. The policy was to offer the peoples of the northwest Caucasus – Ubykh, Circassians and Abkhaz – the choice of relocation, sometimes in the semi-desert and steppes east of the Caspian Sea, or deportation by ship to Turkey (all in the interests of repopulating the eastern Black Sea coast with friendly Christians). In autumn 1859 tens of thousands of Circassians were brought to Kerç to await the ships, or rather hulks, that the government had leased from Armenian brokers to take them to Anatolia. Crimean Tatars realized that the same fate might very well be prepared for them. In spring 1860 Tatars and Noğays, fearing that the issue of exit permits might stop, hurriedly sold their property for whatever they could get, slaughtered their cattle and abandoned spring sowing. (They consoled themselves that in Anatolia they would find a state and a population that respected their religion, language and skills.)

The Crimean governor Grigori Zhukovsky was worried about an impending economic collapse resulting from the exodus of Tatar agricultural workers: he put spokes in the wheels of emigration, reducing the number of permits in the hope that no more than 10 per cent of the Crimean Tatars would leave. Tatars who had sold all their goods besieged the governor's office and Zhukovsky had to give way. Russian landowners, deprived of labour, feared bankruptcy. Russian officials spread circulars denying that there would be any deportations and threatening anyone who said otherwise with arrest. A minister came from St Petersburg in a vain attempt to solve the crisis. It was useless. By autumn 1860 there were 100,000 fewer Tatar peasants in Crimea, whole villages were deserted, fields left fallow. The economic damage, civil servants warned, was worse than that of the Crimean War. Too late, the tsar forbade the issue of passports to Tatars. The loss of population slowed down, but even so by 1862, it was calculated, 180,000 Crimean and Noğay Tatars, half the population before 1854, had gone. Many officials, it turned out, had made fortunes selling passports, charging 25 instead of 2 roubles for each one; others had threatened local Tatars with compulsory baptism and conscription. These corrupt officials then bought up abandoned farms for a pittance.

Official insensitivity was demonstrated in the late 1860s when some 97 Tatar villages were given new Russian names, unimaginatively derived from the names of Russian landowners, replacing the colourful toponyms that the Tatars had devised centuries earlier. The Tatars, once 80 per cent of the khanate's people, were now a minority – less than a third – of the population, while the Russian government desperately tried to fill the gap with foreign immigrants, preferably from Slav countries. By the end of the century the total population of Crimea was nearly 300,000, three times more than after the Crimean War: in towns like Sevastopol Tatars were a rarity. Of the immigrants, the German sectarians from Württemberg were phenomenally successful, growing enough wheat in one season to pay for the land they had been allotted (land which had been cleared of its Tatar owners). The Germans recognized the diligence and skills of Tatar and Noğay shepherds, but were firmly assured of their own superiority, because they grew grain, which was more profitable, and for that reason, they explained to enquirers, the Tatar herdsmen were doomed to die out.

The authorities belatedly realized the depths of their incompetence. Evpatoria, where 75 per cent of the population had been Tatars who did not speak Russian, was now almost a ghost town. Grigori Zhukovsky decided on a policy of integration, summoning Muslim clerics to help in creating an educational system in which Tatars would be compulsorily taught Russian, and in 1872 establishing a Tatar teachers' training college. There was alarm when some of the newly trained teachers, the gendarmerie reported, had revolutionary ideas, but that in itself was a sign of Tatar–Russian integration. The government made its next blunder in 1874, extending compulsory military service to Crimean Tatars, more as a means of Russification and of stopping emigration, than of strengthening the Russian armed forces. The Tatars resisted this not by open revolt, but by evasion.

Tatars who had emigrated to the Ottoman empire did not always fall on their feet. In many areas local conservative Turks were shocked by the freedom given to Tatar girls and women by fathers and husbands to show themselves when unrelated males visited the house. In some Anatolian towns, sick and dying Tatars were abandoned in the streets. Quarantine quarters in Black Sea ports were crammed far above capacity; local porters refused to drag out the corpses for fear of infection. In Rumelia, it was reported, fewer than 5 per cent of the Tatar deportees were still to be found alive thirty years later. The local fevers and, in 1877–8, an invading Russian army had either carried them off or driven them away to Anatolia. Many decided to return to Crimea, only to find that the Russian authorities, despite their policy of repopulating the peninsula, decreed that returning Tatars should be treated as undocumented illegal immigrants. The tsar noted this decision, 'Quite right!' Exceptions could be made only for returning Tatars who could show they had, before leaving Turkey, become labourers bonded to a Russian landowner.

Between 1866 and 1868 the Russian military courts arranged a show trial with such horrific consequences that no Tatar could ever trust a Russian in authority again. A Russian abbot who spent his time confiscating Tatar land and denouncing Tatars for taking wood from the forest was murdered. A Seyyid-Ahmed from the neighbouring village of Taraktaş and his relatives, despite the absence of witnesses and the strength of their alibis, were condemned before trial, then denied lawyers and, when all protests had been silenced, were tried publicly in Feodosia's theatre and hanged. Not a single Tatar was in the crowd witnessing the hanging: all Feodosia's Tatars had closed their shops and gathered in the mosque. This monstrous judicial murder (followed by confiscation of all property from Seyyid-Ahmed's heirs) became a subject of a new genre of Tatar folklore, laments for lost homeland, family, property and justice.

In 1874 the tsar's family built a royal palace at Livadia on the coast near Yalta. The coast now boasted a fashionable string of resorts and palaces: if only for cosmetic purposes, the government hastened to repair some of the damage done to the prosperity of the now landless Crimean Tatars and, after another decade, a system was introduced to buy up land misappropriated by incoming Russians and grant full possession to Tatars. In 1874 the railway reached Simferopol. Although it was extended to Sevastopol, visitors to the south coast had to complete their journey by boat or mail coach (the promised coastal railway has never been built). Doctors began to send, or even bring, consumptive patients to Crimea's reputedly salutary climate. Tatar labour, more plentiful since so many Tatars were landless, was essential to build the villas, drive the carriages, unload the ships, staff the hotels: they won a high reputation from Russian visitors for honesty and industry. Their quiet irony went unnoticed: for instance Tatars built a hospice for terminally ill Russian intellectuals and called it *Yavuzlar* ('The Inexorable Ones'). When Chekhov had an eccentrically designed house erected near Yalta, the Tatar builder called it *Burunuz*, 'As you like it'.

After an abortive experiment in 1845, in 1870 a more liberal administration set about providing Tatars with primary schools in which they were taught, first in their own language, and then in Russian. Gradually Tatar language instruction in these bilingual schools became broader, so that their folklore, if not their literature and history, entered the curriculum. A Tatar teachers' training college was set up in Simferopol. But even by 1913 fewer than 3,000 Tatar boys and girls were attending these 'Tatar-Russian' schools; the *mekteb* gave most other children mostly the ability to read Arabic script and a familiarity with the Qur'an.

Education brought Russians and Tatars closer, and Russian intellectuals in Crimea began to take an interest in Crimean history and culture. Thanks to Mikhail Vorontsov, as early as 1844 the annual *Notes of the Odessa Society of History and Antiquity* began to publish professional and amateur articles on Crimea (these continued until the Bolshevik revolution), and in 1887 this was followed by 55 issues of the *Bulletin of the Tauridean Learned Archival Commission*. An educated and secular Crimean Tatar elite, supported by curious Russian scholars, amateur and professional, took shape.

The change in Crimean Tatar culture is clearest from its folk poetry and songs. In the days of the khanate, songs and lyrics were about war as a calling superior even to love, or about the search for the face of God. The Tatar songs collected in Tsarist times have a frivolity inconceivable in the strictly Muslim culture of the khanate. Women and girls are no longer excluded or secluded. One song popular among Tatars and Karaim proclaims:

> A young girl's life is happiness, a wife's life is slavery
> O times! Our traditions will be destroyed –
> But who then is going to burn with sympathy for this distress?

In another song, a father offers jewellery to his daughter if she will accept the bridegroom he has chosen. She rejects the learned mullah 'because he will make me read a lot of books', and the charcoal-burner 'because he will make me do his accounts'. Angered, her father says he will marry her off to a drunkard. She replies: 'Father, you've guessed what I long for. He will be hungover in the morning and drunk in the evening, and he will keep kissing me.'

There were several popular songs about Eminé, a famous prostitute: 'It's too hot in Alupka,/ If you're asking for Eminé, she's too busy embracing.'[9] (It will be remembered that Evliya Çelebi noted the existence of Tatar brothels in Gözleve; no doubt, urbanization and dispossession had favoured their revival in Crimea.)

When Russia began its 'War of Liberation' against Turkey in the Balkans in 1877, once more the Crimean Tatars found themselves suspected of sympathies with the enemy. They served largely as transporters of food, munitions and wounded soldiers and expressed no open resentment, although the authorities were investigating rumours of Russian revolutionary agents spreading anti-war propaganda. This time, however, there were no signs of any Ottoman agents attempting to recruit Crimean Tatars in the fight against Russia. Tatars continued to irritate patriotic Russians: the influential Bishop Germogen complained, 'Our beloved Crimea! How much of you is unRussian, not yet Orthodox! Tatars are masters here, one is amazed how much local Russians are like Tatars.' The typically antisemitic southern Russian newspaper lies about Jews were now directed at Tatars, who were falsely accused of vandalizing Orthodox churches. German and Finnish visitors noted the opposite: unlike Russians, Tatars never begged and never got drunk – all they asked for was work.

Relief, however, was on its way, as Europe's historians and Russian intellectuals, increasingly cosmopolitan and freethinking, began to show respect for the Crimeans and their khanate. The process began with a history of Tauris by Stanisław Jan Siestrzeńcewicz-Bohusz, a Polish priest, and eventually archbishop of Mogiliov, of extraordinary genius. Towards the end of his very long life (he died in 1826), his history was published in St Petersburg, first in Russian, then in French. Though littered with misunderstandings and omissions, and not particularly sympathetic to its subject, Siestrzeńcewicz's book was a major seminal work. In the 1840s the real initiation for the European public came from Joseph Freiherr von Hammer-Purgstall, whose ten-volume history of the Ottoman Realm, almost unnoticed when published in Pest in the 1830s, appeared in French; this 'Edward Gibbon of Ottoman history' in 1850 published in German a *History of the Crimean Khans under Ottoman Rule*. Hammer-Purgstall had not read everything, and his command of Ottoman Turkish sometimes let him down, but after his books appeared, there was no excuse for dismissing the Crimean Tatar khanate as a nest of savages. Completely persuasive was the 1887 masterpiece of the Russian orientalist Vasili Dmitrievich Smirnov, *The Crimean Khanate under the Supremacy of the Ottoman Porte until the Start of the Nineteenth Century*. Smirnov had read every manuscript available in Russia's and Istanbul's archives. He had academic faults – dwelling on minor mistakes by his predecessors – and he assumed without question that absorption into the Russian empire was the best outcome for the Crimean Tatars. Smirnov's readings and judgements have lasted well and have been reprinted in this century. Moreover, he stimulated the study of the Crimean Tatar language and what was still extant of its heritage.

At the same time, the first internationally distinguished Crimean Tatar appeared: Ismail Gaspıralı (widely known as Gasprinski, this surname being created from Gaspra, the coastal village where his father was born). Born in 1851 near Bağçasaray to a Tatar officer, an interpreter to the Russian governor, he had a mother of Moldavian origin. Receiving noble rank (*dvorianstvo*), Gaspıralı was educated in a local *mekteb*, and finally in Simferopol grammar school. His father sent him briefly to military colleges in Voronezh and Moscow. He tried to leave Russia with a group of volunteers intending to join Greeks in Crete rebelling against Ottoman rule, but he was stopped by the Odessa police. Gaspıralı then emigrated, first to France to study at the Sorbonne (where he wrote his first articles), and then spent three years in Turkey, studying and publishing articles. He had, however, established strong roots in Russian intellectual life. As a cadet he lived in the Moscow home of the Slavophile Mikhail Katkov, the influential literary editor. In Paris he acted as secretary to the novelist Ivan Turgenev. In the Crimea he was already qualified to teach Russian. On his return he became a civic councillor, and by 1879 was elected mayor of Bağçasaray. He published the first long-lived Turkic-language newspaper in Russia, *Tercüman* (Interpreter), printed in Ottoman Turkish that was simplified to make it intelligible to Tatars and Central Asians. He used a reduced alphabet, discarding half a dozen letters used only to render Arabic words; he devised letters representing short vowels – missing from Arabic script, ill-suited to Turkic languages that have many more short vowels than Arabic's three. Gaspıralı's reforms were part of his plan to create a pan-Turkic language, which proved to be overambitious, since Turkic languages, although often mutually intelligible to a degree, nevertheless can vary as much as, say, the Romance languages. *Tercüman* published everything from world news to local advertisements. Despite opposition from conservative Muslims, convinced that all they needed to know was in the Qur'an, *Tercüman* energetically propagated *jadidism*, a Turkic revival movement that instilled in Muslims a modern European outlook and education, without infringing their Islamic faith. Gaspıralı's influence spread to Iran and Egypt. He was surprised to discover that by 1900 he had created the Muslim world's most popular periodical. Gaspıralı's daughter founded a magazine for Turkic women, a comic periodical and eventually a political weekly journal. His publications developed their own fonts, and his colleagues became writers, critics and educators. Russia's Trade Union of Typographical Workers was founded by Gaspıralı. Gaspıralı's aspiration was to develop Turkic education, and his phonetic method of teaching literacy had a phenomenal effect all over Russia's and even India's Muslim world. His own essays, such as 'Islam in Russia: A Muslim's Thoughts, Notes and Observations' of 1881, are remarkably fair-minded: he blamed his fellow Crimean Tatars as much as Russians for misunderstanding 'the other', for emigrating or retreating, instead of seeking common ground. By the end of the nineteenth century, however, *Tercüman* began to lose ground to other Turkic-language periodicals in Russia, particularly in less peripheral and larger Tatar centres, such as Kazan, Baku and Orenburg, but its articles were reprinted all over the Muslim world.

Gaspıralı was also a creative writer. Most of his own fiction now awaits revival: *Letters from France, Letters from Africa,* a utopian *Dar ul-Rahat Musulmanları* (A Muslim Rest Home) – an Islamic Switzerland to be organized into cantons and united by electric trains and telegraph lines – and a book of novellas, *The Grief of the East.* His *Letters from France,* written in Russian and not published until 1887, are of particular interest: they are not only semi-autobiographical (Gaspıralı's persona in these 'letters' is that of an Iranian mullah), but they pose the question of how an observant Muslim can profitably live in Western Europe.[10] Gaspıralı's second wife, Bibi-Zühre Akçurina, known in Crimea as the Mother of the Nation, was his active collaborator.

Politically, too, Gaspıralı was a major force: his All-Russian Muslim Union was liberal and led to a generation of Crimean Tatars acquiring experience in local, national and international politics, their aim being a World Muslim Congress to be held in Cairo (this, too, was overambitious, since Arabs and Persians still tended to see themselves as metropolitans, and Turks as former barbarians, latecomers to Islamic culture). The Russian consul in Cairo admitted with amazement that Gaspıralı now had international renown. The French *Revue du monde musulman* (Review of the Muslim World) recommended Gaspıralı for the Nobel Prize. Neither the World

Ismail Gasprinski (Gaspıralı), left, with Azeri editors, Baku, 1894.

Congress nor the Nobel Prize were forthcoming (although in 1907 the Khedive of Egypt did hold a small multinational congress in Cairo's Hotel Continental). Gaspıralı's funeral in 1914 was attended by large crowds, the first mass event in Bağçasaray; a museum devoted to him still stands in Bağçasaray.[11]

The Russo-Japanese War, the 1905 'first' revolution, the formation of a radical, if powerless, Duma and the reaction that followed in 1907 brought little benefit to the Crimean Tatars. A thousand or more Tatars, including mullahs, were conscripted for the war in the Far East: few returned. The main forces in the 1905 revolution were Russian soldiers and sailors, industrial workers and social democrats, who regarded peasants as hopelessly backward and reactionary, and who thought, perhaps correctly, that the Tatars and other Muslims were interested not in the class struggle, but in Muslim solidarity. The right-wing Russian ideologists looked on Tatars as they did on Jews, as a nationality disloyal to Russia because their ties were to foreigners, whether Ottoman Turks, or to German Jewry. When the Duma was formed, it had a Muslim faction of 25 deputies, but Crimean Tatars played second fiddle to Azeris or Kazan Tatars. Piotr Stolypin's government of 1907–10 was 'a bet on the strong' and favoured profitable Russian farmers; as a Russifying government, it only encouraged a resumption, albeit slower, of Crimean Tatar emigration to the Ottoman empire.

The outbreak of the First World War, with its unprecedented displacement of peoples and unprecedented slaughter on all fronts, stirred Tatar minds. Gaspıralı's pupils and surviving friends wondered if the collapse of Russia might give Crimea back to its indigenous people, even though they now numbered only a third of the peninsula's population. Believing that Crimean Tatars, if not recruited into the army, might welcome the Ottoman enemy to take over Crimea, the Russian army decided in this war to conscript Tatars and other Muslims for active service against Austria and Germany on the Polish front (they dared not use them in the Caucasus, where they might fraternize with enemy troops).

Some eight hundred Tatar horsemen fought from autumn 1914 to autumn 1916 in Belarus, the Prussian borderlands and the Carpathians: they were known for spectacular charges, suicidal when they attacked barbed-wire fortifications with no artillery support. Only half survived. In 1918 they tried to defend an infant Crimean Tatar government against Bolshevik and anarchist sailors in Sevastopol, before joining the Russian White movement. Of this cavalry just thirty men survived to flee from the final Bolshevik triumph in 1920 on a ship bound for Istanbul.

Although the war left the peninsula relatively untouched until 1917, the land had lost its tillers: Tatar women were not accustomed to field work. The troubles of the time are reflected in a story by the Tatar writer Ümer Ipçi, *Aunt Zeynep*: a mortally wounded soldier returns home to die, and his mother then dies of grief. The Russian authorities reacted with a desperate series of repressive measures, removing first all the German colonists, and then scouring the Tatar quarters in Simferopol and Evpatoria to root out mullahs with an anti-Russian bias, looking for a mythical 'fifth column'. The new Tatar press was particularly suspect to the gendarmes. Central Asian Tatars rebelled all over Russia in 1916, attacking tax officials, resisting conscription into an army that forced them to eat pork and buried the dead without prayers. The government's response was to conscript Tatars for forced labour only, still keeping them far from home in conditions offensive to Muslims. One Crimean Tatar song of the time shows how conscription affected them:

> Rows and rows of cauldrons,
> Clerks who don't read.
> They shall not see paradise
> Who conscript us as soldiers.
> Rows and rows of branches and trunks,
> Branches and trunks need water.
> We need slim-hipped girls.

A Hungarian scholar recorded the songs of Tatar foot soldiers: 'If we die in this place/ Who will wash our bodies?/ When spring comes, grasses will grow/ Grass will bury us.' If Tatar folk songs had been first heroic, then lovelorn, and more recently laments for the loss of land and community, now they became protests against war. Many songs (words and music) were collected and recorded by the Austrian scholar Robert Lach, who began the publication of his *Gesänge russischer Kriegsgefangener* (Songs of Russian Prisoners of War) in the 1920s. Ironically, some songs, listing the towns troops had passed through, were exact parallels to songs sung by Crimean Tatars in the Ottoman army, only with different toponyms as the Russian citizens headed west to the Carpathians, and the Ottomans east to the Caucasus. A Crimean Tatar song ran:

> From Sevastopol I set off healthy, well; hell broke out on the
> German border.

> Don't hack, German, don't hack, pity me, Austria's Magyars have
>   hacked my soul.
> My blood flowed, flowed onto the cobblestones, many many
>   greetings go from me to friends.
> Alas, my child, alas, how were you killed, on Germany's border
>   I got to know woe.[12]

A second song, sung with many melismas and rhythmic twists, begins with the same journey from Sevastopol to the Ukraine and the front and also ends with a cry of woe, but it shuns apostrophe and rhetoric, trying to link what is seen, felt and thought between departure and despair with an effectively disordered impressionism:

> Some are wounded, some dying, / at the foot of the bridge is a sharp stake./ A bullet wound doesn't stop the heart./ On Kemal's foot is a bullet wound, now let Austria's Carpathian land burn,/ the so-called Austrians are little lads,/ a Martini rifle on the shoulder, a knife at the waist./ Russia's soldiers do not return,/ Austria's bullets torment a nation,/ from the high valleys, mother, I couldn't make the leap,/ my cartridges fell in the water, I couldn't retrieve them.

When the news reached Crimea in February 1917 that the tsar had abdicated and that the Duma, dominated by liberal and moderate-left ministers, had formed a Provisional Government, hopes were high for an end to the war and the return of millions of soldiers to the land and the factories, as well as for redistribution of land and a more generous treatment of ethnic minorities. Hopes soon faded: even as the front disintegrated, the new government in Petrograd requisitioned every horse and most of the oxen, and confiscated 200,000 cattle and sheep in Crimea for the army, thus paralysing transport and agriculture. To the Crimean Tatars' dismay, Pavel Miliukov, the Minister of Foreign Affairs, still declared his war aim to be the capture of the Bosphorus and Istanbul, and the Provisional Government, while avoiding intensification of hostilities, dared not infuriate the Allies by making peace overtures. The political confusion in Moscow and Petrograd was reflected in disorder, then riots and anarchy all over Russia. Any reform of landholdings was due to peasant acts of arson and seizure. Soldiers returning from the front were deserters, not demobilized forces.

In Crimea the return of Tatar cavalry from the Balkan front, with or without authorization, was a catalyst for transforming Tatar aspirations.

They were little affected by the abdication of the tsar, whom many resented but still regarded as a divinely anointed ruler, and there was little sympathy for Marxist and Social Revolutionary parties that saw society in terms not of ethnic struggles, but of class warfare. Like other Muslim communities in Russia, they aspired at least to self-government, thus arousing in Crimea's majority population of Slavs, Greeks and Armenians the fear that the Tatars intended to restore the khanate.

No candidates for a khanate appeared, but for the first time in over a century the Tatars discovered among themselves ambitious and educated potential leaders. The war had brought home a number of Tatars educated in Istanbul and enthused by the reforms and radical ideas of the 'Young Turks'. Tatar officers back from the front were determined to make fundamental political changes. The most striking figure was Noman Çelebicihan, born in 1885. In Istanbul he founded in 1908, after a brief spell in a Turkish prison, a students' cultural society and then the Tatar Charitable Society. He crossed the frontier illegally to Russia when war broke out, worked in Moscow, then volunteered for the army, returning to Evpatoria in 1917. A second major figure in this group was the younger Cafer Seydamet, a lawyer who went on to study at the Sorbonne, then became an army officer and, when the cavalry came home, an orator and revolutionary in Crimea.

The radical Tatars had little difficulty in displacing discredited traditional Tatar *mirza*s and officials. Çelebicihan challenged the mayor of Bağçasaray to a duel over the underhand appointment of a reactionary to direct the medrese. Very soon Crimea had its own Provisional Government: even the former governor-general and Admiral Kolchak, in charge of the Black Sea fleet, raised no objections. Tatar opinion, nominally radical enough to form a Muslim Revolutionary Committee, was moderate: when the dowager tsaritsa Maria Fiodorovna and her family, virtually under arrest, took refuge in her Crimean villa, she was amazed to find Tatars camped around the palace to defend her from Bolshevik assassins.

In April, under Noman Çelebicihan and Cafer Seydamet, a Provisional Crimean Muslim Executive Committee was formed in Simferopol. It collaborated with the local garrison, thus duplicating the Crimean Provisional Government's military committee. In a fusion of political and religious leadership, Çelebicihan was also elected *mufti* of Crimea.

Aware that they represented only a minority of the peninsula's population, the new Tatar organizations were inclusive: they wanted a federal democratic republic in which all ethnic groups and classes and both sexes had equal rights. Conservative Muslims fiercely opposed female emancipation, while at various Muslim congresses held all over Russia, Tatars often found other Muslims inclined to align themselves with one of Russia's militant political parties, social revolutionaries, if not social democrats; many others anticipated the disintegration of the Russian empire and lobbied for independence.

Women activists, led by Gaspıralı's daughter Şefiqa, came to the fore, travelling all over Russia and making fiery speeches – an unforeseen revolution in Crimean Tatar society. Radical change accelerated when soldiers flooded back from the front. Çelebicihan's committees authorized the desertion, but when the Provisional Government in Petrograd objected and had him arrested, he explained that he was giving permission only for the period of religious holidays. Meanwhile, Simferopol prison was besieged by crowds, and Çelebicihan was released. The influx of angry soldiers also forced the pace of land reform, distributing confiscated and misappropriated land to landless peasants and soldiers. The Crimea's official governor was threatened with prosecution and removed. The Tatar press, in a society where literacy had advanced, now flourished: Tatar-language newspapers like *Crimean Hearth*, *The Voice of the Tatars* and *The Nation* formed radical public opinion.

In May the period of bliss came to an end with naval revolts. In Kronstadt, Petrograd's naval base, Bolshevik and anarchist sailors would murder their officers in July and threaten to start a premature armed revolution. The 40,000 men of the Black Sea fleet at Sevastopol had earned in 1905 an even more violent reputation; now they began their 1917 uprising. Against this ruthless force a small Tatar squadron with the slogan 'Crimea for Crimeans' could not prevail: they pressed for reinforcements from Odessa, Kiev and Kherson, but by the time action was taken in early November (by the European calendar), the Bolsheviks had achieved their own victory in the capital, and the sailors now represented the victorious coup leaders. The officer in charge of Odessa was, ironically, a General Marx, a lover of Crimean Tatar culture, who two years later became a Bolshevik Commissar for Education in Feodosia. In its death throes, however, the Provisional Government allowed the remaining Crimean Tatar cavalry in Russia to return to Crimea to confront the growing anarchy. The effects of the last reforms – a reduction in the working day, prohibition of sales of essential goods and phenomenal inflation – caused hunger riots, and encouraged local Bolsheviks among the Russians and the sailors to inflame the situation to a revolutionary temperature. Tens of thousands of refugees from the even hungrier Russian North, pouring into Crimea, made the situation worse.

The final straw was the return from the Caucasian front of a Russian army, demoralized, despite its defeat of Turkish forces. They reached the Black Sea at Trabzon, where they sold passages in their ships at exorbitant prices to Armenians fleeing the genocide still taking place all over Anatolia, and abducted numbers of Turkish girls. The Armenians found relative safety, if not a welcome, in Feodosia; the Turkish girls were sold off as concubines, a last gasp of the khanate's slave trade.

Çelebicihan desperately tried to mobilize an armed force to defend Crimean Tatar autonomy; the Bolshevik Yakov Sverdlov declared moderate Crimea to be enemy territory, 'a nest of evolutionaries', of 'social-collaborators', that had to be turned into a new Kronstadt. On the other hand, as late as September a congress of mullahs in Bağçasaray complained of the new 'atheism' and demanded enforcement of sharia law: they were banned from the main mosque by the *mufti*, who denounced the mullahs as ignorant, semi-literate degenerates.

Moderate Russian citizens put all their hopes in a Constituent Assembly, meant to be held in January 1918, that would decide the political structure of the new Russia. Crimea began to select its delegates, the Bolsheviks and the Provisional Government each doing so separately. The only point on which the two sides agreed was that 'Muslims are the victims of European imperialism'; they hoped to agree further, but the gap was too wide.

'Crimea for Crimeans' became the slogan for the Crimean government that eventually came into existence in December 1917. It was remarkably similar to the government of the new First Georgian Republic: progressively Social Democrat, with a policy of equality, nationalization and tolerance that would have created a paradise, had there been the funds and the armed force to establish and protect it. But it was futile when faced by a determined totalitarian neighbouring enemy and by the indifference of the European powers, supposedly benignly reorganizing fair ethnic boundaries in Europe and the Near East. The gates of hell, not of paradise, were about to open in Crimea.

Leaders of Crimean Directorate (Milliy Firqa) by the Iron Gate of Bağçasaray Palace, 26 November 1917: (left to right) Seyid-Celal Hattat, Asan Sabri Ayvazov, Noman Çelebicihan, Cafer Seydamet.

10

SOVIET RULE

As the Bolshevik coup opened Russia's gates to hell, Crimea's youthful and euphoric Tatar intellectual elite formed a constitutional assembly to determine, under Tatar leadership, how a secular, democratic Crimea would be governed. On 1 December the 79 delegates opened a *qurultay*, the first time this ancient Turco-Mongol parliament had been held in Crimea since 1706, when Khan Ğazı III Giray convened one in Gözleve. This *qurultay* was held in Bağçasaray town hall, but also met in the khan's palace, only recently returned to the Tatar community. Noman Çelebicihan, Şefiqa Gaspıralı (the daughter of Ismail Gaspıralı), Cafer Seydamet and two others were elected to the præsidium of the *qurultay*. There were only minor disagreements: Cafer Seydamet wanted to revive the khanate, reformed to meet modern standards; Çelebicihan believed the urgent task was to avoid imminent bloody conflict by compromising with all active factions in Crimea; Aivazov insisted that the Bolsheviks were so dangerous that neutralizing them was the *qurultay*'s primary task. Its most contentious question, the equality of women and men, was settled by Çelebicihan, whose Qur'anic learning enabled him to prove that Islam approved of equality of the sexes.

Within a fortnight the main questions had been answered. There was a constitution: the *qurultay* would function for a year until a *meclis* (parliament) was elected. Meanwhile, Çelebicihan was President and Minister of Justice of the Crimean Republic (and remained *mufti*), Seydamet was Minister of War, Özenbaşlı of education. Fundamental laws were passed promoting equality of class, ethnic nationality and gender, brotherhood, unity, democratic freedoms of expression, workers' insurance and the right to strike, while opposing bloodshed and destruction. Guarantees were given to Russians, Greeks, Armenians and Jews. This was the world's first Muslim secular democracy. It was acclaimed by most of the Crimean press.

Even an acclaimed democracy needs an army, however, and not all of the Tatar regiments, least of all their Russian commanders, who had sworn loyalty to the now abolished monarchy, were willing to serve the newborn republic. Polish intelligence agents calculated that a new Crimean army might have around 7,000 'sabres', elite professionals – enough to alarm, but too few to counter the much larger Bolshevik sea and land forces.

In January a 'Red Terror' began against many segments of the population – officers, soldiers who still obeyed them, civil servants, especially those charged with maintaining order, bourgeois civilians and non-Russians, particularly Tatars. Drunken sailors from Sevastopol and fanatical Bolsheviks from the north were indistinguishable, especially in the towns, from burglars and violent gangsters. Class hatred, ethnic antagonism and pure sadism superseded ideological principles. 'Red' Terror eventually generated 'White'; arguably the latter, targeted against Reds rather than neutrals, was less terrible, whereas the former's default position, that anyone not with the Reds deserved to die, was lethal. Crimean Tatars were in the worst position: they attracted the fury of both sides, if only by their adherence to reason, moderation and compromise. Çelebicihan urged his fellow ministers to negotiate with Sevastopol's and Simferopol's Bolsheviks and form a government combining the *meclis*, the Tauridean Soviet of Nationalities and the Bolsheviks. The *meclis*, shocked by the killings of its deputies, refused to cooperate, and the Bolsheviks stood out as the enemies of peace and security on the peninsula, especially now that they were fortified by a torrent of soldiers fleeing from abandoned fronts in Russia, Ukraine and Anatolia. Greek and Armenian refugees from Turkey were as hostile to the Crimean Tatars as to any other Muslims. Although the hostility was not reciprocated by Tatars, these Christians threw in their lot with the Bolsheviks.

In mid-January the Sevastopol fleet sent hundreds of sailors on gunships and minesweepers to ports where Tatars had wide support: Evpatoria, Yalta and Feodosia. Sailors went overland to Simferopol and confronted the Tatar government. After a landing, an inconclusive exchange of fire, and the killing of officers taken prisoner, Yalta was shelled and, on 15 January, fell into Bolshevik hands. On 17 January both Simferopol and Bağçasaray fell to Bolshevik artillery and machine-gun fire. Armed factory workers joined in the attack on Tatar horsemen. Soon Simferopol's post office and railway station were in enemy hands: the Tatar defenders and the *qurultay* signed an almost meaningless truce, for officers fighting for the Tatar government were executed or forced to flee to the mountains. (There they were hidden by Tatar peasants, sometimes, against all tradition, in the women's quarters, which even revolutionaries were reluctant to search.) Yalta's civilians begged the Tatar squadrons to withdraw and thus spare the city from total ruin. Tatar soldiers and those of the newly formed White 'volunteer' army shed their uniforms and bided their time; those whom the Bolsheviks caught were executed. Noman Çelebicihan was caught. Even though he had resigned from the *qurultay*, he was taken by aeroplane to Sevastopol where his supporters could not get to him. Bolshevik power was now organized: all public buildings – theatres, hotels, courts – were requisitioned, and each major town was assessed for a 'contribution', sometimes millions of roubles from its poorest as well as its richest citizens, to the Bolshevik authorities, who spent the proceeds dining and drinking, free of charge, in Evpatoria's Bon Rivage hotel. (These 'contributions' were paid not only in cash, but with the contents of museums and galleries, which, like the museum and private treasures sold or destroyed by Petrograd's Bolsheviks, either passed to European speculators or vanished forever.)

As more guns were seized and redistributed, almost every male in Crimea with a mission or a grudge was now armed to the teeth and ready to kill. In an Evpatoria hotel the Tatar forces managed to capture an entire social-democrat gathering, but lost them when the prisoners broke the locks and ran out of the back entrance. Evpatoria's artillery defences were finally seized by the port's 'Provisional Military' regime, who won support from Sevastopol's Bolsheviks, sending two warships to shell the prosperous outskirts of Evpatoria, where anti-Bolshevik and Tatar forces were stationed. Six hundred sailors landed and arrested Russian officers and Crimean Tatars. From Sevastopol prison they were taken to ships moored in the harbour, tortured unspeakably, according to their 'degree of counter-revolutionariness', then shot at best, or burned alive or drowned in the ships' boilers, in a conveyor belt of sadistic killing. The Red Guard executioners were constantly supplied with food, drink and tobacco exacted from local Tatar peasants.

Sevastopol's executioners, Diomyshev and a married couple named Nemiche (after whom streets were named in several Crimean towns), organized an executive committee to carry out mass killings in Sevastopol. Yalta was worse, for there the Tatar forces resisted and the Bolsheviks, aided by Greek volunteers, raped, tortured and executed even the army nurses that they captured (for that reason, White Army nurses wore a necklace to which a fatal dose of morphine or cyanide was attached). The corpses of at least one hundred officers, weighed down with metal sinkers, were thrown into the sea. Nearby coastal towns suffered similarly.

The climax came in Sevastopol. (In 1849 a government inquiry had noted prophetically that morality in Crimea was worst among Jews, Greeks and the inhabitants of Sevastopol.) Between 21 and 24 February 1918, 350 prisoners, largely Tatars, were shot: one Bolshevik named Shmakov executed 170 'bourgeois' alone in one night. Others, including relatives of the next *mufti*, were publicly executed in the town centre. Noman Çelebicihan was executed on the evening of 23 February and his body thrown into the sea (it may have been among the unidentifiable corpses washed up on shore a week or so later). Çelebicihan's heritage is that of a national hero and martyr; he also wrote the words of the Crimean Tatars' national hymn, 'I have sworn to heal my nation's wounds.'[1] His dream of turning Crimea into a second Switzerland, where cantons governed themselves and different nations lived in harmony, would never be fulfilled.

In March 1918 the congress of Crimean Soviets formed a Central Executive Committee over which Bolsheviks took control, drowning out the voices of Tatars who supported the less murderous social revolutionaries. Incorporating the Crimea into the Russian Soviet Federal Socialist Republic, the Committee rejected the Tatar name *Qırım* for Crimea and reverted to Catherine the Great's *Tavrida*. Bolsheviks also monopolized the new governing cabinet, the Council of People's Commissars, chaired by a Polish Jew from Petrograd. The bloodiest executioner and richest thief of Evpatoria, the former schoolteacher Diomyshev, took control of that city. Bolsheviks stopped redistributing land to the Tatar peasantry: it was simply 'nationalized' and divided into the first Soviet collective farms (*sovkhozy*), effectively a reinstatement of serfdom, one that compelled peasants not just to feed roaming bands of irregular Red soldiers, but to pay a 30 per cent tax on the assessed value of their produce. This measure provided Russia with as much as 300,000 tonnes of grain. Tatar farmers could starve to death if they refused to join the collective farms.

Hope of relief came at the end of March: Germany, not yet on its last legs, quickly moved to dominate the governments of the newly detached regions of the Russian empire – Transcaucasia, Ukraine, Crimea – to seize the grain, oil and metals such as manganese that they needed to sustain their war effort. Ukraine was their first success; there was a prospect of German troops invading Crimea and restoring order. At first, fear of the invaders merely turned the Bolshevik soldiers into even more ferocious marauders; the Tatars, now desperate, resisted Bolshevik mobilization. On the coast, and then in the east and the mountains of the peninsula, with support from Ukraine and from surviving Russian officers, they rose up against their oppressors, Bolsheviks and Greens. The uprising's best-known leader was a Seydamet Karabiber, a peasant from the village of Taraktaş (where forty years earlier innocent men had been hanged by a Russian military court): Taraktaş's peasants crushed an armoured car with a large rock and shot at sailors from the local revolutionary military committee: for a while Karabiber stayed alive. Other uprisings were machine-gunned during Bolshevik punitive raids. The Black Sea fleet sailors, however, now numbered far fewer and had no cohesion, which inspired hitherto peaceful young Tatars to act. A third group, the Greens, loosely controlled by Nestor Makhno's Ukrainian anarchists, and now present in Crimea, were happy to attack any armed representative of the state, White or Red. They tended to support Tatar irregulars.

Some Bolsheviks, sickened by the violence, let dissident socialists, social revolutionaries and social democrat Mensheviks form their own soviet. The very word 'soviet' was now unspeakable to Tatars; surprisingly, the Bolshevik naval authorities agreed, and dissolved the soviets, only to set up a new one with a monopoly of power. It was too late: 20,000 Germans invaded, overwhelming 22,000 Red soldiers and 8,000 sailors. Bolshevik commissars and executioners fled, shooting their prisoners, burning their papers and loading their loot onto carts. (Not until early May 1918 did the last Red make his way to the Kuban.) Soviet power evaporated; in any case, the Brest-Litovsk treaty, agreed in desperation the previous December by Lenin and Trotsky, left the Germans free to occupy the periphery of the Russian empire, although only their rights to control Ukraine (but not Crimea) had been specifically granted.

The Germans were greeted as saviours: there were concerts in Yalta. True, the Germans executed Crimean Tatars, typically for robbery, or failing to surrender weapons, but they allowed a Crimean Tatar government to form first a 'Tauridean Provincial Commisariat', then a national assembly that elected Prince Obolensky (who wanted reunion with Russia) but heeded the *qurultay* leaders Özenbaşlı and Cafer Seydamet. The former proposed a united multi-ethnic Crimea, the latter a presidential version of the khanate. They feared the revival of Russia and relied on Turkey's and Germany's protection, ignoring the obvious signs that both the Reich and the Ottoman sultanate were on the verge of collapse; the Tatars sought reinforcement by inviting Crimean expatriates to return from Anatolia and Dobruja.

Crimean independence was threatened by the ambitious Ukrainian leader Skoropadsky, who wanted Sevastopol for a new Ukrainian navy. On

5 June 1918 the Tatar *qurultay* went on holiday. The German general von Kosch took matters into his own hands and appointed as prime minister an artillery lieutenant-general, Suleyman (born Maciej) Sulkiewicz, a Muslim Polish *Lipka* Tatar who had served in the Russian army. The Germans promised Sulkiewicz, now known as Süleyman-Paşa, to support an independent Crimea, and at the same time told Skoropadsky that Crimea could eventually be Ukrainian territory. Sulkiewicz governed wisely from the governor's house in Simferopol until November, when Germany collapsed and withdrew. Sulkiewicz's sympathy for Tatar nationalism, however, made him unpopular with Russians in Crimea towards the end of his brief leadership. (He then became General Mamed-Bek in the new Azerbaijani army and earned respect, not least when he stoically endured execution by the Cheka, the Bolshevik secret police, in May 1920.)

As soon as the Germans and Sulkiewicz had gone, Solomon Krym, a Karaim agronomist with impeccably moderate liberal inclinations, but an opponent of Crimean Tatar independence, was chosen to head the Crimean government. His cabinet had not a single Tatar in it. Krym hoped for White Army help in expelling Bolsheviks and anarchists; he was rewarded when General Denikin's White Army occupied the peninsula, taking over the local Crimean forces. Denikin was an uncompromising advocate of a single imperial Russia; all Krym could do was stabilize rules for landholding, establish a university and open more libraries and schools.

On 24 November 1918 uninvited ships of an Anglo-French fleet sailed in and landed 3,000 French, 500 British and 2,000 Greek marines to eliminate all traces of German occupation: Admiral Colthorpe was warmly welcomed by Krym's foreign minister. But Denikin's army now followed the Entente's orders, rather than Krym's: those arrested, such as the left-leaning members of Simferopol's Union of Metalworkers, were shot without trial, and the offices of the Sevastopol newspaper *The Tide* were ransacked. Cafer Seydamet despaired of ever seeing independence and left for Istanbul, never to return: from the very start General Piotr Wrangel, then Denikin's Chief of Staff, despised him as a typical liberal lawyer of no practical use, least of all as Crimean Minister of War. Underground Bolshevik gangs were meanwhile hiding from the Entente's searches in the caves of the coastal mountains and spreading their influence all over the peninsula. The British and French, disillusioned by the Whites, and anticipating a Red reunited Russia with whom they would have to deal, even trade, withdrew their support from Wrangel; they now offered only to provide ships to evacuate Russians to Istanbul and Piraeus. Many Tatars, roused by the prospect of fighting both Bolshevism and Ukrainian nationalism, volunteered to join not their own Crimean forces, but Denikin's army, which aimed to reconquer Moscow and Petrograd from its Black Sea strongholds. The White Army, and the foreign forces, were disorganized and relied on banditry to feed their soldiers, in a country that had already lost its grain to the Reds. The ominous prospects of war in 1919 did not encourage Crimean Tatars to till or sow what land they owned. The likelihood of famine was less of a deterrent than the certainty of confiscation and robbery of any harvest. Even if peasants were paid for grain, Solomon Krym's new 'Crimean Rouble' (a map of Crimea on one side, a Russian two-headed eagle on the reverse) was never a trusted currency. Denikin blamed Krym's 'excessive democratization' and 'Bolshevik subversion' for the failure of the Crimean population to feed itself or to mobilize on behalf of the doomed Russian empire.

By January 1919 the 'Tatar National Party' originally founded by Noman Çelebicihan and Cafer Seydamet was formally proclaimed as Milliy Firqa (The National Party), aiming at independence from all other nations and armed forces: it was left-leaning, but demanded 'Soviets without Bolsheviks'. The word 'soviet' was anathema both to Tatar peasants and to the White Army. Krym held elections to a new parliament, the *meclis-mebusan*, and its 'Directorate', less provocative to the White Army, focused on rural problems. Milliy Firqa still had a mandate, however, but emphasized autonomy, not independence, for Crimea. Within weeks, on 23 February 1919, the anniversary of Çelebicihan's execution, Denikin's officers raided the *meclis-mebusan* and closed its newspaper. Innocent Tatars were shot as Bolshevik rebels. The Crimean Tatars forgot their own differences and joined in an anti-White and anti-Russian uprising. Solomon Krym stood back, aware that the Red Army was approaching Crimea from the north: on 10 April he and his ministers gathered up 10 million gold roubles and boarded a Greek ship. The Entente forces blocked the ship's departure until the gold roubles were handed over (not to the Crimeans, but to the Anglo-French consortium).

The day before Krym and his government sailed off to Piraeus a 'revolutionary committee' rose up and took control of Simferopol. By mid-May 1919 all Crimea was proclaimed a Soviet Republic and part of Russia. The new government included five Crimean Tatars and even recognized, for a while, a free Tatar press and Milliy Firqa's right to exist. A contingent of Tatar communist agitators spread propaganda all over the peninsula, but the widespread famine and new exorbitant taxes occupied the peasants' minds more than a campaign to blame Whites and 'exploiters' (*kulak*s) for the lack of food. While requisitioners combed the villages for 'donations' of 'surplus' grain, rationing was introduced: 200 grams (0.5 lb) of bread a day, less than 1.5 kilograms (3 lb) of potatoes a month.

For the next two months a state of emergency was declared. The Cheka killed as many opponents of the new regime as it could. By 26 June 1919 the Soviet regime was so detested that General Denikin's Whites, now the United Army of Southern Russia, had little trouble retaking Crimea. Denikin was now a dictator: all elected assemblies were dissolved, all laws superseded. Counter-intelligence and the prosecutor's office constituted the government. It was enough to have served in the Soviet apparatus to justify the death penalty. Tatars, whether mullahs or intellectuals, protested at being deprived of even the right to organize Muslim affairs. The newspaper *Millet* was shut down for 'separatism' and pro-Turkish views. Peasants now had to hand over up to 50 per cent of their harvest to landowners. (Red 'contributions' were replaced by White 'requisitions'.) Peasants who complained were flogged or shot and left unburied, until it was reported to Yalta that 'dogs are dragging about and eating human limbs, there are bound to be infectious diseases in spring . . . please bury all corpses at Bagreev's cottage and seal the pits with concrete.' The Whites lost in Crimea all support for the fight against the Reds: both sides of the Russian civil war were equally hated by the Tatar population.

Denikin's immediate subordinate, Major-General Slashchiov, achieved notoriety in spring 1920, when Denikin was replaced by the more sober and less utopian General Wrangel. (The transition was tense: junior officers had demanded it, and Denikin had at first reacted by dismissing Wrangel from all posts.) Slashchiov enforced order by court martial, issuing at least 150 death sentences on Bolshevik guerrillas, known as 'Greens', who tried to control Crimea's forests. By autumn 1920 Slashchiov had cities like Feodosia functioning as in peacetime: 'All the restaurants are lit up, Cossacks, Chechens, officers, ladies dressed to the nines walk the streets.' The famous nightclub poet and singer Vertinsky came and sang. Wrangel seemed to have achieved his aim of making Crimea an island of sanity in an incurably demented Russia. Wrangel was not against a Russia that would consist of loosely federated states, but he wanted to focus on Crimea as 'the basis for a Russian army from which the struggle to liberate Russia might begin', and he regarded Crimean Tatars as a still uncorrupted ethnos who would help him achieve his goals. He prosecuted his own officers when they exploited Tatar peasants, but amnestied former Red soldiers. Unredeemed Bolsheviks were to be deported to Soviet Russia – a sentence that many of them rightly feared was equivalent to execution.

Tatars were recruited, not conscripted, although a soldier's salary of 800 roubles a month was just enough to buy three weeks' supply of bread. Subsidies were handed out to revive Crimean industries, such as tanning. Machinery and fuel were imported from Great Britain. Banks gave loans. The 1919 harvest had been far better than expected, and exports brought in hard currency. On 25 May 1920 a new 'Law on Land' transferred ownership from estate owners to working peasants, to the acclaim not only of Tatars, but of Russian intellectuals, such as the historian Shulgin who had now found refuge in Sevastopol. (The peasants had to pay for their new holdings with a 25-year mortgage, costing an average of 4 per cent of their harvest.) The drawback was that Russian and German farmers accepted the new law, while Tatars were suspicious of a grant that was undocumented until they had paid off their mortgage, and land that (as they rightly foresaw) would be nationalized as soon as the Bolsheviks recaptured the peninsula. In fact, the law had come two years too late, for now there were enough covert Bolshevik agents to intimidate farmers who took advantage of Wrangel's offer. Tatars were warily encouraged by a flood of periodicals, leaflets and posters in Crimean Tatar, by the authorization of a Crimean Tatar representative congress (biased in favour of conservative Muslims), which only twenty (including Wrangel himself) out of 44 delegates attended. The congress's outcome was modest; Tatars would devise their own form of ethnic administration, with a council of sixty – far short of the autonomy they sought. They were able, however, to appoint a new *mufti* to replace a man thought to be the White Army's puppet, and to introduce Crimean Tatar as a language of instruction, alongside Russian, in the main secondary schools. On Wrangel's initiative, the Tauridean University set up a faculty of oriental studies, the first in the south of Russia, thus creating a forum and employment for Crimean Tatar linguists and historians. The Russian historian George Vernadsky even turned down an offer from British universities to become rector of the Tauridean University in Simferopol. Like Georgia in 1920, Crimea appeared to have become a hospitable microcosm of Petrograd and Moscow, with poets, artists, philosophers and actors all finding an arena and an audience. Wrangel himself was still optimistic, even if Denikin had written the Whites' death sentence with his departure and doomed attempt to attack Moscow. Wrangel believed that his respect for Crimean Muslim traditions would win the Volunteer Army support from other Muslim regions of Russia and eventual peace, if not victory.

Whatever Wrangel's aspirations, they were dashed in November 1920 when the Red Army broke through Or Qapı (Perekop). Wrangel had a spectacular, but brief, success in spring that year in repelling Bolshevik attacks by land and sea. The Soviet Army was now all the stronger for Trotsky's brilliant organization, and its hands were freed once its war with Poland was over. The White Army, on the other hand, was irrecoverably demoralized by defeats and fiascos all over Russia. Wrangel's last success was to organize between 13 and 16 November 1920 the evacuation of 100,000 men and women by mainly British ships to Istanbul: he personally toured every Crimean port to calm the chaos and panic of this last Russian exodus, and he left on one of the very last ships.

Many Russians and White Army men, at least 50,000, were abandoned – the wounded and sick, those who believed that triumphant Reds no longer needed to shoot Whites, those who hoped to hide in the mountains or steppe villages, or merge unnoticed with the civilian population. Eyewitnesses report desperate men trying to swim to departing ships, officers shooting their families and then themselves on the docksides.

Statistics are only partially trustworthy: the population of Crimea was about 650,000 in 1914, and had risen to over a million when the Civil War broke out. Under Wrangel, it was said, Tatars formed a majority, but the first Soviet census of 1921 counted only 720,000 inhabitants, fewer than 20 per cent of them Tatars. Certainly, there was a mass exodus (though not of Tatars) in November 1920, followed by a ruthless massacre by the Bolshevik Cheka (soon to be called the GPU) that more than decimated the rest of the population.

Stalin's brother-in-law Stanislav Redens, who oversaw the 1921 purges, reported that Milliy Firqa was not a political party in any Marxist sense, but a loose, pragmatic association of Tatar nationalists. Lenin, however, regarded them as 'a source of future speculation, espionage, all kinds of help for capitalism . . . we'll sort them out and stew them.' Milliy Firqa had some 10,000 members (out of 184,500 Tatars) when the Bolsheviks finally seized Crimea. Earlier in 1920 they hoped for cooperation, if not alliance, with Russian 'social democrats', and at first, right up to 1923, the Bolsheviks tolerated Milliy Firqa, now led by its chairman Seyid-Celal Hattat, by the academic and poet Bekir Çoban-Zade and by other intellectuals, who, aware that they were dealing with unprincipled killers, thought they might yet be spared. The leaders in Moscow were willing to make allowances, to appease foreign Muslim opinion and to prevent further outbreaks of ethnic rebellion all over Russia. They even released a few hundred Crimean guerrillas. Crimea's revolutionary committees, empowered by the declaration of Crimea as a Soviet Republic, were intransigent, however, and launched a campaign against Milliy Firqa as enemies of the people, as a band of outlaws no better than Zionists.

The Tatars suffered at first a less systematic terror than what was meted out to Whites stranded in Crimea. The Hungarian Béla Kun, whose communist regime in Budapest had just collapsed, was admired by Lenin, who made him a leading Soviet chekist, with instructions to execute every White on the peninsula, so that Comrade Trotsky could one day visit a completely purged Crimea. Together with his partner Roza Zemliachka, a notorious psychopath from a prosperous Jewish family who had studied medicine in Lyon, but used her anatomical knowledge only to inflict excruciating torture, Kun described Crimea as a bottle from which no counter-revolutionary would escape. He lured fugitive Whites out of hiding by promising amnesties to those who came and registered with his office. Two thousand officers, over 50,000 soldiers and about 15,000 sick and wounded were tortured to death with indescribable sadism. Russian artists and intellectuals who had failed to flee north were also trapped in Kun's and Zemliachka's 'bottle'. In one November night in 1920 nearly 4,000 were shot. The cities were patrolled and not just 'bourgeois', but nurses (and their patients), priests, dock workers, even stray Bolsheviks, were rounded up for execution. Some were drowned in barges scuttled in the Sea of Azov. In cities like Aluşta the Tatar population underwent the same fate as the White Russians and bourgeois. In a year the populations of Bağçasaray, Simferopol and Yalta fell by half. The population huddled in their houses. Villages with more than nine hundred inhabitants were mercilessly culled. All Tatar women between eighteeen and forty were registered. Survivors were sent off on foot in a freezing winter to forced labour camps or the mines of the Donbas: very few of them survived even the trek. A handful of brave men, notably the Russian poet Max Voloshin who had for years lived outside Feodosia, confronted the chekists, even secured a few reprieves and yet emerged themselves unscathed: they were exceptions. In Béla Kun's award ceremony at the end of 1921, he was thanked for killing '12,000, including 30 governors, over 150 generals and 300 colonels'.

The killings went on all through 1921 and extended to Tatars in the remote mountains. It is now thought that at least 52,000 were executed, possibly twice that number if we count all those who died of cold, hunger and disease in Béla Kun's underground holding pens and on the slow journey to concentration camps in the Arctic. No doubt, Crimea's immense stock of wine was partly to blame, for the Red Army and Cheka executioners could only keep up with the killing by being permanently drunk (they were assisted by Latvian and Chinese execution squads who felt not a glimmer of sympathy for their victims). Simferopol stank of corpses stripped of their clothes and then thrown into ravines and gullies (which would eventually be flooded by a new reservoir, while even in this century the skeletons that floated up have been blamed on Nazi atrocities). Crimea's resulting chaos and loss of manpower precipitated a famine that began in autumn 1921 and lasted until spring 1923, killing 100,000, some 15 per cent of the population. The famine affected Crimean Tatars in the countryside far worse than Russians in the port cities. While the massive famine in the Volga region was alleviated by charitable relief from the USA and from Orthodox Church funds, none of it filtered through to Crimea's revolutionary committees.

In 1922 Lenin's desperate concession to capitalism, the New Economic Policy, allowed limited private and foreign trade and modest capitalist enterprise in Russia. The secret police, now known as the GPU, were given a novel task by Stalin, their main patron among the Bolshevik leaders: they executed far fewer citizens of their Socialist Republics and concentrated on counter-intelligence and on undermining, infiltrating and destroying hostile émigré groups, a direction that required fewer psychopathic executioners and more educated polyglot intelligence officers. Béla Kun's reputation was by now embarrassing even to his masters in Moscow, who explained that they 'had not expected him to use his plenipotentiary powers in such a way'. He was sent to stir up a communist putsch in Germany (he failed and in 1928 was sent back to Russia, where he was shot as a Trotskyist and German spy in 1938).

Even with the onset of a less manic regime in 1923, economic recovery was impossible when the Red Army had confiscated most of the horses and carts and, by specific order, all the saddles, and the town Committees for Requisition and Confiscation had dismantled and removed all the bakeries. Markets were closed and the few traders attacked and arrested. Confiscation was so thorough that Tatar women in Simferopol went about dressed in sacks. Grain, including the following year's seedcorn, was commandeered, and those without party or government connections could easily starve to death. Children suffered worse: some 25,000 orphans tried to survive by begging, and tens of thousands of families had to watch their children die. The helpless famine relief officials reported in spring 1922 that some 22,500 were starving to death every month, that they knew of cases of infanticide and even cannibalism. Moscow took no notice. Trade stopped. The frontier to Ukraine, where conditions were slightly better, was closed to Crimean Tatars. The one untapped source of wealth were millions of tonnes of unmined salt in the north: Lenin gave the military commander Mikhail Frunze instuctions to harvest and market the salt, not to relieve the Crimean famine, but to rescue Soviet finances: 'It is a question of life and death for Soviet authority, for us.' Any object of value vanished: a confiscated Amati cello was retrieved only after the Second World War. Cultural institutions were degraded: the Tauridean University founded in 1918 was renamed after Frunze, the Red Army commander who had done so much to destroy the peninsula (in 1925 the university was downgraded to a 'pedagogical institute').

The university acquired, however, an internationally acclaimed genius who was both a Crimean Tatar and a Communist, Bekir Çoban-Zade. As a teenager, he became a prisoner of war in Hungary, was noticed by the Hungarian linguist Julius von Mészáros and rapidly became a Turcologist, culminating in 1919 by holding two professorships, in Budapest and Lausanne, at the age of 26. Çoban-Zade returned covertly to Crimea under Wrangel and was made rector of the Tauridean University by the Bolsheviks. (He declared that in this new Crimea 'the dead had resurrected.') He was appointed to a chair at Baku, where he led the process of switching the Turkic languages of the Soviet Union from Arabic to Latin alphabets. The argument for Latinization (apart from Lenin's wish) of all the languages of the USSR, except for Georgian and Armenian, was weakened by almost universal opposition from Russians and Ukrainians whose culture was rooted in the Cyrillic alphabet. Turkic languages, however, were ill-suited to Arabic script, which could not represent their wide range of vowels and, with its ligatures and varieties of letter formation, was harder to learn and, in particular, to typeset. The real reason, however, for abandoning Arabic script in the USSR (and shortly afterwards in Atatürk's Turkey) was cultural: Crimean Tatars, Uzbeks and others would be cut off from the Qur'an, from Arabic and Persian culture and from their own past literature. They would now be less contaminated by Islam and more easily adapted to European and socialist culture. After various experiments (for instance, simplified Arabic), Crimean Tatar newspapers and schoolbooks went over to a reasonably phonetic and consistent Latin alphabet. Soviet values infiltrated Tatar culture: traditional Muslim and Tatar names began to give way to names like Lemara (Lenin-Marx), Lenur (from Russian 'Lenin instituted the revolution'), while some traditional names acquired a new sense – Zarema now stood for the Russian 'for a world revolution'. Russified names of towns became permanent: apart from Balaklava, Kerç and Bağçasaray, and the Greek toponyms along the southern coast (Aluşta, Alupka, Feodosia), many place names were changed; only rivers and mountains kept their Turkic names. Districts lost their original names and were called after the leadership: Aqmescit (now Simferopol) belonged to Kaganovich district.

By the end of 1922 a dozen or so guerrilla bands, a *maquis* alarming the Bolsheviks on the southern coast, had all been eliminated. Many succumbed to printed leaflets promising amnesty: they were given a celebratory meal, then arrested and murdered. Others saw the hopelessness of resistance and decided to adapt. The new Crimean Autonomous Socialist Republic needed to have Tatar commissars, not Russians, for appearances' sake and in order to have some authority over the population. Members of Milliy Firqa were, in the 1920s, tolerated as 'fellow-travellers'.

The best of these new administrators was Veli Ibraimov, who had as a boy progressed from being a docker to a typesetter for the newspaper *Tercüman* and was tutored by Gaspıralı himself. The owner of a Simferopol coffee-house, he became an activist in Milliy Firqa, then a Bolshevik and a chekist, but he protested at the horrors of the 1922 famine even while fighting the Tatar guerrillas on the coast. Unlike his chekist colleagues, he honoured the amnesty and befriended some of those who surrendered. He was an ideal choice as president of the Autonomous Crimean Republic, which he per-suaded Moscow to treat as a homeland in which the Tatars, if not the majority of the population, would be the 'core' population. He sometimes discreetly opposed decisions taken in Moscow: he lobbied against the establish-ment of a Jewish 'republic' around Or Qapı; he tried, instead of Jews, to have Crimean Tatars, both indigenous and refugees, repatriated from Bulgaria and Romania and even built villages to accommodate 20,000 of them. In the end, Moscow rejected repatriation from abroad as too open to exploita-tion by anti-Soviet elements. But Stalin, while accepting Ibraimov's plan to move landless peasants from the southern coast and the mountains into the relatively empty steppes of the north, still insisted on a partial resettlement of Russian Jews in the same territory.

Even in 1924 the famine had not abated. A hundred thousand had now died, and some 60,000 had fled. A few dozen wagonloads of provisions from Moscow, a few hundred tonnes of food from Azerbaijan and Georgia, dona-tions from the Netherlands and Germany stopped cannibalism, but little else: an anonymous Tatar composed verses: 'The warehouses are full of American grain/ And mothers are eating their children,/ And don't care if they eat cats and dogs,/ All hopes are on the comrades in Feodosia.'

Meanwhile in Moscow, Nikolai Semashko, the commissar for health, himself a doctor, tried to revive southern Crimea's sanatoria for the overworked Bolshevik generation. The only beds available were in a few refuges for orphans, who were turned out into the street, flooding Yalta and Feodosia with child prostitutes.

Meanwhile, Stalin was kept informed in detail by the OGPU, which detected subversion everywhere, of dissidence and resistance in Crimea: in August 1924 monarchists were said to be plotting a rebellion, and three hundred plotters in Yalta had to be 'eliminated'. Allegedly, in Feodosia and Evpatoria Boy Scouts were in touch with émigrés and conducting religious propaganda; in 1925 a kulak gathering was planning to murder communists and resisting reassignment of landholdings, while mullahs were predicting the fall of Soviet power. In 1926 Yalta's Milliy Firqa loyalists were being supported by local communists, and mullahs were proselytizing and assembling all over Crimea; in Bağçasaray Tatars were campaigning against Russian Jews coming to set up 'a second Palestine' in Crimea, and in Yalta Tatars were assaulting Russian labourers.

Russification gathered pace since every nationality in the USSR, including the Crimean Tatars, knew that fluency in Russian was an entry to universities and elite civilian and military institutes, as well as to the local party and Soviet bureaucracy. With Russian lessons came the ideology of the day, first and foremost a renunciation of religious belief and practice by adherence to an obligatory nationwide godless movement. The Communist Youth movement was a preparatory school for membership of the party, essential for holders of responsible posts, a class now called the *nomenklatura*. Tatars, whatever their private feelings, needed party cards for survival. Adherence to the Crimean Tatar language could result in accusations of Islamicism, of Panturkism, of spying for Atatürk's Turkey. Official policy was to encourage the development of 'minority' and local republican languages, a process called 'indigenization' (*korenizatsia*), but the results were meagre.[2] Crimean Tatar primary schooling was established, but there were almost no textbooks to be had in Crimean Tatar, and very few libraries. Books in Russian, Armenian and Yiddish could be imported from Moscow, but lack of materials, machinery and skilled typographers meant that throughout the 1920s very little was published in Crimean Tatar, let alone Karaim Turkish.

By the late 1920s Stalin had ousted his left-wing rivals and silenced the right wing. The time was ripe not only for collectivization of the USSR's peasantry, but for the closure of the New Economic Policy, the end of free enterprise and any relict of freedom of expression. Worst of all, those who had been acclaimed as leaders of their ethnic group now became criminals for fostering 'bourgeois nationalism' and for contacts with foreign powers. Ibraimov's intelligent and conciliatory rule came to a rapid end: his friend Amit Haiserov, a former White officer, defended him by striking an old enemy of Ibraimov's with a revolver. Next day the enemy was found strangled and Veli Ibraimov, together with a number of colleagues, was tried for 'terrorism' and executed in May 1928, the first (but by no means the last) leader of an autonomous republic to suffer this fate. On the evening of his execution, his wife and son visited Stalin in the Kremlin; Stalin gave the boy an orange, and assured the wife that her husband was being sent as ambassador to a distant Muslim country.[3]

Executing Ibraimov was a pretext for eliminating Milliy Firqa. The head of the OGPU, the exquisite executioner Viacheslav Menzhinsky, warned the Crimean party in December 1928 that an indictment of Crimean Tatar nationalists had been prepared. They would be accused of espionage, separatism, planning with the expatriate Cafer Seydamet to unite with Turkey, forming an economic cooperative Şirket to protect exploiters from the authorities. Tried in Moscow in 1929, 63 Crimean Tatars were accused of fantastic crimes. There were eleven death sentences, five of which were commuted; most were sent to prison camps for three to ten years (in the late 1930s nearly all the latter would receive new, lethal sentences). Milliy Firqa in league with the Bolsheviks were like dogs that had joined a wolf pack, to be annihilated because of their fondness for human beings. Crimea lost most of its intellectual elite (the rest would be killed in the Great Terror of 1937–8); just a few survived this trial, such as the doctor, dramatist and prose writer Ahmet Seit Özenbaşlı, who spent most of his life labouring in the Gulag. What had they achieved? Neither the repatriation of some 20,000 émigrés, nor the grant of autonomy for the Crimean Soviet republic had brought much benefit, apart from partly redressing the balance between immigrant Russians and indigenous Tatars in Crimea: only the ideals of Milliy Firqa would persist for decades to come.

Having liquidated independent intellectual activity, Stalin next annihilated the independent peasantry and farmers, the so-called kulaks (peasants rich enough to hire labour for the harvest, or to own more than one or two horses), by forcing the peasantry to give up their land, animals and tools to collective farms, on which they would be semi-slaves, unable to leave without official permission. The object, allegedly, was to increase production and sell more grain to pay for rapid industrialization; by taking the kulaks and many of the 'middle-range' peasants off the land (leaving the poorest and the landless as the dominant population), a new migrant labour force, free or forced, would be available to build the steel plants, dams and power plants needed for a modern industrial power. The predictable ensuing chaos, of course, produced riots, a loss of production (the peasants feasted on meat before their animals could be confiscated), then famine. The economic crash in the West lowered the demand for Soviet produce.

Crimean Tatars were particularly angered: they had few rich exploitative kulak farmers, least of all in the orchards and plantations of the coast and the mountains. They rebelled: with pitchforks, by hiding flocks of sheep with those of the 'poor' peasants, by composing folk songs that threatened to stab to death the OGPU men who 'chased my sister from the village to beg', and by collecting funds to support those made destitute by accusations that they were kulaks.

In December 1929 there was a serious rebellion against collectivization at Uskut and Tuaka, villages in the Alakat valley near Aluşta. The villagers trusted rumours (possibly spread by the OGPU as a provocation) that Polish, German and Turkish forces were ready to liberate them; they wrote a collective letter to the Turkish embassy in Moscow, complaining of terror, persecution of Islam and unbearable taxation, and asking to be resettled in Turkey. They then collected funds to spread the same protest all over Crimea. A secret police agent easily infiltrated the protesters and some eight hundred were arrested, some resisting by pelting the secret police with rocks. The purge spread all round the Aluşta area, and some 40,000 peasant 'rebels' belonging to a probably fictitious 'Assumption' organization, most of them totally unaware, were interrogated, then deported, imprisoned or executed. The archives have only vague details of the operation, but one rebel escaped by boat to Turkey and gave a full account to the leader of the Tatar exiles, Cafer Seydamet.[4]

After the first wave, temporarily collectivizing 90 per cent of Crimea's farms, the party, 'giddy with success' as Stalin put it, had to back down for a year or two, before recruiting Communist youth and officials to stop backsliding and enforce collectivization more brutally, 'liquidating' groups (74 were recorded in Crimea in 1931) who resisted. In 1931 at least 4,325 kulak families were deported with their children in unheated trains, often without food or water, to Siberian steppes or Ural forests, where no accommodation had been prepared. The OGPU itself reported that 50 per cent were starving to death and incapable of work. The few survivors who completed their 'sentence' were not allowed to leave their place of exile. This deportation of tens of thousands of Crimean Tatars to barren northern landscapes was a rehearsal for a crime twenty times more terrible in 1944.

To compensate for the loss of the best agricultural workers, the Crimean party issued absurd decrees: milk cows were now to be used like oxen to pull ploughs and carts; the death of a horse from overwork and starvation was blamed on kulak saboteurs; children had to publish notifications of disassociation from their parents. The anti-kulak campaign reached a second climax in 1934, when 21 per cent of the repressions between 1929 and 1939 took place. The harvest in 1932 had, in any case, been appallingly small (yet the USSR exported nearly 2 million tonnes of grain): in the worst areas of Crimea and Ukraine, the authorities punitively closed markets, stopped all supplies, made any purchase or storage of grain a serious crime, and introduced new taxes to extract whatever the peasant might have left, such as old jewellery and coins.

Despair was such that Memet Qubayev, Veli Ibraimov's successor as head of the Crimean government, addressed his party audience: 'Moscow is robbing Crimea and dooming the people to die of hunger.' (Qubayev was immediately dismissed and later given ten years in the Gulag, where he died.) Russian poets, horrified by the transformation of Crimea from the paradise they had known during the Civil War, were shocked into silence. Only the great poet Osip Mandelshtam dared in 1933 to revisit Eski Qırım and write 'Old Crimea' (for which he was later accused of slander):

> Nature doesn't recognize its face,
> But the shades are terrible – of Ukraine, Kuban . . .
> On the felted earth hungry peasants
> Lurk by the gate, but do not touch the handle.

The year 1934 brought a good harvest all over the USSR and a relaxation of the wave of arrests and deportations. The following year, however, Stalin replaced the head of the OGPU, Genrikh Yagoda, with the manic 'bloody dwarf' Nikolai Ezhov, and together they planned an accelerated extermination of all enemies, potential and even unimaginable. The OGPU was transformed into an all-embracing People's Commissariat of Internal Affairs, the NKVD. From the end of 1934, after the assassination in Leningrad of Sergei Kirov, charges of terrorism had rocketed, and in 1935 and 1936 trials by *troika* (where no evidence or appeal was heard and where sentences were imposed by a secret policeman, a party official and a prosecutor) became widespread. In early spring 1935 the Leningrad NKVD shot well over 4,000 'former people'. The 'Great Terror', which reached full intensity in spring 1937 and would not die down until the end of 1938, went far further: it set for every region in the USSR *limity*, numbers of persons to be arrested, with one-third to be shot and the rest to be 'turned into camp dust' in the Gulag. The focus was largely, but not exclusively, on those formerly targeted by the regime, on educated males between thirty and fifty, especially 'bourgeois' and those with foreign connections or merely surnames, and anyone who might be friends, employees or dependants of already purged leaders, such as Trotsky, Zinoviev or Kamenev. The Terror did to the professional classes, to industry, the party, the armed forces and the secret police themselves what collectivization had done to agriculture and the peasantry. This time, however, there was no resistance from any source, so cowed and shocked were the victims, now that their families were just as liable to repression.

In Crimea the first target was a former chairman of the Executive Committee, Yuri Gaven, now labelled as a Trotskyist. Crimea's NKVD was headed by a Georgian, Tite Lordkipanidze (himself to be purged the following month). In May 1937 he proudly announced he had arrested 3,000, of whom three hundred were Tatar 'nationalists' and three hundred German 'Fascists'. The next Crimean head of the NKVD, Karp Pavlov, set up a *troika* to process his prisoners and set himself a 'limit' of several thousand. Pavlov was given an initial limit of 1,500, of whom 300 were to be shot (without revealing to relatives when, where or even if). He asked for a bigger target, but was told to wait. Meanwhile Pavlov instituted a process that involved torture, first by non-stop 'conveyor' interrogation from a team of NKVD men, then by physical and sadistic brutality. Those 'convicted', if not shot, laboured in camps for sixteen hours a day.

Pavlov was replaced in the autumn by Artur Mikhelson (no Tatar was entrusted with senior secret police work, for which Russians, Ukrainians, Jews and, later, Georgians and Armenians were preferred). Mikhelson had greater 'limits': by January 1938 he had sentenced over 4,000 (of whom 2,288 were shot), and Crimea's prisons, built for 2,000, held nearly 9,000. Crimea's Germans and Greeks, as potential 'spies' for hostile countries, suffered worse than any other: 2 per cent of them fell victim to Mikhelson, whose 'special' *troika* shot another 1,596 victims in the summer of 1938.

The Crimean Tatar intelligentsia was more or less extinct. The dramatist and director Ümer Ipçi, who had almost singlehandedly created Crimean Tatar theatre and cinema, was repressed (he was kept alive, but unable to work). The greatest Crimean intellectual, Bekir Çoban-Zade, linguist, orientalist and poet, described himself as 'Iron hands, oaken head, soul on fire'

(*Qollar demir, baş emen. Könlüm tolu ateşmen*): he was arrested in January 1937 in Russia and executed, as 'an agent of Turkish and Polish intelligence', in October in Qarasuvbazar.[5] Crimea's notorious NKVD interrogator Mikhelson personally assaulted those he wanted to confess to fictional crimes, breaking chairs over their heads. His colleagues made those they arrested (including their former colleagues) watch others being shot, or forced them to have intercourse with corpses. Like his predecessors, Mikhelson fell victim to his cannibalistic NKVD colleagues; he was replaced by a Ukrainian, Lavrenti Yakushev, who was not just more inventive, but more acquisitive, tearing gold teeth from corpses. Even when the Terror was officially over, with Ezhov's arrest and the restoration of the prosecutor's office as the arbiter of justice, Yakushev could not stop: he forged hundreds of retrospective death sentences and in one November week shot 822, including pregnant women and former colleagues, some personally.

Crimea had lost most of its senior administrators, and the Black Sea fleet had too few officers left to function. Yakushev, however, escaped the fate of his predecessors. He was sentenced to the Gulag, but amnestied when war broke out, became a war hero, and died of natural causes in 1986. The one positive fact about the Great Terror in Crimea was that no Tatar played a prominent role as an interrogator or executioner. Despite the practice enforced all over the USSR, few Crimean Tatars wrote letters to the newspapers demanding the execution of 'traitors and spies', or denunciations of their neighbours and relatives.

After the breathing space of 1939 and 1940, when there were far fewer executions, and even some reprieves, Crimea's poets felt obliged to write a collective poem, a 260-line 'Letter to Stalin', which, translated into Russian, persuaded readers all over the USSR that the Tatars had finally been tamed. It blamed all the horrors of the twentieth century on Turks, émigrés and counter-revolutionaries. Some 213 persons, authors and organizers of the panegyric of Stalin, were given special ration cards that gave them access to provisions – 3 kilograms (6.5 lb) of meat and butter, 20 kilograms (44 lb) of fruit and vegetables, 200 cigarettes – and even clothes that the ordinary citizen could only dream of. Conformist intellectuals were now classed as senior party officials.

On the other hand, Russification intensified. Stalin reversed Lenin's Latinization drive: all written Turkic languages had in the late 1930s to use the Cyrillic alphabet. Thus outdated political literature became unreadable to the new generation, communication with Atatürk's Latinized Turkish became harder, and the transition from using a native language to Russian was smoother. Each Turkic language was given a different way of representing sounds alien to the Cyrillic alphabet; the new letters devised were not at first available on typewriters. A cultural revolution followed: except for some folklore, only Soviet prose and poetry was now published, and four centuries of Crimean Tatar poetry and chronicles became inaccessible. Theatres in Simferopol and elsewhere were not allowed to stage traditional Turkish drama, or even European classics. Ümer Ipçi, the leading author of the 'Letter to Stalin', now dictated the laws of literature and criticism, recognizing only atheistic work by contemporaries who were socialist and 'poor'.

Throughout the 1930s, as Stalin's Marxist approach was replaced by a conventional imperial one, Crimean history, like Russian history, was rewritten, primarily to make Russia seem the saviour of the Crimean Tatars. Islam, however, was harder to eradicate from the past or the present: mosques were turned into secular meeting places; attendance at the surviving mosques, while not as severely frowned upon as observance of Christianity, was discouraged; farmers were forced to produce pork, but this was not enough to eliminate the old Islamic beliefs or to inculcate new socialist ones. The much-loved *mufti* since the early 1920s, Ibraim Tarpi, was not arrested until May 1927: he was exiled to Uzbekistan and in 1936 sent to the Gulag; he died in exile in 1945. Almost all Crimea's senior Muslim clergy, accused of being Turkish and Japanese spies, were shot in 1938.

The interlude in 1939 and 1940 when Stalin was more preoccupied with foreign policy than with identifying internal enemies came to an abrupt end on 22 June 1941. Dismissing warnings from their own spies, the Soviet leadership was shocked first into inertia, then into panic by Hitler's sudden invasion. Hundreds of thousands of soldiers, some even under orders not to fire back, were killed and taken prisoner, and in four months the Nazis, with their Romanian allies, had taken Crimea (only Sevastopol held out for months longer). Stalin's hapless party agent Lev Mekhlis took disastrous control of the response, which resulted in the Black Sea fleet officers evacuating Sevastopol without their 100,000 seamen, the generals around Or Qapı likewise abandoning their soldiers, and the army at Kerç drowning countless men in futile attempts to escape by sea or to counter-attack. Mekhlis concentrated on executing German prisoners of war, while, for the Nazis, General Erich von Manstein tried to cope with 200,000 Soviet prisoners. Like the British in Singapore, the Soviets waited in Sevastopol for a naval attack that never came, and left the hinterland, Perekop (Or Qapı), virtually undefended.

The retreating Red Army's one success was to remove or destroy anything that might support the population when the Germans took over. The 'scorched earth' policy removed or burned grain, cattle, horses, weapons, vehicles, generators, museums and palaces (some centuries old). Stocks of wine that had not been drunk by Russian troops were poured out, turning the Black Sea coast red. The only visible preparation for war, this process had begun the previous winter, so that Crimean Tatars faced starvation when the Germans came.

The first invaders behaved atrociously: the storm troops were followed by *Einsatzkommando* who massacred Jews, party members and any civilians who caught their eyes. After the initial terrible winter, however, as in a few areas of the USSR (notably Pskov in the northwest), the Germans established an efficient regime that gave surviving civilians freedoms they had not known for 25 years.

Hitler, Rosenberg (in charge of 'nationalities') and Himmler had plans for Crimea as a country they intended to call 'Gothenland': they would deport or annihilate the Slav population and, to a limited extent, preserve the ethnic Tatars, on the grounds that the Crimean Tatars had Gothic (that is, Aryan) blood. Eventually, ethnic Germans from Italy's South Tyrol would be resettled in Crimea. Cities would be renamed: Simferopol would be Gothenburg and Sevastopol Theodorichshafen (after the king of the Ostrogoths). Crimea would be a *Volkstumbrücke*, linking up with ethnic Germans in the rest of Eastern Europe, once 127,000 Germans from Transnistria, on the border of Ukraine and Moldavia, had been moved, and after demobilized SS soldiers settled there with their families. Himmler, however, thought the process required the slaughter of most of Crimea's original inhabitants and wanted to start the programme even while war was being waged.

Some sense was brought to this idiotic plan by a relatively humane and expert Prussian, Count Friedrich-Werner von der Schulenburg, a diplomat who had been admired in Russia and Georgia and who guardedly reciprocated this admiration. Ribbentrop, who had a mere glimmer of humanity, also preferred a subtler approach to ethnic cleansing. They realized that, in the battle against Russia, disaffected minorities like the Crimean Tatars might usefully be tolerated. Ribbentrop consulted frequently with von Papen, the Nazi ambassador in Turkey, who advised giving Muslim minorities of Russia independence. Simultaneously, a Turkish delegation including Crimean Tatar exiles, such as Cafer Seydamet, spent months in Berlin, lobbying the Nazi leaders to restore Crimean independence and to support all

Russia's Tatars. Two Tatars from Dobruja, the lawyer Müstecip Hacı Fazıl Ülküsal and the intellectual Mustafa Edige Kırımal, came to Berlin to urge the Germans to free Crimean Tatar prisoners of war and organize them into an anti-Russian fighting force. They were at first fobbed off, since Hitler wanted a centralized Reich, but they did make Berlin's experts in Muslim affairs willing to keep supposedly neutral Turkey sweet by appearing positive towards Tatars. By now, from expatriates, deserters and prisoners of war, several battalions of Russians and Caucasian (largely Georgian) soldiers had been armed (with light weapons only) and were acting as rearguard soldiers and as occupation police with the Wehrmacht. Rather than starve to death, most of the 20,000 Tatar prisoners also put on German uniforms.

The Crimean Tatars recruited by General Manstein were used cautiously: they were not trusted to hunt down Russian or Tatar partisans. An Austrian aristocratic writer, Alfred Frauenfeld, headed the civic administration of Crimea. Hitler had always wanted 'to give something nice to Frauenfeld' and had made him gauleiter of Vienna in the 1930s. Frauenfeld was independently minded and strongly interested in Tatar culture: he reminded older Tatars of the much-loved rule of the German general von Kosch and his Polish Tatar collaborator Süleyman Sulkiewicz in 1918. In a memorandum that would eventually win Frauenfeld a nominal one year's imprisonment after being tried and sentenced by the Allies,[6] he recommended to Himmler an approach to Crimea quite unlike that of Erich Koch, the monstrous ruler of Ukraine remembered for his utterance, 'If ever a Ukrainian appears worthy to sit at the same table as me, I shall have to shoot him.' Crimea, wrote Frauenfeld, needed food supplies, a medical and veterinary service, land distribution to all peasants, regardless of their attitude to Germany, permission for soldiers to have relationships with Tatar women, and paid, not forced, employment for Tatar men (of whom only the very young, very old and the sick had escaped conscription into the Red Army).

Frauenfeld managed just a little of his programme: new Crimean Tatar schools were opened, money was allocated to reviving the use of Crimean Tatar language, and for concerts, dances and theatrical programmes at the Alupka pedagogical institute, even debates on philosophical and historical topics, which drew an audience from other Crimean cities. Frauenfeld boasted after his first year that there had 'not been a single act of sabotage, or wounding or killing of a German'. Later, he wrote that he could walk the length and breadth of Crimea, fearless and unarmed. Unlike the German occupiers, however, Romanian troops, underfed and beaten by their officers, behaved bestially: seven were hanged by the Germans for raping a Tatar girl.

From November 1941 to spring 1942 Muslim Committees were set up. They not only smoothed relations with the Germans, but quietly promoted native interests. They undertook reforms, including a reversion to the Latin alphabet for the language. At least 2,000 young civilian men were recruited into the pro-German Vlasov Russian National Liberation Army. In Simferopol a Russian-language newspaper, *The Voice of Crimea*, was printed for nearly three years, its circulation rising from 3,000 to 80,000 issues thrice weekly; it was followed by the Tatar-language *Free Crimea*: although anti-Bolshevik and antisemitic in tone, it had broad cultural interests and published material on Stalin's repressions and on Tatars in Romania.[7] A Crimean Tatar office (admittedly almost powerless) was opened in Berlin. All over Ukraine and Crimea, to the peasants' relief, Soviet collective farms were dissolved and farmers could often work the land as individual proprietors, although all livestock, even a newly hatched chick, had to be registered. They were often allowed to keep working horses: Germans confiscated

Alfred Frauenfeld (right) with Joseph Goebbels, 1932.

Ewald von Kleist, 1942–4, commander of German forces in Crimea.

horses for a few months at a time, but then returned them. Farmers were paid in 'occupation' marks for produce, and in Crimea the Germans provided seedcorn and three hundred Lanz Bulldog tractors, as well as their massive army horses for ploughing. Under Frauenfeld there was a graduated income tax up to 10 per cent on the admittedly paltry earnings allowed. Trade was limited by severe restrictions on peasants leaving their home village. Communication with Berlin was active: Anton Chekhov's villa in Yalta was carefully guarded by a Major von Baake on instructions from Olga Tschechowa, an actress beloved of Goebbels and who was the ex-wife of Chekhov's nephew, while Chekhov's sister Maria lived in Yalta, safe and secure.

Frauenfeld's work, meanwhile, was undermined by the ss and sd forces who had entered Crimea, terrorizing peaceful peasants as they tried to exterminate partisans, more Russian than Tatar, driving villagers into the forests, where they were hunted down, both by ss in search of rebels and by Soviet partisans in search of collaborators. The Gestapo was merciless, torturing and killing the last remaining intellectuals, among them the young poet Osman Amit. One appalling atrocity was the killing of 7,000 civilians on 2 December 1941 in an anti-tank ditch near Kerç. Jews, whether Ashkenazi Russians or native *Krymchaki*, were slaughtered. Otto Ohlendorf, a doctor of law and the commander of Einsatzgruppe D, is reckoned to have killed 130,000 in his year in Crimea, among his victims being tens of thousands of Tatars (he was hanged in 1951). Ohlendorf was helped by antisemitic Ukrainian auxiliaries, Don Cossacks and predatory Romanian sadists to kill an enormous number of Jews in Simferopol (but he exempted a few Jewish farmers because they provided food for the Reich). Just one Jewish doctor, Tikhonovich, was spared when a crowd of his patients shouted at the SD that the doctor was a Slav, not a Jew. The one mercy German orientalists had obtained from the SS was to exempt from extermination the more numerous Judaic Karaim, whom Rabbinical Jews themselves considered to be heretics. (Some Crimean Karaim even joined German extermination squads.) In Crimea, as in Lithuania (but not in Ukraine), the Karaim were largely spared, as were Georgian Jews in Europe: the fact that they spoke neither Yiddish nor Sephardic, and were indistinguishable in speech, clothing and the community from the non-Jewish population, was their salvation. Crimean Tatars suffered less than Jews, gypsies and Slavs, but they were liable to be held as hostages – sometimes all the men in a village would be held, and fifty would be shot if a German officer was killed by partisans. (Soviet partisans reciprocated with similar brutality.) The population often took the view that the partisan, not the German avenger, was responsible for the massacre of innocent Tatars. In Yalta anyone who had been a Soviet official was taken out of town to *Tiktaş*, a tall stone that once marked a cabbies' halt, and was shot.

Frauenfeld's superior, General Ewald von Kleist, agreed that the Crimean Tatars should be courted, rather than brutalized, but his advice fell on deaf ears in Berlin. Instead, to starve out partisans, the SS and its minions confiscated any provisions they found. The problem for both Germans and Soviets was that family and village ties among the Crimean Tatars overrode political affiliation: a Soviet partisan could meet a pro-German brother, neighbour or friend and give him food and shelter. Villagers, especially in the mountains, tried to defend themselves against all partisan groups, Soviet or pro-German, who threatened their existence. Altogether, the Germans alone burned 115 villages down to the ground, and Soviet partisans (one-fifth of whom were Crimean Tatars) acted with the same ruthless brutality. Denunciations were rare: one notable exception was a Soviet partisan group who regularly sent suspected pro-German collaborators to a contact in Simferopol to be denounced as Soviet spies and shot.

For eighty years, as a justification for their suppression, Tatars have been accused of collaboration with the Nazis (despite the fact that at least a quarter of the Soviet partisans were Crimean Tatars, and numbers increased after the battle of Stalingrad and the hope of victory it brought). There was only one serious betrayal of Soviet partisans to the Germans by Tatars, after a group of Soviet partisans was parachuted into the forest: had the local Tatars not betrayed them, they themselves would have been liquidated by the Germans. Like all occupied populations, they tried to survive and, on pain of death, did as they were told. For most Crimean Tatars, the Germans seemed no more inhumane and unreasonable than Stalin's police and party: villagers even felt that their traditional life could be resumed. They were often given two unpalatable options: a Tatar could become a *Schuma* (a defence worker who policed his country and was an auxiliary for the occupiers), or a *Hiwi* and travel to Germany, usually to work on a farm for the pittance that *Ostarbeiter* were paid. Some Tatar *Hiwi*s were treated well by German farmers, desperately short of skilled farm labour. *Schuma*, however, would have to face the vengeance of the returning Red Army. After Stalingrad, it was clear that the Germans and their collaborators would soon be driven out. Tatars tried to delude themselves with the hope that the Allied leaders present at the summits in Tehran and Yalta would force Stalin to concede an end to repression and collectivization. The unbridled Crimean press that Frauenfeld had allowed to flourish conjectured freely about an independent Crimea, which would emerge under Allied and Turkish protection once Germany lost the war.

In the early summer of 1944 anyone who believed in such fantasies was totally disabused.

11

EXILE AND EXODUS

Vagonlarda balaçıqlar
Saqındıqlar öldüler.
Mezarlıqlar tapalmayıp
Vokzallarda kömdüler.

(In the carriages the little children
Die of suffocation.
There are no cemeteries to be found,
So they're buried at the stations.)
Folk song

From 8 April to 12 May 1944 half a million Soviet soldiers rid Crimea of 200,000 Germans, killing half of the enemy (as many by drowning as by shells and bullets), taking prisoner another third, and capturing their artillery. Civilians, as elsewhere in liberated zones, hoped for a new, liberal Stalinism. They were quickly disabused: even pro-Soviet forest partisans were arrested and flown away for interrogation by counter-intelligence tribunals. Denunciations of pro-German citizens were collected. Tatars (mostly women), for whose opposition to German occupation Russian neighbours would not vouch, were often shot on sight. NKVD police and troops followed, sentencing some 6,000 workers to ten years in prison and 1,000 to death, simply for staying at their workplace, for instance keeping the Massandra wine cellars intact. Thousands of Tatars (largely women, since fit men were at the front) were in May 1944 sent off to the Urals or the Far North for forestry work as slaves in the Soviet Labour Army. The Dobruja Tatar Kırımal (whose pro-German stance invites scepticism) claimed that the trees lining Simferopol's streets were hung with Tatar bodies, killed by incoming Soviet forces.

On 11 May Stalin signed a top secret decree, 'On the Crimean Tatars', prepared by the head of the NKVD, Lavrenti Beria, whose main remit was now the punishment of 'traitor' nations. The Crimean Tatars were accused of siding en masse with the enemy, working for émigré Tatars, persecuting non-Tatars and plotting to detach Crimea from the USSR. Accordingly, all of them (estimated at 190,000) had to be 'resettled' by the NKVD as deportees, 95 per cent of them in Uzbekistan. The points of the decree that were never enacted (and never intended to be) offered concessions: the deportees were each to be allowed to take half a tonne of luggage, provisions and items such as tools; they would be given receipts for the livestock and deadstock they left behind, to be honoured when they reached Uzbekistan; each train-load of deportees would be accompanied by a doctor and two nurses and they would receive hot meals and water; on arrival they would be issued with grain, vegetables and plots of land, and seven-year bank loans provided in order to build houses; the trains that transported them were to have 75,000 planks installed for the deportees to sleep on. Not one of these promises was kept.

The speed of the deportation was astounding. A week later, Beria's gruesome underlings Kobulov and Serov reported that fifty trains carrying 136,412 deportees were already trundling east, and another 30,000 were on their way to the railhead at Simferopol. Lavrenti Beria and his men (largely Georgians) by now had extensive experience of mass deportations to Central Asia and the Urals. Beria began with the North Caucasus Turkic Karachai in November 1943, then in December deported the Mongol Kalmyks from the lower Volga region; in February the North Caucasian Ingush and Chechen peoples, altogether nearly half a million, were sent with special brutality – those in the inaccessible mountain villages were shot or crammed

Deported Crimean Tatars at a funeral, Krasnovishersk, 1944.

into mosques and burnt alive; in March Beria deported the North Caucasus Turkic Balkars. Earlier deportations, notably of non-Muslims, such as the Koreans in 1937 from the Far East and the Volga Germans in 1941, had been carried out with surprisingly low mortality: the Koreans and Germans were eventually welcome in Kazakhstan for their skills and communal solidarity. Beria's actions now, however, led to the death of up to half the deportees, and starvation and freezing cold for the survivors. Some deportations, notably of the Chechen and Ingush, directly benefited Beria's Georgia, which grabbed territory now cleansed.

The Crimean Tatars had little warning of what awaited them after a hurried census by the NKVD, who mapped every village and assigned one of their colleagues with three or four soldiers to round up each group of ten families. Roads were then repaired by forced labour for the NKVD lorries to pass more easily. On the evening of 17 May 1944, soldiers were given a hot supper by unsuspecting victims, after which the hosts were driven by their guests with blows from rifle butts into the street, while their houses were searched. In the morning, forbidden to gather their documents or even a bar of soap, let alone the fictitious half-tonne of supplies, women and children (often families of serving soldiers) were driven with kicks and bayonets into the street again. Many Tatars now thought it pointless to take anything with them: especially when they were herded into the cemeteries, they expected to be shot by Russians, as Jews had been shot by Germans (and a

Deported from Crimea: former inhabitants of the
villages of Otuzy and Shelen, Krasnovishersk, 1948.

Crimean Tatars at a logging site after the deportation
from Crimea, Molotov Oblast (now Perm Oblast), 1952.

few were by trigger-happy soldiers). Crowds stood for hours waiting to be literally thrown into lorries. When the lorries moved off, Red Army soldiers rushed to loot the abandoned houses and slaughter the livestock before the Tatars' Russian neighbours did so. (Most, if not all, Russian neighbours did in fact ransack Tatar homes to take what they could find; none showed sympathy for the deportees, let alone a desire to intervene.)

The wagons the Tatars were crammed into had no planks to lie on, no windows, no water, no lavatories; they were basically cattle wagons, from which even the dirty straw had not been swept out. The deportees were deliberately mixed up, so that as few people as possible from the same village would be in the same wagon. Two hundred were crowded into a wagon big enough for fifty humans. The doors were sealed and, although the trains frequently stopped for hours on sidings while urgent military trains passed, nobody opened a door for three days. When they did, the corpses of children and the elderly who had suffocated or died of hunger, disease or heat stroke (that May was exceptionally hot) were just dumped by the track. Rainwater occasionally came through holes in the roof, and at some sidings (the trains avoided large stations where other travellers might see the deportees, or even post on their letters) it was possible to lower a small child on a belt or rope from the ventilation hatches so that he could search for water.

It never took less than three weeks – sometimes six – for the trains to reach Uzbekistan (a few were diverted to the northern Urals, where Tatar women, many separated from their children, had to fell and trim trees for a new paper mill). Only when a train reached Uzbekistan was hot food – the Gulag's thin gruel of fish heads – given. By then so many corpses had been thrown out that the crowding was less unendurable. Just under 8,000 deporteees died on the trains. Another 60,000, a third of the contingent, would die in their first year of exile.

The NKVD had overlooked a small number of Tatar fishermen and their families on the Arabat spit of land along the east coast of Crimea. Kobulov had them rounded up and loaded onto an old barge; he sealed the hatches and the barge was towed out to the Sea of Azov and scuttled. Machine-gunners watched the sea for hours in case anyone escaped. None did. A few more Crimean Tatars were hiding in the mountain quarries and forests. One group held out until 1947, when their lair was discovered and they were completely annihilated by NKVD hand grenades. One Alpine shepherd was caught in 1946 and sent to the Gulag. Another escapee was caught and taken out to sea in 1947, but somehow survived, returning briefly from the Gulag in 1972 to be belatedly deported.

In Uzbekistan any Crimean Tatar who failed to report to the NKVD every fortnight was punished by a twenty-year sentence in the prison camps. Nevertheless, there was a trickle of escapees who attempted to return, and a handful who managed to hide in Crimea for a few years. Those most desperate were the returning Tatar soldiers, who found that war wounds, medals and epaulettes (confiscated when they returned from Central Europe) were no protection from grim exile in Uzbekistan. When Soviet troops were marshalled in Austria, an officer called out 'Crimean Tatars: three paces forward!', marched the Tatars off, tore off their medals and epaulettes, and sent them under guard to be deported to Central Asia. At least a hundred demo-bilized Tatar officers, unwilling to move to Central Asia, were executed, sometimes in horribly improvised ways. In 1945 about four hundred Tatar officers who demanded that their families be brought back from Uzbekistan were first of all sent to a coastal sanatorium, then, after referral to Moscow, each was escorted out one night by a guard, driven to a ravine and shot. Another group managed to reach Moscow and demanded a meeting with Stalin. They were never seen again. The lucky men were the wounded who were hospitalized: after discharge they were sent by ordinary trains to Uzbekistan.

Even worse awaited those Crimean Tatars who found themselves in the Allied zones of occupation when the war ended. (Some were relieved, for Gestapo officers had started sending Tatars, mistaken for Jews, to extermination camps.) Whether they were voluntary or forced labourers, *Hiwis*, for the Germans, or released or escaped prisoners of war, they faced filtration camps where the dreaded anti-spying organization SMERSH sorted them out for execution, the Gulag or, mercifully, a train ride into exile in Uzbekistan. The Allies, fearing that their own citizens might be held hostage in the USSR, had already agreed with Stalin in Yalta that all Soviet citizens found in Europe, civilian or military, would be repatriated. Crimean Tatars who had never been citizens of the USSR, because they had left the Russian empire for Romania, Bulgaria or elsewhere, were included, regardless, in the forcible repatriation. Some of the Allies, notably the British Foreign Secretary Anthony Eden, were insistent on strict adherence to the agreement with Stalin; others, like Field Marshal Alexander, head of occupational forces in Italy, humanely turned a blind eye to Crimean Tatars desperate not to be rounded up: in Italy their holding camps quickly emptied by night, to the fury of the NKVD men who had, all over occupied Europe, acquired greater powers of entry and arrest than any national police force.

Those Tatars who had once served in the White Army and had then fought with General Vlasov's pro-German forces were treated with especial brutality. After a spell in Soviet prisons, they were hanged in 1947. One of them was a Giray, Mustafa Kılıç, a descendant of the khans and a cavalry hero in 1917. Many thousands of Crimean Tatars, employed or conscripted by the German army, had in May 1944 left Crimea by sea for Constanţa in Romania. Some tried to merge with the long-established Tatar community in Romania. Others applied for visas to Turkey, assuming that this neutral country would give them refuge and not repatriate them to the USSR. Despite the intercession of Cafer Seydamet, the most prominent expatriate Crimean Tatar in Turkey, the Turks adamantly refused such visas: they were reluctant to antagonize a Soviet Union currently trying to annex territory near the Georgian border that had been ceded to Turkey at the end of the First World War. The Romanian Securitate, effectively controlled by Stalin's NKVD, combed refugee settlements and sent every Crimean Tatar they could catch back to the USSR, for imprisonment or worse.

Some 60,000 Tatar men who returned from the war were left to find whoever had survived of their families in various cities and provinces of Uzbekistan. When they did so, they had a chance of meagre earnings that might save parents, wives and children from fatal disease, malnutrition and cold. The first years for Crimean Tatars in Uzbekistan were sheer hell: Soviet propaganda prepared the Uzbeks to receive traitors, cannibals, horned devils. Some trains were met by yelling crowds, armed with pickaxes and stones. Uzbeks in the more sophisticated towns soon realized that these starving, often moribund civilians could not be the monsters they had been told to expect. In remoter areas, however, the deportees were at best ostracized, at worst harassed. They had to dig holes in the arid ground and cover them with branches as shelter from below-zero temperatures; the rations of 600 grams (1½ lb) of bread for workers and 200 grams (½ lb) for the unemployed were not enough to sustain life, and children searched rubbish, stole cattle feed, ate grass and leaves. For three years there were 6,000 Tatar deaths for every 1,000 births and out of a total population of more than a quarter of a million, barely 150,000 were still alive in 1947 – possibly the lowest population ever recorded for this nation, which may have had two million speakers three hundred years earlier.

Uzbek and Crimean Tatar are both Turkic languages, but mutual understanding was difficult. Uzbeks saw Tatars, who dressed like Europeans, had a European fastidiousness about clean water and bedding, and allowed their women to come and go unveiled, as no different from Russians: there was little sense of common Turkishness. Unlike Crimean Tatars who sought refuge in Turkey a century earlier, those who were in Tashkent, Samarkand or some desert village were unlikely to assimilate and lose their identity. Not only were they different in speech, clothing and habits, but they resembled criminals, since they had to report to an NKVD officer once a fortnight and were forbidden to leave their place of registration, on pain of twenty years' imprisonment. There was no schooling in Crimean Tatar: whatever schooling they could get was in Russian. One factor that kept the Crimean Tatars from losing their identity was their abhorrence of marriage to non-Tatars, so that the language thus escaped the attrition that happened all over the USSR when a married couple of different ethnic identities adopted Russian as their family language.

Gradually, after the return of the menfolk, tempered by the hardships of war, life became more tolerable: the authorities, particularly the collective farms, realized that Crimean Tatar skills would raise their productivity, and their crafts would stimulate the economy. But over a decade passed before Crimean Tatars could form their own settlements and improve their conditions, so that they no longer drank filthy water, contaminated with manure and chemicals, from ditches that irrigated the cotton fields, and were free of the lice and bedbugs that infested Uzbek villagers. Eventually, the Uzbeks accepted that the Crimean Tatars were just as profoundly Islamic as they were.

It was only in 1956, when Nikita Khrushchiov's so-called secret speech to the 20th party congress admitted that Stalin was a murderous criminal, that it became possible, if not safe, for Stalin's victims to ask for rehabilitation. A circular was drawn up that conceded the Crimean Tatars had not been a nation of traitors and collaborators; unfortunately, the circular was not widely publicized and neither Uzbeks nor the new Russian immigrants in Crimea took any heed of it. Other deported nations – Chechens and Karachai Turks – were now allowed to return to their homelands, and even helped to re-establish their villages and farms. Crimean Tatars, however, were still forbidden to return to Crimea (the fertile and attractive land was too desirable to give back and, in many cases, had already been appropriated by settlers). Tatars were in effect still confined to Central Asia, and even the women who had survived exhausting forestry labour with only manual tools could travel only to Uzbekistan.

In March 1966 almost every literate Crimean Tatar signed a petition asking the party's 23rd congress to let them return. A year later a delegation of several hundred went to Moscow and was allowed to meet the KGB chairman Iuri Andropov; their reception was deceptively mild. In fact, all that happened was the annulment of decrees declaring them to be a 'traitor' nation, but they were referred to merely as 'Tatars formerly living in Crimea' and most restrictions on their movement remained in force. In 1968 Crimean Tatars in an Uzbek industrial town turned a festival into a protest meeting: the participants were attacked and arrested. May Day 1969 in Tashkent saw demonstrations that attracted international attention. Crimean Tatars realized that they should fight for their rights as part of the Soviet dissident movement which, though violently repressed with prison sentences and compulsory psychiatric 'treatment', drew the attention of the world's media to their plight. The exiled Crimean Tatar leader Mustafa Cemiloğlu, imprisoned in 1966 and now 23 years old, joined forces with Andrei Sakharov, the almost untouchable father of the USSR's H-bomb. Repeated trials, at which he could not be prevented from making fiery speeches, long prison sentences and hunger strikes focused attention on the Crimean Tatars' claims. The only concession Moscow offered was an area of Uzbekistan as a homeland, an autonomous Tatar 'Mubarek' ('Happiness') republic, a proposal that angered both Uzbeks and Crimean Tatars.

Crimean Tatar spirits had recovered, indeed ignited, but the demographic recovery of the Crimean Tatar population in Uzbekistan was slow. Estimates, even census figures, are only approximate, for the Uzbek authorities sometimes confused all Tatars, and Crimean Tatars sometimes claimed they were Russians. In 1979 the population was 117,559, even smaller than it had been in 1944, and less than in 1953; by 1989, however, in less penurious conditions, after Crimean Tatars had established if not integrated themselves, the women as skilled carpet weavers and embroiderers, the men as builders, traders and entrepreneurs, and when perestroika effectively liberated them, the population had grown to 188,772. Shortly after the explicit 'rehabilitation' granted by Moscow in 1967, primary schooling in Crimean Tatar began, a Crimean newspaper, *Lenin's Flag*, and a cultural magazine, *Yıldız* ('Star'), appeared, musical, drama and artistic groups flourished, Crimean Tatars became doctors, architects and professors, and for three days a week there were radio broadcasts in Crimean Tatar. Then the great exodus to Crimea began, and by 2000 only 10,046 were left in Uzbekistan.

Meanwhile, Moscow rewrote the history and geography books, as well as maps and gazetteers. Crimea became a simple province; its inhabitants had no Tatars, and those who used to live there were just Tatars who had migrated to the peninsula from elsewhere. The written Crimean Tatar language no longer existed officially. Even when the authoritative five-volume *Languages of the USSR* was published in the 1950s, the Crimean Tatar language was said to be spoken only in Uzbekistan. Many monuments of Crimean Tatar culture, it was now clear, had vanished since the German occupation and the Russian deportations: for instance, the gigantic four-volume manuscript of Abdul Lûtfulla Ilhaq's *Ocean of Proofs*, given by Khan Selâmet Giray to the Zincirli medrese in 1735, but never published, had disappeared.

A very few Tatars drifted back covertly, to be imprisoned and deported. Only Helsinki Human Rights dissidents supported the Crimean Tatar cause. The most effective was General Piotr Grigorenko, a Ukrainian born in Crimea in 1907. Although a loyal communist most of his military life, he reacted strongly to perceived injustice. As a war hero who had been badly wounded, he was a difficult target for the KGB, but in 1964 he was finally arrested and put first in a psychiatric hospital, then in prison for his protests against the feebleness of Khrushchiov's de-Stalinization. Like the Crimean Tatars, he then found solidarity with the dissident movement in Moscow, and in 1969 went to Tashkent, he believed, to help defend Crimean Tatars: it was a KGB trap to rearrest him. It took two years for him to prove his sanity, during which Crimean Tatars demonstrated outside his place of confinement. Not released until 1974, Grigorenko, and thus the Crimean Tatars' cause, won great publicity and a powerful synergy. Moscow's solution was to expel Grigorenko's son to the USA in 1975 and the general himself in 1977. Grigorenko's statue in central Simferopol is still standing: he remains a unique non-Tatar in the Crimean Tatar struggle.

Mustafa Cemiloğlu,
2014.

Russification was relentless. In 1945 a Simferopol newspaper was ordered to devise Russian names for all the deserted villages: the news-paper office had only two books, a fruit-growing manual and a military history, so Crimea now has villages called 'Quince', 'Apricot', 'Tanks', 'Guards' and so on. Typically, the historic town Qarasuvbazar ('Blackwater Market') was given the banal name Belogorsk (Bilohirs'k, 'White Mountain').

In February 1954 Nikita Khrushchiov transferred Crimea to Ukraine, and for good reasons. Crimea was still wrecked by German invasion and occupation, by Stalin's counter-attacks and by his deportation of the entire Crimean Tatar people. It made sense to let Kiev, closer than Moscow, recon-struct the peninsula. In 1961 the Ukrainians began building a huge canal to take the waters of the Dnepr river down the dry eastern coast of the Crimea, thus replacing the aqueducts and deep wells built and dug by the Tatar khans and wrecked by the Russians. The cost was great: whole villages and much fertile land was flooded by the dam needed to collect the water.

There were nearly 100,000 deserted houses and apartments in Crimea: officially they were now state property to be distributed to new settlers com-ing from the overcrowded regions of central Russia. Fewer immigrants came than expected, and most failed to settle: coming from black earth country, they found the stony soil hard to cultivate. The Soviet press spoke of Don Cossacks, used to farming vineyards in a hot climate, taking over; this was a fiction, since the Don Cossack population had been badly depleted in the

1930s purges of kulak farmers. Houses and land fell into ruin. Even after the break-up of the USSR, the newly independent Ukrainian authorities were reluctant, unbribed, to use these buildings and plots to accommodate returning Tatars and the authorities stood back when Russian settlers bulldozed Tatar shacks.

By 1989, as the USSR began to collapse, there were perhaps half a million Crimean Tatars who might want to repossess their homes. The KGB offered to cooperate, if Tatar leaders undertook to fight to take Crimea back from Ukrainian to Russian sovereignty, should Ukraine become independent. When Ukraine (including Crimea) did in 1991 vote for independence from Russia, the new government failed to make provisions for Tatar autonomy or even for Crimean Tatar language use. The main problem in Crimea, apart from the rampant corruption that infected all Ukraine, was an aggressive Russian majority, given unity by a criminal gang of 'nationalists' who wanted unbridled control of the economy and Russian domination, overriding Ukrainian and other ethnic groups. Tatars had to fight against riot police to reclaim land, against Ukrainian 'special forces' in Feodosia, and against Mafia gangs in Simferopol in 1995: Uzbekistan had toughened them into a force to be reckoned with.

From 2010 to 2014, under Ukraine's most corrupt pro-Russian President Viktor Yanukovich, Crimea became the fief of a gangster, Sergei Aksionov. The Crimean 'prime minister', known informally as the Goblin, grew rich by collaborating with corrupt traffic police (selling car parts from 'confiscated' vehicles), prosecutors (selling exemption from prosecution) and officials (getting leases on restaurants, bars and factories), not to mention running insurance companies. Born in 1972 in Moldavia, he has survived and profited from gangsters' shoot-outs. Versatile, active and laconic, he probably never writes his own political speeches. But their content is ominous: he revives Stalin's accusation that the core population, the Crimean Tatars, are extremists to be tried for treason or deported for undermining Russian rule. Pursuing his policy of suppression and self-enrichment even more vigorously since 2014, Aksionov has been kept in power by Putin. After the 2014 annexation of Crimea by Russia, Aksionov's colleague Natasha Priklonskaya attracted attention, not just for her youthful looks, but for the energy with which she indicted several hundred Crimean Tatars (mainly men) for treason, terrorism and other crimes against the state, securing long terms of imprisonment for them far away in Russia: the 'evidence' was rarely contested by lawyers. It took little more than the possession of a Qur'an, a beard or a T-shirt with a pro-Crimean Tatar slogan for a man to lose his freedom

– unluckier Tatars were simply abducted and never seen alive again. The harmless and democratic *meclis* and *qurultay* were declared by her to be 'terrorist' organizations. (Priklonskaya, however, showed weakness by deploring in a Twitter post the casualties in Russia's war against Ukraine: after failing to be accepted as Russian ambassador to Cabo Verde, or chair of the supposedly 'cultural' organization *Rossotrudnichestvo*, she has left the scene.)

The only Crimean politicians of stature come from the Tatar community. Their leaders, comparable in stature to Nelson Mandela, are Mustafa Jemilev (Cemiloğlu), the retired head, and Refat Chubarov, the new head of the *meclis* (the Tatars' parliament). One of the few infants to survive the 1944 deportation to Central Asia without food or clean water, Cemiloğlu spent 45 years in exile, fifteen of them in Soviet prisons for human-rights activism – he was a founder member of the Initiative Group for Defence of Human Rights in the USSR. (He was not released from his last term of imprisonment, including forced feeding, until 1986.) An irrigation engineer by profession, in 1989 he returned to Crimea and in 1991 revived the age-old Tatar assembly, the *qurultay*. He was elected to parliament in Kiev. In 2013 he ceded leadership of the *meclis* to Refat Chubarov. In spring 2014 he talked to Putin, to Western politicians, to the UN and to Turkey's Recep Erdoğan, trying to stop the annexation and persecution of the Tatar community, and asking for UN peacekeepers. He denounced Aksionov's and Putin's referendum of 2014, which purported to show 82 per cent of the Crimean electorate in favour of Russian annexation (Cemiloğlu's figures suggest 32 per cent as the real number). His best hope was Turkey, where there are four million descendants of Crimean Tatar refugees and deportees, several thousand of whom still speak Crimean Tatar. Turkey, once suzerain over the Crimean Khanate, is now as dependent as Europe on Russia for fossil fuels. Turkey dismissed Cemiloğlu's request to close the Bosphorus to Russian warships. Now Cemiloğlu and Chubarov are banished from Crimea. The Tatar *meclis* is 'a terrorist organization': members are given nineteen-year jail sentences, or just murdered; Tatar television has stopped; Tatar-language schools exist only on paper – the 30,000 pupils registered find they are now taught only in Russian. Since 2014 some 600,000 ethnic Russians have been brought into Crimea as settlers, many living in houses abandoned by Tatars seeking refuge in Ukraine. A new repression worsens, with seventeen- or nineteen-year prison sentences for nothing more than 'thought crimes' being handed out almost weekly.

Hardened by ethnic cleansing, dispossession and dissidence, some Crimean Tatars are determined to defend themselves. Others, including

Güliver Altın, who returned from exile in France to establish an extraordinary Tatar museum, historical and ethnographical, La Richesse near Simferopol, at first decided, with encouragement from the Kazan Tatars, traditional mediators between Russia and fellow-Tatars, that collaboration with the Kremlin is the better option (Altın was promised that his museum would become a major university centre). At the time of writing Altın has not been seen for five years, and his museum has been swallowed up by the state and is closed to visitors: his only proof of life consists of disoriented pro-Russian and anti-Ukrainian Facebook posts.

The 2014 regime established a 'loyal' Tatar party, Qırım birliği, but men like Altın soon left when they found most of its members were FSB or Russian military. Putin and his puppet Aksionov, however, had plans for a World Heritage Site, with the Tatars as mere curators. The southwest, the ancient Gothia, was marked out as a future gambling zone, to encourage oligarchs to launder their money at home. The 2022 Russian invasion of Ukraine, subsequent bomb and missile strikes on Sevastopol, and the damage done to the expensive railway bridge from the mainland to Kerç have destroyed all prospects of tourist income for Crimea.

The history and culture of the Crimea could be written about until 2014, when Valeri Vozgrin, a St Petersburg professor of history, born in Simferopol, published four superbly written and exhaustively researched volumes, a 3,000-page *History of the Crimean Tatars*.[1] He was denounced for 'Russophobia': not a single bookshop in Russia stocks the work, and the publisher Lenur Isliamov, a Tatar media giant, is now in the Ukrainian army.

Of the old *qurultay*, some of its members managed in 2014 to reassemble in Ukraine, but many were arrested, disappeared or dissuaded by Sergei Aksionov, the new dictator of Crimea. Some joined a 'loyal' *qurultay* that met, without an agenda, in Simferopol. Fewer than one hundred *meclis* members escaped to Kiev, not quorate enough to expel the collaborators who stayed in Simferopol. The Crimean *mufti* Aider Rustemov was replaced in Simferopol by a puppet *mufti* Emirali Ablayev: the impostor has a weekly YouTube programme, *The Mufti's Hour*. Isliamov's Tatar-language TV channel ATR and radio station Meydan were closed down and replaced by a Russian-controlled *Voice of Nation and Homeland* (Millet ve Vatan sedası), which, occasionally in Crimean Tatar, presents a limited version of Russian propaganda, for example showing elderly Ukrainian ladies with hand grenades in their shopping bags.

In September 2021 a group of Kazan Tatar journalists visited Simferopol to investigate and encourage Crimean Tatar journalism: they found that once prestigious journals and newspapers, such as *Yıldız* and *Qırım*, had virtually ceased to exist: even when they abandoned paper for online distribution, they were harassed and, for just printing the word *meclis*, fined for 'nationalism'.

Reports from 2021 tell us that of 242 political prisoners involved in criminal cases over the occupation period of Crimea, 173 are representatives of the Crimean Tatar people. On 15 April 2022, in the occupied town of Novooleksiivka of Henichesk district, police stopped a car carrying Eskender and Fatima Fuka and their son Reşat Fuka. Father and son were detained and taken away, presumably to the seventeenth school in the town of Henichesk, where the occupiers conduct interrogations and torture. They were not seen again.

After Russia announced a 'partial' mobilization in autumn 2022, the Crimean authorities distributed conscription notices in Simferopol, 90 per cent of them to Crimean Tatar households. Few Tatars, who prefer Ukrainian to Russian citizenship, would consent to serve in the Russian army and risk, if they stayed, accusations of treason from Ukraine or, if they deserted, severe punishment from Russia. The consequence, as may well have been intended, is for Crimean Tatars to flee Crimea, primarily to Azerbaijan, even to Uzbekistan. The percentage of indigenous Tatars in Crimea is likely to fall still further from its estimated 10 per cent. In autumn 2023 Crimean Tatars of military age were conscripted en masse into the Russian army, forcing them to commit treason by fighting Ukraine, and leaving only those with money with the choice of seeking asylum in Azerbaijan. The last stage of an ethnic genocide is in progress.

As the Romanian Tatar poet Şevqiy Bektöre, who spent much of his life in Crimea, wrote in 1922, 'The whole world is a cemetery for Tatars.'

CHRONOLOGY

CRIMEAN KHANS	OTTOMAN SULTANS	KINGS OF POLAND AND LITHUANIA	RUSSIAN GRAND DUKES AND TSARS
1450 Hacı I Giray 1441–66	Mehmed II Fetih (Conqueror) 1451–81	Žygimantas Kęstutaitis 1432–40	Vasili II 1435–62
Mengli I Giray 1468–74		Kazimierz IV 1447–92	
Nur Devlet Giray 1474–7		Jan I Olbracht 1492–1501	Ivan III 1462–1505
1500 Mengli I Giray 1478–1514	Bayezid II 1481–1512	Aleksander Jagellończyk 1501–6	
Mehmed I Giray 1514–23	Selim I Yavuz (The Grim) 1512–20	Zygmunt I 1506–48	Vasili III 1505–33
Ğazı I Giray 1523–4			
Saadet I and Islam Giray 1524–32	Süleyman I Kanuni (The Magnificent) 1520–66	Zygmunt II August 1548–72	Ivan IV Grozny (The Terrible) 1533–84
1550 Sahib I Giray 1532–51		Henryk Walezy 1573–5	
Devlet I Giray 1551–77	Selim II 1566–74	Anna Jagiellonka 1575–87	Fiodor I Blazhennyi (The Blessed) 1584–98
Mehmed II Giray 1577–84		Stefan Batory 1576–86	
Saadet II and Islam II Giray 1584–8	Murad III 1574–95	Zygmunt III Waza 1587–1632	
1600 Ğazı II Giray 1588–1607	Mehmed III 1595–1603		Boris 1598–1605
Toqtamiş and Selâmet I Giray 1607–10	Ahmed I 1603–17		Dimitri I and II 'False' 1605–7
Canibek Giray 1610–23 and 1628–35	Mustafa I 1617–18 and 1622–3	Władysław IV Waza 1632–48	Vasili IV 1606–10
Mehmed III Giray 1623–8	Osman II 1618–22		Mikhail 1613–45
Inayet Giray 1635–7			

	CRIMEAN KHANS	OTTOMAN SULTANS	KINGS OF POLAND AND LITHUANIA	RUSSIAN GRAND DUKES AND TSARS
	Bahadır I Giray 1637–41	Murad IV 1623–40		
	Mehmed IV Giray 1641–4 and 1654–66	Ibrahim 1640–48	Jan II Kazimierz 1648–68	Aleksei 1645–76
1650	Islam III Giray 1644–54	Mehmed IV 1648–87	Michał I Korybut Wiśniowiecki 1669–73	Fiodor III 1676–82
	Adil Giray 1666–71			
	Selim I Giray 1671–8	Süleyman II 1687–91	Jan III Sobieski 1674–96	Ivan V 1682–96
	Murad Giray 1678–83			
	Hacı II Giray 1683–4	Ahmed II 1691–5	August II Mocny 1697–1706	Piotr I (The Great) 1682–1725
1700	Selim I Giray 1684–99, 1702–4	Mustafa II 1695–1703	Stanisław I Leszczyński 1704–9	
	Devlet II Giray 1709–13			Ekaterina I 1725–7
	Qaplan I and Devlet III Giray 1713–17	Ahmed III 1703–30	August II Mocny 1709–33	Piotr II 1727–30
	Saadet IV Giray 1717–24			Anna 1730–40
	Mengli II Giray 1724–30			
	Qaplan I Giray 1730–36	Mahmud I 1730–54		Ivan VI 1740–41
	Fetih II, Mengli II, Selâmet II Giray 1736–43	Osman III 1754–7	Augustus III 1733–63	Elizaveta 1741–62
1750	Arslan Giray 1748–56			
	Halim Giray 1756–8	Mustafa III 1757–74		Piotr III 1762
	Qırım Giray 1758–69			
	Devlet IV, Qaplan II, Selim III, Sahib II Giray 1769–77			
	Şahin Giray 1777–83	Abdul Hamid I 1774–89	Stanisław II August 1764–95	Ekaterina (The Great) 1762–96
1800		Selim III 1789–1807		

REFERENCES

1 Crimea before the Crimean Khanate

1 A. P. Chubova et al., *Arkhitektura i iskusstvo Khersonesa tavricheskogo* (Simferopol, 2008); A. I. Iakobson, *Krym v srednie veka* (Moscow, 1973).
2 See István Vásáry, 'Orthodox Christian Qumans and Tatars of the Crimea in the 13th–14th Centuries', in Vásáry, *Turks, Tatars and Russians in the 13th–16th Centuries* (Abingdon, 2007), pp. 261–7.
3 See Uli Schamiloglu, 'The Impact of the Black Death on the Golden Horde: Politics, Economy, Society, Civilization', *Golden Horde Review*, v/2 (2017), pp. 325–43.

2 The Crimean Khanate Is Born

1 *Polnoe sobranie russkikh letopisei*, vol. XI (Moscow, 1965), p. 172; D. Kołodziejczyk, *The Crimean Khanate and Poland-Lithuania: International Diplomacy on the European Periphery (15th–18th Century)* (Leiden, 2011), pp. 7–8.
2 E. V. Danilova, *Kaffa v nachale vtoroi poloviny XV veka* (Moscow, 1974), p. 201.
3 L. P. Kolli, 'Khadzhi-Girei Khan i ego politika', *Izvestiia Tavricheskoi Uchenoi Arkhivnoi Komissii*, L (1913), pp. 99–139.
4 Alexandre Bennigsen et al., *Le Khanat de Crimée dans les archives de Topkapi* (Paris, 1978), pp. 33–5.
5 István Vásáry, 'Zhalovannye gramoty Dzhuchieva Ulusa . . .', in *Istochnikovedenie istorii Ulusa Dzhuchi . . . 1223–1556*, ed. M. A. Usmanov (Kazan, 2001), p. 199.
6 Kołodziejczyk, *Crimean Khanate and Poland-Lithuania*, pp. 532–3.
7 Even in the fifteenth century the German servant of the diplomat Giosafat Barbaro could communicate with the Goths of Theodoro.
8 Once freed, these brothers became a serious nuisance: in 1474 Hayder, Melik-Emin and Eminek raided Ukraine (then Lithuanian territory) and brought back cattle and slaves to Theodoro principality, selling the latter on the Ottoman slave market. Mengli disapproved, but refused to intervene, probably because he was offended by a new Polish-Lithuanian treaty with the Great Horde.
9 Bennigsen et al., *Le Khanat de Crimée dans les archives de Topkapi*, pp. 41–4.

10 According to Giosafat Barbaro (who heard the story from a Genoese), Mengli fled to Theodoro, where the Ottomans caught up with him. Prince Aleksei had reinforcements from his brother-in-law, Stefan, prince of Moldavia, and they held out against the Turkish attackers for six months. By December 1475, however, Mangup was conquered. Ahmed-Paşa lost thousands of men. Alexei was shipped to Istanbul, where he was executed, and the principality of Theodoro was abolished; like the Genoese ports, it became an Ottoman province.

11 Bennigsen et al., *Le Khanat de Crimée dans les archives de Topkapi*, p. 55.

12 Ibid., p. 65.

13 Ibid., pp. 70–71.

14 V. P. Gulevich and A. V. Dzhanov, 'Letter of the Crimean Khan Mengli Giray to the Genoese Emissaries', *Golden Horde Review*, VII/2 (2019), pp. 318–32.

15 M. N. Berezhkov, 'Drevneishaia kniga Krymskikh posolskikh del', *Izvestiia Tavricheskoi Uchenoi Arkhivnoi Komissii*, XXI (1894), p. 39.

16 István Vásáry, 'A Contract of the Crimean Khan Mengli Giray and the Inhabitants of Qïrq-yer from 1478/79', *Central Asiatic Journal*, XXVI/3–4 (1982), pp. 289–300.

17 Fıraqıñda menim alım sorar bolsañ eger cana –
Köñlüñde nar közde ab ve dilde ah bolur peida
Seniñ murğ-i hayalıñnı içimde asramaq içün
Bolubdır kirpigim birle qafes bu diyden bina.
Menim ol han Meñli oş-minnet mulküniñ sahı men
Cihanniñ mulk-ü malına ğururım yoq durur asla!

18 In 1513 Selim murdered Aişa's eight-year-old son by Mehmed. Selim had another wife, called Aişa-Hafsa, who was the mother of Süleyman the Magnificent.

3 Tatars as Antagonists

1 Nurun-Sultan was furious and told a Russian envoy that Mehmed preferred carousing drunkenly with his junior wives; Mehmed did drink: a Russian envoy reported that one evening he told a *bey* to report again in the morning, because that evening he was drinking.

2 Elsewhere in his *Notes on Muscovy* Sigismund Herberstein gives a lot of information on the Crimean Tatars, but as it came as hearsay from his interpreters and other informants, it should be treated with scepticism. 'They can go without sleeping or eating for four days . . . They drink horses' blood from the veins . . . Their rations are a cow or a horse for forty men . . . They cook the innards just enough to shake off the manure . . . They suck not just their fingers, but the knife . . . They sit in the saddle with their legs tucked under them so as to be able to turn and fire at pursuers . . . They ride only geldings, and don't use spurs . . . Men and women wear the same clothes . . . The common people wear sheepskin and don't change until the garment is worn out . . . They have no legal system, if anyone wants something he steals it with impunity.'

3 Russian State Archive of Ancient Acts (RGADA), 123, 1, 6, 166; I. V. Zaitsev, 'Pis'mennaia kul'tura krymskogo khanstva', *Vostochnyi arkhiv*, XIV–XV (2006), pp. 82–93. Like some other khans, Sa'adet, after living so long in Istanbul, treated Crimean Tatars as an alien people.

4 Thanks to the Crimean court geomancer and Sufi, Sahib Giray's personal doctor and closest friend throughout his reign, Remmal (the Geomancer, real name Kaysuni-zade Nidai-efendi), we have an extensive biography (albeit a panegyric) of Sahib Giray's reign from its start in 1532 to the khan's burial in 1551. It was written some time after Sahib's death, at the request of Sahib's daughter Nur-Sultan, and, although written in Ottoman Turkish, is the earliest extant Crimean–Tatar historical study of a Crimean khan. For Turkish and French versions, see Özalp Gökbilgin, *Tarih-i Sahib Giray* (Istanbul, 2000).

4 Militant Khans

1 As early as 1524, oaths binding Crimea and Muscovy had been taken by many officials and royal relatives on both sides, without them being any more binding than before.

2 'Yakasın çâk eden berg-i gülün / Gülşen içre nâlesidir bülbülün'.

3 *Semin* in Arabic or Tatar, *Semiz* in Ottoman Turkish.

4 Two hundred years later, Baron de Tott thought Eski Qırım 'no more than a paltry village, where the tombs alone testify its ancient importance'.

5 Particularly in Transcaucasia, the Ottomans collected enemy heads in baskets and sometimes stacked them in pyramids to intimidate the population.

6 See 'Mahur Peşrev - Gazi Giray Han (Karar: Kız Neyi - Dört Ses)', www.youtube.com, accessed 20 July 2023.

7 For a survey of women's roles in Crimean Khanate diplomacy, see A. M. Nekrasov, *Izbrannye trudy* (Nalchik, 2015), pp. 243–50.

8 D. Kołodziejczyk, *The Crimean Khanate and Poland-Lithuania: International Diplomacy on the European Periphery (15th–18th Century)* (Leiden, 2011), p. 785.

9 All the same, Ğazı Giray was famed for his love poetry: 'My soul, come as a wall of love this night/ Let secret wells of love be our candle./ Whoever gives you a bad look, my love,/ May their days be short, their body turn black./ Don't drink wine while my tambour is silent,/ Let a vessel of wine be a vessel of delight.'

10 'Ey bana seng-i melâmetden eden âr diyen/ Benim ol başımı ortaya koyub yâr diyen!' These lines are from a *gazel* by the fifteenth-century Azeri poet Mehmed Çelebi. Whether Fetih Giray was anticipating or provoking his manner of death is not known.

11 'Kâtı zulm itdi bugün Fetih Giray Hâna felek/ Yeridir ağlar ise yerde beşer, gökde melek.'

12 Fuzuli's poem was an allegory in which hashish was personified by Sultan Bayezid, and wine by Shah Ismail; Ğazi's poem may also have had a satirical bent, though it was unlikely to have made a hero of Shah Abbas I.

5 Khans Who Would Be Monarchs

1 Guillaume Lavasseur de Beauplan, *Description de l'Ukranie* (Rouen, 1660), written for King Sigismund III.

2 Szymon Starowolski, 'Pobudka abo rada na zniesienie Tatarów perekopskich', in *Szymon Starowolski. Wybór z pism*, ed. Ignacy Lewandowski (Wrocław, 1991), p. 168.

3   Life, even in the nineteenth century, was grim for a captive of the Noğays: see the fictional, but graphic account in Leskov's 'The Enchanted Wanderer' in *Lady Macbeth of Mtsensk: Selected Stories*, trans. Donald Rayfield, Robert Chandler and William Edgerton (New York, 2020), pp. 160–85.

4   E. Schütz, 'Eine armenische Chronik von Kaffa aus der ersten Hälfte des 17. Jahrhunderts', *Acta Orientalia Academiae Scientiarum Hungaricae*, XXIX/2 (1975), pp. 133–86.

5   Ahmed Giray was Mehmed III's son by an enslaved Moldavian woman: the Girays rarely had children by commoners, let alone slaves. Ahmed was despised: he was threatened with a knife in Istanbul by a son of Ğazı Giray Khan for being a speaker of Moldavian and son of a Christian slave.

6   Such horrors were also perpetrated by Western Europeans. A French contingent fighting for the Ottomans is reported by Na'ima to have roasted their Austrian prisoners of war to death on spits.

7   Surah 4 *An-Nisa*, verse 3.

8   Alphonse de Lamartine in his *Histoire de la Turquie*, vol. V (1854–5) was quite sure of this claim: 'The princes of the Giray Tatar family are the only legitimate successors by blood of the princes of the imperial Ottoman household, if that line should ever become extinct in Constantinople.'

9   Bahadır wrote to the sultan in summer 1639, 'You know the deplorable, desperate state of my country. I have nobody but your generous and lofty lordship and hope you will send me a good, knowledgeable doctor . . . medicines, herbs and plants of proven effectiveness.' Alexandre Bennigsen et al., *Le Khanat de Crimée dans les archives de Topkapi* (Paris, 1978), p. 165. Bahadır's mausoleum has not yet been found.

10 N. Królikowska-Jedlińska, *Law and Division of Power in the Crimean Khanate* (Leiden, 2019), p. 145.

11 F. Tott, *Mémoires du Baron de Tott sur les Turcs et les Tartares*, 4 vols (Amsterdam, 1784), p. 107, states: 'Amongst the Turks, where the executioner does not strike until the sum offered by the criminal be refused, there are instances where the wife has sold the blood of her husband. In Tartary, on the contrary, the wife, who is to plunge the knife with her own hand into the criminal, never lets herself be tempted by any offer; and the law which leaves vengeance to herself, excludes every other sentiment. One of the Prince's officers, his arm raised, carrying a silver axe, leads the criminal and assists at the execution.' Another account from the same time, Ch. de Peyssonnel, *Traité sur le commerce de la Mer Noire*, vol. II (Paris, 1787), p. 292, states: 'The Khan [Arslan Giray] only executes criminals for crimes against the public, robbery and murder on the highway, forging coins, treason . . . When the killer of someone's father, brother or parent is condemned to death, the Khan orders him to be handed to a relative who cuts the murderer's throat himself, or pays somebody to do it, the execution being carried out on a bridge outside the back gate of the seraglio. The relative is free to reprieve the killer and agree on monetary compensation. In 1753 a girl had to deal with her brother's murder, refused a large sum from the killer's parents and, not finding anyone to cut the killer's throat, cut off his head herself, and took it home to contemplate it at her leisure and enjoy her vengeance.'

6 Russia Strikes Back

1 Ch. de Peyssonnel, *Traité sur le commerce de la Mer Noire*, vol. 1 (Paris, 1787), p. 80: 'The air is extremely healthy in Crimea; the life that Tatars lead must help maintain their health, the solid base of which is exercise; doctors rarely make a fortune here, because there are few patients and the few that exist pay very badly . . . there are no apothecaries.' The absence of doctors may be connected with the Tatar proverb: 'The sick man isn't sick, but the person who looks after him is' (*Kefsiz kefsiz değil dir, kefsiz bakkan kefsiz dir*). A. N. Samoilovich and P. A. Falev, 'Poslovitsy, pogovorki i primety Krymskikh tatar', *Izvestiia Tavricheskoi Uchenoi Arkhivnoi Komissii*, LII (1915), p. 57.

2 'Bir Yahudi pîçeye dîn aşkina zerk eyledim,/ Âfrîmler eyleyüp Şeytan tahsîn eyledi.'

3 To this day the businessmen of Kayseri have a reputation for ruthless moneymaking.

4 Josef Matuz, 'Eine Beschreibung des Khanats der Krim aus dem Jahre 1699 [*sic*]', *Acta Orientalia*, XXVIII (1964), pp. 129–51.

5 Guillaume Levasseur de Beauplan, *Description de l'Ukranie* (Paris, 1861), p. 84, notes that richer Tatar horsemen, when riding over ice, shod their horses with cow horn, attached to the hoof with leather.

6 Christoph Augustynowicz, 'Begegnung und Zeremonial: Das Bild der Krimtataren bei Balthasar Kleinschroth und Johann Christian Lünig', in *The Crimean Khanate between East and West (15th–18th Century)*, ed. Denise Klein (Wiesbaden, 2014), pp. 189–210. Possibly, the worst behaviour was perpetrated by Noğay, rather than Crimean, Tatars.

7 W. A. Artamonow, 'Rosja, Rzeczpospolita i Krym v Latach 1686–1699', in *Studia i Materialy z Czasów Jana III Sobieskiego*, ed. Krystyn Matwijowski (Wrocław, 1992), p. 29, n. 64.

7 Disintegration and Restoration

1 A more likely etymology is the German *Faule Metze* ('lazy strumpet').

2 For the diary of Hasan, a janissary clerk who witnessed the entire battle, see Yeniçeri Kâtibi Hasan, *Prut Sefer'ni beyanımdır* (Istanbul, 2011).

3 This allegation gains plausibility, despite Voltaire dismissing it in his sycophantic biography of Peter the Great: it is (according to E. Vozgrin, *Istoriia krymskikh tatar* (Simferopol, 2014), vol. II, pp. 753–7) implied in the unpublished part of the governor of Siberia Fiodor Soimonov's memoirs. Whatever her actual contribution to the tsar's salvation, in 1714 Ekaterina was honoured by Peter with Russia's first female award, the Order of the Saint and Martyr Ekaterina.

4 There may have been some truth in these accusations. The historian Halim Giray, a great-grandson of Sa'adet's brother Devlet II, wrote: 'Sa'adet was generous but pusillanimous and cowardly. He loved hunting and spent most of his time on expeditions in the steppe and meadows, indulging, when supposedly hunting, in the embraces of gazelle-eyed beauties. In his youth he was tall and slim, but he became stout, paunchy and almost unable to walk.'

5 The French were the sole Western European power friendly towards the Ottomans, largely out of a shared hostility to Austria. French Catholics could operate discreetly throughout the Ottoman empire; they had a mission in

Crimea from the 1710s, converting Greeks and Armenians to Catholicism, but until the 1750s they had little cultural or political influence on the khanate.

6 Arkhiv vneshnei politiki Rossiiskoi imperii 123, 1, 1.

7 These ships were largely *praams*, floating flat-bottomed artillery bases. Although they had sails and oars, they often needed to be towed by warships.

8 Jean-Michel Venture (1701–1755) was French Royal Secretary in Levant. He should not be confused with his better-known son, Jean-Michel Venture de Paradis (1739–1799), who held a similar post.

9 Louis Jouvin, French consul on Chios, wrote in March 1760 to the Minister of the Marine in Paris that the only reason for Arslan Giray's dismissal was 'his excessive ardour for war'. The ex-khan was taken from Gallipoli to Chios on a French warship (Archive nationale, affaires étrangères. Correspondance des consulats de Chio, Mytilène, Naxie, Milo et Rhodes, 509).

10 François Tott's father András had been a discreet French diplomat in the Ottoman empire, acting as assistant to Saverio Glavani, consul in Bağçasaray.

11 See V. S. Kashirin, *Nabeg . . . nashestvie khana Krym-Gireia 1769 g.* (Moscow, 2019), pp. 9–106; available at https://cyberleninka.ru, accessed 22 July 2023.

12 Catherine the Great wrote to her friend Dorothea Belke: 'The campaign cost the Khan his life: the Ottomans ordered him and five of the most prominent mirzas to be poisoned, blaming their failure to break into our territory on their bad faith.' The Ottomans, however, never accused the Russians of killing Khan Qırım Giray.

8 The Centre Cannot Hold

1 Louis-Mathieu Langlès summed up Qaplan Giray's end: 'He was very falsely accused of secret and treacherous contacts with Russia, sufficient reason to cause his downfall shortly after his promotion in February 1771.'

2 The word *şum*, from Arabic, can also mean 'unlucky', 'inauspicious'.

3 A. Resmi, *Hulâsatü 'l-i 'tibâr* (*A Summary of Admonitions: A Chronicle of the 1768–1774 Russian–Ottoman War*), trans. E. Menchinger (Istanbul, 2011).

4 W. Eton, *A Survey of the Turkish Empire* (London, 1799), p. 328. Mariupol deteriorated still further until a Greek delegation complained to Tsar Alexander I in 1816 and measures were taken.

5 Feridun M. Emecen, 'Son kırım hani Şahin Giray'ın idamı mes'elesi' ve buna dair vesikalar', *Tarih Degirsi*, XXXIV (1984), pp. 315–46. Consul Dutrouy was offered a new post in Crete, but never took it: he disappeared.

6 Cengiz Fedakar, 'Son kırım hani Şahin Giray'ın muhallefatına dair', *Türk Dünyası Araştırmaları Dergisi*, CCIX (2015), pp. 385–408.

9 Under the Tsars

1 Andreas Schönle, 'Garden of the Empire: Catherine's Appropriation of the Crimea', *Slavic Review*, LX/1 (2001), pp. 1–23.

2 Muhammet Mazı, 'The Sultans of the Countryside: The Girays' Displacement into Ottoman Rumeli and Their Widespread Roles in Networks of Violence (1792–1807)', MA thesis, Central European University, Budapest, 2020.

3 A full account of Napoleon's plans for Crimea and of Rolandre's advice is given in V. V. Adadurov, *'Napoleonida' na Skhodi Evropy* (L'viv, 2007).

Rolandre printed his sixteen-page pamphlet in Metz in 1812: Napoleon's copy is presumed lost in the retreat from Moscow, but the Warsaw Vojewoda Count Stanisław Zamoyski's copy survives in L'viv's Scientific Library (F. 103, 451/IIIc).

4 'Er kün ekim kelir de baqar, / Türlü sıltav ile bizleri yaqar. / "Poshol, durak!" der de turmay o qaçar / Ne al oldı, bu zavallı – Kefege.' L. S. Iunusova, *Krymskotatarskaia literatura* (Simferopol, 2000), pp. 126–7.

5 N. I. Zakrevskii, 'Zapiski vracha morskoi sluzhby', *Morskoi sbornik*, LII/3, pp. 56–61.

6 Fiodor Stulli, *Sobranie povestei i rasskazov* (St Petersburg, 1894), pp. 494–7.

7 Known as Qazıqlı Özen in Crimean Tatar, a short river flowing through Sevastopol.

8 Named after Admiral Thomas Mackenzie, a Scot in Russian service, who acquired a hilltop forest overlooking Sevastopol, known to Tatars as Kök-Ağaç (hornbeams).

9 N. K. Dmitriev, 'Chansons Tatares de Crimée', *Journal Asiatique*, CCXII (April–June 1928), pp. 207–27.

10 Ismail Gaspıralı (Gasprinskiy), *Frantsuzskie pis'ma* (Simferopol, 2003), https://textarchive.ru, accessed 23 July 2023.

11 For a very full account of Gaspıralı's life and work including *Tercüman*, see Giuliana d'Oro, 'Perevodčik-Tercüman di Ismail Gasprinskij. Espressione di dialogo interculturale', PhD, Sapienza Università di Roma: Dipartimento di Studi Europei, Americani e Interculturali, 2022. See https://iris.uniroma1.it, accessed 23 August 2023. A centenary anthology of material from *Tercüman* was published in Turkey: Mehmet Yalçın Yılmaz, *Tercümân IV – Vefatinin 10: Yilinda Gaspirali Ismail Bey'e Vefa* (Istanbul, 2015).

12 'Sivasdobuldan piktim sauluh selamet, Yermanin granisasinda kopti kiyamet. Kiyma Gyerman, kiyema, yazikdir bana,- Austiria majarlari kiydi ganimi. Akti kanim, akti Sagil daglare, Benden Suk puk selam ulsun arkadaslare. Eyvah, balam, eyvah, nasil uruldun, Yermanyanin granitsasinda ahlen bulundum.'

10 Soviet Rule

1 Noman Çelebicihan, 'Anthem of the Crimean Tatar People: "Ant Etkenmen"', www.youtube.com, accessed 23 July 2023.

2 Until 1928, and the trial of Veli Ibraimov, Moscow had pursued a policy of making Crimean Tatars the dominant ethnos, despite their constituting only 26 per cent of the population in Crimea: this was proof to the Muslim world that the USSR valued their languages and culture.

3 There were rumours that Ibraimov, as a chekist in the Caucasus in 1920, had found evidence of Stalin's activity as a bank robber, which explains Stalin's interest in his execution. See N. Semena, 'Delo Veli Ibraimova i Milli Firqa', *Zerkalo Nedeli* (Ukraine), 19 March 1999.

4 There is a monument to the victims on the outskirts of Uskut. See *'Sovershenno sekretno': Lubianka – Stalinu o polozhenii v strane, 1922–1934 gg.* (Moscow, 2001–13), vol. VIII, p. 1313.

5 In his lifetime only one small book of Çoban-Zade's poetry was known. Not until 1999 was a wide range of his uncollected work – nearly one hundred

poems and some prose – published by Ismail Otar (in both Crimean Tatar and Turkish translation) in Istanbul.

6 Uniquely for a gauleiter, Frauenfeld served just one year in prison.

7 Bogdan Gubernskii (pseudonym, perhaps of Gulnara Bekirova), 'Zalozhniki voyny: okkupatsia Kryma 1941–4', 4 and 5 May 2015, see ru.krymr.com/a/26992591.html and ru.krymr.com/a/26995860.html, accessed 15 August 2023.

11 Exile and Exodus

1 V. E. Vozgrin, *Istoriia krymskikh tatar*, vol. 11 (Simferopol, 2014).

BIBLIOGRAPHY

17 Yüzyıl Avrupasında Türk İmajı (Istanbul, 2005)

Abdul'vapov, N. P., *Svod pamiatnikov istorii, arkhitektury i kul'tury krymskikh tatar*, vol. III: *Simferopol* (Belgorod, 2018)

Abduzhemilev, R. R., 'Mekhmed Senai – Krymskii letopisets pri sarae Khana Islam Gireia', *Zolotoordynskoe obozrenie*, III (2015), pp. 102–12

—, *Dokumenty krymskogo khanstva iz sobraniia Khuseina Feizkhanova* (Simferopol, 2017)

—, 'Shedzhere predkov krymskikh khanov: problema interpretatsii', *Zolotoordynskoe obozrenie*, VII/3 (2019), pp. 509–23

—, 'Istochnikovedchesko-kompozitsionnyi obzor "Semi planet" Seyid-Mukhammeda Rizy', *Zolotoordynskoe obozrenie*, VIII/2 (2020), pp. 316–44

Abibullaeva, È. È., 'Meditsina krymskogo khanstva skvoz' prizmu povsednevnoi zhizni', *Zolotoordynskoe obozrenie*, VII/4 (2019), pp. 733–43

Abrahamowicz, Z., 'Dokumenty tatarskie i tureckie w zbiorach polskich', *Przegląd Orientalistyczny*, II/10 (1954), pp. 141–8

Agadzhanov, S. G., and A. N. Sakharov, *Krym: proshloe i nastoiashchee* (Moscow, 1988)

Aksan, V., *An Ottoman Statesman in War and Peace: Ahmed Resmi Efendi, 1700–1783* (Leiden, 1995)

Alieva, S., *Tak èto bylo: Natsional'nye repressii v SSSR* (Moscow, 1993)

Artamonow, W. A., 'Rosja, Rzeczpospolita i Krym v Latach 1686–1699', in *Studia i Materialy z Czasów Jana III Sobieskiego*, ed. K. Matwijowski (Wrocław, 1992), pp. 19–46

Augustinowicz, Ch., 'Begegnung und Zeremonial: Das Bild der Krimtataren bei Balthasar Kleinschroth und Johann Christian Lünig', in *The Crimean Khanate between East and West (15th–18th Century)*, ed. Denise Klein (Wiesbaden, 2014), pp. 75–90

Bantysh-Kamenskii, N. N., *Reestr delam krymskogo Dvora, 1474–1779* (Simferopol, 1893)

Barbaro, Josafa, and Ambrogio Contarini, *Travels to Tana and Persia*, Hakluyt Society, 1st ser. (London, 1873)

Barbour, Philip L., *The Three Worlds of Captain John Smith* (Boston, MA, 1964)

Beauplan, Guillaume Lavasseur de, *Description de l'Ukranie* (Paris, 1861)

Bennigsen, A., and Ch. Lemercier-Quelquejay, 'Le khanat de Crimée au début du XVIe siècle: De la tradition mongole à la suzeraineté ottomane d'après un document inédit des Archives ottomanes', *Cahiers du monde russe et soviétique*, XIII (1972), pp. 321–37

——, 'La Moscovie, l'Empire ottoman et la crise successorale de 1577–1588 dans le khanat de Crimée: La tradition nomade contre le modèle des monarchies sédentaires', *Cahiers du monde russe et soviétique*, XIV (1973), pp. 453–87

——, *Le Khanat de Crimée dans les Archives du Musée du Palais de Topkapı* (Paris, 1978)

Berežkov, M., *Krymskie šertnye gramoty* (Kyïv, 1894)

——, 'Nur-saltan, tsarica Krymskaia', *Izvestiia Tavricheskoi Uchenoi Arkhivnoi Komissii*, XXVII (1897), pp. 1–19

Bordier, Julien, *Ambassade en Turquie de Jean de Constant Biron, baron de Salignac* (Paris, 1888)

Bossoli C., *The Beautiful Scenery and Chief Places of Interest Throughout the Crimea* (London, 1856)

Bredal, Peter, 'Donesenie v kabinet 1737 goda', in *Materialy dlia istorii russkogo flota*, S. Elagin, vol. VI (St Petersburg, 1877)

Broniewski, M., *Martini Broniovii de Biezdzfedea bis in Tartariam nomine Stephani primi Poloniae regis legati Tartariae descriptio* (Cologne, 1595)

——, 'Opisanie Kryma', *Zapiski Odesskogo obshchestva istorii i drevnostei*, VI (1867), pp. 331–67

——, *Im Auftrag des Königs: Die Tartariæ descriptio des Martinus Broniovius* (Mainz, 2011)

Bugai, N. F., *Deportatsiia narodov Kryma* (Moscow, 2002)

Çelebi, Evliyâ, *Seyahatnâmesi*, vol. V (Istanbul, 1897)

——, *Seyahatnâmesi*, vol. VII (Istanbul, 2017)

Cevdet, Ahmed Paşa, *Tarih-i Cevdet I–VI* (Istanbul, 1994)

Chubova, A. P. et al., *Arkhitektura i iskusstvo Khersonesa tavricheskogo* (Simferopol, 2008)

Clarke, Edward Daniel, *Travels in Various Countries of Europe, Asia and Africa, Part 1: Russian Tartary and Turkey* (London, 1810)

Collins, L., 'The Military Organization and Tactics of the Crimean Tatars, 16th–17th Centuries', in *War, Technology and Society in the Middle East*, ed. V. J. Parry and M. E. Yapp (London, 1975), pp. 257–76

Croskey, R., 'The Diplomatic Forms of Ivan III's Relationship with the Crimean Khan', *Slavic Review*, XLIII/2 (1984), pp. 257–69

Da Lucca Chiavari, Giovanni, *Sanctae Congregationi de Tataribus* (Rome, 1634)

Danilova, È., *Kaffa v nachale vtoroi poloviny XV veka* (Moscow, 1974)

Dankoff, R., *An Ottoman Mentality: The World of Evliya Çelebi* (Leiden and Boston, MA, 2006)

d'Ascoli, Emiddio Dortelli, *Descrittione del Mar Negro & della Tartaria* (1634)

Davies, B., *Warfare, State and Society on the Black Sea Steppe, 1500–1700* (London, 2007)

Demidov, A., *Puteshestvie v Iuzhnuiu Rossiiu i Krym* (Moscow, 1853)

Dickinson, Sara, 'Russia's First "Orient": Characterizing the Crimea in 1787', *Kritika: Explorations in Russian and Eurasian History*, III/1 (2002), pp. 3–25

Dmitriev, N. K., 'Chansons Tatares de Crimée', *Journal Asiatique*, CCXII (April–June 1928), pp. 207–27 d'Oro, Giuliana, 'Perevodčik-Tercüman di Ismail Gasprinskij. Espressione di dialogo interculturale', PhD, Sapienza Università di Roma: Dipartimento di Studi Europei, Americani e Interculturali, 2022

Dovnar-Zapol'skii, D., ed., 'Litovskija upominki tatarskim ordam: Skarbovaja kniga Metriki Litovskoj, 1502–1509', *Izvestiia Tavricheskoi Uchenoi Arkhivnoi Komissii*, XXVIII (1898), pp. 1–81

Dubois de Montpéreus, F., *Voyage au Caucase, chez les Tcherkesses et les Abkhases, en Colhide, en Géorgie, en Arménie et en Crimée* (Paris, 1843)

Dubrovin, N., ed., *Prisoedinenie Kryma k Rossii: Reskripty, pis'ma, reliatsii i doneseniia*, vols III–IV (St Petersburg, 1887–9)

Emecen, Feridun M., 'Son kırım hani Şahın Giray'ın idamı mes'elesi ve buna dair vesikalar', *Tarih Degirsi*, XXXIV (1984), pp. 315–46

Eravcı, M., 'The Role of the Crimean Tatars in the Ottoman–Safavi War (1578–1639)', *Historical Yearbook*, IV (2007), pp. 153–60

Ertaylan, İ. H., *Gâzi Geray Han: hayâtı ve eserleri* (Istanbul, 1958)

Eszer, A., 'Die "Beschreibung des Schwarzen Meeres und der Tatarei" des Emidio Portelli d'Ascoli O.P.', *Archivum Fratrum Praedicatorum*, XLII (1972), pp. 199–249

Faizov, S. F., 'Iz perepiski krymskikh khanov s russkim tsarem i pol'skim korolem, 1654–1658 gg.', in *Russkaia i ukrainskaia diplomatiia v mezhdunarodnykh otnosheniiakh v Europe serediny XVII v.*, ed. M. S. Meyer and L. E. Semenova (Moscow, 2007), pp. 438–78

—, ed., *Pis'ma khanov Islam-Gireia III i Mukhammed-Gireia IV k tsariu Alekseiu* (Moscow, 2003)

Fedakar, Cengiz, 'Son kırım hani Şahın Giray'ın muhallefatina dair', *Türk Dünyası Araştırmaları Dergisi*, CCIX (2015), pp. 385–408

Firkovich, A., trans. and ed., 'Sobytiia sluchivshiiasia v Krymu v tsarstvovanie Šagin-Gereia-khana (perevod s sovremennoi evrejskoi rukopisi sochinennoi karaimom Rabbi-Azar'ia synom Ilii)', *Vremennik Imperatorskago Moskovskago Obshchestva istorii i drevnostei rossiiskikh*, II/24 (1856), pp. 101–34

Fisher, A., 'Şahin Girey, the Reformer Khan, and the Russian Annexation of the Crimea', *Jahrbücher für Geschichte Osteuropas*, XV/3 (1967), pp. 341–64

—, *The Russian Annexation of the Crimea, 1772–1783* (Cambridge, 1970)

—, 'Les rapports entre l'Empire ottoman et la Crimée: L'aspect financier', *Cahiers du monde russe et soviétique*, XIII/3 (1972), pp. 368–81

—, *The Crimean Tatars* (Stanford, CA, 1978)

—, *Between Russians, Ottomans and Turks: Crimea and Crimean Tatars* (Istanbul, 1998)

Frauenfeld, A. E., *'Und trage keine Reu': Vom Wiener Gauleiter zum Generalkommissar der Krim. Erinnerungen und Aufzeichnungen* (Leoni am Starnberger See, 1978)

Gökbilgin, Ö., 'Quelques sources manuscrites sur l'époque de Sahib Giray Ier, khan de Crimée (1532–1551)', *Cahiers du monde russe et soviétique*, XI/3 (1970), pp. 462–9

—, *Tarih-i Sahib Giray* (Istanbul, 2000)

Gulevich, V. P., 'Neskol'ko nabliudenii otnositel'no problemy "pozhalovaniia" russkikh zemel' Kazimiru iv . . .', *Colloquia Russica*, I/7 (2017), pp. 369–77

—, and A. V. Dzhanov, 'Pis'mo krymskogo khana Mengli Gireia genuèzskim èmissaram Bartolomeo Campofregoso i Lodisio Fieschi ot 30 dek. 1481 g.', *Zolotoordynskoe obozrenie*, VII/2 (2019), pp. 318–32

Haivoronskyj, O., *Poveliteli dvux materikov: Krymskie khany XV–XVI stoletii i bor'ba za nasledstvo Velikoi Ordy* (Kyïv–Bağçasaray, 2007)

—, *Poveliteli dvukh materikov: Krymskie khany pervoi poloviny XVII stoletiia v bor'be za samostoiatel'nost' i edinovlastie* (Kyïv–Bağçasaray, 2009)

Halim Giray Sultan, *Gülbün-i hânân yahut Qırım tarihi* (Ankara, 2019)

—, A. Hilmi and K. Hüseyinov, eds, *Rozovyj kust khanov, ili Istoriia Kryma* (Simferopol, 2004)

Hammer-Purgstall, Joseph von, *Histoire de l'Empire Ottoman* (Paris, 1844)

—, *Geschichte der Chane der Krim unter osmanischer Herrschaft* (Vienna, 1856)

Hasan, Yeniçeri Kâtibi, *Prut seferi'ni beyanımdır* (Istanbul, 2008)

Herberstein, Sigmund von, *Rerum Moscovitarum commentarii* (London, 1851)

—, *Zapiski o Moskovii* (Moscow, 1988)

Heyd, W., *Histoire du commerce du Levant au moyen-âge* (Leipzig, 1885)

Iakobson, A. L., *Krym v srednie veka* (Moscow, 1973)

Iakushechkin, A. V., 'K voprosu ob obstoiatel'stvakh prikhoda k vlasti Khadzhi-Gireia', *Zolotoordynskoe obozrenie*, IV/3 (2016), pp. 580–601

Ianbay, Iala, 'Letters by Crimean Noblewomen to Sweden', *Manuscripta Orientalia*, VIII/1 (2002), pp. 3–17

Ichli, A., 'Neizvestnye proizvedeniia Bora Gazi Gireiia', *Tiurkologicheskie issledovaniia*, I/1 (2018), pp. 147–71

İnalcık, H. 'The Khan and the Tribal Aristocracy: The Crimean Khanate under Sahib Giray I', in *Eucharisterion: Essays Presented to Omeljan Pritsak on his Sixtieth Birthday by his Colleagues and Students*, ed. I. Sevcenko and F. Sysyn, vol. I (Cambridge, MA, 1980), pp. 445–66

—, 'Shipowners, Captains and Merchants in the Black Sea, 1487–1506', in İnalcık, *Studies in Ottoman Documents Pertaining to Ukraine and the Black Sea Countries* (Cambridge, MA, 1996), pp. 112–55

—, 'Krym pod vlast'iu osman i spor o zakliuchenii soglasheniia', *Zolotoordynskoe obozrenie*, I/3 (2014), pp. 163–73

—, *Kırım Hanlığı Tarihi Üzerine Araştırmalar, 1441–1700* (Istanbul, 2021)

Iunusova, L. S., ed., *Krymskotatarskaia literature: Sbornik VIII–XX vv* (Simferopol, 2000)

Ivanics, Mária, 'Posol'stva krymskix tatar pri Venskom dvore v 1598–1682 gg. (iz istorii krymsko-tatarskoj diplomatii XVI–XVII vv)', in *Turcica et Ottomanica. Sbornik statei v chest' 70–letiia M. S. Meiera*, ed. I. Zaitsev and S. Oreshkova (Moscow, 2006), pp. 226–37

—, 'Enslavement, Slave Labour and the Treatment of Captives in the Crimean Khanate', in *Ransom Slavery along the Ottoman Borders (Early Fifteenth–Early Eighteenth Centuries)*, ed. Géza Dávid and Pál Fodor (Leiden, 2007), pp. 193–219

—, 'Krimtatarische Spionage im osmanisch-habsburgischen Grenzgebiet während des Feldzuges im Jahre 1663', *Acta Orientalia Academiae Scientarum Hungaricae*, LXI/1–2 (2008), pp. 119–33

—, 'The Military Co-operation of the Crimean Khanate with the Ottoman Empire in the Sixteenth and Seventeenth Centuries', in *The European Tributary States of the Ottoman Empire in the Sixteenth* and Seventeenth Centuries, ed. G. Kárman and L. Kuncevic (Leiden, 2013), pp. 275–99

—, 'Die Şirin, Abstammung und Aufstieg einer Sippe in der Steppe', in *The Crimean Khanate between East and West (15th–18th Century)*, ed. Denise Klein (Wiesbaden, 2014), pp. 27–46

Izvestiia Tavricheskoi Uchenoi Arkhivnoi Komissii (ITUAK), 52 vols (Simferopol, 1887–1915)

Jankowski, Henryk, *A Historical-Etymological Dictionary of Pre-Russian Habitation Names of the Crimea* (Leiden, 2006)

—, *Język Krymskotatarski* (Warsaw, 2010)

Kadyrov, R. R., 'Istoricheskaia geografiia Krymskogo khanstva po dannym pis'mennykh istochnikov . . .', *Krymskoe istoricheskoe obozrenie*, II (2020), pp. 87–96

Kançal-Ferrari, Nicole, 'Golden Watches and Precious Textiles: Luxury Goods at the Crimean Khans' Court and the Northern Black Sea Shore', in *The Mercantile Effect: Art and Exchange in the Islamicate World during the 17th and 18th Centuries*, ed. Sussan Babaie and Melanie Gibson (Chicago, IL, 2017), pp. 51–61

Karidis, Vyron, 'The Mariupol Greeks: Tsarist Treatment of an Ethnic Minority ca. 1778–1859', *Journal of Modern Hellenism*, III (1986), pp. 57–74

Karpov, Gennadij., ed., *Pamiatniki diplomaticheskikh snoshenii Moskovskago gosudarstva s Krymskoiu i Nogajskoiu ordami i s Turtsieji*, vol. I: *1474–1505* and vol. II: *1508–1521*, Sbornik Imperatorskago Russkago Istoricheskago Obshchestva 41 and 95 (St Petersburg, 1884 and 1895)

Kashirin, V. S., *Nabeg . . . nashestvie khana Krym-Gireia 1769 g.* (Moscow, 2019)

Katkó, G., 'The Redemption of the Transylvanian Army Captured by the Crimean Tatars in 1657', in *The Crimean Khanate between East and West (15th–18th Century)*, ed. Denise Klein (Wiesbaden, 2014), pp. 91–107

Kazem-bek, Mirza Aleksandr, *Seid Mukhammed Riza Sem'planet* (Kazan, 1832)

Kazimirski M., 'Précis de l'histoire des khans de Crimée depuis l'an 880 jusqu'à l'an 1198 de l'hégire', *Nouveau Journal Asiatique*, XII (1833), pp. 349–80, 428–58

—, *Précis des khans de Crimée*, ed. Amédée Jaubert (Paris, 1833)

Kellner-Heinkele, B., ed., *Aus den Aufzeichnungen des Sa'id Giray Sultān: Eine zeitgen-össische Quelle zur Geschichte des Chanats der Krim um die Mitte des 18. Jahrhunderts* (Freiburg, 1975)

—, 'Who Was 'Abdulghaffār El-Qirimī? Some Notes on an 18th Century Crimean Tatar Historian', *Journal of Asian History*, XXXII/2 (1998), pp. 145–56

Khapaev, V. V., 'Krymskie zemletriaseniia drevnosti i srednevekov'ia: k istorii voprosa', in *Materialy po arkheologii i istorii antichnogo i srednevekovogo Kryma*, ed. Michael Choref Kh, vol. 1 (Simferopol, 2008), pp. 89–117

Khoroshkevich, A. L., *Rus' i Krym: Ot soiuza k protivostoianiiu* (Moscow, 2001)

Khrapunov N. I., 'Puteshestvie po Krymu Stivena Grelleta', in *Materialy po Arkheologii*, ed. A. I. Aibabin et al., vol. XV (Simferopol, 2009), pp. 656–81

—, 'Krymskii poluostrov posle prisoedineniia k Rossii v sochinenii Bal'tazara fon Kampengauzena', in *Materialy po Arkheologii*, ed. A. I. Aibabin et al., vol. XVIII (Simferopol, 2013), pp. 456–73

—, 'Vzgliad izvne: britanskii poèt i puteshestvennik Redzhinal'd Kheber', *Krymskoe istoricheskoe obozrenie*, III (2015), pp. 252–73

—, and S. N. Khrapunova, 'Zapiski Dzhona Smita kak istochnik . . .',
  Zolotoordynskoe obozrenie, IV (2015), pp. 151–68

Kırım Hanlarına Nâme-i Hümâyûn (2 Numaralı Name Defteri) (Istanbul, 2013)

Kırımlı, Hakan, 'Crimean Tatars, Nogays, and Scottish Missionaries: The Story of
  Katti Geray and Other Baptised Descendants of the Crimean Khans', *Cahiers
  du monde russe*, XLV/1–2 (2004), pp. 61–108

—, *Türkiye'deki Kırım Tatar ve Nogay Köy Yerleşimleri* (Istanbul, 2012)

Kizilov, M., 'Slave Trade in the Early Modern Crimea from the Perspective of
  Christian, Muslim, and Jewish Sources', *Journal of Early Modern History*,
  XI/1–11 (2007), pp. 1–31

—, 'Polish Slaves and Captives in the Crimea in the Seventeenth Century', *Acta
  Orientalia Academiae Scientiarum Hungaricae*, LXXIV/2 (2020), pp. 252–65

Klein, Denise, 'Tatar and Ottoman History Writing: The Case of the Nogay
  Rebellion (1699–1701)', in *The Crimean Khanate between East and West
  (15th–18th Century)*, ed. Denise Klein (Wiesbaden, 2012), pp. 125–48

Köksal, M. Fatih, and Emre Berkan Yeni, *Klasik Türk edebiyatında yerlilik*
  (Istanbul, 2021)

Kolli, L. P., 'Khadzhi-Girei-khan i ego politika (po genuèzskim istochnikam)',
  Izvestiia Tavricheskoi Uchenoi Arkhivnoi Komissii, L (1913), pp. 99–139

Kołodziejczyk, D., *The Crimean Khanate and Poland-Lithuania: International
  Diplomacy on the European Periphery (15th–18th Century)* (Leiden, 2011)

—, 'Das Krimkhanat als Gleichgewichtsfaktor in Osteuropa (17.–18.
  Jahrhundert)', in *The Crimean Khanate between East and West (15th–18th
  Century)*, ed. Denise Klein (Wiesbaden, 2014), pp. 47–58

Kortepeter, S. M., 'Ġāzī Girāy II, Khan of the Crimea, and Ottoman Policy in
  Eastern Europe and the Caucasus, 1588–94', *Slavonic and East European
  Review*, XLIV (January 1966), pp. 139–66

Križanić, J., *Politika* (Moscow, 1987)

Królikowska, N., 'Praworządny jak Tatarzyn? Stosunki prawne w Chanacie
  Krymskim na podstawie miejscowych ksiąg sądowych z XVII wieku',
  Czasopismo Prawno-Historyczne, LXV/1 (2013), pp. 121–42

—, 'Sovereignty and Subordination in Crimean–Ottoman Relations (16th–18th
  centuries)', in *The European Tributary States of the Ottoman Empire in the
  Sixteenth and Seventeenth Centuries*, ed. G. Kármán and L. Kuncevic (Leiden,
  2013), pp. 43–66

—, 'Crimean Crime Stories: Cases of Homicide and Bodily Harm during the
  Reign of Murad Giray (1678–1683)', in *The Crimean Khanate between East
  and West (15th–18th Century)*, ed. Denise Klein (Wiesbaden, 2014), pp. 109–24

—, *Law and Division of Power in the Crimean Khanate (1532–1774): With Special
  Reference to the Reign of Murad Giray (1678–1683)* (Leiden, 2019)

Krym: Putevoditel' (Simferopol, 1914)

Kurtiev, Refat, *Deportatsiia krymskikh tatar* (Simferopol, 2004–5)

Lamartine, A. de, *Histoire de la Turquie*, vol. V (Paris, 1854)

Lashkov, F. F., 'Shagin-Girei, poslednii krymskii khan', *Kievskaia starina*, IX (1887),
  pp. 37–80

—, *Pamiatniki diplomaticheskikh snoshenii Krymskogo khanstva s Moskovskim
  gosudarstvom v XVI i XVII vv.* (Simferopol, 1891)

—, 'Istoricheskii ocherk Krymsko-tatarskago zemlevladeniia', *Izvestiia
  Tavricheskoi Uchenoi Arkhivnoi Komissii*, XXI (1894), pp. 59–89

Lekhno, Rabbi David, *Debar Sepatayim: An Ottoman Hebrew Chronicle from the Crimea, 1683–1730* (Boston, MA, 2021)

Lemercier-Quelquejay, Chantal, 'Un condottiere lithuanien du XVIe siècle, le prince Dimitrij Višneveckij et l'origine de la Seč Zaporogue d'après les archives ottomanes', *Cahiers du monde russe et soviétique*, X (1969), pp. 258–79

—, 'Les khanats de Kazan et de Crimée face à la Moscovie en 1521, d'après un document inédit des Archives du Musée du Palais de Topkapı', *Cahiers du monde russe et soviétique*, XII (1971), pp. 481–90

—, 'Les expéditions de Devlet-Giray contre Moscou en 1571 et 1572', *Cahiers du monde russe et soviétique*, XIII/4 (1972), pp. 555–9

Likachiov, D., and B. Chichibabin, *Krymskii al'bom* (Feodosia, 1996)

Liseitsev, D., 'Russko-krymskie diplomaticheskie kontakty v nachale XVII stoletiia', in *Tiurkologicheskii Sbornik*, ed. S. G. Kliashtornyi (Moscow, 2005), pp. 238–82

Litvin, Mikhalon, *O nravakh tatar litovtsev i moskvitian* [1614], trans. I. P. Starostina, ed. A. L. Khorshkevich (Moscow, 1994), available at http://loveread.ec, accessed 20 July 2023

Małowist, M., *Kaffa, kolonia genueńska na Krymie i problem wschodni w latach 1453–1475* (Warsaw, 1947)

Mancall, M., *Russia and China: Their Diplomatic Relations to 1728* (Cambridge, MA, 1971)

Manz, B. Forbes, 'The Clans of the Crimean Khanate, 1466–1532', *Harvard Ukrainian Studies*, II/3 (1978), pp. 282–309

Matsuki, Eizo, 'The Crimean Tatars and Their Russian-Captive Slaves', *Mediterranean World*, XVIII (2006), pp. 171–82

Matuz, J., 'Eine Beschreibung des Khanats der Krim aus dem Jahre 1669', *Acta Orientalia (Havniae)*, XXVIII (1964), pp. 129–51

—, *Krimtatarische Urkunden im Reichsarchiv zu Kopenhagen: Mit historisch-diplomatischen und sprachlichen Untersuchungen* (Freiburg, 1976)

—, 'Les relations étrangères du Khanat de Crimée (XVe–XVIIIe siècles)', *Revue d'histoire diplomatique*, CII (1988), pp. 233–49

Mazı, Muhammet, *The Sultans of the Countryside: The Girays' Displacement (1792–1807)* (Budapest, 2020)

Mechovsky, Matvei (Miechowita, Maciej), *Traktat o dvukh Sarmatiiakh* (1517) (Moscow, 1936)

Milner, Thomas, *The Crimea: Its Ancient and Modern History; The Khans, the Sultans and the Czars with Notices of Its Scenery and Population* (London, 1855)

Moiseev, M. V., 'Azov (Azak) v 1570 g. v donesenii russkogo poslannika Ivana Novosil'tseva', *Srednevekovye tiurko-tatarskie gosudarstva*, XI (2019), pp. 60–66

Mundt, T., *Krim-Girai, Khan of the Crimea*, trans. W.G.C. Eliot (London, 1856)

Murzakevich, N., 'Spisok s stateinago spiska Velikago Gosudaria Ego Tsarskago Velichestva poslannikov: stol'nika i polkovnika i namestnika pereiaslavskogo Vasil'ia Mikhailova syna Tiapkina, d'iaka Nikity Zotova', *Zapiski Odesskago obshchestva istorii i drevnostei*, II/2–3 (1850), pp. 568–658

Mustakimov, I. A., 'Arabografichnye dokumental'nye istochniki po istorii krymskogo khanstva', *Srednevekovye tiurko-tatarskie gosudarstva*, XII (2020), pp. 58–9

Myts, V. L., *Kaffa i Feodoro v XV veke: Kontakty i konflikty* (Simferopol, 2009)

Nekrasov, A. M., 'Zhenshchiny khanskogo doma Gireev v XV–XVI vekax (1998)', in Nekrasov, *Izbrannye trudy* (Nalchik, 2015), pp. 243–50

Nerantzis, N., 'Pillars of Power: Silver and Steel of the Ottoman Empire', *Mediterranean Archaeology and Archaeometry*, IX/2 (2009), pp. 71–85

Osmanlı Belgerlerinde Kırım Hanlığı (Istanbul, 2013)

Ostapchuk, V., 'Crimean Tatar Long-Range Campaigns: The View from Remmal Khoja's *History of Sahib Gerey Khan*', in *Warfare in Eastern Europe, 1500–1800*, ed. Brian J. Davies (Leiden, 2012), pp. 147–72

Otar, Ismail, *Bekir Sidki Çobanzade: Kırımli Türk Şair ve Bilgini* (Istanbul, 1999)

Pallas, P. S., *Bemerkungen auf einer Reise in die südlichen Statthalterschaften des russischen Reichs in den Jahren 1793 und 1793*, vol. II (Leipzig, 1801)

Papp, S., 'Die Inaugurationen der Krimkhane durch die Hohe Pforte (16.–18. Jahrhundert)', in *The Crimean Khanate between East and West (15th–18th Century)*, ed. Denise Klein (Wiesbaden, 2014), pp. 75–90

Peçevi, İbrahim Efendi, *Peçevu Tarih*, 2 vols (Ankara, 1981)

Pečevija, Ibrahim Alajbegović, *Historija*, trans. Fehim Nametak, 3 vols (Sarajevo, 2000)

Penskoi, V. V., 'Voennyi potentsial krymskogo khanstva v kontse XV – nachale XVII v.', *Vostok (Oriens)*, II (2010), pp. 56–66

Peyssonnel, Ch. de, *Traité sur le commerce de la Mer Noire*, 2 vols (Paris, 1787)

Pilipchuk, Ya. V., 'Opasnaia granitsa. Sigizmund I i Girei v 1517–1548 gg', *Istoriia voennogo dela: issledovaniia i istochniki* (2006), VIII, pp. 472–505, www.milhist.info, accessed 20 July 2023.

Pochekaev, Roman, *Tsari ordynskie: Biografii khanov i pravitelei Zolotoi Ordy* (Moscow, 2010)

——, 'Pravovye aspekty otnoshenii Krymskogo khanstva . . . analiz istochnikov XVI–XVII vv.', *Krymskoe istoricheskoe obozrenie*, II (2019), pp 68–85

Podhorodecki, Leszek, *Chanat krymski i jego stosunki z Polską w XV–XVIII w.* (Warsaw, 1987)

——, *Chanat Krymski: Państwo koczowników na kresach Europy* (Warsaw, 2012)

Polnoe sobranie russkikh letopisei, vol. XI (Moscow, 1965)

Pubblici, Lorenzo, *Venezia e il Mar d'Azov: alcune considerazioni sulla Tana nel XIV secolo* (Florence, 2005)

Pułaski, K., 'Trzy poselstwa Piaseczyńskiego do Kazi Gireja, hana Tatarów perekopskich (1601–1603). Szkic historyczny', *Przewodnik Naukowy i Literacki*, XXXIX (1911), pp. 135–45; 244–56; 358–66; 467–80; 553–66; 645–60; 756–68; 845–64; 945–60

Resmi, A., *Hulâsatü'l-i'tibâr* (*A Summary of Admonitions: A Chronicle of the 1768–1774 Russian–Ottoman War*), trans. E. Menchinger (Istanbul, 2011)

Romme, Charles-Gilbert, *Puteshestvie v Krym v 1786 g.*, trans. K. Ratkevich (Moscow, 1941)

——, *Correspondance, 1779–1786*, vol. II (Clermont-Ferrand, 2014)

Sahib Giray Han, *Histoire de Sahib Giray, Khan de Crimée de 1532 à 1551*, trans. Ö. Gökbilgin (Ankara, 1973)

Schamiloglu, U., 'The Impact of the Black Death on the Golden Horde: Politics, Economy, Society, Civilization', *Golden Horde Review*, V/2 (2017), pp. 325–43

——, 'The Rise of Urban Centers in the Golden Horde and the City of Ükek', *Golden Horde Review*, VI/1 (2018), pp. 18–40

Schönle, Andreas, 'Garden of the Empire: Catherine's Appropriation of the Crimea', *Slavic Review*, LX/1 (2001), pp. 1–23

Schütz, E., 'Eine armenische Chronik von Kaffa aus der ersten Hälfte des 17. Jahrhunderts', *Acta Orientalia Academiae Scientiarum Hungaricae*, XXIX/2 (1975), pp. 133–86

Seitiag'iaev, N. S., 'Novye svedeniia ob "Istorii Krymskikh khanov" Khurremi Chelebi Akaia', *Voprosy dukhovnoi kul'tury: Filologicheskie nauki*, I (2011), pp. 162–5

Semena, N., 'Delo Veli Ibraimova i Milli Firqa', *Zerkalo Nedeli* (Ukraine), 19 March 1999

Sena'i, Hadży Mehmed, *Historia chana Islam Gereja III*, ed. Z. Abrahamowicz (Warsaw, 1971)

Seyyid Muhammed Riza, *Es-seb'u 's-seyyar fi ahbari muluki Tatar (Sem' planet)*, ed. I. Kazem-Bek (Kazan, 1832); repr. in Latin alphabet as *Sem' planet v izvestiiakh o tsariax tatarskikh*, vol. 1: *Transliteratsiia* (Kazan, 2019)

Shchegoleva, Tatiana, 'Karaites of Crimea: History and Present-Day Situation in Community', *Jews of Eurasia*, 29 May 2011, http://video-en.jewseurasia.org, accessed 20 July 2023

Siestrzeńcewicz-Bohusz, S., *Histoire de la Tauride* (Brunswick, 1800)

Smirnov, V., *Krymskoe khanstvo pod verkhovenstvom Otomanskoi porty do nachala XVIII veka* (Moscow, 2005)

—, *Krymskoe khanstvo pod verkhovenstvom Otomanskoi porty v XVIII v. do prisoedineniia ego k Rossii* (Moscow, 2005)

Solov'ev, S., *Istoriia Rossii s drevneishikh vremen*, vols VI and X (Moscow, 1989 and 1993)

Soysal, Abdullah Zihni, *Jarłyki krymskie z czasów Jana Kazimierza* (Warsaw, 1939)

Starowolski, Szymon, 'Pobudka abo rada na zniesienie Tatarów perekopskich', in *Szymon Starowolski. Wybór z pism*, ed. Ignacy Lewandowski (Wrocław, 1991), pp. 158–76

Stulli, Fiodor, *Polveka nazad* (Moscow, 1894)

Subtelny, O., 'The Ukrainian–Crimean Treaty of 1711', in *Eucharisterion: Essays Presented to Omeljan Pritsak on His Sixtieth Birthday by His Colleagues and Students*, ed. I. Sevcenko and F. Sysyn, vol. II (Cambridge, MA, 1980), pp. 808–17

Syroechkovsky, V. E., 'Mukhammed-Gerai i ego vassaly', *Uchionye zapiski Moskovskogo Universiteta*, LXI (1940), pp. 3–71

Teisier, B., 'Crimean Tatars in Explorative and Travel Writing', *Anatolian Studies*, LXVII (2017), pp. 231–53

Thunmann, J., *Krymskoe khanstvo*, trans. N. K. Ernst and S. L. Belianskaia (Moscow, 1936)

Tizengauzen, V., *Sbornik materialov, otnosiashchikhsia k istorii Zolotoi Ordy* (St Petersburg, 1884)

Tott, François de, *Mémoires du Baron de Tott sur les Turcs et les Tartares*, 4 vols (Amsterdam, 1784)

Turan, Ahmet Nezihi, 'Sudebnye reestry Krymskogo tsarstva', trans. N. S. Seitiag'iaev, 2002, available at http://dspace.nbuv.gov.ua, accessed 20 July 2023

Türk, Ahmet, *The Crimean Khanate under the Reign of Gazi Giray II* (Ankara, 2000) (Turkish text)

Useinov, T. B., *Qırımtatar edebiyatınıñ orta asırlar deviri* (Simferopol, 1999)

—, ed., *Razmyshleniia o poèzii krymskogo khanstva* (Simferopol, 2005)

—, 'Krymskii pravitel, poèt i prosvetitel Gazı Gerai Khan II (1554–1607)', *Nauchnyi vestnik Kryma*, 1/22 (2019), pp. 1–8

Usmanov, M. A., *Zhalovannye akty dzhuchieva ulusa XIV–XVI vv* (Kazan, 1979)

—, ed., *Istochnikovedenie istorii Ulusa Dzhuchi (Zolotoy Ordy) ot Kalki do Astrakhani, 1223–1556* (Kazan, 2001)

Vásáry, István, 'A Contract of the Crimean Khan Mengli Giray and the Inhabitants of Qïrq-yer from 1478/79', *Central Asiatic Journal*, XXVI/3–4 (1982), pp. 289–300

—, 'Zhalovannye gramoty Dzhuchieva Ulusa, dannye italiiskim gorodam Kaffa i Tana', in *Istochnikovedenie istorii Ulusa Dzhuchi*, ed. M. A. Usmanov (Kazan, 2002) pp. 193–206

—, 'Orthodox Christian Qumans and Tatars of the Crimea in the 13th–14th Centuries', in Vásáry, *Turks, Tatars and Russians in the 13th–16th Centuries* (Abingdon, 2007), pp. 260–71

—, 'The Crimean Khanate and the Great Horde (1440s–1500s): A Fight for Primacy', in *Das frühneuzeitliche Krimkhanat (16.–18. Jahrhundert) zwischen Orient und Okzident*, ed. Meinolf Ahrens and Denise Klein (Wiesbaden, 2012) pp. 13–26

Veinstein, G., 'Missionnaires jésuites et agents français en Crimée au début du XVIIIe siècle', *Cahiers du monde russe et soviétique*, X (1969), pp. 414–58

—, 'Les Tatars de Crimée et la seconde élection de Stanislas Leszczyński', *Cahiers du monde russe et soviétique*, XI/1 (1970), pp. 24–92

—, 'La révolte des mirza tatars contre le khan, 1724–1725', *Cahiers du monde russe et soviétique*, XII/3 (1971), pp. 327–38

Veliaminov-Zernov, V. V., *Materialy dlia istorii Krymsarihine Dair Kaynaklar* (Ankara, 2009)

Vinogradov, A. V., *Russko-Krymskie otnosheniia: vtoraia polovina 70-kh godov XVI veka*, 2 vols (Moscow, 2007)

Vozgrin, V. E., *Istoriia krymskikh tatar v 4-x tomakh*, vol. II (Simferopol, 2014)

Williams, B. G., *The Crimean Tatars: The Diaspora Experience and the Forging of a Nation* (Leiden, 2001)

—, *The Sultan's Raiders: The Military Role of the Crimean Tatars in the Ottoman Empire* (Washington, DC, 2013)

—, *The Crimean Tatars from Soviet Genocide to Putin's Conquest* (London, 2015)

Witsen, Nicolaas, *Moscovische Reyse, 1664–1665*, 3 vols (The Hague, 1966)

Yılmaz, Mehmet Yalcin, *Tercümân IV – Vefatinin 100. Yilinda Gaspirali Ismail Bey'e Vefa* (Istanbul, 2015)

Zaitsev, I. V., *Mezhdu Moskvoi i Stambulom (XV–XVI vv.)* (Moscow, 2004)

—, 'Pis'mennaia kul'tura krymskogo khanstva', *Vostochnyi arkhiv*, XIV–XV (2006), pp. 82–93

—, *Krymskaia istoriograficheskaia traditsiia XV–XIX vekov* (Moscow, 2009)

Zajączkowski, A., *La Chronique des steppes kiptchak Tevarih-i dešt-i qipčaq du XVII-ème siècle* (Warsaw, 1966)

Zakrevsky, N. I., 'Zapiski vracha morskoi sluzhby', *Morskoi sbornik*, LII/3 (1863), pp. 62–94

Zapiski Odesskogo obshchestva istorii i drevnostei (Odessa, 1844–1919)

Zinkeisen, J. W., *Geschichte des Osmanisches Reiches in Europa*, vol. V (Gotha, 1856)

Archives

France Affaires étrangères. Correspondance des consulats de Chio, Mytilène, Naxie, Milo et Rhodes.

509 Jouvin à Berryer, secrétaire d'État et ministre de la Marine, Azilan-Guerey, ancien khan des tartares, relégué à Chio. Administration. Héritage de l'empire ottoman. Kapoudan-pacha ; présents. Voïvode de Tchesmé; avanies ; bâtiments français. Dépenses de l'échelle de Chio. Nation de Smyrne. P. J.: 'Dissertation sur l'exil du khan des tartares', 17 March 1760.

1247 Dutrouy, nouveau consul, à De Castries, Persécution de Guerey, khan des tartares; protection de France; troubles; menaces contre le consul; négociations; administration; fin tragique de Guerey, Consul de Russie. 1 August 1787.

Russia Arkhiv vneshnei politiki Rossiiskoi imperii 123, 1, 1.

ACKNOWLEDGEMENTS

I am very grateful for generous help in obtaining books, papers and information from Poland, Bosnia, Crimea, Turkey and French archives to Hanna Dettlaff-Kuznicka of the British Library, to Andrea Lesić-Thomas of the University of Sarajevo, Thomas Bédrède, an Iranologist working for TV France24, my son Gabriel and his wife Irem Arf in Brussels, to the Canadian historian Virginia Aksan at McMaster University, Refat Chubarov of the Crimean Tatar *meclis* in exile, the late Evgeni Vozgrin, the Petersburg and Simferopol historian, and all the Crimean Tatar historians who in very difficult times have energetically uploaded to the Internet a vast number of hitherto inaccessible materials. Unfortunately, a number of Russian scholars who have been helpful cannot yet be named in these politically dark times: my gratitude must remain anonymous.

For a treasure house of high-resolution illustrations I am indebted to Tatjana Štefanič of the Ptuj Ormož Regional Museum, with its unique collection of portraits of Tatars, and to Ian Williams, curator for the Sri Prakash Lohia Hand Coloured Rare Book Collection for reproductions of Carlo Bossoli's Crimean scenes.

Finally, I am thankful to Robert Chandler and to my wife Anna Pilkington for insistently encouraging me to persist with this history, despite the increasing and discouraging obstacles to free enquiry that have arisen in the Crimea over the last ten years.

PHOTO ACKNOWLEDGEMENTS

The author and publishers wish to express their thanks to the sources listed below for illustrative material and/or permission to reproduce it. Some locations of artworks are also given below, in the interest of brevity:

Collection of Gulnara Bekirova: pp. 309, 310, 311; from Carlo Bossoli, *The Beautiful Scenery and Chief Places of Interest throughout the Crimea* (London, 1856), photos courtesy of Ian Williams, Sri Prakash Lohia Hand Coloured Rare Book Collection: pp. 183, 184; © d-maps.com, www.d-maps.com/carte.php?num_car=92577: pp. 10–11; David Rumsey Map Collection, David Rumsey Map Center, Stanford Libraries, CA: pp. 214–15; Institute of Manuscripts, Azerbaijan National Academy of Sciences, Baku: p. 273; collection of Nicole Kançal-Ferrari: p. 280; photo Malik Mansur, VOA: p. 317; National Library of Russia, St Petersburg: pp. 179 (*top*; MS F.IV.232, fol. 872v), p. 179 (*bottom*); Österreichische Nationalbibliothek, Vienna: pp. 110, 162, 170, 304; private collection: pp. 177 (*top* and *bottom*), 182 (*bottom*); Ptuj Ormož Regional Museum: pp. 180, 181; State Hermitage Museum, St Petersburg: p. 182 (*top*); Topkapı Palace Museum, Istanbul: pp. 178 (*top*; MS Hazine 1523), 178 (*bottom*; MS Hazine 1517).

INDEX

Page numbers in *italics* refer to illustrations